The
KENT & SUSSEX
WEALD

The High Weald at Stonegate near Burwash. The beauty and tranquillity of this typical scene in a landscape of partial woodland clearance is also redolent of adverse farming conditions. (Reproduced from a painting by Tim Pryke.)

The
KENT & SUSSEX
WEALD

PETER BRANDON

 PHILLIMORE

2003

Published by
PHILLIMORE & CO. LTD
Shopwyke Manor Barn, Chichester, West Sussex, England

ISBN 1 86077 241 2

Printed and bound in Great Britain by
BUTLER & TANNER LTD
London and Frome

*Dedicated to the men who rested on their ploughs
and said nothing*

A timber tug. 'Slow progress laboured forward, then the check …' (Sackville West, 1946). The scene is almost certainly near Paddock Wood, Kent. Depicted is a team of massive horses hauling oak out of grudging Weald Clay in winter. The wagon wheels have sunk into the sodden ground and the photographer has caught the horses at the precise moment when their continued exertions have moved the load. The waggoners are sturdily gaitered and booted. (From The Times *picture page in the 1920s).*

Contents

List of Illustrations

Acknowledgements

Many people helped me to express the identity of the Weald and my grateful thanks are due to Michael Wickham to whom I am indebted in more ways than I can recount. Ann Money introduced me to places I should have known with her most observant eye for detail. Ann Winser read and criticised my drafts and again took on the onerous task of compiling the index. It has been a pleasure to have the permission of John Malton to include a number of his drawings. I also desire to express my cordial thanks to Dr Phil Betts for kindly making available the muniments held by Frittenden Parish Council; to Sue Rowland, the cartographer-extraordinary of Sussex University, for the welcome assistance of her superbly clear and accurate maps; and to Clive Chatters for his ecological expertise. I also owe grateful thanks to Bob Edgar of English Nature, Diana Chatwin, Kay Coutin, Geoffrey Mead, the staffs of the East Sussex and Kent Record Offices, the planning departments of the County Councils, and of the London Library without whose collections this book could not have been written. Henri Brocklebank of the Sussex Bio-Diversity Unit has been unfailingly helpful and Bob and Ann Spencer have been most hospitable at Stockland Farm. I also express my gratitude to the many others who provided me with information including Liz and Robin Beeney, Christopher and Vivienne Blandford, Mrs Elizabeth Carey, Geoffrey and Audrey Cohen, the late Dame Jean Dowling, Daphne and Tim Drabble, Dr J.M. Gurney, John Hardcastle, Peter Harris, Philippa Hewitt, Richard Holt, Tom and Ann Knowles, Stephen and Hebe Pritchard, James Overy, Robert and Judith Ruthven, Air Marshal Sir Freddie and Lady Sowrey, David Spearing, Sylvia and Bob Tidey, Miss J.M. Tate, David and Sheila Walters, Margaret Wheatley, Graham Williams and Mrs Laurie Woodcock. As usual Noel Osborne and Nicola Willmot of Phillimore have given me every help and support. Finally, I also wish to put on record my early debt to Fred Tebbutt ('Teb') whose brilliant field work around Ashdown Forest freshly opened my eyes to new aspects of the Weald and who was also a mentor and long-standing friend.

The author is grateful to the following individuals and institutions for photographs and other illustrative material and giving permission to reproduce them. Photographs not listed were taken by the author:

Mick Aston, 25; Bedgebury School, XXVI; Michael Bennett, II; John Blair, 28; Bury Art Gallery and Museum, XXIII; the Trustees of the British Library, 43, 106, 107, 138; The Trustees of the British Museum, 142; The Courtauld Institute, 137; East Sussex Record Office, 20; Peter Herbert, 75; Jason Hawkes Aerial Photo Library, I; Kent Centre for Local Studies, 61, 63, 78, 90, 102, 116, 118, 140; Kent

Messenger, 150; Richard Loder, 147; John Malton, 30, 45, 46, 76, 98, 101, 104, 109, 121, 128, 129, 149; Dr Harry Montgomery, 26, XIV; the National Trust, 119; Chris O'Brien, 142; Phillimore & Co., endpapers; Portsmouth Museum and Art Gallery, 136; Tim Pryke, title page; Sue Rowland, University of Sussex, 3, 6, 11-16, 32-4, 38, 42, 49, 50, 52, 67, 69, 70, 72, 89, 99, 115, 131, 132, 135; David Saunders of East Sussex County Council, 35-6, 151; Air Marshal Sir Freddie Sowrey, IV; the Tate Gallery, XXIV; Times Newspapers, frontispiece; Wealden Buildings Study Group, 27, 51; West Sussex County Council, 110, 134, XIX, XX, XXI, XXIV; Ann Winser, 5, 10, 17, 19, 21-3, 29, 31, 37, 54, 56-58, 60, 71, 73, 74, 86, 88, 114, 123, 125, 130, 131, 133, 139, III, V, VI, VII, XI, XII, XV, XXII.

Preface

The Weald is not easy to know. The concealment of its old iron works and mills, myriads of ponds, straggly greens, and one of the biggest concentrations of timber-framed buildings anywhere in Europe amidst heedlessly exuberant trees, makes this a landscape of hidden surprises. Yet the hiddenness greatly stimulates the quest, and residents secure in their guardian woods are not so exacting in their notion of privacy as to resent the enquiries of the curious passer-by. The only way to familiarise oneself with their intensely private retreats is to travel on foot in one of the most entangled and crookedest mazes of steeply banked lanes, bridle ways and footpaths. The aim to see personally every place and feature mentioned in this book has meant walking along many ways into deep recesses over splodgy fields and damp, rushy meadows and through extensive woods. This tested map-reading skills and ardour to its limits. Yet it is only by this means that some of the threads in the complexity, both natural and man made, can be teased out to make meaningful patterns. In the process this singular landscape casts its spell, delights the eye, warms the heart and feeds the soul.

A principal theme of this book is change, because landscape and society are constantly evolving. The rise and fall of the cloth, iron and glass industries are examples of change which transformed agricultural communities into industrial communities and back again. Yet continuity in the Weald was as pervasive as change. For a variety of reasons the Weald was one of the slowest changing regions of Britain until just about the 1950s when ways of life which had hardly changed for centuries became altered out of all recognition in the space of a single generation. This makes the early 20th century seem a long time back. In several respects over past times an unchangeableness almost amounting to stasis held the Weald firmly in its grip. Whatever yardstick is deployed – ways of farming and equipment used, the management of woods, or the small beer of everyday doings and happenings – we find a remarkably unchanging rural economy and society over hundreds of years committed to such things as a cashless economy, unspeakably bad roads, ox ploughing and threshing with a flail. It will be demonstrated how little the system of agriculture changed over more than seven centuries and the astonishing degree to which field shapes and sizes and, of course, the hedges around them, have persisted for the same length of time. As Oliver Rackham has remarked, the popular notion that the English landscape has been continually changing is less than a half-truth.

Moreover, with much land economically marginal, the Weald has responded more slowly to the progressive amelioration by man than any other region of the South East. Far from being a steady advancement in farming achievement, it has been a hard-won battle with repeated setbacks. The history of each individual farm is invariably one of a family's victories over unkindly soil followed by another's defeats, and parts of the region have never been really tamed. Kipling brilliantly conveys this theme in his poem *The Land* by means of Old Hobden, representing generations of Wealden farmers and labourers who have repeatedly tried, but failed, over some hundreds of years, to bring the meadows in the Dudwell valley at Burwash in Sussex into a secure farming system.

Amongst the general public the Weald is more closely associated with fiction than fact. An example is the legendary belief, which still has a huge popular following, that the Tudor and Stuart iron industry was the main agency responsible for destroying the woodland cover and creating the present pattern of settlement (*Country Life*, 8 February 2001). Pits are always mine pits and all ponds are hammer ponds; byways were constructed to carry cannon from the foundries; every country house was an ironmaster's whose successors laid out the farms once the industry's voracious demand had denuded the great woods. This is romantically picturesque but it is not history. Until comparatively recently scholars more or less agreed with this still popular view but over the past forty years or so the Weald has been the subject of a great deal of new research which has greatly modified this and many other aspects of Wealden history.

A major topic which is repeated and developed throughout this book is the Wealdsman's relationship to his still densely wooded landscape which has been largely played out to the present day as the interaction of man with trees. The story begins as a saga of man against forest, the principal characters being those who wrested a living from the forest by subduing and cultivating it to make a new farm. Apart from every generation's inclination to fight back against the old enemy the wood, a system of farming was evolved whereby trees, livestock and crops were all raised on one piece of land. The guarded acorns sprouted into prodigious bits of timber for the nation's warships and coppice produced a truly remarkable amount of sustainable wood fuel for the iron and glass industries. Traditionally, too, oakwoods and coppices sustained rural communities with materials for a wide range of handicrafts and for the region's unrivalled legacy of timber-framed buildings. Much of the woodland was saved from the forester's axe for hunting, hawking and shooting. From the 17th century trees were felt to be desirable as well as useful and landed estates have been beautified according to current fashionable design. Notably, Victorian and Edwardian *nouveaux riches* introduced so many exotic trees in pineta, arboreta and 'wild gardens' that farming rapidly declined. In few other parts of England have trees and their tending and grubbing been more closely interlinked with human life.

This book seems to have been with me forever. Before 1959, when I began to study the Weald for my doctoral thesis, I had been inspired by Wooldridge and Goldring's *The Weald* (1953) (the only substantial book written on the region in the past fifty years) and become fascinated by a region with a thoroughly bad name during almost all its history but now perceived as England at its most delightful and enjoyable by those to whom suburbia, industrial towns or moorlands are not what England is.

I

A Perspective

FEW FAIL to be seized with an uplifting of spirit as the beauty and wonder of some thirty or more miles of England at its most glorious come into view from the crest of one of the bordering hill ranges of the Weald. By accidents of landscape evolution within this crumpled stretch of the earth's surface, the North and South Downs are for the most part near the horizon circle and frame a huge bowl of exquisitely modulated space. Against this long spare skyline sunrises and sunsets are often breath-taking and views are amongst the most extensive in Britain. Seventeenth-century climbers of Goudhurst church tower were thrilled with a view of 30 parish churches (fewer today are seen because of denser tree cover) and through a telescope at his observatory near the summit of Crowborough Beacon (796 feet above sea level) 19th-century Dr Leeson Prince

1 The view across the Weald from Blackdown, beloved by Tennyson. On a clear day forty miles of densely wooded countryside is visible along the long axis of the Weald, a landscape identical to Norman bocage.

saw 'considerably more than one hundred'. Vaughan Cornish has remarked that 'To live where the outlook is on such a scene endows the ordinary man with poetic feeling, however inarticulate he may be' (*The Beauties of Scenery*). Certainly those who had praised Italian scenery to the uttermost on the Grand Tour and wondered how they could ever again live without it, delighted in scenery which they could imagine as the sweeping backdrop of their Italian models (p.219). The awe-inspiring beauty of these broad prospects induced people to build houses from which to look out upon them, such as the nature-loving poet Tennyson on Blackdown. The owners of Chapledown on the margin of Ashdown Forest rotated their bed on a turntable so that before rising they could take in 360 degrees of deep green country. In his declining years at Chartwell, Winston Churchill dreamt that the lines of continuous folds stretching beyond his dining-room window were the ocean views he had seen on wartime crossings by Cunard liners.

It is a scene which has profoundly stirred scientific enquiry. Around 1800, geologists began to explore the departure of the central dome of chalk which once overarched the landscape (the reason for the present sense of spaciousness) and to unravel how, and for how long, natural forces had taken to shape it into its distinctly different present-day aspect, a matter of excited controversy in a religious age grappling with a new cosmogony. Moreover, it was in the Weald that Mary and Gideon Mantell discovered in 1822 the fossil teeth of a then unknown reptile in a quarry near Cuckfield, which proved to be the remains of a large herbivorous dinosaur, the first found anywhere in the world.[1] Since then the Weald has attracted some of the acutest environmental observations on record and, as natural scientists wrung more and more meaning out of it, the region has become familiar to those absorbed in geographical discovery the world over.

2 *Gideon Mantell (1790-1852), a brilliant and indefatigable geologist, whose discoveries in the Weald brought him fame but no real satisfaction and first undermined his marriage, then his medical practice and, finally, his health. The contemporary researches of Dr Fitton of Hastings were also outstanding and have been given inadequate recognition (see p.23).*

Although the Weald has been conceived as a natural marvel for some two centuries, it is only recently that man's story as played out in this distinctive natural arena has justly become recognised as a human epic. The still great wooded distances as seen from vantage points around the Weald – a rarity in the English lowland – are the key to the decipherment of the region's history. In contrast to the more open Downs which border it, and which were settled so much earlier, the land clearance and settlement for agriculture of the Weald, the largest forest remaining in England in 1086, is a human achievement without parallel in medieval England and one of the longest-running and best recorded examples of the unremitting labour of generations of farmers to clear and settle a great expanse of wild country.

3 The Low and High Weald formed the historic Weald, a district of heavy soils, the natural habitat of the oak. The sands and sandstones of the Greensand ridges on its borders were normally excluded. A sharp distinction was made between settlements on the latter formation, such as Sevenoaks, Sundridge Upland and Boughton Malherbe Upland and the later colonisation in the Wealden portion of these parishes called Sevenoaks Weald, Sundridge Weald, and Boughton Malherbe Weald.

The name 'Weald', akin to German 'Wald', meaning 'forest' was bestowed by Saxons and Kentish Jutes on the immense wooded area that then occupied much of Surrey, Kent and Sussex. For millennia the forest shaped the history of south-east England by functioning as grazing land exploited seasonally by human communities on its more habitable fringes, in the manner of similar extensive areas of mountain, bog and forest in Britain and on the continent. These considerable natural difficulties made the land marginal, i.e. close to the minimum return below which farming became unprofitable. It is uncertain to what degree the Wealden forest was cleared and colonised in the prehistoric and Roman periods but the growth of civil disorder and barbaric invasions, together with epidemics, seems to have led to a conspicuous drop in population in south-east England accompanied by an increase in forested land in the Weald. In historic times a gradual resumption of land clearance occurred, notably when the better land on its fringes ran out around the tenth century.

Thereafter the history of Wealden colonisation at the expense of the forest becomes steadily clearer. The Saxon poet addresses the man who drove the plough on the edge of the forest-waste and daily, bit by bit, wore his way into it, as *Har Holtes Feond*, 'the old enemy at the wood'. His successors reclaiming the wild for new farms were known as assarters who went forth into the wastes at times of land hunger resulting from population pressure, most notably from the 12th to the mid-14th centuries, when widespread agricultural land clearance projects organised by royalty and feudal magnates shrank the forest dramatically. From the second half of the 14th century famine and devastating plagues did away with more than one third of the population. This returned large areas cleared over previous centuries to woodland, scrub, and derelict fields. Tudor and Stuart assarters renewed the onslaught on uncultivated wildness when population rose yet again, recovering, little by little, what had been previously lost, and on seeking to make something out of fresh wildness. Although assarting subsequently petered out, and the old forest was only a fraction of its former existence, there still remained pockets of 'wild' on which a hardy pioneer impelled by dire necessity could start a family. An example was the 'assart of Rushlake Coppice' in Warbleton, let for grubbing and cultivation in more then fifty parcels on the Ashburnham estate as late as the 1820s[2] or the contemporaneous proliferation by the poor on the bleak ridges in the vicinity of Waldron, Heathfield and Burwash of hundreds of smallholdings and cottages, mostly illicit encroachments by squatters ('cribs'). Assarting persisted longest along the margins of Ashdown Forest where cribbing was an old story before the forest became finally regulated in 1866. Thus the assarter's extraordinary achievement makes him the most representative of Wealdsmen. In responding to the perpetual challenge of making a new farm and a new freer life, he is the personification of the region's hearts of oak.

This late and persistent, but incomplete deforestation by land-hungry settlers has created a distinct and uncommon species of English and west European countryside. Climbing to the windmill on Argos Hill near Rotherfield one has a characteristic view of it (Fig.III). The residual scatter of woods, patchwork of little hedged fields, and wide belts of timber known as shaws, together with sparse, scattered and well hidden settlement, betokens a special human landscape, of

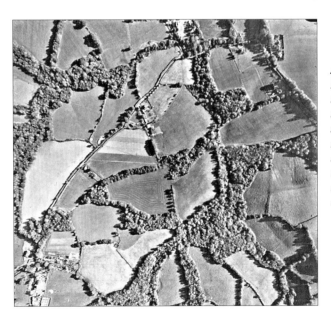

4 *An aerial view of part of Wadhurst parish. This reveals the classic character of a landscape of woodland clearance. The residual woodland is a remnant of one former extensive wildwood. The principal linear woods are ghyll woods, probably never cleared by man. The crooked hedges and the patchwork of small fields are very evident.*

woodland clearance, which represents the vestiges of a more or less continuous tract of forest eaten away piece-meal.

This landscape shaped after clearance by man is known in Normandy as 'bocage' – land wrested from woodland in historic times but with a high proportion of woodland left uncleared owing to inferior soils and difficult topography. After the Conquest this term was adopted in Norman-French and applied to some places in the Weald such as Plumpton Boscage, a former wooded outlier of Plumpton manor near West Hoathly, and lands named 'Boscage' which belonged to Alciston manor in Hellingly. To a remarkable degree the present Wealden landscape with its little dandelion and broomy fields, deep hedgerows and scrabby and splodgy bits linked by shady lanes has changed remarkably little from that produced by the medieval farmer, his wife and a helper or two by 1400, although most of the commons are gone (and almost all the commoners); fields are generally now rather larger, woods rather more extensive, and hedges perhaps wider than they were. This makes it special as a vestige of the much older England of centuries ago, which has largely disappeared almost everywhere else under urban, industrial and agricultural development since the 18th century. Thus to many, the Weald has come to embody England at its most characteristically English.

The individual human scale of almost everything in this landscape is small. All is good to look upon and feels instinctively right and comfortable, making it easy to feel at home and to have the peace of mind that goes with it. The writer H.E. Bates thought it conveyed the 'friendly tranquillising effect of a familiar room'. This smallness was implanted on the landscape by the region's traditional small family-run farms and the active management of timber and underwood for centuries in small woods in comparatively small estates. Yet there was no planning as we understand it now and no striving to produce a beautiful effect. Each individual instinctively did what he felt to be right. The result is a great deal of harmony everywhere. The Weald has always been relatively free from the influence of the 'big house' and the titled estate so that in the Weald proper there is little that is glamorous, bombastic or showy. Instead, small farmers took over a countryside and held it with tenacity and simplicity in relatively adverse circumstances and adapted it in a homespun way to their own hand. For several centuries they remained in isolation with scarcely a voice of their own, nor did others trouble to write of them. Remarking on the landscape pattern of great beauty created by these farmers, John Halsham (C. Forrester Scott) more than one hundred years ago observed that it was, 'Surely in its entirety one of the most notable pieces of man's handiwork which the world has seen'.[3] It is only within the last fifty years that the perceptiveness of his observation has become more generally recognised.

Yet although the weald landscape has been beautifully man-made, some of its charm and ecological value is due to residual features of former forest surviving amidst the artificial shaping of man. These comprise craggy rocks, scrabby hillsides, heaths and remaining woodlands not yet eradicated, including those in the ravine-like valleys ('ghylls'). Being more lately and incompletely settled, these natural features are more abounding than in most English landscapes. These 'wilder' elements intermix with the domestic, garden-like character of farmland tamed from forest, both types of landscape being present by turns at almost every place and melting into one another. This admixture of extensive woodland alternating with cultivation – an unfinished aspect in a human landscape – was excoriated by agricultural 'improvers' down the ages but for the past hundred years or so has come to be regarded as most unusual and delightful scenery where people can come into close contact with nature rich in human, animal and plant communities. Leslie Stephen wrote 'The grandest scenery is not that in which man is altogether absent, nor that which he has tamed and broken, but that in which his victories have been won by submission.'[4] This last is the distinctive quality of the Wealden landscape. It could not fail to leave a mark on Wealdsmen themselves who in so many ways lived close to nature and worked in different conditions with resilience and a deep respect for their soil. Increasingly, this is being regarded as vital to our sense of well-being and fulfilment in the modern world. The appreciation of Wealden 'wildness' only came into public consciousness with the sense of its widespread loss with the growth of London and industrial cities. As long ago as 1898 Forrester Scott advocated protection 'for whole heaths, woods, hillsides and rivers' in the Weald as a foil to advancing London.[5] A step towards this realisation was the designation of the High Weald as an Area of Outstanding Natural Beauty in 1983 but it is only recently that the modern conservation movement has begun to deal seriously with Scott's vision.

The old forest land provides types of unusual landscape with a special charm of their own. The 'ghyll' woodlands have already been mentioned (and see p.22). The innumerable ponds in the Low Weald, particularly in west Kent around Bethersden, also bestow remarkable distinctiveness. Another ubiquitous feature is the woodland-clearing or glade found in the many former deer-parks, on the forests and on wooded pastures once used for common grazing, best known at Ebernoe Common, now a National Nature Reserve, or Mens Wood near Petworth or Markstakes Common in Chailey. One also stumbles across everywhere little meadows (laggs) on tributary streams which are bright with wild flowers in spring and summer, the woods on their steep valley sides being known as 'hangers'. The clack of the mill-wheel is now silent but several hundred former water-mill sites have been identified and their leats, now silted, still traverse their valley floors to the benefit of wildfowl.[6] The streams, quiet in summer but raging in winter, also provided the power for the cloth and iron industries, but the valleys have always been frequently visited by land floods which repeatedly swept away bridges. The failure to bring the meadows into a secure farming system is a recurring theme of Kipling, for example, in his short story *The Friendly Brook* in which Jim Wickenden's response to a full flood in the Dudwell valley contrasts making a living on the land and making money out of it: 'I ain't going to shift my stack a yard. The brook's been good friends to me and if she be minded to take a snatch at my hay, *I* ain't settin' out to withstand her.'

The straggly and isolated footpaths and bridleways that often vanish into green tunnels are amongst the most distinctive and charming features. Their origin was the need for every little farm to have its own access to a cart road or pack-way to link it with its church, mill, common, woods, markets, furnace and forge. Many of these small lanes had to be duplicated as the more direct 'summer roads' were usable only in drier weather. This network of very minor ways feeds into a remarkable tree-like system of byways, which was denser in the past than now because numerous ones became obsolete with road improvement from the 18th century (see p.180 and fig.135). The system thus represents an enduring monument to the culture of the small family farm and harbours many past associations. Walking along these abandoned lanes that cannot be seen from the outside, so entrenched are they by their high hedges of roses and honeysuckle in early summer, is to find how the small farmer put his mark on his land, field by field, copse by copse, and pond by pond.

The Wealden landscape is a product of traditional systems of farming management never rashly abandoned for new fashions and one in which farmers worked with nature, accepting inevitable limits imposed on production, rather than against it, with a too masterful hand. It thus offers a refreshing alternative to modern monolithic and dull countryside, as single-mindedly devoted to production as a modern car assembly plant.[7] The Weald stands out as a place where the destruction that threatens the variety of interest elsewhere – extermination of wildlife, over-mechanisation and mass-production, spoiling of natural beauty, obliteration of cultural traditions and extirpation of small features such as little fields, hedgerows, ponds, copses, and green lanes, has only minimally occurred. It is, therefore, visually more attractive and culturally and biologically more diverse than the Orwellian world which is now much of lowland England. There the ploughing up of chalk grassland, draining of water-meadows, grubbing up of miles of hedges, loss of ancient woodland and excessive use of chemicals has shredded once varied and beautiful landscapes almost to extinction. So much remains unharmed, secluded and unspoilt in the Weald that it offers environmental and social benefits hard to find to the same degree anywhere else in today's overcrowded England.

Apart from creating a special type of landscape, pioneer farmers also established a distinctive type of rural community, primarily cattle-breeding, but also industrial. In a land not easy to settle and cultivate, combining pastoral farming with forest-based industry or some other by-employment was a good way of supplementing income. Unlike arable farming, the routine of pastoral farming involved hard, but seldom unrelenting, toil throughout the year. There were periods during the day and year allowing people with small grass holdings to create second jobs. For example, handicrafts based on local materials such as clay, wood, bark, hides and skins, iron and cloth which flourished from the 13th century in villages founded by artisans and traders, not farmers as in most of England. These handicrafts attracted people to the region from more open countrysides with fewer opportunities of earning a living and by Tudor times they transformed the Weald from a once poor and backward 'frontier' community into one of the wealthiest districts of England. This human handiwork intimately woven into the fabric of rural life centuries ago is kept alive today by the many craftsmen still practising traditional wood crafts.

In their extraordinarily wooded landscape Wealdsmen have been woodsmen
and land-breakers to the very core of their being for over a thousand years. Boys
were traditionally taught to coppice and pollard trees (for this is young men's
work), and the farmer was as skilled with hedges, clearing trees or managing them
for fuel and timber as with his cattle. The skills and customs thus evolved in the
winning and working of land were often handed down in the same families for
generations. In few other parts of England have woods and their tending and
grubbing been more closely inter-linked with human life.

The Wealdsman has also long had a loving and proprietorial relationship with
the English oak, for which the region was long celebrated. The pride and glory
of the forest, it was yet so common as to be nicknamed the Sussex weed. For
ships and buildings there was little other timber comparably so strong as Wealden
oak. This exceptional quality was attributed to its growth in ferruginous clays. The
scientific proof of this is still lacking, but John Hardcastle, a retired forester of
Whiligh in Wadhurst, itself for centuries a famed nursery of oak, has implied its
correctness with his assertion that the ferruginous Weald and Wadhurst Clay 'is
to oak as mustard is to beef'.[8] The acorns of Sidney's oak, supposedly planted
at Sir Philip Sidney's christening in 1554, but in fact much older, have been planted
round the world by the 1st Viscount De L'Isle and, as a result of cloning, saplings
genetically identical to the tree are to be planted on the Penshurst estate. Pope's
oak, under which the poet wrote the 'Rape of the Lock' in the former West
Grinstead Park, is also revered. In the Weald the oak is king and its people are
proud to have cherished numerous veteran trees which no one has had the heart
to fell.

Gliding by Eurostar, or travelling by motorway or commuter train through
what is increasingly becoming part of London's rich businessman's world, it is
hard to imagine how remote and divergent the Weald was compared with bordering regions until comparatively recent times. Families seem seldom to have moved
out of the circle of hills and often kept together for years within the boundaries
of a single parish (but see p.168). To the young Frank Kendon near Goudhurst
in the 1860s the strange and unimagined world of the North Downs and places
beyond to London 'were all names on the lips of travellers, as far away from us
as the Americas.'[9] Similarly, only faint vibrations of the outer world reached
Siegfried Sassoon's family at Matfield c.1900. It was the 'sleepy miles' to the county
town of Maidstone in his intensely local and limited world which implanted in him
in later life a sense of heartache for little cock-crowing farms, deep-rutted lanes,
mist-coiled waterways and hedgerows sparkling in the sunshine after early
morning showers under which the cattle drowsed.[10] Edmund Blunden has noted
of Yalding at about the same period that 'London was within fifty miles of us,
but troubled most of the inhabitants hardly more than the mountains of the
moon.'[11]

The concept of the Weald as a region has meant different things to people
at different times and has been variously imagined and rendered. Early Anglo-
Saxon annalists viewed it with hostility and a sense of alienation. They pondered
a desolate scene, symbolically charged with an aura of mystery, into which people

took refuge for concealment, so untouched and dangerous that people preferred to settle its borders. Bede's eighth-century description is of a region 'thick and inaccessible, the abode of deer, swine and wolves'. The impression given by such Saxon writers is that man had hardly left any mark on the Wealden forest and that no effort was being made to tame it. This we now know was both true and untrue (p.45). In actuality, its parishes were gradually evolving from pig pastures owned by manors on the fringes and increasingly succumbing to colonists with axe and plough. Yet there was still much clearing of forest to be done by medieval churchman or lay magnate whose belief was that the only good wood was a wood cleared and settled. Lambarde, the first historian of Kent, writing in 1570, echoed this sentiment by declaring the Weald of Kent to be 'a forest now wholly replenished (thank be God) with people'.

Successful pioneers are typically sturdy, adventurous, hard working and resourceful persons who tend to be independent and ruggedly individualist. The medieval pioneer farmer was of this type. To him the forest offered food, clothing, shelter, heat and light and a sense of security and freedom. He reacted positively to the challenge forests have always posed to resilience ancl ingenuity and might well have thought of it as a training for life. Enveloped in his not easily traversible woods within encircling hills and the sea, the Wealdsman also tended to be secluded and near-isolated from the outside world. It was not easy in such a close-knit rural community of small family farms, exposed to the eye and criticism of neighbours in like circumstance, for anyone to break with tradition, and isolation limited the opportunities for doing so. Steeped in old customs which offered strong resistance to new ideas, the small farmer did not adopt the materialistic outlook measuring everything in terms of profit. Like that of other late settled forests, his society was one in which individuals had a great deal of freedom from manorial control.[12] Moreover, and in this respect like all forest communities, the Wealdsman's tended to be naturally insubordinate, at times not easily governable and inclined towards nonconformity in religion. The maxim of the Sussex labourer, 'We won't be druv' is almost certainly Wealdish. In this respect the Wealdsman tended to contrast with the rural society in bordering villages more strictly controlled by lords where there was more respect for authority. In these cicumstances, the Weald, particularly the Kent Weald, became the classic home of the yeoman. Visually, the most impressive evidence of that freedom today is the extraordinary legacy of substantial yeomen's houses, some having been owned by rebels who were the mainstay of Cade's revolt in 1450, and descendants of supporters of the Peasants' Revolt in 1381, a number of whom had been Lollard followers of John Wycliffe.

Despite this general freer element in the Weald, there were important cultural differences between the Sussex (and Surrey) Wealds, on the one hand and the Kent Weald on the other, which are reflected in their respective landscapes ancl societies. Wealden Sussex is not Wealden Kent although the soil is much the same. Moving towards Sussex or into Surrey from Kent the richness fades near the borders and the aspect is less soft. The hop gardens and orchards begin to thin out. The intensity of farming and the fecundity is no longer there; the landscape

5 A late 19th-century iron overshot waterwheel at Newbridge Mill in Ashdown Forest. This probably originated with the pioneer farmers of the 13th century, for example at Suntings Farm, who would have needed to grind their flour locally. The site is near that of the blast furnace and forge introduced into Sussex in 1496, which is regarded as the birth-place of the English iron industry (see p.129).

has much more bracken, gorse, heather and broom. There are also fewer half-timbered farmhouses of the 15th and 16th centuries and they tend to be smaller and less designed to impress.

Apart from the significant natural differences across the Sussex border, culturally there was greater wealth accumulation in the Kent Weald, promoted by tenurial differences to the advantage of Kentish peasants. Whereas in the medieval Surrey and Sussex Wealds manor lordship was a powerful force, siphoning off peasant wealth as it accumulated, in Kent, as Lambarde stated, 'in a manner every man is a freeholder and hath some part of his own to live on'. The freehold, family-sized farm was a bulwark to the agricultural economy and to democratic ideals. The wealth of the Kentish yeoman early became proverbial, and the custom of gavelkind dividing land amongst male heirs, ensured that the relatively small freeholder was typical of Kent. It also meant that with his sense of security and status the Kentish farmer tended to devote more attention to the care and improvement of his own land[13] and was often relatively richer than his counterparts in Sussex and Surrey. Furthermore, society was more mobile and individualistic, and thus more readily able to develop agricultural production for market and to initiate new industries than elsewhere in the Weald (pp.141-152). Thus passing from the Kent Weald into that of Sussex (and Surrey) was in some ways like passing from one society to another and the landscape reveals this in various subtle ways.

Although the Wealdsman had a sense of satisfaction with his unobtrusive and domestic homeland, outsiders in past times were more likely to be detractors, most of whom, however, were snobbish fools. The poorly farmed, muddy Weald was imperfectly known and seemed about as welcoming as Afghanistan is today. Forests were generally despised in the 17th century and earlier as 'wild and rude places' and were contrasted unfavourably with rich and plentiful open country of the fertile plains of north-east Kent and coastal Sussex rolling inland from the sea until they met the Downs adorned with great flocks of sheep. Such places had elegant country seats, were 'plenteously peopled', and being 'unblemished' by great woods and wastes, everything could be turned into profitable use.[14] Moreover, in the early 17th century 'lewdness and rudeness' of people was specifically attributed directly to the presence of extensive woods and wastes; it was said at the same time that Sussex needed more magistrates than any other county on account of the woods and the sea.[15]

The civilisation of a district was tested by such criteria as the state of its agriculture and condition of its roads; both being found antiquated in the Weald for several centuries, these negative connotations were extended to the community living with them, and the Weald consequently became distinguished largely by the degree of stigma attached to it. Until the era of good roads, journeys up and down the Weald's 'impracticable hills' were at the hazard of one's bones and the Weald was known more for the danger and discomforts of travel than the merits of its scenery. When the ordeal and even danger of crossing it in winter and wet weather was being gradually alleviated by turnpike roads, visitors discovered obsolete agriculture, a 'wilderness' near at hand and people who had long followed a country life of a much slower and different rhythm from that of much of their surroundings. They found themselves in a little world whose way of life was stuck in the distant past. To borrow a phrase of Thomas Hardy's, the Weald was 'a place which had slipped out of its century generations ago …' and where 'the busy outsider's ancient times are only old, his old times are still new, his present is futurity'.

For centuries, in fact, to the harm of its reputation, the Weald was defined in the eyes of contemporary outsiders as a region where landscapes and life were on the wrong side of the divide between the civilised and uncivilised, the refined and the unrefined and the beautiful and the forlorn. In modern jargon, the Weald had a fundamental image problem. Criticism came to a head in the 18th century with the laments of agricultral improvers and tourists fresh from exclusive London or Tunbridge Wells clubs, theatres and coffee houses. Horace Walpole's travelogue, which turns the region into a stage set of barbarism, smuggling and unbelievably bad tourist and travelling facilities, gives the impression that the Weald had little changed from the time when its thick forest was inhabited by pig-keepers (pp.45-6). Outsiders had it in for the Weald so strongly that this sentiment is expressed by Jane Austen in her unfinished novel *Sanditon* (1817) which opens in the High Weald. Her evocation of the dirt and dangers of a road traversing matchless scenery is masterly topographical drawing. The response to an enquiry about a place by the rescued occupants of a carriage which had overturned in a little-used by-way was the reply, '[… It is] quite down in the Weald'. 'And we, sir,' he added, speaking rather proudly, 'are not in the Weald.'

Edward Hasted, whose *History of Kent* was published between 1778 and 1801 and who had the tastes and prejudices of the Hanoverians, disliked the salient features of its scenery which have been admired since the Romantic and Picturesque movements. Dark woodland places and rocky outcrops filled him with gloomy thoughts; the now justly prized half-timbered houses were to him 'mean and old-fashioned'; ponds only signified wet miry clay; and he had no notion that woodlands which smell so sweetly in the morning give one great pleasure, well-being and a sense of the 'wild'. Although, for example, Rolvenden and Benenden were deemed pleasantly situated in the ups and downs of their

Weald, parishes such as Frittenden, Marden, Headcorn and Shadoxhurst were regarded as dull and inaccessible.[16] Dearn (1814) and Ireland (1829), who plagiarised extensively, reiterate Hasted's opinions.[17] The Weald remained largely unexplored by the pleasure-seeker or the artist. A new romantic note was early struck by an excursionist from Maidstone to Tonbridge who never saw 'sweeter country even in Devon'.[18] It was not until a generation later that Nasmyth (1758-1840) made it known to art, the Barbizon school of romantic painters began to paint in the forest of Fontainebleau and John Linnell sketched in Balcombe Forest.

The marked change of attitude favourable to the Weald which increased steadily from the early 19th century was in part created by improved roads, and later by railways, which made the formerly inaccessible Weald readily reached from London and the growing coastal resorts. But primarily the changed appreciation of the Weald arose in the minds of the ordinary visitor struggling to cope with the effects of industrialism and, in particular, the rapid expansion of London to become the world's largest city. People concerned at overcrowding, bad housing, poverty, disease, dirt and noise and haunted by the disappearance of 'Old England', brought newly-opened eyes to a peaceful region bearing no scars of these changes. They began to recognise it as the distinct species of human landscape that it was, and discovered its powers to refresh mind and body wearied by the dual shocks of industrialism and urbanism to such a degree that they took the Weald to their hearts as a dream of tranquil English scenic beauty (see Chapter 28).

On the threshold of the 21st century, the Weald is one of the landscapes crying out for a prominent place in the tired, overworked countryside of Britain. For Wooldridge, who wrote his inspiring *The Weald* in 1953, it was a region to which we could turn as much for solace of mind and spirit as for scientific studies 'in the fitting and valuable endeavour to see ourselves as one with our past and part of nature' (p.4.) Doing this is still as realisable at as deep a level as when Wooldridge was writing, but the need to follow his example, and to ensure that the landscape is sufficiently protected to enable us to do so, is more vital than ever now that in so much of England this experience is unattainable.

It is therefore unsurprising that Nigel Nicolson, son of Vita Sackville-West (with the modern development of the Medway towns and the rest of the Kent coast and estuaries in mind), should regard the Weald of Kent as the cultural heartland of his county;[19] or that Ashdown Forest, which William Cobbett perceived as the most villainous place God made, should now be regarded as a jewel for the recreationist.[20] How astonished those 16th-century antiquaries, William Lambarde and William Camden, would have been at this modern high regard for the Weald, in which they had found little historic or other interest. Englishmen over the past hundred years or so, with an enthusiasm bordering on the rhapsodic, have proved the old image of the Weald to be an anachronism. Will the renaissance lure so many people that the Weald's special character will be destroyed?

2

The Historical Bounds of the Weald

GEOGRAPHICALLY the Weald is hard to place for many Britons. This is because it is widely famous for not being famous; unlike the South Downs, the Cotswolds or, say, Dartmoor which have become icons among the general public. Yet it has one of the longest-lasting of the regional names of Britain and has always had a distinct identity within south-east England. Today it is usually thought of as one of the most plainly marked areas in England, the oval-shaped area covering more than one thousand square miles of expressively-shaped countryside lying within the outer rims of the North and South Downs which is divided administratively into the Wealds of Kent, Surrey and Sussex with a tiny part in Hampshire.

This is the Weald of the geologist which only became common currency after a handful of natural scientists from the late 18th century stretched it to unify all the expanse formerly covered by the Wealden dome, the over-arch of chalk subsequently eroded to reveal older rocks forming its core within the present chalk rim. This structurally compact natural region makes a rational unit for geologists and geographers and has been adopted by planners and others.

Yet although this concept of the Weald is now rooted in common parlance, the historian's Weald is more limited in extent. When Saxons and Jutes bestowed the word 'Weald' it was equivalent to the German 'Wald' meaning forest. They applied it to ancient untamed oak forest broadly identified with the area which has many place-names in 'hurst', 'ley' and 'field', indicating cleared woodland; and other place-names which betoken closely-wooded country such as 'den' and 'fold' where in summer great droves of swine were attended in the glades by swineherds from older established places on the periphery. This is the district of tenacious and obstinate soil, the natural habitat of the oaks for which the Weald was famous. This area is now known as the Low and High Weald which geologically lie on the Hastings Beds and the Weald Clay respectively.[1]

Anciently excluded under the term 'Weald' was land cleared of forest and settled earlier, such as the rich Vale of Holmesdale running like a ribbon immediately below the escarpment of the North Downs, and the corresponding line of villages in the scarp foot zone below the South Downs. Also excluded were the more lightly wooded sandstone hills on the Lower Greensand formation to the north and south, probably more open, where beech would have been interspersed with heath. They also appear to have been settled earlier. Also excluded were Romney Marsh and the Pevensey Levels which were sea and alluvial flat when the term 'Weald' was coined.

In this book, the name 'weald' has been used mainly in its more limited historical context although the wider meaning has been adopted for the sake of contrast and to bring out when necessary the interaction between the historic Weald and its surrounds. The wider definition has also been used when dealing with some events from the 19th century because it would have been pedantic to have done otherwise.

Thus landscapes, customs and practices have not been ascribed to people in any period who did not consider themselves Wealdsmen. An example will make this point clear. Wynne Thomas's engaging study of cricket is subtitled *From the Weald to the World* but it is evident that early cricketers played in the shade of a great house or on the squire's village green and aristocrats mingled with artisans on the field of play. In the Weald there were plenty of artisans but hardly any aristocrats and thus the earliest cricket grounds were invariably not in what contemporaries recognised as the Weald but on its bounds where quite different social and economic conditions were more favourable to the game's origin.

This question of the historic limits of the Weald is of particular significance because, possibly uniquely in England, 16th- and 17th-century inhabitants claimed that the Weald's boundaries could be defined according to whether tithes were payable on woodland or not. By immemorial custom before the Tithe Commutation Act of 1836 woodland in the Weald was exempted from tithes whereas in bordering districts it was accountable. The ancient exemption of the Weald's woodland from tithe presumably indicates that until the voracious demand of the iron- and glass-makers in the 16th and 17th centuries, timber and fuel was not saleable owing to the distance and inaccessibility of markets and that woodland was considered to be awaiting clearance by would-be farmers where crops would then have been titheable.

The main issue contested in these tithe disputes was whether or not the boundary of the Weald lay below the sandstone hills on the Lower Greensand formation to north and south. In east Surrey and Kent this range of hills had its own ancient district name of the Chart Country. It was also known variously as the Red or Ragstone Hills and they are now being popularised as the Quarry Hills. A similar terrain is repeated in West Sussex. Along this northern range of hills, as Hasted implied and Furley observed in 1871, the Weald's boundary was generally accepted as following the crestline on which Kentish parish churches such as Boughton Monchelsea and Linton are located. The hills that overhang the Weald were never considered part of it.[2]

Local juries did not always agree with the conventionally accepted boundary. Generally speaking, however, the Weald's boundaries for tithe purposes did not extend beyond the Weald which was still largely forested in Saxon times. This is evident from the Tithe Awards for parishes straddling the reputed boundaries of the Weald which invariably distinguish woodland on Weald Clay as exempted from tithe.

3

The Natural Setting

The Low Weald

The low-wooded and watery Low Weald, which wraps round the High Weald in the form of a horseshoe and interweaves the other landscapes together, is the least known and most misunderstood part of southern England. It is usually thought of as an undiversified muddy plain but is in fact gently undulating and has many delightful scenic qualities. A succession of low east-west ridges traverse it in which there are subordinate beds of sand and sandstone locally which include sites of Mesolithic hunters, now the haunts of badgers. These produce a topography of small swellings and ridges, some affording wide views over the extensively wooded countryside. Near Billingshurst (Fig.6) is a geologically important exposure of a succession of such strata which becomes finer in texture upwards. This is interpreted as a deposit by a swollen river entering the Weald from the region of Cornwall bearing floating debris of trees which grounded on a former bar in a delta. Subsequently, finer sands were dumped on top by the river in a quieter period. Abundant fossil remains are preserved including gastropods, fish, reptile bones and plant and tree fragments.[1] Soils derived from the Paludina are of considerably greater fertility than their surrounds and they and the other little eminences are invariably the sites of farmhouses, the land nearest the barns being the main arable land and pasture: meadow and woodland traditionally occupied the wetter and heavier ground in the valleys. Okehurst and Rowner farms in Billingshurst illustrate this.[2]

   The pleasant undulations of this charming sylvan landscape can be viewed, for example, from Sharpenhurst Hill at Itchingfield near Horsham. Although this hill is less than 300 ft. above sea level, it gives sudden outlook over the plain of alternating low folds with distant prospects on the skyline (Fig.7). Writing of this view at the end of the 19th century, Wilfrid Scawen Blunt (1840-1922) thought that 'no more perfect picture of peace could be imagined, nothing more absolutely beautiful'.[3] For all his espousal of progressive causes, he was at heart a wistful traditionalist who, in old age, could not experience happiness without his local anchorage, and found it difficult to recognise beauty anywhere other than in the Weald. His tomb, in an avenue of yew trees on his estate, bears the lines of a virile youthful sonnet declaring his passion for this particular part of the Sussex countryside:

> ... Dear checker-work, of woods, the Sussex Weald!
> If a name thrills me yet of things of earth,

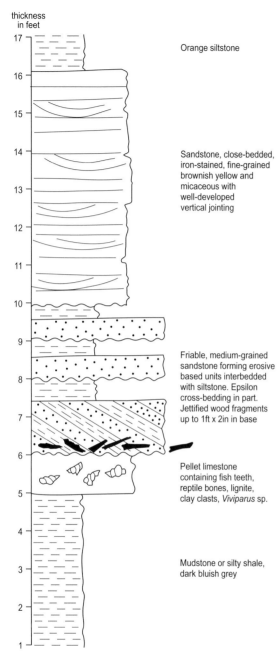

thickness
in feet

Orange siltstone

Sandstone, close-bedded,
iron-stained, fine-grained
brownish yellow and
micaceous with
well-developed
vertical jointing

Friable, medium-grained
sandstone forming erosive
based units interbedded
with siltstone. Epsilon
cross-bedding in part.
Jettified wood fragments
up to 1ft x 2in in base

Pellet limestone
containing fish teeth,
reptile bones, lignite,
clay clasts, *Viviparus* sp.

Mudstone or silty shale,
dark bluish grey

6 A geological section through the upper strata of the Weald Clay at Okehurst, Billingshurst. The intervening strata between the clay appears at the surface locally and makes low ridges of lighter and warmer soil.

That name is thine. How often have I fled
To thy deep hedgerows and embraced each
    field.
Each lag, each pasture – fields which gave
    me birth
And saw my youth, and which must hold
    me dead.[4]

The densely wooded little valleys on this Surrey-Sussex border strongly appealed to Hilaire Belloc and to the novelist George Gissing who wrote in 1889 of Chiddingfold that 'More beautiful country cannot be found … I suppose there really is no part of England more richly wooded and more tempting to people wanting absolute quietness …'.[5]

It is still the Weald at its hiddenmost. One enters narrow lanes with few of their old bends and curves smoothed away so their verges are amongst the most flowery in the Weald. The most ancient hedges have up to ten wooded species in 30-yard stretches and include ancient woodland indicator species such as midland hawthorn, field maple and spindle which have glorious autumn colours. A particularly characteristic feature is the greenway, an obsolete highway trending north-south used by drovers herding pigs and cattle, between villages on or below the Downs and Wealden pastures. Of a close network of these, the finest preserved is the 40ft. wide one on which stands Crookhorn Farm in Shipley (Plate xv). This is a precious ribbon of wildlife conveying an illusion of an unchanging countryside. Where sand lenses occur in the clay these old lanes are hollowed into the rock, twisting many feet below field surfaces. It is a thickly coppiced landscape with wide shaws and great swards of bluebells of the deepest hue and of such an overpowering scent as to make one feel drunk. Another delightful characteristic is the hanger, the wood on the flanks of the ghylls intersecting the landscape where sandstone outcrops of Weald clay are occasionally exposed in stream banks. In winter most of the meadowland and rush-fringed ponds are flooded by the main rivers and their

7 Wilfrid Scawen Blunt's tomb in his grounds at New Buildings, Shipley.

8 Bluebells, Shelleys Wood, Itchingfield. The land falls gently in the wood to display the flowers to perfection, with lovely views to the Surrey Hills and the South Downs.

tributaries and myriads of small stream-lets. So sparsely settled is this country-side that one can spend hours in this quiet, wild, hidden country of extensive woodland and river and canal pathways with a sense of being alone with cuckoo, nightingale and kingfisher, butterflies and rampant wildflowers.

Ebernoe is one of the most inter-esting places in this neighbourhood. It is almost unpeopled, with one biggish house and two or three farms scattered over a mile of wild country in the heart of the Sussex Weald. Yet it has an old school house and a church. It was famed for its Horn Fair, held in June, and its cricket ground is unique in Sussex, being cut across by the only road, leaving some outfielders on the other side. It is now notable for its wood common which has become a national nature reserve and SSSI.

The Low Weald of Kent has simi-larities but considerable contrasts. The Eurostar to Paris and Brussels now glides along the straight and perfectly level track to the channel tunnel, a railway which when first constructed in 1844 opened this formerly isolated area. The land is low, frequently flooded and the soil has a rubber-like quality in winter and a concrete-like hardness in summer. No one would call this naturally good land but assiduous yeoman farmers have mellowed their grudging soil over generations by marling and other means to enable it to produce good crops of corn and grass. This more intensively worked land than in the equivalent Weald clay belt in West Sussex is very evident near Bethersden and Smarden where past digging of Bethersden 'Marble', marl, and clay for tiles and bricks has resulted in an extraordinary profusion of reed-filled, tree-lined ponds (Fig.16). The area covered with alluvium from the rivers Medway and Beult was one so rich in hops and fruit as to be accounted part of the Garden of England.

9 An abandoned 'summer' road between Bethersden and Smarden. These former highways on deep clay were unsuitable for use in the winter.

The High Weald

Travel in any direction across the varying rocks between East Grinstead, Uckfield and Cranbrook brings dramatic visual contrasts. This district is composed of alternating sandstones, sands and clays of the Hastings Beds, aptly described as a 'multi decker sandwich'. It is much faulted and folded, and deeply furrowed,

10 A graveyard of hop poles, Rolvenden, a widespread sign of the rapid collapse of the hop industry.

11 The High Weald woodland species. The oak remains the predominant tree but birch has rapidly colonised land formerly used for grazing and neglected coppice. (Forestry Commission, Alice Holt)

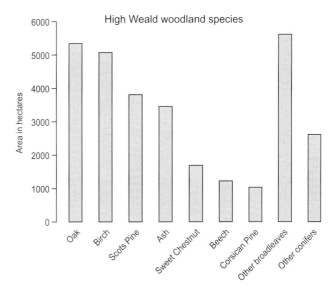

with some 300 ravines in headwater valleys known as ghylls containing swiftly-flowing streams in winter which once powered cloth mills, furnaces and forges (Fig.13). Superimposed on this markedly 'up and down' landscape is the remarkable patchwork of little fields.

Amongst the most interesting natural feature of the High Weald is exposure of sand rocks which rise, usually from the sides of ghylls, as deeply fissured crags up to 30ft. high in the vicinity of Tunbridge Wells. They bring an unexpected element of 'wildness' to within thirty miles of Piccadilly, the topography in places being reminiscent of Exmoor or even Wales. Only a few are widely known, such as Eridge and High Rocks, and the famous Toad Rock at Rusthall, which E.V. Lucas rather exaggeratedly remarked, 'Is to Tunbridge Wells what the Leaning Tower is to Pisa'. There are 75 significant such rock exposures and hundreds of lesser ones in private grounds, like those hidden in dense woodland on an estate at Heron's Ghyll near Uckfield bearing early 17th-century graffiti. Generations of later visitors also discovered that the rock is so soft that initials can be carved on it almost as easily as on a tree, yet sandstone blocks used for masonry hardened with dry storage within a year or two. There are only three other areas of soft sandstone rocks in lowland Europe – the Forest of Fontainebleau, the Petite Suisse in Luxembourg and at Elbsandstungeberg on the Czech-German border.

Most of the cliffs occur in the Ardingly Sandstone, a massively jointed bed within the Lower Tunbridge Wells Sand. They are broken by widened vertical joints or Gulls which separate the sandstone into a series of blocks. In many locations the cliffs are strikingly undercut at their base and are pitted by masses of circular hollows. This honeycomb pattern is considered to result from weathering from salt carried inland from the coast in rain.[6] As the only natural rock faces within easy reach of London, in the 19th century, the most precipitous and accessible, such as High Rocks near Groombridge, became popular venues for artists and sightseers and are today major tourist attractions; although all the ascents are short, some are of sufficient technical difficulty to challenge even experienced climbers. The base of many cliffs is often strikingly cut into caves. Some isolated blocks have been so extensively undercut that they form pedestal rocks. The best known is Great-upon-Little, an isolated block of 400-500 tonnes which stands on a narrow pedestal just in front of a cliff near West Hoathly.

The woods, sheltered by these rocks, are the main stronghold of many 'oceanic' or 'Atlantic' species, both vascular plants and bryophytes. Such woods were invariably owned and managed by landlords on tenanted farms but owing to their inaccessibility most such habitats have remained virtually undisturbed by man for millennia, although exploitive clearances presumably were made during the period of the iron industry, for example, at Hendall. Dense trees in these narrow valleys, such as alder and ash, which form a closed canopy, together with the damp sheltered sites, create a warm, humid micro-climate unlike anywhere else in south-east England. Rose has examined at least 200 woods and demonstrated that in this special habitat grow plants general in the South East during the 'Atlantic' period of climate some 5,000 years ago but now usually restricted to the West Country. The most striking plant of the ghylls is perhaps the hay-scented fern known in about 100 sites from Warninglid eastwards to Tenterden in Kent. The ivy-leaved bell-flower is also found in some ghylls amidst varieties of uncommon liverwort, mosses and innumerable rare lichens. The beautiful coral-root is plentiful on Wadhurst clay. Fairlight Glen is famous as the only location east of Devon for the 'tropical-oceanic' liverwort *Dumortiera hirsuta*, plentiful on wet rock faces, both at the head of the glen and on wet boulders near the stream. Of the massive sand rocks the most interesting site is Philpots Rocks, unique in England east of west Somerset for its extraordinary flora of

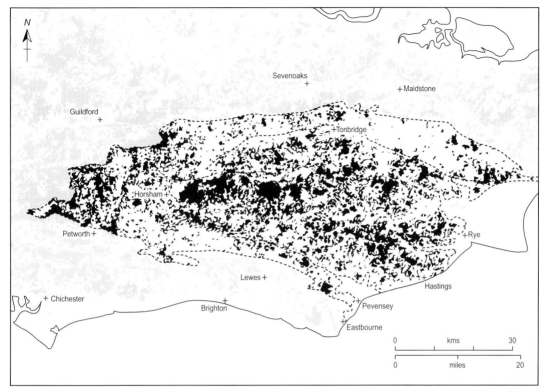

12 Distribution of woodland greater than two hectares in the Low and High Weald, 2002 (Forestry Commission, Alice Holt). The total area is 65,351 hectares, of which 38,262 is broadleaved woodland (mainly oak and birch), 8,000 is coniferous and 4,189 coppice. Ancient and semi-natural woodland covers 28,253 hectares and ancient replanted woods 13,758 hectares.

oceanic bryophytes. By 1987 a massive infestation of rhododendron *ponticum* and the spread of beech and holly was damaging the bryophyte flora. The great storm of 1987 swept up the ravine and uprooted at least 70 per cent of the trees. This proved to be a blessing in disguise because the extra light has been beneficial to most of the important bryophytes on the main rock faces. Examples of these linear woods in Kent are Robbins Wood, Combwell Wood and Parsonage Wood near Tunbridge Wells.[7]

Exceptionally interesting are other 'ancient' woodlands which have never been cleared, or retaining a continuity of woodland cover since at least the Middle Ages. Such ancient woodland is identified from its special 'old woodland lichens' and vascular plants. House Copse near Crawley, significant botanically and historically for its woodland, includes the small leaved lime (*tilia cordata*) which some 5,000-7,000 years ago was a common component of Wealden woodlands but has now almost disappeared. Almost uniquely in southern England, the lime was managed with hornbeam as coppice under oak standards.

The nature of the soil profile is an excellent indication of a site being wooded throughout most of its history. Sites long under agriculture will usually have

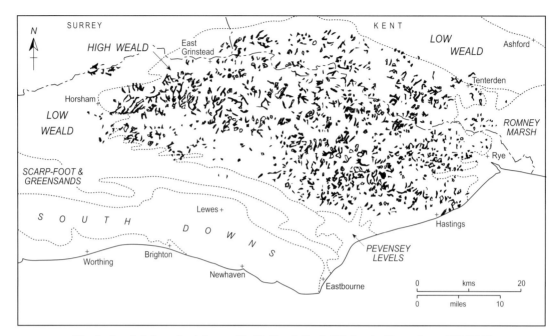

13 Distribution of ghyll woodlands (surveyed by Dr Francis Rose). (Biodiversity Centre, Sussex Wildlife Trust, West Sussex County Council)

evidence of soil erosion and fertilising. Sites bearing long-continued woodland are normally on deeper, non-calcareous soil, often with much iron oxide present, giving the soil profile a reddish brown colour. Such sites correlate positively with old documents or estate maps indicating long continued presence of woodland.

The ground and shrub flora of a woodland also give positive or negative indications of the age and continuity of the woodland cover. Most important is the presence of so called 'indicator species', certain plant species unable to re-colonise newer woodlands except over a long period of time. These include plants such as butcher's broom, wood spurge, wood sorrel, wood anemone, sweet woodruff, herb paris, solomon's seal, moschatel, yellow archangel, etc. A list of species known to correlate well with old woodland in a particular district can be used as a guide to examine woodlands of uncertain age. Some insects, particularly those beetles and bugs associated with old trees and decaying timber, appear to give excellent indications of probable ancient woodland. It is the epiphytic lichens, however, that are perhaps the most valuable and reliable indicators of the age and continuity of woodland because nearly all of them are slow colonists.

Ashdown Forest

This is an area of great individuality of almost true highland where the shape and sweep of the hills reminds one of the Yorkshire Moors. It is a tract of singular loveliness, the largest remaining part of Andredesweald or Forest of Anderida and thus one of the few surviving vestiges of the pristine England where the wildness pushed back by medieval backwoodsmen elsewhere in the Weald still continues to hold out. It lies on the silty sandstones and silt of the Ashdown Beds in the highest part of the Weald where poor drainage, rainfall higher than the average for south-east England, and shorter growing season, have throughout history made these soils difficult to cultivate.

During the Middle Ages Ashdown was used for hunting as a royal Forest until in 1372 granted as a free chase to John of Gaunt as part of the Duchy of Lancaster. The Forest core was specifically reserved for harbouring deer but the surrounding fringes were commonable to tenants of the Manor of Duddleswell. Between the 16th and 19th centuries a robber economy prevailed on the Forest. Probably never extensively wooded, the remaining trees were stripped for iron works, and pared turf for fuel. Periodic burning of heather, to improve grazing and cutting of fern, gorse and broom to litter barns for manure, progressively degraded and depleted the soils and turned the Forest into heathland. Large tracts of the Forest core were enclosed under the 1693 Decree but the commoners' dogged resistance ensured that 10 square miles were reserved for common grazing. Another fierce resistance by the commoners occurred in 1876-82. For this lovely portion of England, now seen as the crowning glory of the Weald for recreational purposes, we owe much to the stubborn resistance of the 'Forest men' over the past three centuries.

The Cliffed Coastline

The cliffs between Hastings Castle and Pett Beach constitute one of the most scenically outstanding stretches of undeveloped coastline in south-east England. As viewed from East Hill or other vantage points along it, this complex coast is of great scientific interest on account of its geology and the plant life in its glens. Geologically, its outstanding scientific significance has been recognised ever since the pioneer studies of Dr William Fitton, a Hastings resident, in the 1820s and there is still no better place to examine the geological evolution of the Weald.[8] The sandstones of the Ashdown Sands in the upper part of the cliffs are well exposed and the base of the overlying Wadhurst clay is a prominent feature. Root traces and plant debris, including soil beds with *Equisetites* are traceable, some overlain with thin brown coal. The variations between the hard sandstone and soft clays stretch inland to form the alternating high ridges and narrow valleys in the High Weald. A number of plant habitats are also represented, protected by an SSSI, including woodland (mostly ancient), scrub, maritime grassland and a vegetated shingle beach. These support a number of rare bryophytes (mosses and liverworts), lichens, flowering plants and beetles.

STAGE I   The early Mesozoic sea invades the Palaeozoic platform and the Mesozoic trough begins to form

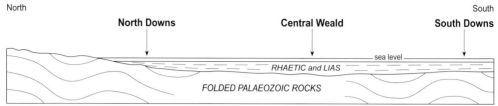

STAGE II   Subsidence of the trough continues throughout Jurassic and early Cretaceous times with sporadic emergence of the margins of the trough in the north

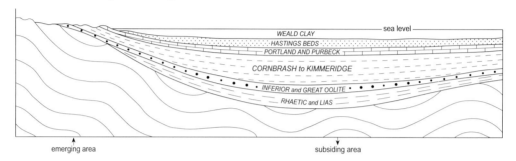

STAGE III   Differential subsidence ceases and the London Uplands are submerged beneath the Gault and later Cretaceous transgressions

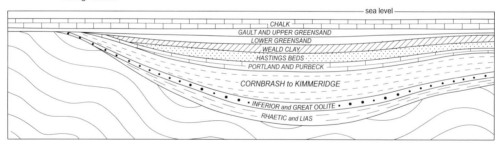

STAGE IV   Tertiary folding and subsequent subaerial erosion erosion produce the present day structure and topography

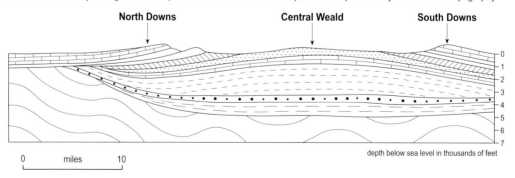

14 Geological evolution of the Weald (after Allen).

4

Soils and Earth History

THE rocks within the saucer around the Weald are not found anywhere else in Europe except in its now three truncated continuations. These are the northern half of the Isle of Wight; the Boulonnais near Boulogne; and the narrow arm of the Pays de Bray, an eroded anticline like the Weald in which rocks older than the chalk lie in an elongated hollow within lovely beech-covered chalk escarpments rising to 750 feet in the uplands of Normandy and Picardy. It had important iron-making connections with the Weald (p.130) and has a pretty bocage landscape with towns appropriately twinned with Hailsham and Heathfield in Sussex though it is not as densely hedged as the Weald, and so does not retain a 'cosy' appearance to the same degree.

The variability of the rocks is a keynote of the Weald and observers have long been struck by it. The naturalist Gilbert White of Selborne, the most celebrated worshipper of the Weald's *Genius Loci*, distinguished in the 18th century nine successive belts of soil, each with its distinctive crops and trees, within the bounds of his single parish, including one 'producing the brightest hope', another a rank clay 'that requires the labour of years to make it mellow' and one on which trees grew large but fell to pieces in sawing.[1] On a day's ride through the Wealden countryside in the 1820s William Cobbett encountered the extremes of 'six of the worst miles in England' in St Leonard's Forest followed near Maidstone by the finest seven miles he had ever seen.[2] The Rev. Arthur Young, author of a book on Sussex farming, considered that the juxtaposition of chalk of the South Downs and Weald clay provided the most vivid contrast in English farming.[3]

Underlying the rocks' diversity are the varying qualities of the soils and in turn these permeate the whole of the Weald's social and economic history for, although the effect of geology on soils is not one of simple determinism, the human landscape developed on each soil type tended to be shaped by people of different backgrounds and objectives, whether we are considering sandy heaths in Surrey, rich loamy 'ragstone' around Maidstone, or the cold, heavy clays of the Weald.

High Weald soils are so amazingly varied that the usual geological or soil map does not do justice to them. The soil will commonly vary between farms on the same geological formation and the plough may turn up soil of almost every consistency within a single field. Sticky clay, say, on low ground might give way to a stratum of more workable, crumbly soil, itself giving way higher up into thin stony land (where the ploughshare has to be lifted to avoid sandrock) and then perhaps becoming clay again. In ploughing an acre the ploughman becomes attuned to changing sounds and different stresses as the share travels over a field. A whispering noise betokens a bed of wet sand, a rasping one thin soil above bedrock and a slowing down means that he is driving deeper into heavy clay. When freshly ploughed, the varied colours of such a field look like a 'smeared palette'.[4] The Weald farmer will point to his best spot in each field. Even on the Weald clay, which is much more uniform in composition, a farm will usually include 'earlier' fields on rather lighter soils derived from river alluvium or subordinate sandstone, and drainage is often a matter of slope. On the clayland at Billingshurst, for example, sand turns up unexpectedly in gardens in the High Street and there is a bed of rather lighter land to the west of the village. At Gatwick Airport mudstones some five metres below the surface clay were useful in putting in foundations.

These varied soils, hard and soft, gritty and waxy, are largely due to the underlying geology. Again, remarkable variations occur not only in the different strata comprising the Weald, but within the same bed of rock and even within the same horizon. Topley first drew attention to this in his classic monograph on the Weald (1875).[5] He noted the abruptness with which a particular rock would change, for example, from silt to fine sand, to coarse conglomerate or to pure clay. When digging for ironstone on the Wadhurst clay near Heathfield in the 17th and 18th centuries, eight distinct layers were found in shafts less than 18 feet deep. Eighty different strata were distinguished in 1809 at Cooden near Bexhill in a borehole dug some 160 feet below the surface including 'strong coal' at the base (which was later found to be lignite!), nine ironstone beds at varying levels, sandstone, sand, clay and loam.[6] Expression of this on a single farm can be illustrated with reference to Little Pell Farm, in the High Weald at Wadhurst. The richest and deepest soils tend to be at the bottoms of fields, due to downwash. In several fields sandstone bedrock protrudes at or near the surface and the plough has to be adjusted to plough shallower. One field has four different soils, one more fertile than the rest. On steep fields, land slippage may occur after periods of heavy rain, when clay topsoil is liable to slip downwards on sandstone bedrock. Such landslips have also occurred on the Wadhurst clay around Wadhurst, at the junction of the Wadhurst clay with Tunbridge Wells sands on neighbouring farms after heavy rainfall or during a thaw following prolonged frost where slopes are steep and seepage occurs.[7] Its signs are steep valley sides bulging and dropping in places. (Landslips occur also around the Weald's northern and western rims at the junction of the Lower Greensand and the Gault and such slippages are recognised by a vertical scar at the head, and hummocky ground ending in a steep bank on the downward side.)[8]

The ways in which the rocks were originally laid down explain this diversity. Those in the core of the Weald comprise the Wealden Series, broadly divided into Hastings beds and Weald clay. The Hastings beds are divided into five major sandstone and mudstone divisions. The Weald clay has subordinate layers of sandstone, sand, 'Sussex Marble' and Horsham stone alternating within great thicknesses of clay, estimated at a maximum of 450 metres. These complex sequences were laid down 146 to 132 million years ago when the Weald was nearer

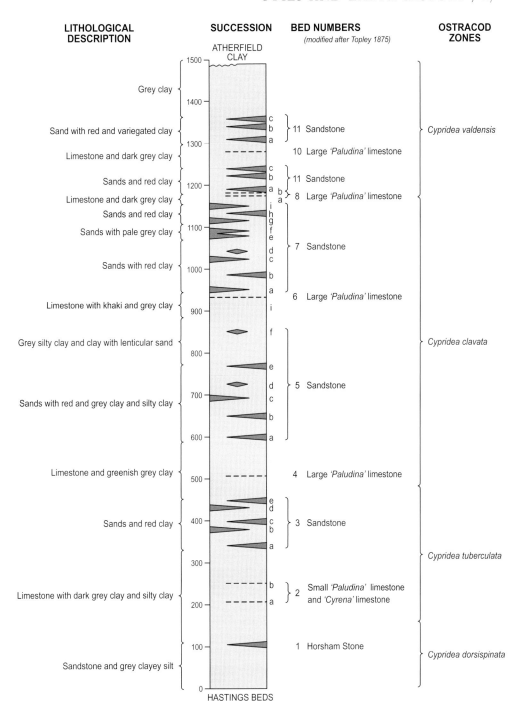

LITHOLOGICAL DESCRIPTION	SUCCESSION	BED NUMBERS *(modified after Topley 1875)*	OSTRACOD ZONES

ATHERFIELD CLAY

Grey clay — 1400

Sand with red and variegated clay — c b a — 11 Sandstone — *Cypridea valdensis*

Limestone and dark grey clay — 10 Large *'Paludina'* limestone

Sands and red clay — c b a — 11 Sandstone

Limestone and dark grey clay — b a — 8 Large *'Paludina'* limestone

Sands and red clay — i h g f e — 7 Sandstone

Sands with pale grey clay

Sands with red clay — d c b a

Limestone with khaki and grey clay — 6 Large *'Paludina'* limestone

i

f — *Cypridea clavata*

Grey silty clay and clay with lenticular sand — e — 5 Sandstone

d c

Sands with red and grey clay and silty clay — b a

Limestone and greenish grey clay — 4 Large *'Paludina'* limestone

Sands and red clay — e d c b a — 3 Sandstone — *Cypridea tuberculata*

Limestone with dark grey clay and silty clay — b a — 2 Small *'Paludina'* limestone and *'Cyrena'* limestone

1 Horsham Stone — *Cypridea dorsispinata*

Sandstone and grey clayey silt

HASTINGS BEDS

15 *Geological section through an immense section of the Weald Clay (after Gallois).*

the equator than now. Their rare fossil plants – mollusca, small crustacea, fish and reptiles – indicate relics of life on land in an environment of fresh or brackish water also embracing much of present southern Hampshire, the Isle of Wight and the Paris Basin. Subsequently, other rocks were laid down – mainly sandstones and chalk – over a period up to 65 million years ago.

Ever since the discoveries of the pioneer geologists, W. Fitton, Gideon Mantell and others, the Weald has been the subject of increasingly detailed ecological and palaeontological investigation, reconstructing the world in which creatures such as dinosaurs, crocodiles and turtles lived in a tropical climate like Sumatra's today. The Weald has been variously described at different times as a former great estuary, an extensive lake, a huge delta, or a combination of all three. Since 1939 oil drilling has brought much new evidence of the origin of the Wealden formation. The discovery and correlation of many more soil beds and their plant fossils in the original position of growth near the base of the Wadhurst clay in the Hastings beds, hitherto unrecognised with certainty, has greatly increased knowledge of the extent of the reed swamps and the environmental conditions in which they grew. Recently attention has been drawn to the fossil insects of the age of the dinosaurs by Ed Jarzembowski who has studied a spectacular lacewing reported by Roy Crowson in 1946 with a wing span of about 64mm.[9]

The current model of the formation of the Wealden rocks is that of P.G. Allen who has devoted more than fifty years to its study. He explains the alternating sandstone and mudstone formations as representing repeated phases when rivers eroded lofty mountains (horsts) on the site of the present Thames valley, and deposited sand which so accumulated that the rivers became sluggish and deposited the lighter sediment of mud and silt instead of sand. Subsequent earth movements rejuvenated the uplands and the cycle started over again. It is this variable sediment which has accumulated over half a mile thick which constitutes the Wealden beds. Possible present-day analogies are the Maracaibo basin in Venezuela, the enormous Mississippi delta and the braided streams of the middle Brahmaputra. Present-day features of deposition by heavily loaded rivers in these river basins are being examined to throw light on the Weald's origins.

At times of uplift rivers eroded deeply, forming braided river systems, bringing down coarse sediments (now mainly sandstones through pressure from above). There were also periods of subsidence, resulting in the deposition of finer sediments (clays and silts) and leading to complex systems of muddy lakes, lagoons, bays and meandering channels. The Weald clay is generally composed of clay and silt, representing alternating freshwater, brackish and occasionally semi-marine environments in a lake which was sometimes in contact with the 'East Anglian Sea' to the north. Spasmodically, the uplift of surrounding highlands resulted in short-lived river channels and deltas which extended into the lake. These river channels are represented by the subordinate beds of sandstone. The underlying Hastings beds are dominated by the coarse sandstones, indicative of severe erosion and braided river systems. Within the Hastings beds, however, are rocks composed mainly of silt and clay elements; for example, the Wadhurst clay, evidence of a period of subsidence when rivers flowed in deeply filled channels across a wide flood-plain to a shoreline of very varied habitats. The full story is still far from realisation but a clearer picture of alluvial plains, mud swamp, levees, lagoons, sand and gravel banks, bars of sand, shoals, lakes, deltaic fans and estuaries is emerging. In places fossils change abruptly in the same formation between brackish, fresh water and marine, suggestive of changing shallow water lagoonal conditions. Ripple marks on rock and footprints of dinosaurs suggest that, for much of the period, the Wealden water lying on the surface was so shallow that 'the Iguanadon and its relatives could have paddled 30 miles across it with ease.' In the Wealden 'lake' is stored away a vast treasure house of fossils.[10]

Certain sites in the Weald are enormously important for unravelling this complex history. Part of the Hastings-Pett Beach cliff-line has been designated a Site of Special Scientific Interest (SSSI). It is also proposed to bid for its recognition in a new category of conserved sites known as Special Conservation Areas (SCAs). The bedding planes within the sandstones show them to have been formed in a great delta and the variations between the hard sandstones and soft clays stretch inland to form the alternation of high ridges and narrow valleys in the High Weald. Severed subsequently by the English Channel is the eastern prolongation of the Weald in the Paris Basin known as the Pays de Bray which has a similar landscape on the same strata as the Weald. The Weald cliffs rest on a solid platform of sandstone that is streaked with black seams that look like coal, so much that bore-holes were drilled near Bexhill in 1809 for a fruitless search for coal. The black streaks are thin layers of lignite formed from wood and other

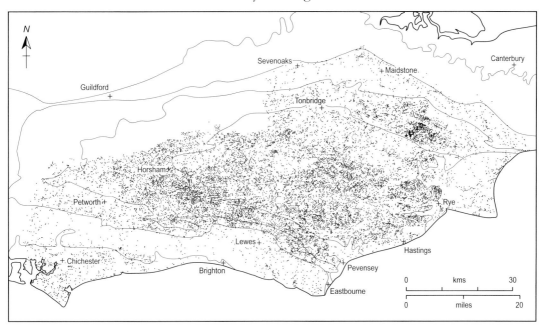

16 Distribution of ponds in the Sussex and Kent Wealds, at their most dense in the Low Weald. (Biodiversity Centre, Sussex Wildlife Trust, West Sussex County Council) For an explanation see p.30.

vegetable matter that once floated in the shallow waters of the great Wealden lake.

A site at Northiam is being elucidated to understand the nature of the river channels crossing the flood plain. A site at Lower Dicker is disclosing a source of minerals from the Cornwall area. A quarry near Battle has already yielded a fascinating 'bone bed' with fish scales, coprolites, bones and teeth and remains of reptiles, including crocodiles, turtles and dinosaurs (Megalosaurus, Cetiosaurus, Iguanodon and Hylaeosaurus) intermixed with water-worn pebbles. The Philpots and Hook quarries at West Hoathly have been used by Allen and others for fresh interpretations of the complex history of the origins of the Weald. In Kent, Southborough Pit intermittently shows a section of rock with the aquatic horsetail *Equisetes lyellii* in its growth position, and Pembury Cutting is also vitally important for interpreting episodic river flow conditions.

The economic use of Rocks and Minerals

The Weald has been dug over to an unusual degree for various stones, minerals and clays for some two millennia. In consequence, its landscape is peppered with small pits and quarries, many of which have developed into ponds. There are 12,500 ponds in Sussex alone, mostly in the Weald. Their depth, generally up to 20 feet, indicates an origin in some extraction industry. In the clay country everyone cried out for stone. The densest concentration of ponds occurs where subordinate beds of stone in the Weald clay were quarried for building, or making stone causeways and paths, without which it would have been impossible to venture out in wet weather. Near Bethersden, Kent, small reed-filled and tree-fringed ponds are so multitudinous as to create a remarkable little local 'landscape of many ponds' (Fig.16). Most are presumably old workings for Bethersden 'Marble', though marl would have been a useful by-product because the rock is calcareous (p.59). The 'Marble' was the most important stone bed in the Weald clay. It was not real marble but a fossiliferous limestone, a conglomerate of fresh-water shells of snails and molluscs in thin beds, seldom more than one foot thick. Commonly in the Weald clay are two beds of this 'marble', differing only by the shell size, and separated by an intervening bed of calcareous clay which was dug for marl (the large and small Paludina). The hardest beds are quite durable and have been used in paving, as around Staplehurst, and in building, notably in the Perpendicular church towers of Headcorn, Smarden, Biddenden and Tenterden and in the inn at Pluckley railway station. As the 'Marble' takes as good a polish as Purbeck marble, it was much favoured for interior use in churches (including Canterbury Cathedral), as floors, altars, pier bases, shafts and stairs. It was also favoured from the 12th century for medieval tomb slabs and memorial tablets, and for domestic mantelpieces. In and near Bethersden parish it would appear that quarrying the stone, as at Tuesnod, a hamlet of half-timbered houses, was apparently long combined with farming (and medieval iron-making). The Bethersden 'Marble' beds extend intermittently towards the top of Weald clay right across into Sussex and Surrey, and wherever it occurs there are signs or

17 Tuesnoad, a dwelling in a hamlet which was an important centre for quarrying Bethersden 'marble'.

mining activity, notably in Kirdford near Petworth, though not so intensively as in Kent where it was a lively business of freeholding yeomen. In this western part of the Weald it was variously known as Laughton stone, Sussex marble and Petworth marble. Like the Bethersden 'marble', it took a fine polish and its interior use as pillars and fonts is commonly found in local churches, such as at Boxgrove, Trotton, Arundel, Ardingly and West Chiltington, and as innumerable old farmhouse mantelpieces. In the Sussex Weald, softer beds were dug for marl (pp.59-60) but not to the same degree as in the Kent Weald.[11]

Also occurring in the West Sussex Weald clay is a 'flaggy' calciferous sandstone known as 'Horsham Stone'. This came out of the quarry in natural flat grey slabs of varying thickness. The stone, four to five inches thick, was used for roofing churches, manor houses, barns, water-mills and dove-cots, and was impervious to rain and so durable that many existing old buildings still retain their original covering. This is so hospitable to lichens that it weathers to beautiful green and orange tints. On account of its excessive weight the roof had to be low pitched, typically at an angle of 45 degrees but, even so, the stone bore heavily on a specially strengthened timber frame, and a sagging ridge on buildings roofed with it is a common feature. Again, because of its weight, it is not commonly found far from navigable water. Thicker slabs were worked as pavement or crushed for road metal. Stammerham, in Saxon 'the home of the stone masons', on the site of Christ's Hospital, and Nuthurst had extensive quarries but former Horsham stone quarries can be found by the walker in many out-of-the-way places and in one or two cases the quarry face is not too

18 A roof of Horsham stone, probably 15th-century or earlier, being relaid at Kingston Buci church, 1982.

overgrown to discern symmetrical layers of clay and stone like a sandwich cake. The last workings were around 1880.

An important source of building stone was the quarries on the Lower Greensand hills on the northern rim of the Weald. At Limpsfield, quarrying is recorded in Domesday Book. In east Surrey the Upper Greensand had some 20-30 ironstone and hearthstone mines between Brockham and Godstone, the last of which only ceased working in 1961 after 1,200 years. This stone was used in the earliest churches and was sufficiently important to come into Crown ownership in medieval times. It was also in demand for lining lime kilns and hearths. This stone also occurs near Petersfield, and Gilbert White described its use. In its final phase the workings were a source of hearthstone for whitening doorsteps, hearths and floors. Wren used large amounts for rebuilding St Paul's. Softer stone called Reigate or Merstham stone was used for interior purposes from the Middle Ages.

The most important source of building stone in the Lower Greensand was 'ragstone' from outcrops near Maidstone which was used for the walls of Roman London and numerous medieval City and Essex churches. It was also popular with Victorian architects: Topley (pp.375-6) lists 33 London churches built with it in the mid-19th century. In the Godalming district Bargate stone was quarried, at its best similar to Kentish rag, as were also Pulborough and Petworth stone from the corresponding outcrop in Sussex. From the Folkestone beds came Carstone, a hard ferruginous sandstone which because it cleaved in flat pieces was much used for walling and rough pavement. Gilbert White believed that it never became slippery in frost and rain, but it appears to do so with wear: salt has to be applied on Thakeham church path in West Sussex on winter days. Carstone was also chipped into small fragments, the size of the head of a large nail, and stuck into the mortar of a freestone wall, a practice known as galleting in Surrey and Sussex.

Some of the loveliest 'country stone' in the region is the golden sandstone streaked with ruddier iron veining from the ferruginous Hastings beds, although owing to transport difficulty it was only used locally. This stone was used in Old Pembury church and at Bodiam Castle, Wakehurst Place, Penshurst Place and

1 *Bocage landscape of the East Kent Weald, looking towards the North Downs.*

II *The great bowl of the Weald seen from the tower of Goudhurst parish church. The ridges are almost entirely wooded and a patchwork, largely green, wraps round the brick-built village, a former seat of the cloth trade. The loss of hop fields is evident. Much of the view was in the great estates of gentry at Bedgebury, Combwell and Finchcocks. (Michael Bennett)*

III *A southwards view from Argos Hill, Rotherfield (see p.4) with the South Downs in the far distance.*

IV *Seventeenth-century graffiti on sandstone exposures at Heron's Ghyll near Uckfield.*

V *(overleaf) A former highway at Hadlow Down, one of innumerable abandoned roads in the Weald.*

19 Twineham church, of 16th-century local brick.

manor houses such as Marshall's Manor near Maresfield (*c.*1575). Tilgate stone, a calcareous grit, was much used as roadstone. Philpot's Quarry, opened in the 19th century, supplied stone for Lancing College which has not proved so durable as anticipated when exposed to salt. Iron-ore diggings are discussed on p.132.

Of special interest are brickworks and tileries sites, because Kent has produced some of the best brickwork ever made in England and its tilework and that of East Sussex is even more memorable.[12] The red bricks of west Kent, generally regarded as the finest of all, come from the brown and blue clay of the Weald, with the reddening of iron. On the Weald and other clays the sights and smells of brickfields, tileries and potteries were formerly familiar, now marked mainly by extensive diggings of an acre or more in extent, and deep pools. In their most unpretentious form common house bricks were roughly manufactured of clay of any description, mixed with cinder, and dried in 'clamp' kilns erected on the spot. Such small-scale works were once ubiquitous for small Wealden farmers leased land to brickmakers who supplied London and suburbs. With the coming of railways, large-scale brickworks were established near railway stations, as at Pluckley, Kent and Keymer Junction in Sussex. A brick works near Frittenden still produces hand-made, finely textured facing bricks and roofing tiles. Pottery was also manufactured at numerous places including the Dicker Common, Chailey, Crowborough, and Ditchling, where the main speciality was ceramics burned to the famed colour of 'Sussex Red'. Terra-cotta ware was also a local industry apparently dating from its use on Laughton tower in the 1540s.

20 *The Dicker Potteries, Lower Dicker, near Hailsham, supplied popular everyday brownware.*

The mineral with the most powerful effect on industry was iron ore (p.132). With the re-location of the iron industry from the end of the 18th century to its new indispensible complement, coal, the ore deposits lay idle and useless. 'Could Sussex but be shown to have Coal!' became the cry of industrialists, and their hopes were raised of workable deposits by the presence of black strata of lignite, which burns with a blue flame, and by a superficial resemblance of the Wealden surface and its rocks to the Belgian and West Midland coalfields, where coal and iron-ore were being mined together from the same pit. As early as 1809 Thomas Pelham of Laughton licensed prospectors to search for copper, lead, and coal on his estate.[13] The erection of barracks at Bexhill early in the 19th century led to a deep bore being sunk there in an abortive search for coal, and the discovery of a 'black stratum' in Waldron parish about the same time again led to disappointment amongst local people who had themselves dug with spades and shovels, although the smith was happy with the lignite burnt at his forge.[14] In the 1870s a deep bore at Netherfield failed to find coal but the excellent source of pure white crystalline gypsum was discovered. The failure to find coal led to investigations as to whether iron-ore could be shipped to the coalfields and as recently as 1908 Lord Sheffield received an adverse report on a proposal to smelt ore with imported coal in the vicinity of Sheffield Park![15] Clearly the dashed hopes of coal had profound consequences for the present landscape.

The geological structure of the Weald is conducive to reserves of oil, generally thought to be produced by the decomposition of plant and animal remains which, subjected to great heat and pressure over millions of years, migrate through porous and permeable rocks. Conoco made an exploratory drilling at Burnt Oak Farm in Rotherfield in 1984. Natural gas has been found in small quantities but not in economically viable reserves.

5

The Wildwood

I⸤ᴛ⸥ was Benjamin Harrison, the village shopkeeper of Ightham, Kent, a keen naturalist, who, persevering in fieldwork with heart and soul, found a much greater antiquity for man than the six thousand years customarily accepted in the mid-19th century. Using Topley's *Geology of the Weald* (1875) as 'bible and encyclopedia in one', the 'little grocer' searched for flint implements in the valley gravels of the Strode stream passing through his village on the sandstone rocks of the eastern Weald and on the elevated chalk plateau around Ash. His discoveries of flints which appeared to have been chipped and worked by human hands, made the hair rise on end of cautious archaeologists and those who were reluctant to look the question of man's antiquity in the face.[1] Professor Prestwich's paper interpreting his discoveries read to the Geological Society in 1869 was the greatest day of Harrison's life and the Civil List pension he subsequently received set a seal on his scientific work, proving that the occupiers of Oldbury Hill and the surrounding area were shaping their stone tools more than 25,000 years ago while sheltering from intensely cold tundra conditions at the margin of an ice sheet extending as far as Norfolk.[2]

Analysis of the proportion of pollens of different tree and plant species preserved in peat and other sediments, suggests that over some 4-5,000 years from the beginning of warming about 11,000 B.C. the first colonisers of the landscape were birch, aspen and sallow, which can withstand cold and had light seeds. Then followed in descending order, with the progressive amelioration in climate, pine and hazel; alder and oak; lime and elm; holly, beech, hornbeam and maple. The mosaic of tree communities in present-day Wealden ancient woods, notably oak, ash, alder, elm and hornbeam, appears to have made up the regional wildwood about 5,500-3,000 B.C. but two native species of lime, the small-leaved and the large leaved, possibly the commonest trees of all, have mysteriously become almost extinct in the Weald, despite their exceptional longevity and powers of survival. Place-names including *lin* or *lind*, e.g. Lindfield, indicate that they were apparently at least still locally present in significant numbers in the early and mid-Saxon period. Beech was a relatively late arrival, increasing rapidly in the Bronze Age, *c.*2000 B.C. Cleere has shown that it was used for charcoal at Roman ironworks and there are many references to it especially in the High Weald in later centuries.[3]

As a result of climatic amelioration almost all the surface of Britain became covered with natural woodland, in Rackham's dramatic term, the wildwood, i.e. not significantly altered by human activities.[4] This began to be cleared by man from Neolithic times *c.*3500 B.C. and had largely been grubbed as an obstacle to cultivation at a time so remote as to be beyond historical record. The South Downs, the Sussex Coastal Plain and the open lands of north-east Kent are examples of woodland clearance occurring two or more thousand years ago. Exceptionally, recalcitrant tracts remained wild country with a few islands of farmland as late as the Saxon period, the Chilterns, the Forest of Dean, and parts of the Welsh border amongst them. By far the largest of these wooded areas was the Weald, some ninety miles by thirty, then occupying much of Surrey, Kent, Sussex and part of Hampshire.

We can now outline early man's occupation of the Weald against this background. The long-held view, expressed authoritatively by E.C. Curwen in his *Archaeology of Sussex* (second edition, 1954), was that the Weald was avoided by prehistoric man as unattractive and unworkable with his agricultural equipment, and hence unoccupied except for seasonal hunting expeditions. The Weald remains little studied by archaeologists because of the scarcity of arable land available for field walking, and the heavy nature of the soils which limits the season for searches and is not very productive of soil or crop marks. Gardiner also noted in 1990 that, despite these limitations, the potential for aerial photography had not been fully realised.[5] Nevertheless, recent work has destroyed the long-standing myth that the Weald was an uninhabited waste before the Saxon clearings and it is now becoming apparent that it was exploited for millennia beforehand in a manner and to a degree hitherto almost unsuspected. These revolutionary new insights result from the combined application of field walking, aerial photography and environmental archaeology.

A seminal study on the prehistoric occupation of the Weald was by C.F. Tebbutt. He began to notice from 1966 humanly struck flint flakes and implements while walking over Ashdown Forest. Tebbutt's survey was extended to surrounding farmland, where he found widespread flint on areas suitable for searching. No one had previously realised the significance of flint flakes, cores and 'pot boilers' which indicated where prehistoric man had lived, at least part of the year, if not permanently. Tebbutt concluded that in and around Ashdown Forest prehistoric occupation of some permanence was widespread, and that his study, taken at random, was hardly likely to be atypical of the rest of the Weald. This truth had not emerged before because of the scarcity of field workers.[6]

Mesolithic hunting camps *c.*6000 B.C. often used the overhang of rocks and caves, part natural, part artificial, to shelter from the weather. Sloping timbers placed against the vertical rock-face extended the shelter outwards, niches to hold the supports being sometimes clearly visible. Some sites were particularly favourable, having had a southern aspect, proximity to water and commanding a long view of wild animals coming to drink. The first such rock shelter to be discovered was in Tilgate Wood, Sussex, in the 1930s, though likely ones at West Hoathly had also been recorded. By 1990 the total had risen to eleven. At High Hurstwood rock shelters, 4,000 pieces of struck flint have been radio carbon dated to *c.*5500 B.C. At High Rocks charcoal patches have been dated to *c.*4500 B.C. (Fig.21).

The rock shelter camps may perhaps be attributed to seasonally occupied, small hunting parties, probably composed only of men, whereas sites on the

21 Mesolithic rock shelters, Buxted.
22 Mesolithic rock shelters under overhang, High Rocks, near Groombridge.

Greensand of Surrey and Sussex may have been longer-stay home bases, involving both men and women. From these sites come scrapers and stone axes, suggesting skinning of animals and forest clearance. The largest concentrations of flint working waste, as at Farnham and Selmeston, possibly indicate home bases where microlithic points were manufactured in quantity for use in longer distance hunting trips into the Wealden forest, for wild ox, red and roe deer and boar as well as nuts and berries. The densest Mesolithic distribution located to date is on the chalk-bounded heaths on the Lower Greensand in south-west Surrey. Hunters dwelt typically beside streams or meres and their most characteristic legacy in the landscape is the chipping floor, where flint derived from the North Downs was prepared by flaking into flint points for arrow shafts, knives, saws, gouges and scrapers. The many thousands of such implements collected from the Surrey heaths (then more wooded than now) is evidence of intensive hunting activity. One site has yielded more than 85,000 artifacts, mostly waste flakes produced in making small worked flints called microliths.[7] It was once thought that Mesolithic people had little impact on forest clearance. More recent research suggests that they began the process of pushing back the trees, probably through the use of fire in trapping game.

The not inconsiderable number of polished stone axes now recorded in the Weald is evidence of woodland clearance. Late Neolithic woodland clearance, local in extent, has been detected at West Heath, Sussex. More general clearances occurred in the succeeding Bronze Age. At Iping Common, Sussex, the destruction of hazel woodland has been associated with human activity, which led to soil impoverishment, creating a heath environment and leading to wind erosion. Very significant are discoveries resulting from environmental archaeology. Scaife and Burrin have examined river valley sediments in East Sussex and have found evidence of woodland clearance as an accompaniment of agricultural use which caused significant soil erosion, creating substantial alluviation. Of particular interest is the presence of cereal pollen and that of *Graminbeae* and *Plantago Lanceolata* at Mayfield, dated to the Neolithic or post-Neolithic period and suggesting the practice of agriculture.[8] There is growing evidence from cereal pollen of Wealden agriculture in the Bronze Age, at Rackham and vicinity, for example. Additional Wealden evidence comes from polished stone axes (Neolithic) and Bronze-Age barrows in Ashdown Forest and in Ewhurst, East Sussex. Research on Wealden Iron-Age sites has been almost confined to hillforts which, with the exception of Castle Hill, Tonbridge, were not occupied until the end of the period. Recently, aerial photographs commissioned by I.D. Margary during the 1920s have been re-examined and an extensive system of enclosures and boundaries has been found on Ashdown Forest on uncultivated heathland, 'a little known and almost unrecorded fossil landscape'.[9]

This leaves us at present with a very vague and generalised picture. Perhaps in the Iron Age we should envisage a picture of scattered farmsteads in areas of localised clearance. I.D. Margary's investigations of the Roman roads in the Weald in the 1920s and '30s developed from the discovery of a length of Roman road on his estate at East Grinstead.[10] They were the most important ever undertaken in England up to that time, convincingly establishing 'lost' sections of a number of routes known either vaguely or hardly at all, including the 'London-Brighton', 'London-Lewes', the Sussex Greensand Way and the 'Rochester-Maidstone-Hastings' route, together with lesser roads. One of the most famous sections unearthed was the stretch at Holtye constructed of iron and iron slag, as hard as modern roads. This is exposed to public view. A remarkable relic which Margary considered almost unique in Britain, the Roman paved ford at Stream Farm in Benenden, was destroyed in the exceptional floods in the autumn of 2000.

Roman villas are mainly on the periphery of the Weald but also occur at Chiddingfold in the Low Weald and Wiggonholt and possibly at Holmstreet, both near Pulborough. It has been suggested that small towns existed at Pulborough and Hassocks. It is unclear at present what economy was practised at these sites. The Roman villa discovered at the edge of the Weald at Barcombe, Sussex, by an aerial photograph, is in the process of excavation. Margary suggested that centuriation was responsible for the gridded landscape near Ripe, Sussex, but definite proof is lacking.

The Roman Iron Industry

The Wealden iron industry was a large-scale operation during the Roman period, perhaps second only to that of Noricum in modern Austria, and there is the presumption that it was at least partly a state enterprise. Caesar refers to iron manufacture in the area in his *Gallic War* before the Roman Invasion of A.D. 43. It was based on the carbonate ore of the Wadhurst clay, a reducible material with an average iron content of 40 per cent. This very heavy clay also produced the forest cover which generated excellent charcoal and the clay itself was refractory enough for furnace construction. The Roman iron industry began immediately after the Roman invasion in A.D.43 in the Hastings-Battle-Sedlescombe area but by the mid-second century the ore and fuel resources here were considerably depleted and apparently the industry began to move to between East Grinstead and Wadhurst. This survived until the mid-third century, when deforestation and over-exploitation of the ore appears to have resulted in a virtual closure, apart from some small sites such as Withyham which survived until the end of the Roman period, by which time the Forest of Dean was apparently the main iron-producing centre. The scale of the working at Beauport Park near Hastings is remarkable. It is estimated that 50,000 tons of slag existed before being largely quarried away for road metalling in the 19th century. Some central authority is indicated by the finding of tile fragments stamped with the CL BR[11] monogram of the British fleet at Beauport Park, Bardown in Wadhurst and also at Cranbrook.

The ore occurs at the base of the Wadhurst clay in the form of carbonate nodules varying from 2in. to 18in. across. The ore was dug in open-cast pits, very common in the Weald and usually filled with water. It is an easily reducible material and thus easy for the ancient ironmaker to smelt it. Early smelting furnaces are known as 'bloomeries'. The earliest type was probably a simple hollow in the ground lined with clay, filled with ore and fuel and blown with bellows – the 'bowl-furnace'.

Cleere's experimental iron-making was based on a group of early third-century Roman furnaces excavated at Holbeamwood near Bardown, constructed of clay and standing as excavated one to two feet high with an internal diameter of 12-15 inches. The ore was roasted prior to charging in the smelting furnace, which was built three feet high and after building with clay was left to dry in air. A fire of green wood was lit and kept going for about six hours. On the following day the fire was rekindled and stoked with charcoal. A tuyere, a clay nozzle, was made and inserted into the aperture at the base for the bellows and to run off the molten slag which cooled as a spongy 'bloom' of iron. An ore-charcoal ratio of 1:1 gave the best results. Cleere estimated that a furnace would last for at least a dozen smelts and that the 12 actual examples at Holbeamwood had been rebuilt at least forty times, and averaging 40 lbs. of iron in each bloom at each smelt, a minimum production of eight tons of iron could be estimated from that group of furnaces. He also postulated that five to six persons would be needed to man a furnace, working in shifts.[12] These and subsequent experiments by the Wealden Iron Research Group led by Roger Adams gave some indication of the hours of effort which went into the production of a bloom and left the participants with a tremendous admiration for the expertise of early iron workers.

Field walking in a study area of 162 square kilometres in the central Weald revealed the remarkable number of 246 bloomery sites (represented by waste slag

23 Barcombe, Roman villa site. This has a southern aspect and lies on the edge of the Weald facing the South Downs.

heaps, some of enormous size which had accumulated over long periods), a density of 1.4 per square kilometre, although this total certainly fell far short of the actual number.[13] The majority of the sites which could be dated were Romano-British. The conclusion was that this project confirmed the previous impression that a large and intensive Roman industry geared to export contrasted with a small medieval operation mainly satisfying local needs.

The project also threw light on the siting of these bloomeries. The typical bloomery was situated on the banks of a small stream which had cut a deep channel through the base of the Wadhurst clay, thus exposing the ore to a prospector. The ore was then quarried back from the stream until the overburden

24 *Members of the Wealden Iron Research group experimenting with a simple bloomery of the type used in Roman and Saxon Sussex.*

of rock became too great. The site of the ore was an obvious place to smelt as charcoal was also at hand.

There is no evidence as to how the wildwood was exploited by early iron-makers. Cleere suggested little management of woodland but Rackham has challenged this view, suggesting that a form of coppicing, known elsewhere in the Roman world, was being implemented in the Weald during the Roman period.[14] Examination of charcoals indicates that there was little, if any, selection of wood for charcoal burning. Enormous refuse heaps existed in the Battle-Sedlescombe area. Roman ironmaking sites roughly fall into two groups; coastal such as Beauport Park, Crowhurst Park, etc.; and High Weald sites such as Bardown, Cansiron, Knowle Farm, Minepit Woods, Oldlands, Ridge Hill with an extreme western outlier at Broadfields. Main production is between the late first century and the middle of the third, a period of less than 200 years. All Roman sites lay within 3.5 km of a known Roman road. The Broadfields site may have supplied London. Of Romano-British sites only Bardown has been excavated in any detail. Cleere has stated that by the end of the third century only Oldlands and Broadfields in the western group of sites and Footlands in the eastern were still functioning, and little later fourth-century material is known from any of these settlements. 'The last furnaces were quenched by the end of the century and the last settlers moved out, and the wildwood moved back to the clearings *to reclaim its own*.'[15] There is no incontrovertible evidence of permanent occupation of the Weald during the sub-Roman period. The general picture is one of desertion, the Wealden forest being the resort of fugitives and hunters. It was not until the seventh century at the earliest that the seasonal swine pastures of the Downland Anglo-Saxon settlers began to be occupied permanently, and the earliest records date to the middle of the eighth century.

We can now come to some tentative conclusions as to the Roman and prehistoric Weald. The ancient primeval Weald does not appear to have survived on the scale considered likely by earlier historians. It is hard to escape the conclusion that the population increase in the Iron-Age and Romano-British periods led to a gradual colonisation ever more deeply into the Weald. The extent of this can easily be exaggerated, however. There is little in the Weald to hint at substantial colonisation such as that complex overlay of prehistoric and Roman tumuli, lynchets, and settlements characterising the South Downs nor anything remotely suggestive of the rectilinear planned landscape of the south Essex clay plain, of Roman or pre-Roman date, which we now know to have been farmed intensively in the prehistoric and Roman periods.[16]

Conversely, the dramatic population decline now being postulated between the third and seventh centuries can scarcely have failed to have left its mark in the abandonment of the more marginal land previously opened up. We should perhaps no longer regard the woodland clearances discussed in these pages as assaults on *primeval* woodland or *virgin* lands, but as *recovery* by man of previously lost farmland when a rising population was turning back on its old paths and filling up again some of the spaces abandoned centuries earlier.

Very pertinent in this context is Professor Glanville Jones's hypothesis, based on the 13th-century custumals of the Archbishop of Canterbury's manor of South Malling, that the loosely clustered small family farms on shared yardlands of customary land are survivals of Romano-British or even earlier *Clachans*, which had then been integral parts of multiple estates, as they were later. This stimulating suggestion still awaits testing archaeologically. The present author has explained the hamlet-like nature of much of Wealden rural settlement on a fundamentally different basis, as a cycle of rural development associated with a young 'frontier' type of community in the early Middle Ages (p.87). According to this theory, the hamlets evolved out of relatively large and mostly unimproved pioneer holdings, held singly, into a cluster of small family farms held by members of the same kin, as an accompaniment of population increase and gradual improvement of the original holding. These continued to be so held through successive generations into a period so relatively recent that it was within the knowledge and experience of the mid-14th-century scribe responsible for the Rotherfield custumal, who noted that the original ferling holdings had evolved into clusters of settlement. Such an evolution of rural settlements is consistent with the known population increase and regional inclination of the Weald towards land clearance between *c*.900 and *c*.1280-1325. The superficial resemblance of the Wealden hamlets to Celtic clachans is not surprising, given that both types of hamlet probably resulted from a basically similar process, the reclamation of the waste by a group of pioneer farmers.[17]

6

The Saxon and Jutish Andredesweald

THE immense, multi-centuried wooded area which the Saxons and Jutes inherited
was called *Anderita* or *Anderitum* by Britons during the Roman occupation and a
variant of this name first appears on a fourth-century road map of Roman Britain
as *Anderid(t)os*, the name of the Roman fort at Pevensey.[1] By the name of Andred
the forest was taken over by the invaders and it is thus mentioned for many
centuries in English annals. The Anglo-Saxon Chronicle under A.D. 477 records
a Saxon expedition into Sussex which slew many Britons 'and drove some of
them to flight into the wood which is called *Andredesleag*'. This is taken to be the
forest of the Weald. As a forest name it continued for many more centuries, being

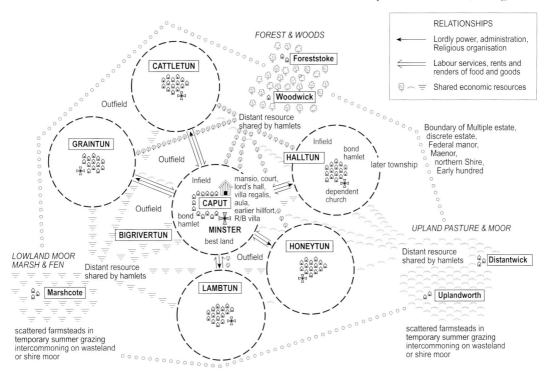

25 *The discrete estate (after Aston). The headquarters (*caput*) of a large multiple manor on or near the Downs and coastal
plain and its fragmented outliers in the Weald provided the framework for economic and social development in south-east England
to the end of the Middle Ages. The diagram shows the circumstances of the early 13th century when there were still immense
areas awaiting colonisation. The origin of such estates was in Saxon and possibly earlier times.*

called the *Desertum Ondred* in the *Life of St Wilfrid* (c. A.D. 700), and simply as *Andred* in 785 and 893 in the *Chronicle*. In 1018 the forest is referred to as *Andredsweald* but afterwards the old British name was finally dropped. As Weald it enters English nomenclature in Domesday Book (1086). Thus the name Weald, with its British predecessor, has been imprinted on the national consciousness for more than two thousand years.

Nowadays the term 'wald' is usually translated as a wood or forest but recently it has been suggested that its meaning in the Middle Ages was broader and signified a largely uncultivated wilderness where livestock were grazed on leaf fodder and mast, food for bees was found and wood collected.[2] It has hitherto been widely believed that such wildernesses as the Weald were dark, impenetrable, closed canopy forests until cut down by farmer colonists to make arable fields and pastures for cattle. We now know more about the relationship between the large herbivores such as deer, wild horses and cattle and their habitats. The purely anthropogenic view of landscape-shaping has been challenged and the effects of grazing by wild and domestic animals over long periods is considered to have resulted in a park-like landscape before the introduction of agriculture, consisting of a mosaic of grassland, scrub, solitary trees, groves and more extensive areas of forest. The closest analogy in historic times is thought to be 'wood-pasture', the type of wooded landscape used by commoners for grazing, which was characteristic of the Weald and still remains at places such as Mens Wood, Ebernoe and Markstakes Common near Chailey. Droves of swine, cattle and sheep were driven up into the wilderness when there was little room for grazing in the arable fields of the peripheral villages. Thus the Weald was not an unexploited wilderness but was integrated into the system of farming from prehistoric times.

We are told a little about the extent of the forest in A.D. 892(3), when the Anglo-Saxon Chronicle relates that the estuary of the Lympne is at 'the east end of that great wood which we called Andred. The wood is from east to west 120 miles long, or longer, and 30 miles broad'. To understand this annal we must reconstruct the geography of the local shorelines which have greatly changed since the embanking of Romney Marsh. It has been plausibly suggested that the 'estuary of the Lympne' and the river which 'comes out of the Weald' must refer to the Eastern Rother before it assumed its present course to Rye. The older course of the river probably followed the line of the disused Military Canal. There is little difficulty in accepting the annalist's estimation of the Weald's breadth. A straight line drawn from Egerton near Ashford to Hailsham in Sussex across the greatest width of the Weald approximates to thirty miles. The stated length is less easily understood without attempting to reconstruct the possible distribution of woodland in south-east England at the end of the first Millennium. The distance between Lympne and Petersfield is about 90 miles. To extend the Saxon Weald to its stated length of 120 miles, 'or longer', we need to prolong it westwards across Hampshire into the New Forest. This is plausible because the name *Andret* occurs in the Domesday Survey of the Forest's eastern end, so that it might have linked up in an easterly direction with the Forests of Bere and Waltham in southern Hampshire before passing into the Weald.

Seasonal Settlement

With the paucity of archaeological sites, our best hope of understanding the forest and its associated human activities, or lack of them, over six obscure, but formative, centuries up to the Norman Conquest is by combining the study of Saxon charters and descriptive place-names.

Thus we discover the Weald functioning, as it had done doubtless for millennia, as a great undeveloped area exploited by the human communities on its more habitable fringes. A pastoral stage of human occupation prevailed, in which the communities on the periphery of the Weald used it mainly seasonally as summer pasture by a system of transhumance involving annual movement of livestock and people tending them between the more anciently settled parts of manors around the forest, and detached 'outliers' held by these manors in the forest itself. These places were commonly ten to fifteen miles distant; in Kent, which is built bigger, they were further apart, and exceptionally as much as 35 miles.

The whole of the Kentish Weald was divided into the swine pastures of manors on the fringes of the Jutish kingdom. The uniformity of this pastoral organisation and the degree to which it was used over a long and unbroken period is reflected in the more than 500 swine-pastures which have been identified, mostly still bearing the place-name ending in *-den*, a swine pasture. As Everitt has remarked, no other area in England has such a concentration of swine-pasture names, or in which a primitive economy has had such an impact on the present landscape.[3] In the Sussex and Surrey Wealds place-names in *-den* are uncommon,

26 *Ebernoe Common, one of the best known wood pastures. The Sussex Wildlife Trust have recently acquired additional land to expand the habitat.*

suggesting that its forest management evolved on different lines. This is incorrect. An identical system operated there under a Saxon nomenclature, the name *-fold*, for example, being equivalent to that of a *-den*. It is, however, likely that the forests on the highest ridges, including St Leonard's, Worth, Ashdown and Dallington, were never brought under the standard manorial system and thus not divided into outliers of coastal manors, presumably because they were early appropriated for hunting by the South Saxon kings. Moreover, in Hastings and Pevensey rapes the older pattern of manorial swine pastures was largely broken up by Norman overlords for military considerations (pp.91-2). For this reason, although there are seven or more *-den* place-names in Ticehurst parish, only difficult detective work can relate them to the coastal manors that formerly held them.

Very characteristic of the West Sussex Low Weald, and also of the adjoining parts of Surrey, are place-names with the suffix *fold* (OE *falod*) which later denoted the sites of Saxon and early Norman churches and their attendant farmsteads. The probability is that the *fold* names were given to pastures or shelters for animals by the men who came to and from the outlying grazings by the network of drovers' roads, which still lace together the parent centres to the backwoods sites. Many such pastures or shelters appear to have subsequently developed into homesteads (commonly moated) or villages, thus making the *folds* correspond to Kentish *dens*.

It will have been noted that the place-name elements considered are older than the villages themselves now bearing the same name. This is usual in the Weald, where the site chosen for a human habitation generally had earlier borne a well-known name as a seasonal pasture. This evolution from temporarily occupied huts associated with seasonal pasture, before they were being permanently occupied by farmers cultivating the land within hedged fields, is one of the most distinctive and fascinating characteristics of Wealden settlement history.

Particularly valuable in this connection are place-names with the element OE *(ge)sell*, meaning a group of shelters for animals, herdsmen's huts, or both. This term *gesell* is one of the oldest Sussex place-name elements which appears to have early gone out of use, so that it takes us back to the stage when man was erecting his first buildings in the Wealden landscape. They are mostly in eastern Sussex and are chiefly drawn from Saxon charters, for example, Boarzell in Ticehurst, Breadsell in Battle, Bremzells in Herstmonceux and Drigsell in Salehurst.

The most remarkable legacy of this transhumance to outlying pastures is the survival in the present-day landscape of an extensive network of roads and byways created by herdsmen. Everitt pointed out that droves could not have originated as cart-tracks because their passage over the downland escarpment is too steep for horses. A small-scale map will bring out clearly Witney's observation that because the Weald is roughly elliptical and drove roads normally took the shortest route into the deep Weald from the peripheral habitations, they change direction, crab-wise round the circumference of the Weald. They trend south-west/north-east in the Surrey part of the western Weald, then roughly north-south in the east Surrey/west Kent area, before turning on a south-west/north-east axis in east Kent, reverting to a north-south direction in central Sussex.

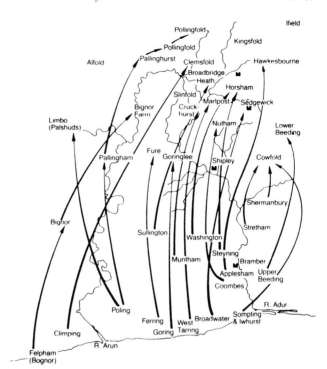

27 *The pattern of droveways in central Sussex (after Wealden Buildings Study Group).*

Archaeologists currently believe that the droveways were probably inherited by the Saxons and Jutes from Romano-British herders and indeed still earlier ones. Witney has shown how the droveways dictated the siting of churches in the Kent Weald, notably at river crossings, and how eventually traders gravitated to the churches, so founding villages and, in some cases, market towns. Kentish examples of churches are Bethersden, Headcorn, Leigh, Penshurst, and a dozen or more others: Cranbrook, Benenden and Rolvenden churches lie at the convergence of droves from surrounding dens; Cranbrook, Tonbridge and Tenterden grew into market towns.[4] In Sussex the churches of Shipley, West Grinstead, Ashurst, Thakeham, Shermanbury and Ditchling lie on droves. The role of droveways in determining the present pattern of the landscape can be taken further for they have guided the siting of many farmsteads and the shaping of their fields and boundaries. Thus to a remarkable degree, the evolution of the Weald landscape, both urban and rural, has up to the present day been fundamentally within this framework of roads, fields and farmsteads created by a pastoral society centuries ago.[5]

It is instructive to trace with the aid of a topographical map the courses of these droveways, now surviving intermittently; for example, how herds reached Broadwater Lane near Horsham, from Broadwater, near Worthing; or Lower Beeding from Upper Beeding; or Marlpost Wood in Shipley parish from West Tarring, near Worthing. To do this one needs to know the site of the parent manor's headquarters. Yet much useful work can be done by noting the courses of

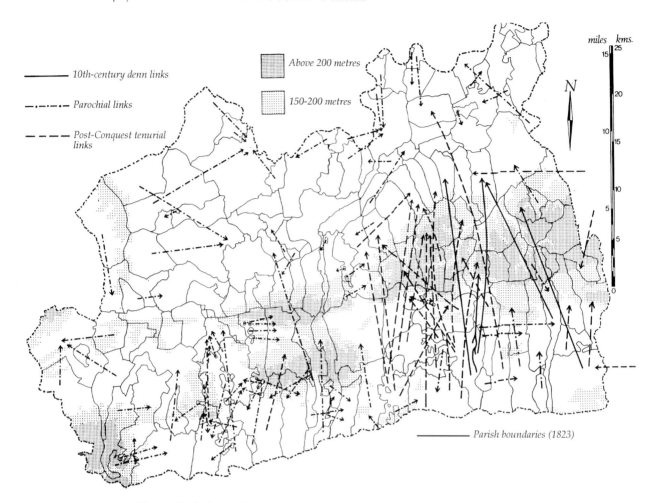

10th-century denn links

Parochial links

Post-Conquest tenurial links

Above 200 metres

150-200 metres

miles kms.

N

Parish boundaries (1823)

28 *Territorial links between the Surrey Weald and manors in the earlier colonised north (after John Blair).*

the droves themselves. Droveways are not the only vestigial survivals in the present landscape of old pastoral society. The woodcommons, which are a particular feature of West Sussex, are in this category.

The Primitive Landscape

The value of Saxon and Jutish descriptive place-names is their survival to the present day long after the features they had described have disappeared. They can, therefore, be used to reconstruct something of the primitive landscape. The distribution of place-names in the Kent, Sussex and Surrey Wealds ending in *-feld* 'open land within sight of woodland'; *-leah* 'woodland, glade or clearing'; *haep*, or *hap*, heath; *fearn*, bracken; *-den(n)* 'woodland swine pasture'; *hyrst* 'wooded hill', and the like, provides cumulative evidence that trees began to thin out on the High

Weald ridges, yielding only a sparse cover on their summits and that, on sandier tracts, clumps of trees and bushes probably stood above a continuous cover of bracken or, more rarely, grass. Clearly, no more than in any medieval forest was the Saxon Weald an unrelieved woodland.[6]

At this point it will be useful to consider local and regional words used by the Saxons and Jutes to denote different types of woodland, the meaning of which has been lost or has varied over the centuries. *Holt* was used for a single-species wood. It is rare in the Weald, an area of mixed woodland. *Hangra* meant a hanger wood, hanging on a hillside, *fryth* (Frith, in Kentish dialect *fright*, 'land overgrown with brushwood, scrubland on edge of a forest'), as in South Frith in the Lowy of Tonbridge and Fright Farm in Rotherfield; *hyrst* (*hurst*) is the characteristic name for a wood in the later settled Weald, occurring in more than 200 Kentish place-names,[7] in Sussex in 20 major names out of approximately 125, and in Surrey in three out of 72 (excluding names not recorded before 1500, and field names). It seems likely that *hyrst* names are of relatively late origin and may be in areas not recognised by the earlier Saxons as appropriate to arable farming. *Grava*, grove, is considered on p.51. In their modern spellings, copse and spring refer to coppice. *Toll* signifies a grove or clump of trees, usually on a hilltop.

Moreover, although Wealden place-names overwhelmingly perpetuate the former existence of woodland, the considerable number of early 'open land' names in localities where on geological grounds one would have expected natural woodland is striking. Examples are Fairlight, in East Grinstead, 'the bracken clearing' and Lindfield, 'open land by the lime trees'. Additionally there are other 'open-land' place-names recorded in the earliest Saxon charters, such as *Baere Leah*, 'the pig clearing', *Citangaleahge*, 'clearing of Cita's people', and the unidentified *Hafocungaleahge* mentioned in a charter of *c.*765-771 relating to places in or near West Hoathly. Such place-names, and numerous other examples, testify to a considerable thinning of the woodland in the deepest recesses of the Sussex Weald as early as the eighth and ninth centuries and in some cases had clearly resulted from permanent settlement in the forest.[8]

Other South Saxon place-names offer direct evidence of change in vegetation, presumably due to early human interference. Several names, compounded with hazel, such as Hazelwick in Worth and Hazelhurst in Ticehurst, presumably record this shrub's vigorous growth and abundance of fruit, when stimulated by the clearance of overshadowing trees such as oak, ash and beech. Hazel would also have formed a pioneer woodland phase on any abandoned land.

There are also two place-name elements recording some of the earliest cultivation sites in the Weald: *etisc*, 'a cornfield' (possibly unenclosed), and *ersc*, a later form, meaning ploughed field or stubble. The first element is an extremely archaic word-form, represented on the continent in the *esch* names of Westphalia, Oldenburg and Holland but it quickly dropped out of use with the Anglo-Saxons and is found in very few places in England outside the extreme south-eastern corner of Sussex, where in Icklesham and surrounding parishes it is preserved in such 'exe' names as Cleeve Axe and Platnix. Ekwall regards these 'exe' names as being the main characteristic of the place-name of the Hastings district. They occur in the most favoured farmland of the people called the *Haestingas* and evidently mark very early settlement on the fringes of the Weald. In the Surrey Weald there are two possible *-etisc* names. The *ersc* form is also mainly confined to east Sussex. Ticehurst has a sprinkling of these names: Hazelhurst, 'earsh land grown over with hazels', is mentioned in 1018, *Birchen Ersh*, meaning 'earsh land overgrown with birch trees' mentioned in Cowfold in a late Saxon charter, and formerly considered lost, is identifiable with a field known as 'Birch and Ash' in the Tithe Apportionment. In the Surrey Weald there are 11 *-ersc* names. These 'earsh' names appear to mark an early stage in the recurrent theme in Wealden history of cultivated land subsequently abandoned to scrub or forest, awaiting a favourable moment for reclamation.

The *-feld* names bring us back to east Sussex, that is to the part of Sussex dominated by the *Haestingas*. We have already noted how the element *feld* tends to occur on the higher, bleaker ridges of the High Weald. The question now arises as to what light they throw on social organisation and settlement evolution. Dr Margaret Gelling has recently suggested that when *feld* was in living use in the language of Berkshire the term may have been used for belts of heathy common pasture. This attractive idea is certainly worth considering in a Sussex context. Implicit in her suggestion is that villages eventually developing on the *felds*, such as Cuckfield, Heathfield, Mayfield, etc. were later in origin than the surrounding farms once inter-commoning their livestock on sites subsequently becoming villages.[9]

Permanent Settlement

As already noted, most Wealden settlement, both isolated farms as well as hamlets and villages, evolved from temporarily occupied huts and shelters associated with seasonal pastoral farming before being permanently occupied by farmers cultivating land within ring-fenced fields. Thus most Wealden place-names are much older than the farms, villages and towns that bear them. It is also clear that fully-fledged farms were evolving from summer pastures in the 10th and 11th centuries. Early antiquaries concluded that the original Wealden settlements were on the ridgeways and that the deep, densely wooded valleys were cleared subsequently. The reverse appears to be the case. Pioneer farms were invariably sited in the sheltered hollows with deep mould under woodland which had earlier been used for seasonal grazing and pig-rooting. Ridge-top settlements, including numerous and well-known compact villages, did not begin to cluster around once-isolated central churches until later.

Stages in the Colonisation

We must, however, be aware of the limitations of the documentary evidence at our disposal. Although the contemporary sources have little to say about permanent farming settlement we must not assume, therefore, that it had not substantially happened even by the eighth and ninth centuries. On the contrary, the evidence of Saxon charters and place-names suggests that considerable permanent settlement had spread to every part of the Weald long before earlier historians had thought it likely. We may conclude that the partial winning of new land was one of the main gifts of the Saxons and Jutes to posterity. Yet to questions such as 'When did seasonal settlements turn into permanent ones?', 'What was the extent of permanent settlements by Domesday?', 'Was it then already ancient or was it recent and expanding?', 'Was there any continuity between Saxon and Jutish and earlier Romano-British settlement?', it is difficult to provide answers with our present knowledge.

As an example of the difficulties in the interpretation of Saxon documents we turn to the *Haeselersc* charter of 1018. This is of undoubted authenticity and is clearly and carefully written.[10] It records the grant to Archbishop Aelfstan by King Cnut of land in Ticehurst 'in the famous wood Andredesweald'. The land granted is referred to in Latin as a '*Silvule Nemus*' and bears an endorsement in contemporary Anglo-Saxon that this is a den. The translation of *nemus* presents a difficulty. It has been translated as a 'small wood', but in this instance the bounds included an area of more than a square mile. The word 'grove' has also been proposed but this is one of the English woodland words whose exact meaning is lost. Thirteenth-century and later medieval recordings of the word are now considered to mean 'coppice', i.e. managed woodland, which is unconvincing in an early 11th-century context in the deep Weald. We are helped by Alan Everitt's suggestion that the Old English word *grav* often came to signify a woodland pasture as well as the wood itself.[11] This appears to have been the meaning of this *nemus*, i.e. a den in English. Thus the land granted was apparently then a rough unenclosed woodland pasture for cattle and pigs. The bounds of the land granted were identified by Gordon Ward as being in a corner of Ticehurst bordered by Whiligh and including what is now Lower Hazelhurst Farm. It may have been the scene of an earlier abandonment of cultivation (p.50). When granted the land appears to have been unpeopled but, unusually, the gift of a den was made apart from the manor to which it was presumably attached, making subsequent colonisation of the den difficult to trace. The 'Haslesse' entry in Domesday Book records land worked by 11 ploughs, 10 villeins and two cottars already served by a church. This is not, as is commonly supposed, the same area as that of the 1018 charter.

For Kent, two documents roughly coeval with Domesday Book furnish supplementary information greatly modifying and expanding our knowledge of 11th-century geography. One, *Domesday Monachorum*, deals with properties of the Archbishop of Canterbury and Bishop of Rochester, amongst others. Its most important information in the present connection is a list of 104 churches in places unrecorded in Domesday Book making payment to Christ Church Canterbury, mainly lying in the eastern Weald.[12] The *Textus Roffensis* complements this with a further list of 48 churches otherwise unrecorded in the bishopric of Rochester, mainly in the western Kentish Weald.[13] Omission of settlement on this scale is a striking demonstration of the limitations of Domesday Book. Of particular interest is that 37 of the 11th-century churches (and some others which have not been identified) lay in settlements in the Kentish Weald subordinate to the great multiple estates centred outside the woodland. They are fairly evenly distributed over the Kent Weald and Romney Marsh, across an area left blank on the Domesday map as seemingly uncolonised forest and marsh.

For Sussex we can fill in to some extent the nameless tracts of the Domesday map from the late 11th-century charters of Lewes and Sele priories which reveal that churches unmentioned in Domesday Book existed over the central Sussex Weald. These sources indicate that the historical evolution of the Wealds of Kent and Sussex was a process stretching back in time infinitely more remote than was formerly considered likely. Blair has discovered that Surrey also underwent the same development in pre-Conquest times.[14]

What should now be our revised estimate of the extent of late 11th-century settlement in the Weald? If we had lists of Sussex and Surrey churches as comprehensive as those of Kent they would almost certainly show that their Wealds were far more thoroughly settled than Domesday Book suggests.[15] In 1962 it was Darby's view that the old impression of the uncolonised Weald 'must be modified, but not fundamentally changed; even with the additional names, the Weald remains a relatively empty area'. The outcome of this discussion remains controversial and has not ended. Bearing in mind the enormous extent of post-Norman colonisation on cleared woodlands to be discussed later in this book, Darby's conclusion appears to be still the correct one. Even if we spread out the Domesday data of settlement amongst the backwoods (as in the extensive Archbishop's manor of South Malling), the 11th-century clearings do not appear to have developed beyond an initial stage when they were insufficient to maintain more than a small group of families in each parish. Some of these settlements may well have been ancient and some failed settlement has been noted. Altogether, the evidence supports the belief that the Weald was in the late 11th century grossly under-exploited, and was still a sort of appendage to the much more developed zones on its borders.[16] It also supports, whatever may be the case in other parts of England, the traditional view, held by Professor Loyn, that the story of Saxon and Jutish settlement in the Weald is one of 'the saga of man against forest'.[17]

7

The 'Custom of the Country' – Agriculture

SO many forestry and farming practices continued largely unchanged for centuries that it is desirable to discuss them before proceeding with a chronological approach.

Woods not only provided timber and fuel. During the Middle Ages farmers evolved a system of farming adapted to their circumstances which stood the test of centuries. A cardinal principle was to integrate farming with forestry. On freeholds the farm and its woods would be managed as a whole, the artificial distinction between farming and forestry broken down, and on tenant farms, where timber belonged to the landlord, trees, livestock and crops were nevertheless all raised on one piece of land instead of separately, a flexible method of land use for the small farmer working under natural difficulties. It is often

29 Semi-derelict woodbank, Markstakes Common, Chailey. Commonly found in the Weald, woodbanks protected young coppice and young tree seedlings from cattle and deer browsing.

supposed that cattle and sheep *prefer* grass to *all* other kinds of vegetation. On the contrary, they show a great liking for the leaves of many trees and will turn aside to eat common dock, mint, nettles, thistles and other coarse weeds to balance their forage. (Modern farmers are being asked to tolerate nettle, beloved by the conservationist.) The Wealden farmer took advantage of this along ditches, the margins of hedges and shaws on headlands, and on patches of wet ground. Cattle and sheep browsed on foliage; swine were fattened on mast in woods; cattle were pastured in coppice woodland as soon as the stools of trees had regrown out of the reach of browsing; sheep and geese grazed orchards in summer and pigs cleared up the fallen apples; vegetables and other crops were planted between the rows of fruit; hedges were used for medicinal purposes and provided nutritious food for half the year – hazel nuts, crab apple, bullace, blackberries and acorns. Thus a single field might supply a crop of grass, plus hedgerow timber, domestic fuel, litter from verges for laying down in barns, wild fruits and medicines.[1] This system of farming is still practised over extensive areas of central and eastern Europe and its environmental benefits are so indisputable that it is being promoted in Britain as agro-forestry. *Pace* Arthur Young and William Marshall, vociferous 18th-century critics, deriding such practices as sowing under trees and alongside wide hedges and shaws as being hundreds of years behind the times. Recent trials have shown that produce is actually increased in such conditions during dry summers because of reduced evaporation and the growing season is extended by up to a month. There are also fewer problems with aphids. Were the much maligned Wealden farmers after all more right than their detractors? Certainly they contrived a harmonious balance between farming and forestry as a source of mutual support when one or the other was in difficulty.

Various features on the face of the landscape originated from agro-forestry. Impressive earthworks around former coppices attest to woodmen's efforts throughout history to protect their crop of wood from browsing creatures which would damage the growing tip of each coppice shoot. The standard practice was to exclude cattle and deer until the coppice shoots had grown tall enough for their tips not to be browsed. The cattle were removed when the herbage of the woodland floor was shaded out by the closing coppice canopy. Cattle would then be grazed in another compartment which had been cut more recently. This required a woodbank and ditch of about four feet wide. A thick live hedge, 'well brushed up', was planted on the bank to act as an efficient fence.

Domestic animals were also grazed in high Forest on wood commons, the ancient royal forests and in medieval deer parks. This was associated with the pollarding (coppicing) of trees. Young oak and beech trees pollarded at a height of a few yards formed a broad crown, low down on the trunk, and produced a richer mast at an earlier age. In former wood pastures trees with several stems are found. Young trees were planted in bundles in one planting hole. The subsequent overdeveloped crown gave increased mast production and when protected with spiny scrub species there was no need for special devices to ward off grazing animals. Controlled pig grazing, together with managed cattle grazing, assisted woodland regeneration in two ways: firstly, by the planting of oak and beech as

30 Town Hill, Lamberhurst, a settlement in Sussex (Kent since 1895), which has grown up on the margins of several dens owned by Battle Abbey. Some of the dwellings appear in the Survey of Lamberhurst Manor in 1568 (CKS U 47/42 M12) when a number of them had detached kitchens (see p.109). (John Malton, May 2002, pen and ink with watercolour wash, 19 × 14cm [7½ × 5½in.])

mast-bearing trees and, secondly, by the loosening of soil through the grubbing activities of pigs, creating appropriate germination conditions for young trees.[2]

The Weald's unforgiving clay, with its coldness, retentiveness, flatness, floods and tenacity is no ordinary clay. The 18th-century agricultural writer Arthur Young (writing before the widespread under-draining from the 1840s) found nothing so rank as Sussex clay on his journeys in France and to William Cobbett the Surrey version was 'bottomless' and as condemnatory.[3] For Wilfrid Scawen Blunt the spatter of brown clay fallow on a dark green plain was the quintessence of his Sussex birthplace. To Vita Sackville-West, the Weald farmer is a wrestler who broke with 'the unkindly spirit of the clay' in battle and plodded over it in a steady and unhurrying gait until the clay crept into his bones before its due time.[4] The clay indeed weeds out all but hard-working farmers, the toughest of foresters and the most dogged of huntsmen and ramblers. Only G.K. Chesterton, who had fierce pleasure in things being themselves, professed love for the 'unutterable muddinesss' of its mud.[5]

The Weald, indeed, has always been a region of antonyms. Its wonderful impression of fecundity and tranquil beauty, 'trim as a garden plot', has always belied grudging clays wearily farmed to the very limits of practical credibility. On clay soils (and, as we have seen, on the fine silts and sands of the High Weald when wet), even minor changes in the weather have exaggerated consequences. Clay particles expand when wet and prevent downward drainage; during a hot, dry spell they contract, leaving cracks on the surface. Both types of weather result in smaller crops. Pasture quickly becomes poached in wet weather, resulting in a severe loss of grass. Moreover, clay soils are more difficult, and thus more costly, to plough than others; when dry, clods are difficult to break down into a reasonable tilth for sowing, and in wet conditions only winter frosts make the soil friable, so a hard winter is a blessing. Its sticky nature meant that, whereas two horses (or four oxen) had sufficient strength to plough the lighter downland soils, the Weald was considered 'three-horse' or even 'four-horse' land or an eight-ox team, at considerable extra cost and effort. (Early 20th-century farmers using only two horses were generally cultivating only their lighter or best-drained fields.)

Better soils, suitably ameliorated with marl (pp.59-60), were capable of producing good crops of wheat or beans, and, in a good season, oats, but all sowings were highly dependent on favourable weather at the time of ploughing and sowing, and also during the growing season. The indispensible fallow was crucially dependent on a good season and fine weather made a great difference to yield. The mark of the good Wealden farmer thus became, and has ever remained, his timeliness in farming to the weather, shown by his seizing the most

31 Flooded marl pit, now a fishing lake, Hadlow Down. Marl dug from such pits was the indispensible means of fertilising land in the Middle Ages.

favourable moment to get the land into condition for the fittest corn, and the choice of an 'early' field to nurture crops through a wet, cold spring. For a spring crop, the farmers' aim was to plough before Christmas to enable frost to break clods down. On account of the unpredictable sowing conditions, the prudent Wealden farmer practised 'sow as you go'. He would stop ploughing in mid-afternoon, unhitch two of his three horses, and sow the half-acre or so he had prepared straight into the furrow by hand, his mate following with the harrow, using a single horse. A continuance of this method day-by-day, season after season, reduced the ever-present threat of crop failure. Even now that tractors are used, some farmers play safe with 'sow as you go'. On the Downs the practice was to plough all the fields that had to be ploughed, till all were done.[6]

Coarse sandy soils have open drainage, and thus dry out rapidly in drought. They are 'hungry', being extremely short of foodstuffs, potash, potassium, phosphate and lime but they warm up readily in spring and are easily ploughed and sowed if liberally manured. Soils derived from the Hastings Beds have a dual personality, being close and sticky when wet but dry out to sands liable to wash under heavy rains. They have the disadvantages of clay in that they work heavily in the wet. Their up-and-down character also tested the judgment of ploughmen and carters and the muscles of oxen or horses. Generally speaking the Weald lacks loams, the best all-round soils, better drained and aerated, easier to plough and capable of growing any crop. In the Weald the expense of cultivation could almost equal the value of the moderate produce. The drenched clay land of a wet autumn would leave an unreaped harvest rotting in the field, the corn sprouting in the sheaf, and the next season's crop could not be sown. When the winter wheat was drowned by winter rains the farmer sowed oats in its stead in spring. Peasant families presumably went hungrier. Conversely, dry weather at the spring sowings quickly shrivelled the crops into nothingness. As a whole, despite his efforts, the yields of all grains were lower and more erratic than those from sheep-and-corn districts on the better drained soils bordering the Weald, and in bad seasons the grudging soils in early times probably left communities verging upon dearth. Historically, cow-keeping and woodmanship have been more profitable activities than arable farming.

Consequently, the Weald needed strength, toughness and craft to work it. To keep a family in some degree of well-being, one had to have an unlimited capacity for work, strenuous exertion paid for with stiff muscles, an aching head and sweat pouring over one's skin. Older men lifted themselves stiffly from the plough-handles. With extraordinary vitality a farmer might struggle untiringly in bad times and remain ambitious and enterprising; others submitted to adversity by cutting down on farmwork and more or less withdrawing from the fight with nature.[7]

The System of Farming

The farmer was to discover that even strenuous labour of both men and animals, and its great expense, could not readily reduce his strong, stiff, cold clay to a good tilth. The first ploughing brought up immense slags of earth which even after

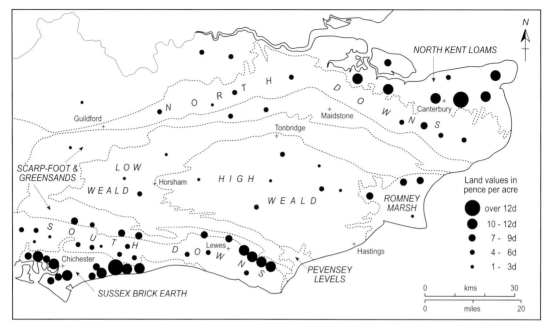

32 Land valuations, early 13th-century (Source: Inquisitiones Post Mortem). The low Wealden valuations reflect mediocre soils and inaccessibility to markets; the high valuations represent naturally fertile land near tidewater, allowing carriage of crops to market by sea and river.

being cut transversely by a second ploughing, left the field covered with huge clods, in dry weather as hard as a brick. When a little softened by rain, a third, and frequently a fourth, ploughing was made but this still did not reduce the hard remaining lumps to the requisite friability for sowing. To pulverise the clods further, repeated harrowings between ploughings were necessary, and by itself this was insufficient. A man went behind plough or harrow to hack the cloddy surface with an iron implement much like a carpenter's adze after each ploughing. At the final ploughing the farmer would make a cross furrow to assist drainage but on flatter surfaces this was insufficient to allow rain to escape. So the farmer ridged up his lands into round-backed ridges which the rain could run off as it would from an umbrella or roof of a house. Even with the prevailing use of the turn-wrest plough with its movable wrest (which normally ploughed flat), land could be ridged by simply not moving the wrest at the end of a furrow.[8] (Although ridging was general in later centuries a form of under-draining was possibly practised in the Middle Ages, centuries before 18th-century farmers thought it probable, see p.117.) After sowing and harrowing he would break up all remaining large lumps with a strong wooden mallet or maul. After all this ploughing, hacking and mauling there were still weeds to be pulled when half a finger high and loose stones to be gathered for walling or paving which would otherwise have damaged the plough next season. The expense of cultivation, for a moderate return, was the main cause of decline of Wealden demesne farming from the end of the 13th century.[9]

This laborious method of cultivation adopted in the Middle Ages stood the test of time, basically unaltered up to at least the 18th century. Few parts of Britain needed a greater exertion in husbandry. From the late 18th century the improved technology was the heavy roller drawn by two horses and the scarifier drawn by one which finally ended the hacking and mauling. This alleviated, though did not resolve, the difficulties of cultivation.

Another cause of exceptional exertion and expense was fertilisation, always given the highest priority. Gervase Markham aptly observed of the Weald in 1625 that '... it was of a very barren nature and unapt for either pasture or tillage until that it be holpen by some manner of comfort as dung, marl, fresh earth, fodder, ashes or such other refreshings'.[10] This was as true of medieval times as after. The pioneer farmer quickly learned that his land soon wore out and needed periods of rest. Moreover, it needed some mechanical aid to produce a good tilth in the form of a combination of large increases in fertility and improvement of soil texture, together with recuperative periods under grass. This fertility had to be searched for on and around the farm. The Weald farmer was by necessity 'manure mad'. He fed the lean soil as one crammed chickens. Dung, compost, sleech (ditch clearings), and seaweed were pressed into service and, in later centuries, lime, guano, soap-ashes and rape-cake, but unquestionably the cornerstone of Wealden farming for at least six centuries was marling.

From the chemical point of view the basic deficiency of most Wealden soils is carbonate of lime. The first step in making them workable was a heavy application of some calcareous substance. In the days of narrow, miry lanes and packsaddles it was impracticable to get lime from the chalk hills on the Weald's borders. Experiencing dear carriage and cheap labour, farmers made the marl-pit do the duty of the lime kiln. The readiest method of marling where calcareous strata were at hand was to open a pit at the corner of almost every little field. An underlying bed of calcareous clay was then winched up in buckets and carted

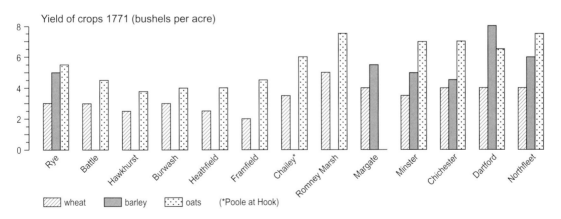

33 *Yields of crops, 18th-century. (Source: Arthur Young,* A Farmer's Travels through Eastern England, *1771.) The disparity between the Weald and its borders would have presumably been a factor throughout history.*

to fields to be liberally spread and ploughed in to enrich the soil, an application of 3-400 cart-loads in the 17th century being regarded as effective for up to three or four sowings of corn. Many of these marl-pits went into oblivion when filled in during the 19th-century under-draining and land improvement, when the object was to make unevenness even (p.190), but myriads of them, dimpling fields, usually water-filled ponds still survive to bear ample witness of farmers' extraordinary assiduity. On some farms one or two pits centrally placed were dug, to serve the entire holding and with repeated use over centuries these became 'great yawning pits … deep enough to drown the weathercock on a church steeple and wide enough to accommodate the church as well'. These ancient marl-pits, now overgrown with trees and filled with water, are valuable refuges for wildlife.

Markham in 1625 noted 200-year-old trees in marl-pits and young trees, of one hundred years old in the 1780s, were indicative of the decline in marling from 1400 and its subsequent revival which ended with the coming of lime. In some districts, as in the Kentish Weald around Bethersden and Smarden where marl was dug in association with 'marble', pits are so ubiquitious as to cover the whole landscape with little ponds. Many soil pits also occur in localities without calcium carbonate, but we cannot attribute the medieval farmers' high regard for marl to its chemical properties alone. On the sandier soils of Surrey, for example, non-calcareous earths were spread to improve the water retention of the soil. In such instances 'marl' was being used as a soil conditioner, rather than as a fertiliser.

Marl was regarded as so essential to Wealden tillage that some 13th-century landlords aimed at regular marling of the entire arable demesne, each field being heavily marled about once in a generation. Such a requirement was built into farm leases. The Earl of Arundel, for instance, who was leasing out parts of his demesne at Cuckfield and Keymer in 1343-4, granted an additional parcel of land to those who marled, as compensation for costs, and others took land on the basis of 'half-marling' in which case the earl presumably paid the remaining expenses. This could only be done by a high labour and capital input.[11] Other lords who continued to work their demesne directly were ardent marlers. At Chalvington, near Lewes, where the whole arable was regularly dressed (subject to a sufficiently dry summer), 11½ acres were dressed in 1347 by seven men and six boys, mostly hired persons, for eight weeks, at a cost of 7s. an acre, a good season's work, but a costly operation considering the price of wheat. The long-term beneficial effects of marl on soil fertility are evident from the valuations placed on land so manured (*Terra Marlerata*) in the late 13th century – as much as treble, or more, the value of unmanured land.

Modern geologists have asserted that much medieval marling was a wasted exercise because samples contained little calcium. It is, however, nonsense to believe that farmers, not only in the Weald but elsewhere in Britain and all over western Europe, had deluded themselves, generation by generation (in some instances over two thousand years), and that their extraordinary exertion did not pay in higher yields. Wealdsmen became very conservative, preferring a heavy plough when a lighter implement would have done better, for example, but they did not engage in mindless routines.[12]

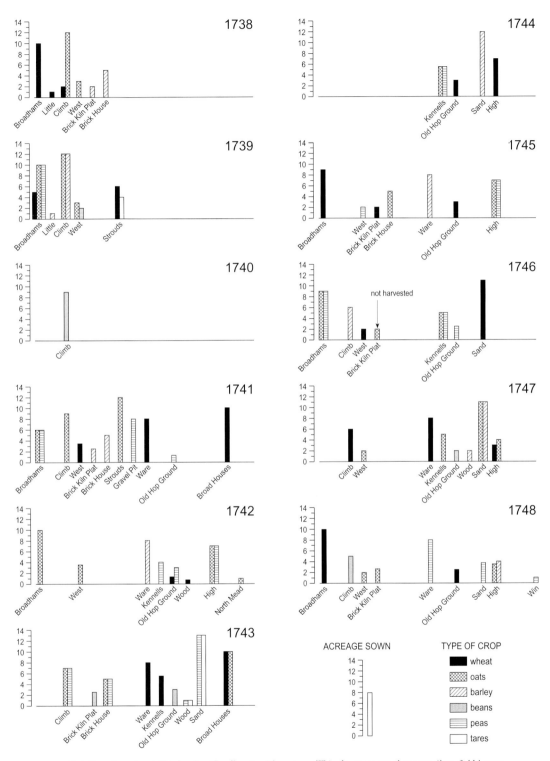

34 *Rotation of crops at Finchcocks, Goudhurst, 18th-century. This demonstrates that some 'best fields' were intensively cropped between fallows whilst other fields were only occasionally brought into arable cultivation when, for example, old pasture was broken up. This system of husbandry prevailed from earliest farming settlement.*

Another highly-prized source of fertiliser amongst commoners was 'litter', cut in autumn. This comprised anything on commonland that made good bedding for beasts in barns (straw being scarce on small farms) which could afterwards be ploughed in as dung. An annual supply of 'brakes' (bracken and fern) or 'litter' (mainly young heather) was indispensible for the maintenance of a little farm, and even larger properties made use of it. The small farmer's family would descend on a common, the men scything, women and girls raking, and boys swinging their own little hooks. Seasonal labourers, fresh from hop-fields and orchards, cried, 'Master, can I cut any heather for you' and doubled their money cutting for commoners, if they could get away with it, by illicitly selling heaps to the highest bidder. It was, however, hard work: a man might spend a day or more cutting a wagon load but its value would be reduced by a long haulage back to a farm. Litter had other uses apart from bedding and fertiliser. Old heather went for road-making and was also used as a roof over a charcoal burning. On Ashdown Forest extensive and chaotic litter cutting led to one of the greatest Victorian disputes over commoners' rights (pp.228-31). The two wagon loads of heather and litter cut by Miles for Bernard Hale, which was the immediate cause of the dispute, illustrates its versatility.

Hale, in reply to counsel:

> The litter went to Suntings Farm and the brakes came up to Holly Hill House and formed the thatch for a pile of mangel-wurzels and finally this covering went back to Suntings Farm and together with the litter were matured into dung and put into the ground with the turnip crop.
>
> Counsel: I hope it produced a good crop
>
> Hale: I do not think it did.[13]

The pioneer had also to devise a particular type of cultivation for average or below average soils. Outside the Weald, fields were cultivated either biennially with a summer fallow in between (the 'Two-Field System') or twice in three years, with an intervening fallow (the 'Three Field System'). Thus arable would normally comprise either fifty or sixty-six per cent of land in any one year. The Weald failed to reach even this modest degree of agricultural development. For example, on sandy soils at Wotton, near Dorking, only 80 acres were cultivated out of 200 in 1280, and only 40 in 1300. Similar examples of low-intensity arable exist for the medieval Surrey Weald, as for the Wealds of Sussex and Kent. The Wealden farmer had very significant amounts of under-used land for, except on heavily marled land, his fields quickly became full of weeds and exhausted and required long periods of rest. His normal method was to keep quasi-permanently cropped the small fields nearest the barns, for these could be more readily manured and marled. He then took the plough round each of the remaining fields until they 'ran out', usually in two to three years, except on heavily marled land, when it was left to swarth again on its own account, in which condition it remained for up to ten years. Thus no distinction was made between arable and grassland (convertible husbandry is the term adopted by modern scholars), the main difference being the land use of the relatively small acreage of fields near the homestead (designated *infield*) and the much larger acreage of sporadically cultivated land (*outfield*). The Abbey of Westminster's farm at Westerham was farmed thus between 1297 and 1350,[14] and the Abbey of Battle had a similar system at Barnhorne, near Bexhill. There does seem to have been an idea of a beneficial rotation of crops. Wheat followed a summer fallow of beans; oats rounded off cultivation before putting down a field to grass. An identical system was adopted in one 18th-century farm (Fig.34).[15]

The foundation of Wealden cultivation for centuries was a bare summer fallow. Fallowing as a preparation for wheat was considered indispensible in days of broadcast sowing to rest land before a demanding crop, and the best mode of cleaning the ground of weeds which on the heavy soil choked fields. Tedious and expensive fallows in earlier ages, strictly prescribed in leasehold covenants, became an argument for their continuance as late as the early 19th century, by which time there was abundant evidence that they could be abolished provided that under-draining had been undertaken.

A regional custom which persisted for centuries was a mode of land-breaking known as burn-beating. This involved bringing under production either newly-won land from the waste or the re-cultivation of old, worn-out grassland. The farmer would cut weeds close to the ground, using a paring plough or shovel to clear off turf. Roots were stubbed and everything combustible was piled up into heaps and burned night and day under sods of earth. In May he would spread and plough in the ashes.

It will be apparent that farming based on exceptionally little closes suited the needs of the small family farmer, lacking extra labour. In the pioneering stage of woodland clearing, or in subsequent intakes of waste, he could only tackle a small acreage, season after season. This also applied to hedging, ditching, draining and sporadic land-breaking. Small fields were also ideal for regular marling, done field by field in rotation year by year. The advantages of small fields offset the shade and wet resulting near hedgerows and shaws. It was not until under-draining became practicable from the mid-19th century that the Wealden farmer grubbed up hedges to enlarge fields.

These difficulties of arable farming had a significant and early impact on commercial agriculture. By the second half of the 13th century, a number of church institutions had given up cultivating the Weald directly on account of the expense, and handed over the unenviable task to tenants. Thus Robertsbridge Abbey, farming at Lamberhurst, reported in 1258 that half of its arable was 'sterile, or almost sterile, which no one takes into account because of its condition' and of *Otefeld* in the manor of Charing it was said in 1268 that 'it has long been untilled, being fitter for the growth of broom and fern rather than corn'. Larger landowners evidently held this view for in May 1264 a report during Simon de Montfort's rebellion climaxing in the Battle of Lewes stated that 'from a deficiency of victuals in that barren province many persons wasted away from want of food and the cattle were lowing and falling all round from scarcity of pasture'.[16]

A sense of adversity in arable farming is offset by glancing at fruit culture. It is clear that fruit-growing and horticulture had clearly already made the Weald a land of gardens in the Middle Ages on sunny hill-slopes. The older farmed fringes of the Kent Weald on the Charts were plentifully furnished with vineyards in the 11th and 12th centuries. Gradually the Weald proper was also plentifully endowed with varieties of pippins and other fruits, solely for domestic consumption. For want of good barley (an unsuitable crop on the heavy soils) an orchard for cider and apple-butter was well planted with fruit trees on the lords' 'great gardens' and doubtless on Kentish yeomen's farms as well. At Yalding where the lord's garden was seven acres, the value placed on its fruit and herbage was high. At Petworth the Earl of Northumberland had 251 apple and 24 pear trees planted in 1347-8 and the gardener accounted for crops of 'genetz' pears and 'Wardonns' as well as walnuts from the subsidiary manor of Duncton and produce from two herb gardens. The latter were so extensive that parcels were let out to towns-people for sowing their vegetables. In Surrey, gardens attached to manor houses were also on a considerable scale. Other farms had fruit for subsistence purposes. Throughout the Weald larger farms possessed a cider press, and cider-making was one of the great festivals of the farming year. Doubtless, early peasant farmers also found room for a few fruit trees – probably originally 'sports' from the woods on the sunny side of their cottage.

35 Young sweet chestnut coppice shoots.

The long period, during which the 'custom of the country' established in the Middle Ages held the Weald farmer in its grip, becomes readily apparent when the husbandry covenants in farm leases are examined through the ages. Here is a selection:

A lease for seven years from April 1408 between the widow of the lord of the manor of Frant, Lady Joan Brenchesle and two husbandmen, Richard Longeligh and Laurence Wymondesherst, whereby the lessees took over 12 acres of wheat and 18 acres of oats and covenants required to them to sow no more at the end of the term, the wheat to be on a summer fallow. Implements included a matchet, doubtless a clodding-bill.

Lease, 29 Sept. 1483. Walter Roberts to John Kyppyng of Benenden, term 7 years, Boarzell, Springetts and Cuckys. Four hundred cartloads of marl to be applied; no field to be sown two years together with oats; no meadow to be sown within last 2 years of term; within last 2 years not to sow more than 10 acres of wheat and 20 acres of oats.

10 March 1691. Walter Roberts of Boarzell to Joseph Blewett of Cranbrook, 140 acres (same land as in 1483), not more than 40 acres to be ploughed and sown in the last 3 years of the lease; not to sow oats upon oats grattent [stubble] 300 loads of marl to be applied after three crops of corn.

John Roberts to Thos. Pavy at Horsmonden, husbandman, 1709. No more than four crops before amending with 300 cart loads of marl. No wheat to be sown but on a summer fallow.

1756 Samuel Roberts to Gabriele Down of Ticehurst yeoman, marl 300 loads after three crops of corn. No more than thirty-five acres to be ploughed in any one year.

Hammerden Farm, Ticehurst, 1916; Preparation for Mangolds after Oats. Maize and Cabbage; 3 ploughings and 5 cultivations with four horses, 4 rollings with four horses, 4 rollings with 2 horses, 4 drag harrowings.

1918 Annual tenancy, Beauman's Farm Wadhurst; not to take two crops of corn without having first well manured the land from which the crop is taken and in a husbandlike manner not to sow wheat after oats or oats after oats, nor to take more than two cereal crops in succession. In the last year of tenancy to leave one-fourth of the arable in a summer fallow or other preparation for wheat.[17]

Oxen were the main draught animals. A good team, always yoked in pairs of similar size, and gait, ploughed in a day as much and as well as a team of horses. Moreover, they thrived on straw, roots and a modicum of meal – a diet that starved a working horse – and made prime beef when sent to the butcher after their working life. In hilly districts they drew a load up a steep bank at a steady pace, whereas a horse would rush at the work and then stop, start again with a snatch, break something or strain itself – or jib at the job altogether. The ox-cart was also very suitable for the small farm, the animals needing no harness of any kind and being so tractable as to follow the farmer exactly along the line he took. They are often thought to have been slow, but their stride is longer than it looks and their pace is deceptive in consequence.

Hedge and Shaw

A hedge is a man-made linear feature of trees, shrubs and plants generally enclosing a field, farm, manor, hundred or parish. The Weald's intricate hedgerow pattern is due to the pastoral economy which was the backbone of the small family farm, with short interludes, for hundreds of years. The hedge was also used to stabilise hillsides. Wealdsmen feel in their bones that hedges are part of their history and reckon that there is no kind of fence which is half as good as a live fence or so enduring and beautiful.

The ubiquitous Wealden hedge is unusually thick and of great age. Often unrestrained with swarths of intertwined branch and bramble, its dense foliage runs lavishly to many species of shrubs, trees, wild flowers, mammals and song birds as a sign of slowly-acquired wealth. Many Wealden hedges doubtless originated as the deliberately planted hedges by the pioneer farmer in the Age of Clearing. Hawthorn and blackthorn were the most suitable: other species valued were hazel, ash (both coppiced for long poles), maple, willow and hornbeam. Other useful trees were introduced as required for some special purpose. The guelder rose and elder quickly filled gaps.

Generally speaking, the most prominent Wealden hedges define manorial, parish, and other ancient territorial boundaries. With a high bank and deeply-cut ditch, their formidable earthworks are important historical monuments. An example is the hedge near Huggett's Furnace Farm in Mayfield, marking the boundary between the Royal manor of Rotherfield and the Archbishop of Canterbury's manor of South Malling, both of mid-Saxon origin.[18]

One sign of the great age of a Wealden hedge is its crookedness. The ploughman walked on the near side of his four or eight ox-team, guiding them with his whip first inwards and then outwards so that they could turn more easily at the headland. This tended to make furrows in the form of an inverted S. More recent hedges are generally straighter (as well as more timid) because from the 18th century horse-ploughing became general and needed less space to turn in at the end of a furrow.

The great age of Wealden hedges is also indicated by another characteristic. Research by Dr Max Hooper has demonstrated that hedges tend to acquire additional species as they age, and old Wealden hedges tend to be more species diverse than recent hedges. Hooper concluded that one additional species of shrub colonised a hedge about every one hundred years. This provides a simple rule-of-thumb estimate provided that a number of procedures are observed. The species count of the manorial hedge previously referred to gave totals of seven, seven, and eight along successive thirty-yard lengths and, from this, Streeter concluded that the hedge may not be as old as the boundary, even though a medieval origin is indicated. Bearing in mind a possible wide margin of error, Streeter has observed that the technique of species count would be sufficiently sensitive to distinguish between a medieval, or earlier, a Tudor or a 19th-century hedge. This is borne out by the fact that hedges laid in 16th- and 17th-century clearances, such as the enclosure hedges in St Leonard's and Worth Forests, have since been colonised by fewer species of shrubs. Relatively modern hawthorn hedges often indicate the grubbing up of old hedge-lines to amalgamate two or more small fields or to straighten out awkward boundaries, a practice common during under-draining in the second half of the 19th century. The identification of ancient hedgerows derived from species counting is now a vital part of countryside conservation. It should be borne in mind that the rich mixture of shrubs which were probably used by the pioneer farmer to make the initial hedge means that Hooper's dating method must be used with caution.

Traditionally, the Wealden field hedge is exceptionally broad. Streeter and Richardson discovered that the profile of a Sussex hedge was as much as 2.5m. in breadth and five times or more wider than the Essex variety. This difference is explained by the traditional maintenance of a Sussex hedge to provide a continuing supply of underwood for both farm purposes and sale and, consequently, the hedge was deliberately left untrimmed, letting it increase in height and permitting it to spread in width a considerable distance beyond the line of the ditch and bank which becomes deeply buried. It was apparently with this type of hedge in mind that medieval officials of the Archbishop of Canterbury's manor of South Malling measured land assarted on the manor by a rod of 18½ feet, 15 per cent greater than a statute acre. On account of the exceptional width of most Wealden hedges, a land surveyor since the 16th century has distinguished the 'plain', or interior, i.e. cultivable measurement of a field from its outside measurement including the hedge. This kind of hedge provided a formidable windbreak to shelter livestock, the Weald farmer's principal source of income, whereas the Essex hedge was in the midst of a countryside intensively managed for agriculture, and underbrush was normally cut close to the field boundary.

The exceptional width of the Wealden hedge enables it to support more woody and herbaceous plant species than lesser hedges. These include such ancient woodland indicator species as wood anemone, sweet woodruff, wood sorrel, dogs mercury and greater stitchwort and woody species such as midland hawthorn, wild service and small-leaved lime, and in turn this appears to host high diversities of associated mammals, birds, invertebrates and their predators. Hedges, being linear, have a useful ecological role acting as corridors for wildlife to larger habitats.

The wide hedgerows and the extremely small and irregular fields which add so much scenic beauty have long been considered by the improving farmer as baneful. Grant, studying Tithe apportionments in 1845, found that near Exeter hedgerows occupied between seven and 10 per cent of the land surface. They shaded at least half as much; harboured birds and vermin which injured the crops and were nurseries of weeds. Moreover they were expensive to maintain and prevented the free circulation of air and were obstacles to the drainage of soil, the roots found in them frequently choking the drains. So many small enclosures required many more gates which had to be maintained and caused a much greater number of small lanes and cart-tracks leading from one place to another. The fences being crooked, and fields being irregular, the labour of every operation of the farm, particularly ploughing, was most materially increased. 'It will be self-evident', he wrote,

> how utterly impossible it must be for the farmer of such densely wooded districts
> to compete with those who are living on more open, and therefore, more
> productive farms, in small enclosures, under five acres, the deterioration that
> ensues to the crop is very great … in many cases depreciating the produce from
> 10 to 20 per cent.[19]

The same problems faced the Weald farmer. A computation from the Tithe maps of Framfield and Buxted parishes in the 1840s reveals that the percentage under hedge and shaw was higher than in Devon, being 11 per cent. A quarter of the working day must have been lost by recurrent turns at ends of too-short furrows. These hedges and shaws to which Wealden farmers clung so obstinately were early targets for agricultural improvers.

Another distinctive feature of the regional landscape is the shaw in East Sussex and Kent, and a few further west – a linear strip of woodland around the fields, too wide to be termed a hedge, and normally owned by the lord. It is surprising, given their significance, that little research has been done on their origin and development. Speculation about them is traceable to William Marshall (1798) who considered them as a belt of trees left round the edges of fields cleared by pioneer farmers in lieu of a hedge.[20] This is unconvincing, for the resulting hedge would not have been stock-proof. Ground surveys indicate that shaws lie on either side of a field lynchet of a clearly defined bank and ditch. It seems likely, therefore, that the pioneer would have planted up his hedge on a bank in the usual manner to secure a field boundary against animals. It thus seems that shaws were created at a later date, either by natural seeding from the hedgerow, or, more likely, by planting.

The growth of trees beyond a former hedge line represented an encroachment on to the borders of one or more fields. This would have resulted from neglect or dereliction but also by intent. It appears that in bad times for farming, hedges, formerly well-trimmed, were allowed to run wild as shaws across the former ploughed edge and were cut back when corn prices were favourable. At certain periods of history, as during the Wealden iron industry in the 16th and early 17th centuries, shaws were apparently brought under a form of woodland management by landlords to produce underwood for charcoal or fencing. This suggests that it was more profitable than the value of field crops lost as a result (p.157). Thus tenant farmers would have benefited because woodland was kept in hand by landlords. Cartographic testimony confirms that many once-hedged fields later came to be bounded by shaws for ornamentation, game preservation (well-managed shaws were ideal for shoots), and for additional protection to hop gardens and studs.

It would thus seem that the shaw should be seen not as a static but as a dynamic feature, expanding or contracting over time in response to economic or other considerations. Many should doubtless be regarded as hedgerows run wild and to which a match might be put when the produce from fields rose as in the 1840s and 1850s and again in the post-war period under the Agriculture Act 1950 after the long agricultural depression from the 1870s. Whatever the origin and history of shaws they were a reality and consequently the field surveyor from the 16th century distinguished between the outside breadth of a field, including the shaw, and the cultivable acreage inside. The Tittensors found that shaws were often two rods wide (33 feet) and deliberately sown with oak and elm, and that they might contain as many as 15-22 species of tree and shrub, including fruit trees such as bullace, crab apple, wild pear, cherry and damson.

8

The 'Custom of the Country' – Woodcraft

THE Weald has always been regarded as one of the finest timber regions in England due to its moisture-retentive soils and equable climate. Nature speedily overruns with wood any neglected field. The easiest way to create a wood in the Weald is to take a piece of land and do nothing with it. 'Every berry soon becomes a bush and every bush a tree', and within a space of ten years there will be a naturally regenerated young wood. A characteristic of the woods has always been the variety of tree cover – alder, crab apple, ash, beech, birch, wild cherry, elder, elm, hazel, holly, hornbeam, field maple, oak, plum, whitebeam, willow and yew. Soil conditions, however, have an important influence on species, oak being characteristic of clays, for example, whilst beech is more adapted to Tunbridge Wells and Ashdown Sands.

The most distinctive form of tree-farming to emerge was enclosing woods managed as 'coppice-with-standards' for two specific purposes, wood fuel, and timber for shipbuilding and construction. Coppicing was a highly sustainable method of producing truly remarkable growth which may reach 1.5m. in the first year after cutting and continuing this enormous regeneration for centuries without the need to replant. Most hardwood trees coppice freely when regularly cut down near ground level, by reproducing fast-growing shoots from the stump (stool) which could be readily used in a multitude of ways. The earliest reference to coppice in south-east England is that to *Silva Minuta* in the Kent Domesday Book and this management is recorded on the Archbishop's manor of South Malling in 1273 and appears to have been a major element in woodland management from the 13th century. The principle of the cyclical cutting of underwood on a rotation of 14 to 20 years, depending on species, condition of the soil, and thickness of timber required, was, however, apparently fully understood in England thousands of years earlier. The practice of growing standards (mainly oak and beech trees) above the lower storey of coppice in the same wood, so producing the

36 Present-day mature sweet chestnut coppice, used for building purposes.

highest possible sustained yield of timber, was another thread of woodmanship. This entailed careful management, because standing trees grown too closely thinned out the underwood and, conversely, underwood had to be thinned out to provide light for young trees. By the 15th century, and probably before, it was found that both coppice wood and standards grew best by deliberate thinning of oaks to about twelve to an acre which were not allowed to grow very large before felling, so that they might neither hinder each other's growth, nor cast too much shade for too long on the underwood. In high forest oaks grew tall and straight with little crown and were used for construction purposes. Shipbuilding, which required crooked boughs, known in the trade as 'knees' and 'elbows', was best served by widely placed trees which grew large crowns in hedgerows or parkland and not as standards in coppice which tended to grow taller and straighter. Oaks were cut at about 120 years old on average, although in the Napoleonic Wars this was reduced to about eighty. The demands for coppice by the iron and glass industries followed by the expanding hop industry seem to have greatly reduced standard growth for shipbuilding (p.160). Coppice-with-standards woodlands are (probably) mostly direct descendants of the primeval wildwood, modified by centuries of management. In the early Middle Ages coppice was probably mainly oak mixed with other native woody species such as ash, field maple, thorn, alder and willow in wetter patches, and birch and hazel where dry. In Kent hornbeam would also have been present.[1]

Everyday life depended on coppice-with-standards because its products satisfied a vast array of peoples' needs and because they were valued, and trees and underwood were cared for and sustained employment, whereas many were mismanaged and neglected for much of the 20th century. Underwood was used in many ways. It was the major fuel for iron and glass makers and mast and foliage provided fodder for pigs and cattle. Hazel, which can grow five feet in a year, was highly appreciated by foresters; whippy young stems provided material for hurdle-making and the binders or hethering were used in hedge laying; older growths made smooth, straight stakes, thatching spars, and wattles which were covered with clay (daub) to make panels for buildings; ash supplied pegs, gates and handles for tools and weapons; oak was used for laths and fencing materials; willow supplied baskets and cricket bats; elder, skewers; hornbeam, troughs and screws; maple was favoured by the cabinet maker. Large timbers were used for building wooden frame houses. The growth of a market for underwood promoted the practice of single-species coppice. It is not clear when sweet chestnut, which grows faster than hazel, was introduced. Everitt considers it possible that it has formed a major part of the Wealden landscape for more than a thousand years. The main market for sweet chestnut was hop poles. There is evidence of the extension of chestnut coppice on to poorer agricultural land in the 17th and 18th centuries and Kent came to have a larger acreage of chestnut coppice than the rest of England put together, a remarkable influence on the Wealden landscape by London brewers. Varying ages of coppice growth affect the type of end product. Seven-year-old hazel is ideal for hurdles while 15-year-old growth is more suitable for hedge stakes.[2] Most coppices in addition to being managed as a wood were deliberately grazed by domestic livestock (p.72).

37 The Sidney oak at Penshurst, one of the oldest living Wealden oaks.

The woodward would allocate parcels (cants in Kent) of coppice to be cut, marking any standards to be left uncut. The felling of timber was normally winter work but for oak it was timed for 'bud burst' in early spring, when the tan bark is at its softest and can be axed or peeled away very easily. After the winter or spring felling came the conversion of misshapen branches and small wood into fire-wood billets. Men and women bound these into faggots for domestic fires or bavins tied with binds (wifts in Kent) of sallow, and used for quick heat in bread-baking ovens. Finally, fences were repaired round the newly cut area to prevent deer or cattle from eating off the young undergrowth. Oxen were used at this period for carting. Woodcutters would spend the summer making up the harvest into saleable items. Coppice workers tended to lead quite isolated lives, often tucked away deep in the woods with few people knowing of their existence. Throughout the year deadwood was sought for fuel. Nothing in the woodland was wasted. Unlike today, the woodlands resounded with activity. Charcoal burning has a history from the pre-Roman period; wood was dried for a month or two before burning between March and October. It was carefully stacked into a dome and covered with litter, wet sand and turf. Wood colliers found sites in clearings. They spent several months a year living in their conical huts of poles, brushwood and turves because the woodstacks could not be left unattended during a burn for several days' duration.

Ancient coppice and other woodland usually has an earth bank around it, always with the ditch on the field side. On the bank was planted a thorny hedge to keep out cattle. In the case of coppice woodlands the object of the banks and fences was to keep deer and cattle *out* until the new shoots were growing strongly from the stools. In the case of medieval deer parks and some common wood-pastures the object was to keep animals *in*. In some instances there are internal banks within common wood-pastures, indicating that parts were periodically fenced, to allow for the regrowth of trees after cutting. A wood without earthworks around it is thus unlikely to be an ancient wood.

The remarkable continuity of woodland management and preservation can be illustrated with reference to the Whiligh estate in Ticehurst and Wadhurst. In the 1390s substantial quantities of pedunculate oak were supplied for the vast hammerbeam roof of Westminster Hall which for ingenuity of construction and delicacy of detail has been described as quite without a rival anywhere in the world. Further large consignments of oak were sent for the restoration of the roof between 1915-23 and additional supplies in 1941 to make good German bomb damage. These two last consignments of oak were from the Happy Valley on the estate. The great storm of 1987 blew down several of the largest remaining oaks and others showed signs of incipient decay. It was decided, therefore, to preserve the stand with its unique historical associations by fencing in the wood and sowing no acorns or plants grown from seed other than the Happy Valley trees themselves. Direct sowing of acorns, two to a quill, proved to be a cheap and effective way of planting under the Woodland Grant Scheme. The uneven age-structure of the wood was thus ensured and high quality timber should continue to be produced and amenity preserved for the future.[3]

9

The Medieval Woodland

WOODLAND is the natural habitat of the pig and their grazing of woodland (swine pannage) was its oldest use. Its importance in the Weald is indicated by the measurement of the surface area of woodland in Domesday Book by the number of pigs it could sustain during the seven weeks until Martinmas (11 November) when most were killed and salted. All inhabitants in a settlement, craftsmen as well as cultivators, engaged in pannage which clearly then filled the lord's coffers more than any other form of forest exploitation. A pig fed on a peck of acorns a day increased in weight one pound a day over the two-month fattening period to produce valuable protein, an essential source of energy during winter. Mast (pig fodder) also included beech and hazel nuts, chestnuts, rose-hips, the wild cherry, pear, apple and sloe. Additionally pigs were also grazed in woodland outside the pannage period. Payment was customary for both pannage and grazing. Manorial lords convened annually an Aves Court to receive tenants' payments and regulate the practice, the tenants testifying on oath as to the number of pigs they had sent in.[1] The rooting pigs (by which they turned over the soil looking for worms, insects, slugs, and other animal food to supplement their diet) would have injured the growth of young trees and bushes (p.83).

Manors on the Weald periphery had detached swine pastures to which they sent pigs. In Kent there were about 700 swine pastures, mainly in the Weald, which belonged to distant manors, including Thanet, forty miles away. Such long distances would have been outside the herding range of swine and it is possible that they were out-stationed at places on the way. There is, however, an important difference between Kent, on the one hand, and Sussex and Surrey, on the other, regarding the scale of pannage recorded in the Domesday folios. Witney computes the pannage dues owed at Domesday to lords in Kent at 7,350 swine which, at the rate of one pig in ten surrendered to the lord, implies a herd of some 70,000 in a good mast year, when the system of pannage was probably already past its peak on

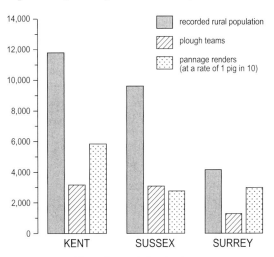

38 Domesday statistics of swine pannage.

39 Medieval swine herder knocking acorns from oak trees to fatten pigs at a Wealden 'den' in autumn. (Corpus Christi Coll., Ms 285)

40 Slaughter of fattened swine at coastal manors on arrival from a Wealden 'den'. The pork was salted for winter food. (Corpus Christi Coll., Ms 285)

41 Deer Park pale, Eridge Old Park. Such prominent banks and ditches were erected round all deer parks.

account of accelerating colonisation. The majority of these pigs would have been fattened in the Kent Weald. This compares with the renders for Sussex and for Surrey, despite the combined area being twice that of the Kent Weald. Population difference does not appear to be behind these figures: it is more likely to be due to a wealthier population in Kent, able to keep more pigs.

Pannage entailed particular tree management. Young oaks were often cut at a low height so that they produced at an early age acorns which could readily be beaten down for the pigs by the swineherd. Oaks planted for mast were generally surrounded by thorns to keep off cattle and deer; 'The thorn is the mother of the oak', is an old saying. By the late 13th century the encroachment on woodland had greatly reduced swine pannage which was declining as a source of revenue to lords and the basis of rural life. Earlier, the large swine-renders recorded in Domesday Book for the manors of Otford and Wrotham in Kent and South Malling in Sussex imply tenants' herds of 1,500-2,000 swine. The High Weald of Sussex continued to be an immense larder in which swine were left to shift for themselves. The Crown regarded Ashdown Forest and Tonbridge South Frith as great storehouses of pig-meat for the king's military campaigns, when droveways were thronged with animals being driven to the port of New Shoreham, the main provisioning centre for archers. Oak forest was the most favoured ground, for acorns were more dependable than beech mast, which ripens only in warm summers, on average about one year in three. In years when the mast failed, tenants were obliged to pay a due to the lord known as *danger*. Payments for herbage to the lord outside the pannage period were also made in 1086.[2]

Medieval Forests, Chases, Deer Parks and Warrens

Few parts of medieval England reveal a greater reverence for hunting than that bestowed by lords and knights on the Wealden woodland. Moreover, to the lord, agricultural holdings were for hunting over. Appropriately, the oldest English book on hunting, *The Master of Game*, was translated from Gaston de Foix's *La Chasse*, by the 2nd Duke of York at Pevensey Castle, *c*.1403-4. By then hunting had become a highly organised ritual. Whilst hunters were eating a hearty breakfast and arraying themselves in their richest apparel, grooms were preparing their mounts and the kennel man (*valets de limiers*) was silently tracking down deer with his *limiers* on a leash. On his return the chase began to the accompaniment of a succession of different airs on horns recording each episode during the hunt, such as 'hounds cast', 'several deer sighted', 'hounds running well', 'hunted stag', 'he has crossed the stream', right up to the climax of the kill when horns sounded *les honneurs*, and the three long notes for the withdrawal.[3] A huge acreage in the Weald was devoted to deer parks and forests (excluding Chases [see below]) in the Middle Ages, probably more than one-fifth. But for the tight limits set by kings and aristocrats on forest clearance for farming so as to save woodland for pleasure hunting, the face of the present-day Weald would have a much less sylvan aspect.

Hunting grounds comprised forests and chases. A medieval forest was a Crown possession and was so called by Normans long before the word forest had its modern meaning of a place of trees. The term is derived from the Latin *foris*, meaning 'out of the jurisdiction of the common law'. Thus the term was applied to an area of rough land set apart for the preservation of game at a king's pleasure which was regulated by special laws, and subject to the jurisdiction of special courts, drawn up, stated Stubbs, the constitutional historian, 'rather to insure the peace of the beasts of the chase rather than of the king's subjects'. Forests were enclosed by a pale, a prominent earth bank. A ditch was dug to perhaps a metre, with its spoil banked on the *outer* side to present the greater height from within the park, to lessen the chance of deer escaping on to farmland. Deadwood was piled on the top of the bank to complete the pale. This enclosing bank was the opposite in construction to other traditional boundaries which marked property in general and coppiced wood in particular. Peasants had certain commonable rights over forests, which they had to exercise so as not to hurt the vert (cover) or venison. Forests were not all woodland but divided into woods and plains. Enclosed woods had a wood-bank around them, plains were grasslands, grazed by deer and set with ancient oaks, maples, hornbeams, and ashes. Scrub was a third element: thickets of hawthorn and young trees. Six great forests existed on the highest ground in the Weald and comprised in the 13th century some 50,000 acres, about one-tenth of the whole area of the Weald: St Leonard's, Worth, Ashdown, Waterdown, Dallington in Sussex and the Frith across the border in Kent.

A chase was similarly devoted to the hunting of beasts normally reserved for the king and held by some magnate at the express grant of the Crown or some other authority which did not confer on the holder the right to hold forest courts or enclose it with a pale. So great was his passion for the hunt and respect for its status symbol that 13th-century Richard Waleys, a knight of Glynde, successfully defended his rights of chase of hare, fox, wildcat, badger, otter, squirrel and rabbit, pheasant and partridge in South Malling against the archbishop.[4] Such chases would probably have covered most of the Weald outside deer parks and forests, and the hunt was allowed to pass at will over farmland sown with so much pains.[5] For example, the bishops of Chichester had deer parks and a chase over all their lands in Henfield, Cowfold, Warninglid and Albourne, including holdings of their tenants who must have cursed them heartily. Further east, also on the Weald Clay, were the chases of the Shortfrith, Freckbergh and Cleres for nobility and gentry around Lewes which similarly embraced woods, common pastures and agricultural holdings. On such hunting grounds ranging deer destroyed crops, and numerous regulations were enforced against tenants in case pheasants and partridges should suffer.[6]

Deer parks of some kind had existed before the Norman Conquest but essentially they owe their origin to Norman deer husbandry to provide the luxury of venison at table. Their number increased rapidly with the 12th-century introduction of fallow deer from the Near East, which were easier to keep within a park pale than the wilder native red and roe deer. After the legal disafforestation of King John, possession of parks became a status symbol and their ownership moved downwards from the great magnates, both lay and ecclesiastical. Indeed, not to possess a park was a visible sign that one was not a gentleman, and thus even poorer knightly families each laid out a small park. A pre-requisite for enclosing deer in a park was a licence from the Crown. The granting of these rose to a peak in the late 13th century but continued as a trickle into the late Middle Ages and even into the first half of the 16th century, by when the general trend was disparking for agricultural use.[7] Over one hundred deer parks existed in the Weald, the great magnates each owning several apiece.

The optimum shape of a deer park was circular or oval giving the maximum internal area for a minimum length of fence. Most medieval parks had such an outline and consequently a space devoid of old farm buildings and other settlement can often be regarded as *prima facie* evidence for the possible site of a medieval deer park. The average-size park was about 100-150 acres. There is a strong indication that deer parks were originally surrounded by a fringe of trees called a 'haga' which was afterwards replaced by a fence. This was maintained by the owner's customary tenants, each township given a specific stretch to repair. Additionally, the archbishops of Canterbury required tenants 'in the Wood' to assist with the hunting for six to 12 days annually. They so valued sparrow hawks' nests (valued at 40s. each, about twenty times a labourer's weekly wage) that tenants were expected to guard them from theft and damage at a halfpenny per season.[8]

As deer are primarily woodland animals, parks were well wooded; but as deer are also grass feeders, parks also comprised 'wood pastures' in Oliver Rackham's phrase, consisting of trees and pasture intermixed. Domestic animals were consistently agisted in parks during summer, though never in the 'fence' period, i.e. usually one month at midsummer following the fawning season. Sheep and goats were commonly excluded from parks (and from forests) because their grazing habits interfered with the keeping of deer. The ancient common right of pannage generally continued in parks. Fishponds were commonly constructed in parks and building timber, bracken (for litter) and wood fuel were important secondary products of deer parks. Timber production has had a major effect on tree shapes for they were commonly standing trees pollarded successively for ships' timber, and bore great spreading crowns for this purpose and for pannage. Imparked land was not necessarily protected from the plough. During intense population pressure on land in the half century before the Black Death, some parkland was brought under cultivation, notably by the monks of Westminster at Westerham.

Nevertheless, many medieval parks, or substantial parts of them, were enclosed from the wildwood and have survived as relatively unmodified plant habitats for several centuries, during which time human interference has successively reshaped the landscape outside. For this reason a number of former deer parks retain plant species which are prime examples of relict woodland and their associated lichen flora is the richest in the region.

The best remaining medieval deer park relic is at Eridge Old Park, recorded in Domesday Book and which was a deer park for some 800 years, until economic pressure sadly forced the estate to remove the deer in 1956. Half has been converted to farmland, but the northern half has survived undisturbed. It is by far the richest remaining site for lichen epiphytes of ancient forest in England east of the New Forest. Other important ancient deer parks or their remains still existing in the Sussex Weald include Ashburnham, Heathfield, Buckhurst, Danny and Parham, similarly containing plants indicating a continuity of woodland cover over the past 5,000 years.

Ashdown Forest, which was granted in 1372 as a free chase by Edward III to his son John of Gaunt, had been impaled with a prominent bank and ditches before 1273 enclosing some 15,000 acres of land. The line of the pale normally

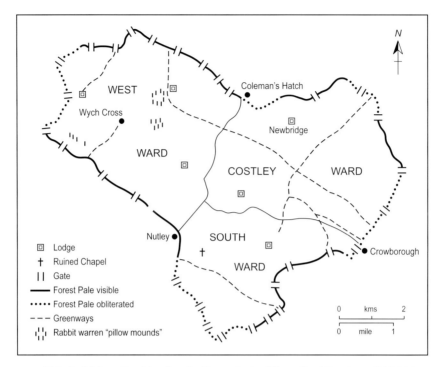

42 *Map of Ashdown Forest based on the Decree of 1693. The medieval Forest was divided into Wards. The Forest pale, often overtopped with holly and beech, is now traceable intermittently round the former enclosed area.*

runs along a distinct break of slope; beyond this boundary were commons over which Forest Law also extended, these being the more featureless parts of the forest which could not be protected. To meet the costs of impaling, it was customary to sell dead wood and birch as firewood. At numerous intervals the pale was broken by deer-proof gates known as hatches. For administrative purposes the forest was early divided into three wards, originally called Waldhatch (or Westhatch), Heselwode and Lampole. Each ward held its own woodmote and Aves Court (dealing with pannage) and receipts from each ward were separately distinguished in accounts. Meetings of the forest officers traditionally took place at the point where the three wards met. Nearby, on some of the highest ground, was the King's Standing, now a square embanked enclosure planted with firs but containing a mound directly past which deer were driven. The core of the forest, containing the hunting lodges, was specifically reserved for the harbouring of deer. This was described in accounts as *In Defenso*. Agistment cattle were taken into this part and the owner had the right to the mast therein up to Martinmas (11 November) after which what remained could be used for pannage by commoners.

Rights of common at the end of the 13th century were enjoyed by some 300 'customaries' except between Michaelmas and Martinmas (the time of pannage) for as many beasts as they could winter on their lands. Of these 208 were 'old customaries', others numbering 58 (presumably assarters on the forest fringe), paid for their common by the year at the rate of one halfpenny for each beast. A third group of 20 were *extranei* who paid at double the rate of new customaries and are explained in later documents as occupiers of tenements of some manor other than the principal royal manors of Duddleswell and Maresfield, but living within the 'liberty' of these two. Many commoners' names are listed in the forest accounts and are also to be found in the 1296 Subsidy in parishes into which the forest extended.

The earliest extant custumal is that of 1273. Sheep and goats were not commonable, presumably because they deprived the deer of herbage, but pigs could be grazed all the year round except during the fence month when pigs above six months old were excluded. Commoners were entitled to windfall wood as fuel and to cut fern, heath and broom, the purpose probably being litter for layering barns and subsequently applied as dung to fields. The pasture could be improved by burning, provided no damage was done to trees. In 1520 the right to 'mend lands with fern' was specifically enumerated as was the right to dig marl for mending lands, heath to thatch their houses, loam to daub their walls and stone to underpin their houses (see pp.228-31).[9]

Considering the poor pasture, the forest was quite heavily stocked. Apart from large numbers of deer – which sometimes exceeded 1,000 – the commoners at the end of the 13th century, judging from the rents, were putting in between 1,500-2,000 cattle a year and additionally certain ecclesiastical estates had pasture rights, e.g. at the ancient enclosure of the Vetchery (Vachery). A century later many vacant holdings resulted in a reduced demand for commonage and in the latter half of the 15th century, judging by the receipts, the average yearly number of cattle grazing the forest was reduced to only half that in the 13th century, a clear indication of the depressed state of the Weald at that time. Pannage receipts from the Forest in the late 13th century were substantial. Some 100 tenants put in 400 pigs between them in 1292 and 'strangers' (*extranei*) at this time put in between 2,000-3,000 pigs. The names of two of the three men paying for 'strangers' pannage are to be found in the 1296 Subsidy Roll among those taxed at the port of New Shoreham, which suggests that they were grazier-butchers, and purveyors of salted pork to Channel traders and Edward I's war fleet. The commoners' swine were fattened on beech mast, the strangers' on acorns. Eventually acorn pannage died out altogether. This is confirmed by a survey of the forest of about 1500 when the forest is described as a barren heathland with beech trees in some of the coverts and with very little underwood. A further sign of the extending heath cover was the growing practice to let out parts of the forest as rabbit warrens.[10]

Normans introduced the rabbit (known as a coney) and a warren was an enclosure within a close pale fence composed of a series of long mounds up to 150 yards long, six feet high and 20 feet broad. The rabbits burrowed into the soft, dry soil and were taken with the aid of a ferret, by spreading a net along the side of the mound (Fig.43). These 'pillow-mounds' proliferated from the 13th

43 Medieval women rabbit-warrening. Note that the rabbits are burrowing into an artificially constructed 'pillow mound'.

century in parks and forests. For example, a warren was established at Nutley in Ashdown Forest early in the 15th century, and at Petworth Park 'mending the conyghere' and the repair of the gates leading into the warren necessitated 14th-century payments, young trees being coated with tar to prevent them being nibbled by rabbits.

VI *The sandstone outcrop of Bowles Rocks near Eridge offers good climbing for beginners.*

VII *'Oceanic' lichen and ferns on a sandstone rock outcrop in the ghyll wood at Hendall near Maresfield.*

VIII *Reproduction from an illuminated manuscript of Count Gaston II of Foix (see p.75). The huntsmen wear heavy leather leggings to protect them from thorns and brambles. Around their necks hang the horns for calling the hounds and at their belts are daggers used for skinning animals and long swords for killing stags and wild boar.*

IX *Medieval herders driving swine to and from fattening grounds in autumn.*

X *Rowland Hilder's Kent Weald, when hop-farming contributed much to the beauty and prodigality of the Garden of Kent.*

XI *The Causeway, Horsham: a street of great distinction untouched by the modern development of the town.*

XII *East Grinstead has one of the best groups of old buildings in the Weald.*

10

How was the Land Won?

It is quite important even to guess at who first broke up [land to make] a farm, and subdued it, and cultivated it.

William Cobbett, *Legacy to Labourers* (1834), 51.

How was the wildwood destroyed? How was its destruction organised? How many man-hours did it take to clear an acre? What did people live on while they were doing it? These are questions, which although relating to one of the greatest achievements of our ancestors, have rarely been asked. Oliver Rackham, who did, was unable to supply the answers because the conversion of woodland into farmland in England usually belongs to an age far beyond record or memory. The Weald is a special case. Because its woodland clearance was largely deferred until the age of written records, there is rather more information, though there are still tantalising gaps. It is quite impossible even to guess who first cleared, subdued

44 *Okehurst, Billingshurst. A fine example of the Wealden vernacular of the 15th and 16th centuries on one of the numerous low ridges of warmer soil in the Low Weald. (John Malton, July 2002, pen and ink, 24.5 x 15.5cm [9½ x 6½ in])*

and cultivated a particular patch of forest but in general terms we can learn from this something of how the Saxon and early medieval peasant shaped the wild to his needs and in some degree was himself shaped by it.[1]

In the Weald the story of the farm begins with land clearance. Its piecemeal character up to as recently as the 19th century must have been a familiar scene. In Saxon and medieval times it was primarily a response to population pressure, in almost all cases probably an individual undertaking. It was also seen as a long-term activity, the laborious task being dependent on a farmer's own physical ardour and such circumstances as the weather and nature of the land. This steady expansion of cultivated land was the hallmark of the energetic farmer and for more than a generation it would have given a pioneer character to his holding. The ease, speed and profitability of land clearance would have depended upon three factors: the nature of the vegetation, whether tree, scrub or bush cover; the nature of the soil, for example, the vegetative covering would normally have been denser on a heavy clay soil and stumps would have been more difficult to remove; and slope would have been important because this would have affected drainage, ploughability and the amount of sunshine. Destruction of extensive areas of the forest by fire would have been impracticable on account of the climate but controlled burning of felled and cut-over patches, known as burn-beating, would have provided valuable ash for manuring successive crops.

The work of woodland clearance would thus have been directly related to the density of small trees and bushes and the number of large trees which had to be felled and stumps removed. Present-day derelict woodland on heavy clay soil is varied in aspect, depending on past management and the length of dereliction. It may be a dense tangle of about 500 trees and bushes to the acre between 12-19 inches in diameter and ranging up to 30ft. in height. Today the reclamation would be done with specialised machinery including bulldozers, an undercutter, lifting-comb and a heavy cultivator. With the primitive tools available to the pioneer farmer, the clearance of large tree stumps and bushes, together with the removal of roots and the burning of debris, would have been herculean even in favourable weather.[2]

Present-day derelict woodland, however, probably gives a misleading impression of the uninhabited Weald of A.D. 800-1200. The dense oakwoods had already been subdued before large-scale colonisation began. As previously noted, the mixed oak forest was early developed by Saxons and Jutes as an immense larder providing rich sustenance for herds of rootling swine which furnished excellent bacon. The pig's snout appears to have been the main agency in the clearing of the once all-covering forest in advance of its conversion into agricultural land by pioneer farmers. Pannage, continued for centuries, would have been very destructive of oak and beech wood for most of the mast which survived was eaten or crushed under-foot by pigs and any that struck root would have been devoured by deer or wild ponies. Very slowly, but surely, all replenishment of the growing stock of trees would have ceased and all younger trees and much of the underwood would have been eaten down. As Edlin has remarked, 'Pannage stands as a classic example of how to eliminate a forest.

45 *Upperton, near Petworth, attractive stone-built cottages in a compact village contrast with the Weald proper.
(John Malton, August 2002, pencil sketch, 18 × 14.5cm [7 × 5¾ in.])*

Simply cut off the seed supply and wait'.[3] The felling of timber for fuel and
building would also have been a cause in the slow but persistent deforestation.
Much remaining woodland on a particular holding would not have been cleared
manually but by throwing it open to grazing, browsing and rooting by the
pioneer's domestic animals. '… What pig snout had begun to clear, peasant was
avid to plough' as Eleanor Searle put it.[4]

   Much of the arduous task of clearing the forest had thus been done for the
pioneer farmer by grazing animals. Nevertheless, we must not underestimate the
work of painstaking clearance that remained. Documentary evidence fails us as
to the details of the pioneer farmer's winning his fields, but the following
sequence, suggested by 17th-century colonisation in North America, may have
prevailed. When the would-be pioneer tramped from his parent village bearing
a heavy sack containing his food, a cooking-pot and a few basic implements, he
did not think of any part of the Weald as a no-man's-land or any-man's-land, but
as 'waste' within some lordship. The lord's officers would have selected the
locality to be settled and supervised it, so he would not have settled willy-nilly.
Yet the choice of the actual site for his homestead and first fields was probably
his alone. He would have taken into account aspect, drainage, water supply and

soils, judging their capability by examining soil exposed along the banks of a stream or where a tree had blown down. Mould enriched with the rotted wood and leaf fall of centuries would be an object of his search. The potential of a site would probably not have been determined by the eye alone, but by the feel of the earth under foot. He would have avoided the stiffest clay, swampy ground, or where there was nothing but sand. Slopes with a south-facing aspect where oak and beech grew would have been his first choice. First comers went instinctively to hollows in the hills – the -dens, -leys and -folds – which held the deepest soils. In the Low Weald the 'rising lands' would have been preferred to any other site. Late-comers took 'pot-luck'.

Once a suitable dry place with good water had been found, the pioneer's most crucial decision was made. Now stretched before him years of unremitting toil. The strong young fellow and his wife would have built a hut for themselves and then begun clearing with axe and spade, yard by yard. Both would have had to go right in amongst tough, hard trees, *ridding* (grubbing) the smaller, ring-barking the larger, chopping others down and burning them up with the brushwood when dry. Then by ditching and throwing the spoil up into a bank within the belt of trees the pioneer had left round the edges, he planted a hedgerow, gathering the diverse species of shrub readily to hand. He would then have levelled between the tree stumps as best he could, reducing sods of earth with his spade or bare hands. Then one still calm day (perhaps religiously working bare-headed), he spread the ashes and sowed rye or wheat, stirring the seeds into the mould as best he could with a makeshift rake.

What help had he from his wife with the mingled hopes and hardships incident to the first years' pioneering? We can but speculate, but it is probable, bearing in mind what was expected of a farmer's wife in the early 16th century (p.111), that from the very outset the wife helped her husband in all the manual work she could in addition to looking after the cow and the few goats and sheep that they eventually might have had. There was still more land-breaking to do, perhaps no more than an acre or two each season, and the couple would have cleft timber for a simple timber-framed dwelling of two rooms. The frame was raised with the help of neighbours and the heavy roof beams secured before the autumn rains. Any animals then had the former hut as a barn. After garnering his frugal harvest the farmer became a woodsman again, felling trees to the stumps for another field and levelling a slip of land by the stream for a meadow (lagg) fit for next year's first cow. He had by now acquired a pick, a saw and fork but was still harrowing in seed without ploughing. Stumping (stocking), would have involved the different operations of felling, ring-barking, pulling, piling and burning. The pioneer would have lacked initially ox or horse-power to remove tree stumps. He probably grubbed by hand with a mattock, ringed the stumps, and removed them when dead several years later. In the interim what animals he had were pastured on cleared areas to check the growth of shoots. On rocky ground he would gather stones and pile them up on the edges of new fields. Later he would make a scythe and rake for hay-making. He would soon need to share a yoke of oxen and a plough with his neighbours. He had still to build a little

Old Manor House
Tillington

46 *Tillington, on the Greensand ridge, has quite different building styles from the Weald. (John Malton, August 2002, pencil drawing, 19 × 14cm [7½ × 5½ in.])*

barn with a threshing-floor, a hay-loft and granary. The pioneer would have experienced three or four of the hardest and roughest years he had ever encountered in his life. In imagination, for documents fail us, we can perhaps see him sitting on the door sill with his wife and new-born child, looking with pride and relief over their little fields. As the years passed the pioneer would perhaps have noted changes in wild life. Seagulls would have made an appearance from the coast searching for worms on the ploughland; woodmice and swallows would have got into the storeroom. Crows came and badgers made their sett on the edge of a field. As his children grew up they would have had little choice but to marry and set up farms within the limited community in which they were born.

In the Weald, Norman lordship to a very large extent preceded peasant settlement but at Domesday there are signs of rapid and recent colonisation. For the right to have holdings on the old swine pastures, peasants paid dues in money and kind to their lord. They were also required to perform services (lighter than those in older settled districts because of the impracticability of enforcing them from the long distances from parent manors) and make payments for pannage in autumn and another for pasturage *De Herbagio* for the right to pasture swine in the forest during the main part of the year. Economic inducements, apart from reduced services, were offered to such settlers. Rents were kept low, even nominal. Initially, most peasants seeking wilderness holdings were allocated a holding of a virgate in size, a flexible measure of land which in the Weald was four or more times the acreage of that outside it, this being reckoned the acreage or unimproved ground sufficient to maintain a backwoods family in the initial stages of land clearance. This was measured by a 'customary' acre, larger by up to 20 per cent than a 'standard' acre. Although this comparatively large holding of inferior soil in an inhospitable district needed back-breaking work to get it into a state of reasonable cultivation, its possession presumably gave a sense of pride and freedom to peasant households. Furthermore, lords in Pevensey and Hastings rapes, notably the Count of Eu and the Abbot of Battle, intent on speeding up colonisation in sparsely inhabited districts for reasons of defence and income, eased taxation for tenants. It was accepted by lords that a newly settled virgate was unable to bear the tax burden of a fully established holding of the same size. On the banlieu of Battle Abbey new tenants paid no taxation at all for a time, then half tax for a period, before liability for the full amount. That this was not a Norman innovation but had also been an inducement in the late Saxon period of colonisation is indicated by the repeated phrase in the Domesday folios that holdings in newly settled areas had never paid tax (geld) in the time of King Edward.

As previously noted, the historic pattern of agricultural settlement in the Weald was not the village, characteristic of downland farming communities. The Weald villages were not primarily agricultural and did not make an appearance until communities began to evolve from a 'frontier' phase in need of traders and craftsmen from the 13th century. Over extensive areas of the Weald farms exist in isolation. Such single habitations were invariably the creation of post-Domesday freeholders, men of some substance who may well have engaged a pioneering party to perform the arduous task of clearing, and to perform the earliest farming operations.

Another type of settlement consists of farms in small clusters. These small hamlets originated in a clearing and were apparently the creation of peasant farmers who shaped their lands according to the needs of colonisation by farmers of limited means which, in the main, apparently occurred before single farms were created by freemen. They could not have existed unaided. They probably came in families and alliances of families. They would have wisely helped themselves by helping one another – organising hunting parties to extirpate wolves and sharing expertise and an ox-drawn plough until their amount of arable increased. They may have mutually cleared new land and erected their dwellings. Certainly they would have needed the support of lord and neighbours during the tug and toil of the first few years. Consequently, two or more adjacent peasant holdings were usually created simultaneously in a clearing. Families invariably took their surname from their virgate. Such clusters of farms tended to be separated from other similar groupings by 'islands' of intervening waste used for common grazings. Over time such family units became more productive and original holdings were subdivided by inheritance, alienation or purchase and additional dwellings would be built on the fragmented properties. In the 13th and 14th centuries this basic agricultural layout might be somewhat obscured by the growth of a village at the hands of immigrant artisans and traders and perhaps by the erection of a chapel subordinate to the parish church or the construction of a new watermill for grinding corn or fulling cloth. By then there would have been small assart tenements on the edges of the commons ('waste-edge' settlement) and the original clusters of farmsteads would have grown into larger hamlets.

The subdivision of a former virgate by the end of the 13th century, and by implication the probability of some additional dwellings, can be illustrated by *Betesfeud* (185 acres) in Wadhurst, within the archbishop's manor of South Malling *c.*1273:

> Matthew le Freke, one twelfth share; Widow of Absolom and Frankelyen, one sixth share; John de Ecclesia, one eighth share; John Robyn, one eighth share; Richard de Betesfeud, one eigth share; John Betesfeud, one quarter share.

Some of these persons had evidently won their interest by inheritance or purchase.[5]

Other evidence for splitting the original virgate holdings is from Rotherfield manor. The Custumal of 1346 explains that each peasant farmer originally held a ferling (i.e. a virgate, or a quarter of a hide), a division of land varying from 100 to 150 acres. By 1346 these holdings had been sufficiently improved to support several families each in their own dwellings, so creating, for example, the hamlets at Hamsell and *Gilderrigge* (now represented only by Gillridge farm in Withyham). The latter was provided with a chapel in 1292 because the inhabitants successfully claimed that they were unable to reach their parish church in Buxted during winter. Collectively, such evidence of split virgates infers that the pattern of land-holding represents the working of partible inheritance in a newly-settled society and may be the mode of original settlement of much of England. As the centuries progressed, more cottages would arise with population growth, increase in specialised occupations and some urban growth.[6]

In parts of the British Isles, for example Dartmoor and the island of Sark which are examples of 'suspended' or 'arrested' development, the cluster remains the characteristic agricultural settlement to this day. Even in the Weald with its much greater changes, the pattern has not been entirely overlaid. An example is the district now known as Highbrook near West Hoathly which in medieval times was called Hammingden. This place-name probably means 'Hemele's swine pasture'. This part of the Weald was known as Plumpton Boscage, an outlier of Plumpton manor extending into Ardingly and Wivelsfield.[7] In one former clearing and lying adjacent to one another are still existing farmhouses which in origin were medieval halls – Battens, Hammingden, Willards and Highbrook. Close by is Sheriff Farm which was also probably a medieval tenement (Fig.48). It should be noted that from the 16th century smaller farms split off from the original virgates tended to devolve back into larger holdings and thus a former hamlet might become a single farm, as is the case of present-day Hamsell and Gillridge. It is this process which doubtless has given rise to the notion that the isolated farm was the original form of settlement. The traditional cluster type settlement, without the communal obligations demanded of common-field villagers in the Downs and with relative freedom from manorial control, laid the foundations for the notoriously independent society of the later Weald.

The reconstruction of medieval Hammingden is, however, over-simplified, for a number of smaller tenements would probably have co-existed with the ones identified and so it would be wrong to confine reconstruction only to medieval buildings which survive in the present landscape. Furthermore, it gives a misleading impression of the stability of farm extents and boundaries in past times. Although fields were hedged from the beginning of colonisation, farms were not necessarily consolidated into permanent blocks of land. Fields in early documents are often described as 'pieces of land' and an owner and occupier might hold them dispersed in quite limited areas with other tenements in between. This arose in part because a single occupier invariably held land by different tenures, e.g. freehold, bondland (copyhold), assart – old, middle and new – and shareland. As noted previously, this suggests land cleared from the waste at different periods. Secondly, the different tenures were subject to varying inheritance customs. On the Archbishop's manor, the eldest son or daughter was normally admitted to assart land on the death of the holder, whereas the youngest son or daughter inherited bondland. Thirdly, population density in the beadlewick appears to have been much greater in the later Middle Ages than today; holdings were more numerous and smaller. Accordingly, the process of assarting which added fresh land and could itself lead to a re-organisation of existing holdings and re-siting of farmhouses, together with the effects of inheritance laws and opportunistic selling and buying of individual fields could lead to splitting and subsequent integration of virgates and other tenures which means that the size and boundaries of farms could vary from generation to generation. Underlying the deceptively unchanging field pattern of the Wealden landscape, previously noted, is therefore a constantly shifting pattern of holdings.

The history of each Wealden farm will be unique to its place, but an historical approach makes it apparent that in broad terms most will have undergone the same recurrent trends. The evolution of Stockland Farm at Hadlow Down, before the Reformation within the 'Borg in the Wood' in the beadlewick of Mayfield on the Archbishop's manor of South Malling, may be used as a microcosm of the common experience of a typical Wealden tenement. At the Tithe Survey in 1843 it encompassed 136 acres; in 1949, 88½; in 1982, four acres and at the present time, 140 acres. These fluctuations in its boundaries were also a feature of past times. It is clear from 16th-century and earlier documentation that the farm is an amalgam of a number of smaller, medieval and 16th-century tenements which were subsequently opportunely combined to make a larger holding. Two of the field names record their occupation by persons listed in the Subsidy Rolls of 1296-1332. Rado Selter and Robert Selter being presumably identified with Salters (Tithe 1843) and Gillbert Coggere with Cockers (Tithe 1843). William Dyker's 16th-century holding comprised a house called *Stokke*, a barn, orchard and croft, together with 30 acres of land consisting mainly of old and new assart but including a small portion of a virgate or bondland. The information given in the document suggests

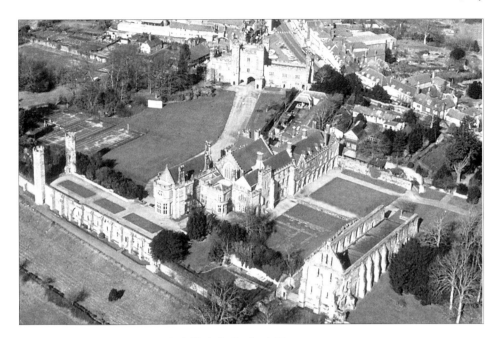

47 The site of Battle Abbey on the field of the Battle of Hastings.

48 The present-day character of a former farm cluster established in a medieval woodland clearing at Hammingden, West Hoathly.

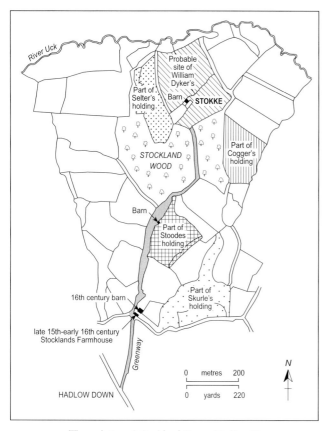

49 *The evolution of Stockland Farm, Hadlow Down.*

that the house and barn lay north of the present farmhouse on old assart known as Barnfield. Here a barn, since demolished, existed in 1843 and the site also suggests an abandoned farmhouse. The re-orientation of the farm to the present site of the farmhouse, which became known as Stockland, is on part of Hadlow Down assarted towards the end of the Middle Ages (Fig.49). Documentary evidence suggests, and structural examination confirms, that the present farmhouse was built at some time between 1498 and 1560. *Stokke* was accessible only by means of a 24-foot-wide greenway. The new farmhouse was sited along this same route but nearer Uckfield, the nearest market town.

Another ancient settlement pattern which developed subsequently to the cluster with assarting from the early 13th century was the 'waste-edge' straggly line of cottages and small-holdings along the edge of a common. A remarkable number of these still have faint traces of their origins as back-woods settlements. The best examples are the little holdings around Ashdown Forest. Stone-built farmhouses, cottages and barns cling to the sides of steeply wooded hills, such as Sweethaws in Buxted, Cackle Street in Maresfield, and Chelwood Common. In the 19th century smallholding and cottage-keeping was the way of life at such places until the Second World War and several, like Sweethaws, had their own little tiny chapel. There is still a faint touch of Exmoor about them. High Hurstwood is another example of a former colony of small farms of assart origin which still retains a little flavour of it.

A remarkable survival from the age of pioneer farming is Polebrook Farm sited on the banks of a small stream in the Low Weald near Sevenoaks. Its 31 acres are divided into 15 fields, a layout believed to have remained unchanged since the woodland clearance possibly nine hundred years or so ago. The hedgerows have many shrub species indicative of their great age, including pendunculate oak, ash, hawthorn, willow and field maple. Midland hawthorn, spindle and aspen are also present together with dog rose and brambles. The shaws tend to have been managed as hazel coppice under a canopy of standing oak. The five little ponds within the farm probably owe their origin to marl pits.[8]

II

The Great Clearing c.*1050-1348*

As much of the Weald only succumbed to the axe and plough during the period of written records, we can trace the evolution of its landscape and society in a unique degree of detail over the course of centuries. In its borderlands, and in most other parts of England, the medieval historian studies a landscape which had long existed and can only surmise earlier changes. The Weald had quite a different evolution. From surviving documents we can observe the countryside and society in constant movement and subjected to continuous alteration. This means that we can trace the actual becoming of places, and their growth and development under our eyes, so to speak – an unusual and exciting experience in landscape studies. Broadly speaking, as we have seen, the transformation of the swine-pastures tended to pass through a sequence of distinct but overlapping stages of human occupation between that of sheds used as swinecotes and temporary huts of swineherders, to permanent farms, water-mills, churches, hamlets, villages and market towns. Each of these stages marked a certain type of rural settlement and a distinctive type of rural economy and society. Each succeeding stage added new elements which were absorbed into the earlier ones.

The Normans' arrival greatly accelerated Wealden colonisation. At Domesday there are many signs of a rapid expansion of newly-settled land in full swing, owing to the Conqueror's deliberate plan to speed up the colonisation of the sparsely inhabited parts of Pevensey and Hastings rapes for defence. His unopposed landfall at Pevensey and march to the site of the Battle of Hastings convinced him that the lack of local settlers was a strategic weakness which needed remedying. When in 1076 he granted to his newly founded Abbey of Battle in *banlieu* or 'leuga', a circular estate, three miles in diameter centred upon the high altar, it appears to have been virtually uninhabited, 'a desert surrounded by swampy valleys and by forest out of which only a few homesteads had yet been carved'.[1] The Abbey was not solely founded to save the souls of penitential conquerors; it was also intended as an important bastion protecting the sparsely inhabited and thus weakly guarded route into England William himself had taken. Through the Abbey, settlers and resources quickly flowed in. At Domesday, 21 bordars (small peasants) are shown as living in the 'leuga' and under Abbot Ralph (1107-24) the demesne farm was extended and intensified. Moreover, by 1110 a town of 109 households had arisen on the present site of Battle. By 1124 the Abbey had quadrupled the rental value of its 'leuga'.[1]

A similar motive lies behind the major new colonisation immediately after the Conquest by the Conqueror's cousin, the Count of Eu, in his rape of Hastings.

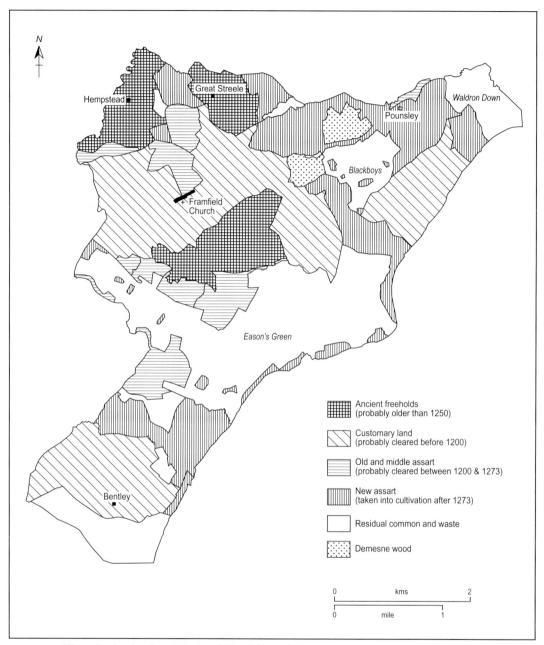

N

Hempstead

Great Streele

Pounsley

Waldron Down

Blackboys

Framfield
Church

Eason's Green

Bentley

Ancient freeholds
(probably older than 1250)

Customary land
(probably cleared before 1200)

Old and middle assart
(probably cleared between 1200 & 1273)

New assart
(taken into cultivation after 1273)

Residual common and waste

Demesne wood

| 0 | kms | 2 |

| 0 | mile | 1 |

50 The medieval and earlier colonisation of Framfield parish. See p.127 for an explanation of the reconstruction.

He revolutionised the old pattern of Saxon estates by splitting off outliers from parent manors in order to create new lordships held by military tenure on which to plant his loyal knights from his own home district of Normandy (who owed castle-guard at Hastings) so as to protect other weak places in the 'Channel

March' and make subsequent invasions less easy than the king's own. To prosper, the knights had to find tenants, which they quickly did. The main beneficiary of such undeveloped estates was the Count's steward, Reinbert, who was *Vicecomes* of the rape and progenitor of the locally important family, the lords of Etchingham. His enormous estate recorded in Domesday in the northern part of Hastings rape lay in sporadic clearings in which he had only 14 demesne ploughs and a handful of peasants paying such low rents that Reinbert was given generous exemption from taxation. By the mid-12th century the potential was beginning to be realised. His successors, as lords of Etchingham, had increased their rent roll with the same success as Battle Abbey. These little knightly estates were to be an unusual characteristic of the Weald and to have a marked social impact for centuries. Their dominance, so readily observable in the 17th century, is also clearly evident in 13th-century Close and Patent Rolls, and in the records of Battle Abbey (p.169). A further project was also successful as a new defence of the route to London. King William's second cousin, Richard Fitz Gilbert, was granted a huge estate, of which the key element was the Lowy at Tonbridge, on which a castle was created and colonists planted, on land apparently previously inconsiderably settled. It would seem that earlier woodland clearance had been impeded by the difficulty of ardent pioneer farmers to find the protection of a willing lord. The coming of Norman lordship to the Weald opened it up at last.[2]

The last stages in medieval clearing brought in the assarter. Lords were no longer willing to make land grants to peasants of farms. The need had grown to furnish communities with traders and smallholders supplementing their income with craft activities. The new wave of pioneers who entered the Sussex High Weald from *c.*1240 took up small parcels of assart land for a nominal money rent. They brought into existence the familiar 'waste-edge' pattern of straggly settlement, characteristic of the fringes of Ashdown Forest and many other places. These peasants began to supplement their hard-won living from the land by various kinds of handicrafts such as the making of cloth and leather, the hammering of iron, wood-turning and pottery manufacture. These migrants were the first of the farmer-artisans who were to be a feature of rural life for centuries. The pioneer initially survived by subsistence farming. This evidence of extensive assarting by small to middling peasants in the High Weald was probably due to their aim to progress beyond mere subsistence. Farming more intensively their little holdings would have been more costly than taking up additional intakes of fresh land from the commons and wastes as pasture for beasts which

51 A reconstruction of a medieval market place.

could have been sent to market on the hoof. This is borne out by the detailed survey of Rotherfield manor in 1340.

This 'folk-flow' was associated with one overlapping with it, and continuing slightly later, comprising tradesmen setting up in business in the growing neighbourhoods, when the supply of available frontier land for agricultural colonisation was running out. They added cottages to the formerly isolated churches, so creating characteristic wealden villages such as Cranleigh, Mayfield, Heathfield, Hawkhurst, Cranbrook and Goudhurst. At the same time settlers were arriving to create the first market towns serving the now bustling interior e.g. Horsham, East Grinstead, Uckfield and Tenterden.

A number of place-name elements were current in Middle English to signify 13th-century clearances:

Brech(e). Breach. Land broken up from waste for cultivation
Hurne. A corner of such land. These names occur in the Surrey dialect in some
   of the oldest Middle English verse, ' The Owl and the Nightingale':
         'Þe nightingle bigon to speche
         In one hurne of one breche'.
Holne. Innome. An intake of land from commonland for separate (private)
   cultivation.
Rede or rud from Ridde. Land taken in from waste and grubbed for agriculture.
Inhok. A hook, i.e. a hook-shaped piece of land resembling a sickle carved out
   of waste, presumably often with difficulty, hence expression 'by hook or by
   crook'.
Reue. A modern, new row or line of anything, a hedgerow or belt of trees.
Shau(w)(e), a thicket or strip or trees in lieu of a hedgerow.

These newly introduced field-name elements help us to chart colonisation across the waste. 'Rede' is commonly found in East Sussex, as is 'rud', the variant in West Sussex dialect. Later estate maps show that 'reedings' or 'riddings' often denoted a new intake scooped out of the shrinking waste, marking the enlargement of an existing farm. In Middle English 'riedlond' can also mean the creation of small-holdings, and Rede in East Sussex appears as a term used for assarts throughout the 13th century. Numerous wealden farms bear the name Rede, e.g. Great and Little Broad Reed, Stile Reed and Wood Reed farms near Mayfield. The verb 'to rid' was also in general use in the Weald for 16th- and 17th-century clearances.[2] Another field-name denoting clearance of waste at this time is 'innome'. Words with a similar meaning are Breche (breach) and Inhok (hook) and Hurne. These terms were apparently in use slightly earlier than the Rede names. Fields bearing such names are traceable on tithe maps and some are retained to this day.

Documentary evidence invariably records a striking colonisation of the waste between the Domesday survey (1086) and the Black Death in 1348, after which land clearances virtually ceased on account of the heavy mortality. It is useful to begin with the large manor of Rotherfield for which there is exceptionally good documentation. This was held by Earl Godwin before the Conquest and subsequently it became a royal manor before being acquired by the Clares of Tonbridge. The laconic entry relating to Rotherfield in Domesday Book records 'In lordship 4 ploughs. 14 villagers with 6 smallholders have 14 ploughs, 4 slaves ... and a park'. Clearly Rotherfield was not a large settlement but, nevertheless, was the most considerable manor separately recorded in Domesday Book for the Sussex Weald.

During the Middle Ages Rotherfield grew spectacularly. We can get from documents some idea of the size of the rural community in 1262 and again in 1346. A very substantial, but uncertain, expansion under villeinage had occurred between 1086 and 1262. More definite information exists for two other classes of tenancy, freeholds and assarts. Freehold land won from the waste from 1086-1262 amounted to 478 hectares. By then the number of tenants had risen from the 20 recorded in Domesday Book, to a total of 364 individuals and it can be deduced that in total about 15km sq. of land in Rotherfield manor was cleared and portioned into farms and smallholdings between 1086 and 1346. The vigour of clearances right up to the eve of the Black Death is striking. From 1319 Rotherfield had a weekly market and a number of its citizens were cap-makers (capello). The survival of a map of the manor dated 1664, redrawn from one of 1597, throws valuable light on the location of the various classes of land-holding which in turn is an indication of when it was taken into cultivation. Land settled before Domesday Book and held in villeinage appears to have been in the northern part of the manor on the comparatively good agricultural soils of the Medway Valley. Post-Domesday clearances lay south and east of the park, on up-and-down country rising to the highest altitude of cultivated land in Sussex on the flanks of Crowborough Beacon.[3]

We can also establish more or less precisely where some of the other medieval colonists were settling, in what numbers, and what they did for a living. In the Low Weald of Surrey, where Saxon settlement was considerable, sporadic surviving wastes were still lacking agricultural colonists in the early 13th century. Here peasants were taking up small parcels of customary land as woodland clearings (breaches or rudings): Henry de la Breche, Richard le Brechere, Walter atte Rud, etc. As early as the 1320s the little community of Ruckenham, in the wildwood of Albury manor near Ockley, had grown sufficiently to warrant two new water-mills. Numerous woodland clearers at Ruckenham were part-time farmer-artisans, including Godfrid le Verer (glass-maker); Thomas and Robert Faber, possibly, as their name suggests, smiths or iron-makers; Walter le Chaboner (charcoal burner), and Thomas le Denere, a holder of 'pot-lands', i.e. places of pottery manufacture.

At roughly the same period the monks of Sele priory were settling smallholders on their demesne at Crockhurst, near Horsham, another place-name signifying pottery manufacture. Similar evidence of a pottery-making community is the collection of tithes by the priory and convent of Selborne, Hampshire, from hand-dug plots on the edge of Alice Holt Forest, including 'ye dykers croft, ye potteris crofts, ye Carpenters crofts'. These various communities of wealden potters made both coarse pottery from Weald clay and superior quality pitchers from white clays in other strata and were probably serving both a relatively thriving and expanding local market in the Weald and also the old-established market towns on the Wealden periphery.

The clearance of the waste in the Sussex High Weald was a long process of attrition. Before *c.*1240 it was still a region of forest clearings. Lack of transport is probably the chief reason for its settlers remaining backwoodsmen rather than farmers, longer than any others in the South East. Beginning *c.*1240 a new wave of pioneers entered the region as assarters (Old French, *essarter*, to grub up trees), holding land by money rents. The most dramatic gains of this vigorous colonising effort were in the archbishop's manor of South Malling. In its beadlewicks of Mayfield (including Wadhurst) and Framfield, constituting about half the land 'in the wood', some ten square miles were newly colonised between *c.*1240 and the onset of plagues from the mid-14th century. Of this clearing, *c.*3,600 acres is attributable to the final phase of this movement after *c.*1273.

In some parts of the High Weald we can see places evolving in some detail. Thus at Heathfield, Sussex, on the outlier of Bishopstone manor near Seaford the earliest pioneers were probably no more than half-a-dozen families dispersed over half-cleared places within walking distances of their once solitary church. Shortly before 1257 this little colony was expanded to include 32 new assart tenements on 310 acres of freshly cleared ground. By 1300 the number of assart tenements had doubled and in 1379 the tally of assarters was 72, of whom 47 had built cottages. As little hedge- and shaw-bound fields spread their lines up the freshly cultivated hillsides, tradesmen moved in and set up businesses. By 1257 a miller, a smith (*faber*), a baker (*pistor*) had taken up residence and three other tradesmen had opened up stalls (*selda*). Meanwhile, the church was enlarged to accommodate the fast-growing congregation, a pest house was built and the Bishop of Chichester obtained for the new community the grant of a market and fair. Here then was the emergence of a fully-fledged community. Robertsbridge *c.*1280 was another example of a new town which had textile workers and fullers as well as smiths and other artisans.[4] This kind of evolution at roughly the same period was probably the experience of the other wealden ridge-top villages in the Kent and Sussex Wealds, such as Hawkhurst, Cranbrook, Goudhurst, Mayfield, Wadhurst and Rotherfield.[5]

Surnames indicating handicraft occupations are interesting. In the woodland portion of South Malling in 1273 surnames such as Weaver (Texter), Dyer, Glover, etc. are found. At Uckfield and Wadhurst, where fulling mills had been established, no fewer than eight tenants were designated Le Fuller. Each farming family probably spun its own wool and passed it on to cottage weavers in the locality who in turn brought it to local fullers and merchants.[6] Another leading manufacture was that of iron. Its widespread existence is indicated by the 12 tenants of Framfield, Mayfield and Wadhurst bearing the names 'Fabrica' (smith). Others were called Le Stel and Le Colyer, that latter doubtless making fuel used by local smiths in bloomeries and forges.[7] The custumal of Rotherfield manor dated 1340 also gives evidence of glovers and smiths, and Robertsbridge was a bustling little town with various artisans in the cloth and metal trades *c.*1280.[8] Unfortunately, this kind of evidence throws little light on the scale and organisation of industrial activity. Much local craftsmanship probably catered merely for the growing local market but the textile and iron industries seem to have had a greater significance. It should be noted that the cloth industry pre-dates the alleged introduction of Flemish weavers in 1332 by King Edward III.

12

The Retreat of Settlement

THE Great Famine of 1315-17, the Black Death in 1348-9 and a further succession of epidemics in the later 14th and 15th centuries resulted in a fall in population from a national total of some five or six million in 1300 to about three million in the early 16th century. The effects of this on the age-old Wealden colonisation was dramatic. The persistent deforestation over several preceding centuries virtually came to an abrupt end at the Black Death in 1348-9. After this pandemic the High Weald manors in Sussex which still had extensive colonisable reserves now lacked men to clear them. The tide was beginning to turn even before the plague, for there is evidence of a reduction in tilled land between 1291 and 1340, for example, at Hellingly, Ticehurst, Heathfield, Burwash, Itchingfield and numerous other places. This reduction is ascribed largely to natural disasters and to imparking rather than a decline in prosperity.[1]

The Black Death not only stopped colonisation but led to rural dereliction. Broadly speaking, the only persons taking up fresh land in the late 14th and 15th centuries took tiny plots, clearly the needs of those setting up a house, inn, shop or smithy on the highway waste. Such persons were probably not primarily engaged in agriculture, but possibly in iron-working. Our knowledge of the Wealden medieval iron industry is very fragmentary, and direct proof of its influence on colonisation is lacking, but it is significant that iron-working sites were becoming larger with the use of water-power to lift the hammers at forges (even before the introduction of the blast furnace in the 16th century).[2]

Not only did assarting dwindle to negligible proportions but numerous properties lacked tenants. The worst affected areas were on the borders: Dallington Chase, Ashdown Forest, and Waterdown Forest in Kent where small-holdings reverted back to waste. Some of the marginal land assarted in the last phase of Wealden colonisation was also left tenantless, e.g. the rocky land in Rotherfield manor near Crowborough. There was not, however, the widespread reversion to woodland and waste that overwhelmed groups of farms and buildings in central Europe at this time. Assart land, held for a money rent, was probably attractive to peasants in the Downs and Coast who were liable for carrying and other services to the lord. The 15th-century Weald also offered expanding opportunities for various handicrafts. The full picture, however, may not yet have emerged. In the course of extensive field walking, C.F. Tebbutt noted apparent house platforms in many parts of the central Weald and suspected that they might be the sites of deserted medieval farms. One such site, at Faulkner's farm near East Grinstead, was partially excavated to reveal a half-timbered building and sherds of medieval pottery, which points to the abandonment of the site about the mid-14th century. The present farmhouse probably dates from the second half of the 16th century. So far, this appears to be the only depopulated medieval farmstead located in the Weald.[3]

The more common effect of recession was probably less drastic. As already noted, wealden agriculture, based on the principle of convertible husbandry, was especially adaptable to fluctuations in economic climate. In economic depressions the plough simply went less frequently and regularly round the farm. The whole landscape would have told its own story; weedy, abandoned fields, ruined worn-out land and neglected woodlands. A sward of ever-deteriorating pasture would have been colonised by docks, thistle, bramble, broom and furze, followed, in cases of extreme neglect, by the encroachment of scrub and woodland where men had formerly harvested corn. We may presumably imagine fields far from supplies of manure degenerating into under-used and rough pasture, hedges growing wider and sometimes thickening into strips of wood (shaws), ditches silting up, causing bad drainage, walls and fences breaking down, and buildings needing repair.

Above all, one would have seen woodland on the march, as it always is in the Weald, if not kept under by the plough. A hedge neglected for 20-30 years begins to encroach far over the field it enclosed and, if abandoned for 100 years or so, would become part of scrub forest and indistinguishable from it. We should probably envisage the Weald during the 15th century as a new landscape of neglected pasture overrun with furze and wood, with arable shrunk to the lowest for centuries. This scenario is consistent with the early 17th-century observations (p.114) and we shall have ample evidence of the back-breaking effort with which the work of field reclamation had to begin over again in the better farming conditions of late Tudor and early Stuart times.

One should not, however, take a gloomy view of the period as one of unrelieved decline. A new social order began to emerge. Better-off tenants took advantage of the economic situation by accumulating a number of formerly separate holdings. Very notable in this process was the rise of minor gentry and larger freeholders.

It is appropriate at this point to survey changes in the distribution of regional wealth and population in previous centuries with that of the early 16th century. In so far as this can be measured from taxation evidence, three cross-sections in time are available: the Domesday Survey of 1086, the 1334 Lay Subsidy return (particularly valuable as it enables us to see the situation on the eve of the Black Death), and that of 1524-5. As we have noted, although the Domesday Survey gives a misleading notion of the Weald's economic development, men's actions had made a limited impact in comparison with the more highly-productive soils on the periphery. It was the achievement of generation after generation of medieval farmers and craft-workers to transform the relatively poor and backward community of the Weald into one of the wealthier districts of England by 1500. The progress can be fascinatingly illustrated by the Lay Subsidy rolls of 1334 (Fig.52). The association of backwardness of the Weald and development of the

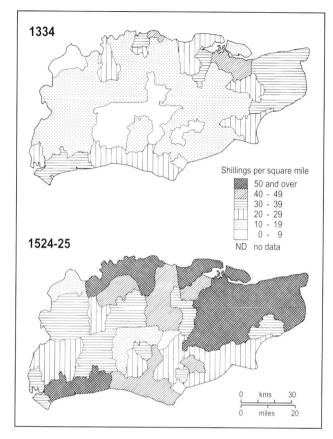

52 *Changes in regional land values 1334-1525 (after Glasscock 1965 and Sheail 1972)*

coastal belt still held good in several respects. The most striking feature of the 1334 map is the comparative poverty of the Weald and Romney Marsh relative to north-east Kent and coastal Sussex (which would have shown a still greater disparity had the Cinque Ports not been exempted from taxation). One must bear in mind that the Weald's tax returns probably under-record its economic activity for many taxpayers earning income from its resources were taxed at places of 'most resort' outside. This 'colonial' character of the medieval Weald must therefore be allowed for. The lowest values in the Weald were on the Weald Clay and on the poor ridge soils of the central Weald. The forests remained primitive areas supporting a subsistence way of life to a greater degree than anywhere else in the South East. The poorest parts of the Weald were being left more and more behind with the economic and social advancement of other districts.

The 1524-5 tax subsidy reveals the spread of prosperity into the Weald. The Kent Weald, in particular, is revealed with high tax assessments reflecting the growth of cloth, glass, tanning and iron-making industries. The highest taxed districts were those closely identified with the production, preparation and marketing of cloth and iron, notably the Cranbrook district, such towns as Godalming and Guildford, and the Petworth and Midhurst district. In each of these areas considerable numbers of aliens were present. As already noted, it was the development of handicrafts, such as the cloth trade in the 13th century, that led to the creation of villages and market towns, and also enlargement or rebuilding of parish churches. Yeoman farmers supplying wood and other products to these growing industrial districts shared in the increased prosperity. The headwaters of the Medway and its tributaries, the Teise and Beult, are lined with water-mill sites, relic features of the time when the district's villages were full of cloth workers and water-power was used for fulling cloth.[4]

The incidence of floods, largely marine in origin, was such a remarkable phenomenon in coastal Sussex during the later Middle Ages that this weather hazard deserves particular attention. Along the coast early forerunner floods such as the 'great flood' at Apuldram in 1275 were manifestations of a rapid submergence which led to the destruction of Old Winchelsea in 1287 and severe flooding all along the Channel coasts. Major flooding is again reported as recent in 1331-2 and the amount of land lost from this cause, and from erosion, between 1291 and 1340 is notable. It is uncertain, however, to what extent flooding between 1291 and 1340 resulted in permanent loss of land. The drainage of Hooe, for example, was restored in the 1380s and not again abandoned until the 1420s.[5]

The testimony of account rolls indicates that sea floods persisted throughout the period of recorded weather, 1340-1444, but a significant trend is detectable in their intensity. Between 1340 and 1367 numerous floods occurred at Barnhorne and Dengemarsh and other coastal sites but did not reach disaster proportions. From 1368 the incidence of severe floods markedly increased in Sussex and winter inundations became common events on low-lying ground. As a result of a series of recurrent encroachments, most notable in 1369, 1374-5, 1378-9 and 1386, and for some years after, the cropping of coastal marshland became hazardous. At Fodiland there was no pannage of pigs in a meadow at Bodiam because it was in the lord's hands and lay under salt water.

These late 14th-century floods were succeeded by more catastrophic events in the first quarter of the 15th century. The great floods of 1401 and 1402 were followed by the major flood of 1409 and devastating floods of the 1420s, precipitated by the outstanding disaster in the autumn of 1421 and followed by lesser occurrences in 1422, 1423 and 1429. At Barnhorne these floods were the 'coup de grace'. The initiative previously held in matters of sea defence by the Abbey of Battle, which had staved off the previous disasters by its superior resources, was finally and utterly lost. The steadily deteriorating drainage of the Pevensey Levels appears to have been unchecked until 1455 when a major attempt to improve the drainage of the Hooe Level was made, but reports of severe flooding in the 1460s and 1480s make it clear that no effective remedy had been discovered. These floodings of the Romney and Pevensey Marshes would have been disastrous for upland farmers in the Weald whose wealth was largely derived from the rich summer grazings there.[6]

13

Timber-framed Buildings

ALTHOUGH stone such as Reigate Stone, Kentish Ragstone from the Hythe Beds and sandstones from the Hastings Beds was available, it was normally used in the Middle Ages only for churches, public buildings and larger houses. In a forested area like the Weald timber was undoubtedly cheaper than stone, and was thus normally the first choice for manor and smaller houses.[1] Thus the ancient vernacular tradition of domestic building in the Weald is not of stone, as in the Cotswolds, or cob, traditional to Devon, but timber-framed houses with exposed timbers and an in-filling of lath and plaster.

The method used to construct timber-framed buildings in South-East England was the box-frame (Fig.53). The space between one pair of principal posts and the next was called a bay. The system was very flexible, for although a three-bay house was standard, an owner could have as few or as many bays as desired and another range of bays could be built across the end of a building to form a crosswing. The box-frame supported a number of roof types which evolved over the centuries. The simplest was the coupled rafter, or sans purlin roof, where pairs of rafters were connected by collars. To counteract the leaning

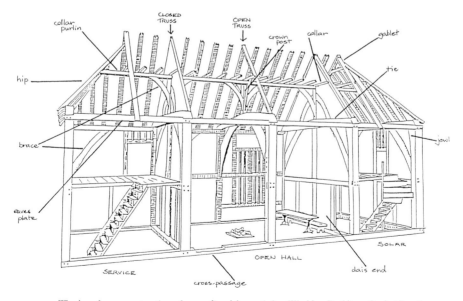

53 The box-frame construction of a medieval house (after Wealden Buildings Study Group).

of rafters, the crown post roof was introduced where a collar purlin runs the whole length of the building immediately under the collars and is supported at each bay division by a crown post (Fig.53). Further rigidity to the box-frame was provided by braces. Other ways of strengthening the roof were also introduced in the South East.[2]

The majority of the region's medieval houses have the roof ends hipped, which provided the most stable form of construction, and have a small open gabled section at the apex known as a gablet. Between the principal posts the walls were formed by upright studs and horizontal rails. The panels were commonly filled by wattle panels, usually of unbarked ash or hazel daubed on both sides with a mixture of wet clay and cow-dung, tempered with chopped straw or cow-hair. A coat of limewash gave added protection against the wet. Later, a thin coat of plaster, a mixture of lime, sand and cow-dung, was applied as protection. From the 17th century brick-nogging became a popular way of replacing defective wattle and daub panels. The wooden framework, however, was always an important visual element. Nails and bolts were not used in construction: wooden pegs held the various timbers together. Mortice and tenon joints were the most common form of carpentry.

The predominant timber used in framed houses was oak, with its matchless strength and resistance to rot. Oak was used unseasoned because it is much easier to cut when 'green'. Carpenters were careful to select the smallest possible tree for a particular purpose to avoid too much cutting. A study made by Dr Oliver Rackham of a 16th-century farmhouse in West Suffolk has shown that new fewer than 330 trees were used in its construction, mostly very small. Current studies suggest that in the South East larger trees were used, one tree being sawn into four or six joists.[3] Larger timbers were squared with an axe, then trimmed with an adze. Sections of the building were prefabricated on the ground and 'reared' or raised on the site, symbols known as carpenters' marks being incised on the beams to aid identification on erection. Principal posts often have a wedge-shaped depression high up on their outer face, for use when propping up the post during assembly.

The extremely simple sans purlin roof was likely to have been the most common type up to the mid-13th century, when crown post roofs began to be constructed, with possible origin in Normandy (though only for superior buildings initially).[4] In east Surrey, east Sussex and Kent most of the surviving hall houses have crown posts. Many of the oldest houses are aisled, because long timbers were not easily available and a span of 20ft. was the maximum that could normally be achieved. An aisled hall exists in Rudgwick, Sussex, which has round arcade posts surmounted by beautifully preserved carved stiff-leaved capitals which can be dated to about 1220-40.[5] As arcade posts were an obstruction in the open hall, a method of dispensing with them was to use base crucks for the central hall truss as at Chennells Brook Farm in Horsham. Such aisled houses were especially popular in the 13th and 14th centuries and were very practical as long as all the accommodation was on the ground floor, as the roof continued down so far as to restrict headroom on an upper floor.

54 Headcorn Manor, a 'double Wealden'.

Freeholding yeomanry, especially in Kent, were able to build a larger and more luxurious house in greater numbers and somewhat earlier than elsewhere in England. By the later 14th century the archetypal medieval open hall house had come into being. This had a two-bay hall, open from floor to rafters, a service end with two ground-floor rooms, a buttery for storing wooden and pewter vessels, pots and barrels of beer and ale, and the pantry where food was kept, and ground-floor rooms for the family on the other side of the hall. First-floor chambers were also normally constructed over the two ends of the farmhouse. The tie-beam in the centre of the hall often had elegant arch braces and the crown post above was decoratively moulded. Tenon and mortice joints were made firm by the use of pegs through the joint in a hole cunningly offset so that when the peg was hammered home it increasingly drew the shoulders tighter.[6] The fire burned on an open hearth in the centre of the hall. At one end was the high table raised on a low dais. An elegantly moulded beam, known as a dais beam, was added to high status houses. A cross-passage was sometimes separated from the hall by wooden screens known as speres. Above the 'high-end' was the solar, or main bedroom. The other chambers above the service end would have provided sleeping accommodation for members of the household, and farm servants, these reached by ladders from the hall. Windows were tiny oak-framed openings with shutters, and floors were of beaten earth. Smoke from the fire eventually found its way out 'via the eyes of everyone in the room', through openings at the ends of the ridge as well as through tiles or thatch and the triangular gablets at either end of the roof which were left open for this purpose. Over the years smoke from the hearth stained the roof timbers with soot. Hall houses were occupied by the rich and people with more modest means alike. The size and quality of the building and its internal mouldings help to distinguish the better-built dwellings. Houses of the less well-off often had only one floored end, which combined service rooms below and the owner's private room above.

Amongst the finest examples of timber-framed architecture in England are the 'Wealdens', so called because they are found principally in the Weald, though they have a wider distribution.[7] As the timber-hall of the house was enlarged with a wide and higher hall, the increased weight of the hall's roof or its loftier walls without buttresses posed a construction problem. The 14th- and 15th-century solution was found in a combination of the tie-beam and the use of flanking units as buttresses for the hall roof. This produced the apparent recessing of the hall front between the wings of the house. Actually, the front is not set back but the first storey of the wings is jettied outwards so as to carry a continuous plate-beam supporting the hall rafters for the hall-front which were relieved of thrust. The overall effect was a most elegant and distinctive facade which attracts the eye as pleasingly as when it was first built. An important element, notes Coutin, 'is the highly skilled carpentry and generous use of timber. The dais beam, crown posts and tie-beam of the open truss display mouldings and decoration which indicate not only the affluence and a desire to impress but also appreciation of fine crafts-manship'.[8] This lavish and lovely use of timber adds greatly to these houses' charm. Roberts has also stressed the wonderful flowering of English carpentry

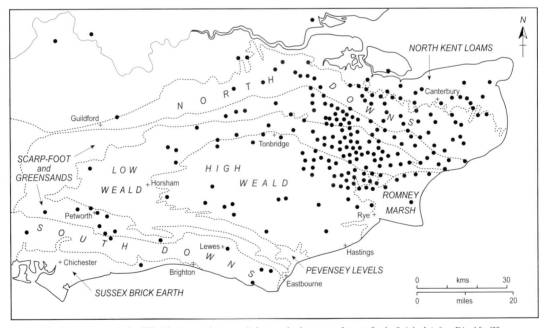

55 *Distribution map of the 'Wealden' type of yeoman's house, the largest and most finely finished (after Rigold). These were almost as plentiful in the Kent Weald as on its borders and, although they spread into Essex, Surrey and Sussex, they are comparatively sparse.*

and wood carving which depended on the medieval craftsman's long tradition of 'feel' for his material. The result is a house of simple and practical layout with an attractive and impressive outline. These houses have several variations in design and plan. The ultimate development is the 'double-wealden', jettied in the same style at both front and rear, as is Vane Court, Biddenden, Headcorn Rectory and Pattenden, all in Kent, the two last being jettied also at the sides.[9] The largest and most ornate 'Wealdens' made fine homes for the gentry, and for the yeoman less elaborate versions were striking evidence of status and prosperity. Houses of this kind would have had lesser buildings nearby, a kitchen and a brewhouse, perhaps, and a barn and sheds. However, there is now little trace of these contemporary structures, apart from the barns. Coutin and D. and B. Martin have demonstrated that, although it is the freestanding Wealdens in the countryside which attract most attention, over half are in towns and nearly a quarter in large villages, mostly near the Kent-Sussex border. They are of a standard not found elsewhere in England until much later.[10] The heaviest concentration of these houses between the 14th and 16th centuries was not in the historic Weald, but immediately south-east of Maidstone (Fig.55), a classic area of small but highly productive yeomen freeholds on lighter soils. Numerous examples are also found on the heavy soils of the Kent Weald and in Romney Marsh, notably in the cloth district around Cranbrook, Goudhurst, and Biddenden. The east Sussex and south-east Surrey examples are only one-fifth of those of Kent: here non-jettied halls were the most common. They are also, however, quite plentiful in the west Surrey and Sussex cloth district around Guildford, Godalming, Petworth and Lodsworth. Rigold detected a kinship between the timberwork of Kent 'Wealdens' and that of Normandy, particularly the Pays d'Auge, which also has steep overall hipped roofs and close-studding with concealed braces, and was inclined to the view that the origin of the recessed hall must be sought there.[11]

Martin has found a correlation between the proportions of hall houses and the extent of the holdings which maintained them. On the whole, a substantially-built house with a ground floor of 70 to 150 square yards would be supported by a freehold or copyhold tenement of some 50-125 acres (excluding woodland), while larger holdings were capable of maintaining proportionally larger buildings. Few medieval houses survive for holdings less than 50 acres, suggesting that they were of inferior construction and have been replaced. The still flimsier cottages of the poor have similarly not survived.[12] An alternative suggestion of Chatwin is that these small houses were demolished not because they were poorly constructed but because they were difficult to adapt into larger ones.

The simplest Wealden houses and their sparse furnishing are only glimpsed in 15th-century records. At Hooe and Barnhorne, for instance, little homesteads comprising only three rooms, hall, bedroom and kitchen, were apparently single-storeyed houses with a service room at either end of the hall. William Creche's little house at Hooe was furnished with only the barest necessities – a table, two benches, a form and a chair. His kitchen housed the cooking equipment brought back and forth from the hall fire and in the bedrooms were two plainly furnished beds, a bench and 'two coffins in readiness'.[13] Bell's Farm, Slaugham and

Hashland Farm, Horsham are similar surviving farmsteads. In medieval seaports well-constructed vernacular architecture is sparse, doubtless because of their impoverishment in the later Middle Ages. At Hastings, for example, Martin has noted some very low-quality 15th-century buildings skimped in almost every particular.

A high proportion of medieval town houses has survived, as in Burwash, Robertsbridge, Sedlescombe, Ticehurst, Cranbrook and Goudhurst. Roberts-bridge was a 'new town' in the early 13th century and beginning with long burgages and having avoided severe contraction or expansion, 50 of these medieval houses survive. Close by Battle Abbey's precincts is the terrace lining the High Street, of 'Wealdens' built to form a continuous row. Each unit comprised a one-bay hall and a solar bay with jetty. These terraces, which would have brought an air of distinction to a street, appear to be speculative building to be let to tradesmen and craftsmen by, or on behalf of, the Abbey.[14]

Analysis of the size and other features of these houses apparently shows that many occupants of small wealden market towns had attained a high standard of living by the later Middle Ages, almost certainly considerably better than that enjoyed by the majority of the rural population, as Martin has noted. Very few economies in building design have been found, although costs were reduced in some cases by using close vertical studding for aesthetic effect only on the front and sides, the rear walls being constructed with large daub panes.

In East Sutton parish alone from 1400, wealthier yeomen during three genera-tions built nine 'half-timbered' houses which remain listed in the gazetteer of the Royal Commission for Historic Monuments. The first owners were either limbs of the august St Leger family at Ulcombe or newly wealthy cloth and farming families.[15]

'Wealdens' were built for well-off families who needed a house reflecting their superior position and having the space to accommodate the extended family and farm workers. It is likely, in the main, that builders of the largest timber-framed houses were supplementing their agricultural incomes with cloth or other craft activities, but this remains to be proved. During the 15th century some new social and economic trends, or an accumulation of old ones, opened the door of oppor-tunity to yeomanry and gentry who were able to amass little complexes of private property by shrewd business methods. In Kent this was a process already possible and familiar in the 13th century, if not earlier, but now intensified through greater opportunities of social mobility. Even in Sussex and Surrey, the more feudalised life-style did not prevent the rapid break-up of holdings and their re-consolidation into larger sizes. Certain areas of the Weald became lands of the yeomanry and gentry *par excellence*. Amongst these was north-west Kent where there was a notable gravitation of population with business and political interests in London. The process by which the London merchant infiltrated the Kent Weald can be clearly discerned as far back as the early 14th century when John Pulteney, draper and four times Mayor of London, acquired the whole manor of Penshurst and in 1340 constructed its magnificent beamed domestic hall. Another instance of wealthy immigration into the Kent Weald is around Knole, an

56 Hendall Manor Farmhouse and its great stone barn, Herons Ghyll, early 17th-century, the home of the ironmaster family of Pope. See p.138.

enlarged estate which by its example attracted the successful around it. Kent was the most popular choice of the wealthy immigrant, partly because the land was held in gavelkind tenure and could be alienated at will and so was freely negotiable on the land market.

A prominent feature of the wealden landscape is the moated homestead, fashionable between *c.*1100 and 1500. Although this is now more adequately recorded, it has received insufficient attention from archaeologists as yet for its social and economic significance to be fully understood.[16] The county lists of moats suggest that the Weald contained fewer moats than Essex with its more expansive clays, although the Kent Weald has 86 sites. More systematic research would increase these figures. Typically, the enclosure is roughly square or rectangular, though circular ones are not uncommon. All are usually surrounded by a single ditch. One of the very few sites excavated is the small one at Pivington near Pluckley in Kent.[17] The earliest dwelling within the pentagonal moat is assigned to the mid-late 13th century. About 1300 this was adapted and in the early or mid-14th century a new dwelling was constructed on the site of the old with a short cross-wing and earthen outshot. In the early 16th century this building was in turn demolished, and on the level raised by debris a new hall house was built which lasted, with modifications, until destroyed after the middle of the 17th century. The second dwelling might have had a base-cruck construction but this is hitherto unrecorded in Kent, although it has been traced at Dunster's Mill, Ticehurst, and at Chennells Brook, Horsham.[18] The 14th-century replacement was a 'Wealden' type, but simpler than the fully developed yeoman's farmhouse, the hall being only 17ft. wide internally, and so comparable with only smaller timber-framed houses of the time.

An analysis by Mike West of the size of moated sites in West Sussex reveals that the great majority of sites of known acreage were less than one hectare in area.[19] This is also true of the Kent examples. It is probable, on the basis of the slender evidence, that the characteristic Wealden moated site contained a relatively humble dwelling, such as Batchelor's Farm, Edenbridge, comprising an ordinary farmhouse with room for a cattle byre within the moat. This type might characterise the many homesteads cleared from woodland on large farms by freemen (franklins) in the 12th and 13th centuries, but the period of moating of most sites is inconclusive at present. Further light on the social status of the initial occupiers is West's reckoning that over 50 per cent of the West Sussex moated sites were probably manorial or connected with church or castle.

Historians have long debated the purpose of moats without coming to one agreed conclusion, and, as Joan Thirsk has observed, in the course of 400 years, moats doubtless served more than one purpose.[20] The majority of Wealden ones associated with the early colonisation of waste had doubtless a defensive function when farmers settling on remote sites required moats to defend themselves against marauders and wolves, whose harassment is reflected by place-names such as the Wulfa Biorh (Wolves Hill) in a Saxon charter of c.934, Woolfly in Henfield (Overlie in Domesday) and Woolborough Farm in Ashington. Such sites would have needed provision for guarding livestock at night. In the Arun valley is a long string of large moated enclosures, mainly manorial or sub-manorial, where barns and other farm buildings lay within the moated enclosure, still leaving extensive room for livestock. Other moats resulted from licences to crenellate, as, for example, the double moat fed by the river Eden surrounding Hever Castle. Later sites may be connected with the need for a regular water supply or for stocking fish. In the 15th century moats were increasingly being used to store carp, pike, tench and bream for both commercial and domestic purposes. By this time, too, moats seem to have acquired a status symbol.

The Post-Medieval House

From about 1550 new houses were built with a smoke bay rather than the earlier open hall. This was a narrow bay for confining smoke in a space some three or four feet wide open from the floor to rafters. In some cases a partition was built to form an entrance lobby giving access to the first floor. By the end of the 16th century new houses with brick chimney stacks were being built by those who could afford them. The chimney could be placed centrally or to one end of the building. Chimneys were superior to smoke bays not only because they were more fire-resistant and took up less room, but because they could provide several hearths instead of the single one linked to a smoke-bay. Meanwhile, owners of open halls began to insert chimneys and to floor over the hall to provide more living accommodation upstairs. This was a gradual process; in a few instances, such as Hempstead near Uckfield and Duke's Place near West Peckham, the hall remains open to the roof.

Sixteenth- and 17th-century probate inventories indicate that the once out-housed farming activities, such as cheesemaking, dairying, and brewing, were then normally carried on in specialised rooms of the farmhouse, the lofting over of the hall having provided more domestic accommodation. More accommodation for labourers was also provided. With the advent of brick chimneys cooking

57 Hapstead Farmhouse, Ardingly. The stone and tile exterior hides a timber-framed house which retains one complete bay of an open-hall house built in the late 13th century.[21]

58 A room in Hapstead Farmhouse in part of the late 13th-century portion of the house.

could safely take place inside the farmhouse without risk of fire and a bread oven was incorporated into the structure. Nevertheless, the change and detached kitchens are mentioned at the end of the 16th century in village houses at Robertsbridge and Lamberhurst. A few former detached kitchens survive, such as at Aldhurst Farm in Capel, Surrey.[22]

In the 18th century the exterior of the upper floor was generally covered with weather-boarding or tile-hanging, giving added insulation and water-proofing. A further impetus to this was given by the Georgian dislike of exposed timbers, a prejudice continued into Victorian times. At first plain tiles were used, but increasing use was made of shaped tiles, producing a wide variety of decorative effects giving an added charm to wealden buildings. The ground floor was often 'brick-nogged' or modernised completely with a new front façade with a brick skin at the same time. Timber-framed farmhouses which were not given this treatment were generally covered with plaster to conceal the framing. Around 1900 the fashion for exposed timbers started again: Loddenham in Staplehurst was one of the first to have the plaster stripped off to reveal the original framing.

An example of the sincerest form of flattery is Peter Shaw's reproduction of Bayleaf, now at the Weald and Downland Museum, as a modern residence.[23] Half-timbering is a technology with many advantages over less traditional brick cavity wall construction. The traditional Wealden model provides for an open-plan living system with rooms that can be used flexibly for formal entertainments and

59 Disguised Wealdens at Steyning resulting from conversion of houses to shops and the use of brick and plaster in place of wattle and daub.

60 Barn under conversion at Burstye Farm, Ardingly, using traditional methods and materials of craftsmanship.

for day-to-day living. The Wealden provides this with its central hall opening from the front door and a large kitchen and living rooms off it on either side. Shaw builds as closely to the medieval construction as building regulations allow. As the oak needs no treatment, the outside of a Shaw house should need no maintenance at all. The overall effect is of a house already having a mature character and atmosphere, blending into the wealden landscape. Meanwhile, a traditional Wealden house has been designed at Dunsfold; architect Ken Hume is giving a lead in the raising of small frame buildings of sweet chestnut in the ancient vernacular tradition of domestic building; and Ben Law, a woodsman at Lodsworth, has recently built a timber frame house out of timbers in his own and surrounding woodlands, the roof covered with individually cleaved sweet chestnut shingles, load-bearing frames from sweet chestnut round wood and walls constructed of straw bales.[24]

14

The Age of the Improvers, c.1550-1650

In the 16th and 17th centuries the pace of economic life quickened and market forces appear to have penetrated more deeply and permeated more widely than before. As a result of population increase, the rising prices of corn, cheese, butter, meat and other farm products encouraged landowners and tenant farmers to bring more land under agriculture. 'Stub up rough woody ground and convert to arable and pasture' was the slogan between 1550 and 1650. A good deal of land reserved primarily for sport in deer parks and forests, and not previously considered fit for anything else, was reclaimed and put 'to better uses' with revived agricultural techniques, such as 'devonshiring' (p.117). So, also, was much of the land which had lapsed since the recession in the late Middle Ages.

Apart from the disparking of deer parks, a strong movement for the enclosure of commonlands is also characteristic of this period. The impetus came from the increased profitability of agriculture and the aim to raise more timber and wood fuel for industry. It was facilitated by the Crown's sale to wealthy merchants and holders of Crown office of ecclesiastical property at the Reformation. Another factor was the boom in the iron industry, following the introduction of the blast furnace and the casting of cannon in early Tudor times. This was directly responsible for some enclosure, and capital acquired from the iron industry was put into land improvement, notably in St Leonard's Forest. These various causes were responsible for an unseemly scramble for commons, which evoked violent opposition from commoners. Moreover, as Joan Thirsk has noted, because of the improved market, the gentry were being persuaded anew to manage their home farms directly and to take more interest in their estates generally, including the renovation of fishponds and establishment of orchards, vegetable and hop gardens. The new landowners and yeomen farmers coming into the Weald also wanted to learn how best to farm it.

This new chapter in Wealden farming was one of great activity and prosperity. Fitzherbert's *Boke of Husbandry* (1534) assumes that the farmer's wife will work as hard on the farm as her husband. After religious devotions she should:

> first swepe thy house, dresse up thy dyssheborde, and sette all thynges in good order, within thy house: milke thy kyne, suckle thy calves, sye up thy milke, take uppe thy chyldren, and araye theym, and prouyde for thy husbandes brekefaste, dynner, souper, and for thy chyldren and servauntes …

Fitzherbert then mentions (in addition to other household duties):

> It is wyues occupation, to wynowe all maner of cornes, to make malte, to washe and wrynge, to make heye, shere cornes, and in time of nede to helpe her

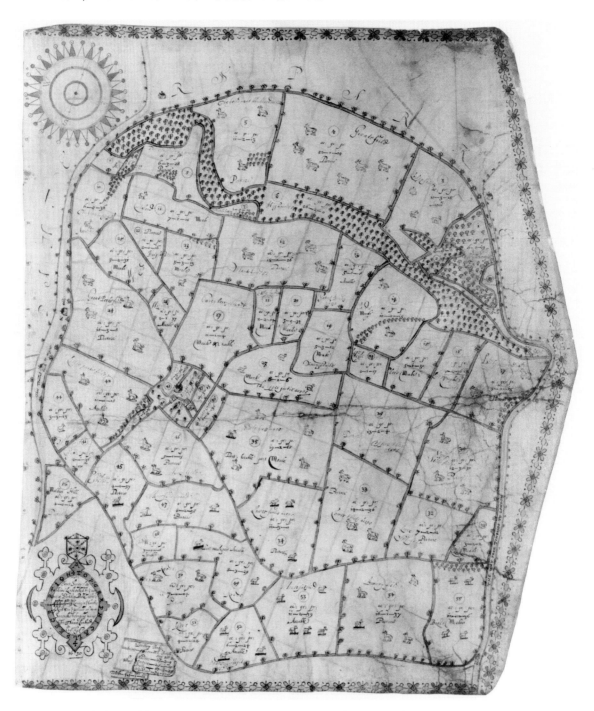

61 *A map of the disparked deer park of Panthurst Park at Sevenoaks Weald belonging to Thomas Lambard, 1630. Over 400 acres had been enclosed into large fields most of which have drawings of domestic animals. (CKS U 442 P102)*

husbande to fyll the mucke wayne or dounge carte, dryue the ploughe, to loode hey, corne, and suche other. And to go or ride to the market, to sel butter, chese, mylke, egges, chekyns, capons, hennes, pygges, gese, and all maner of cornes [see p.167].

Leonard Mascall of Plumpton in Sussex was one of the best known Elizabethan writers on husbandry who supplied the new demand for farming manuals. His chief work, *The Government of Cattell*, first published in 1587, was very largely a compilation, but nevertheless represented the best practice of the day, and continued in vogue until far into the succeeding century.[1] The author had a herd of red Sussex cattle but also bought black Welsh cattle, presumably at local fairs. He broke oxen into labour at three years, worked them until ten years of age, and then fattened them for slaughter in true medieval fashion on vetches, peas and beans. He fed sheep on 'wild' grass and in winter hay and tares eked out by browse of elm, ash, and other leaves, a practice also recommended by Fitzherbert's *Boke of Husbandry*, which advised cattlemen to fell underwood or trees a little at a time in winter so that cattle could eat the fresh browse, which, as we have seen, was a custom probably not new in the Saxon Weald (p.44).

Mascall also wrote the first printed book on poultry keeping (1581). Earlier he had written on the planting and grafting of trees for the orchardist (1572) (a traditional craft in the Weald), which was largely a translation of French and Dutch literature and, in a book on fishing (1590), claimed that an ancestor had introduced carp and pippin apples to England. Unusually, for a writer on agriculture, Mascall appears to have farmed successfully as an improving landlord at Plumpton. His wide range of farming interests, including his fish ponds, hemp,

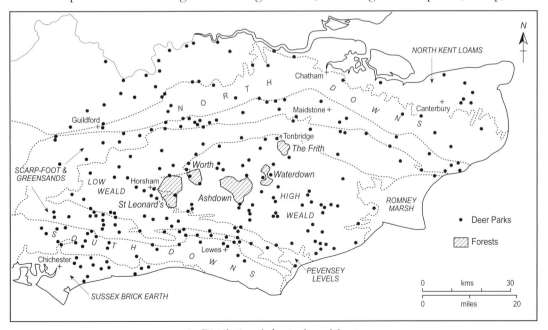

62 *Distribution of deer parks and forests.*

and cultivation of hops as early as 1595, implies an outstandingly progressive mixed farmer. With his advice to let 'lands lie high on the ridge' on cold, wet clay, the wealden farmer would have been in complete agreement.[2]

The foremost early 17th-century writer on country matters appealing to the wealden squire and yeoman was the outdoors man, Gervase Markham. His two books most relevant here, *Inrichment of the Weald of Kent* (1625 and several later editions) and *Farewell to Husbandry* (1638), demonstrate the greater literacy of the Wealden farmers of his day, but they are often mistakenly regarded as being a populist advocacy of new practices in agriculture.[3] Although his advice on improving barren claylands embodied the most improved techniques of his age, in actual fact what Markham recommended by way of good husbandry in the Weald had been practised by many previous generations of farmers. Markham has two main principles of good farming, as applied to the Weald – convertible husbandry and assiduous marling. Both, as previously noted, had been adopted as cornerstones of Wealden husbandry centuries earlier. It is thus noteworthy that Markham advocated little diverging from the standard medieval farming practice at, for example, Westerham or at Barnhorne in the Pevensey marshes in the 14th century (p.63).

Markham explained that his *Inrichment* was based on the writings of 'a man of great eminence of worth' and 'painfully gathered for the good of this island'. His source was possibly Sir George Rivers, resident at Chafford in Ashurst, Kent, to whom his book was dedicated. According to Markham, Rivers had built a large, imposing new manor house, and his estate is said to have employed many people in farming and related activities to the great advantage of the poor on fair to good soils of Markham's 'hazel mould' type in the gentle valley of the upper Medway. His house was destroyed by fire, but an immense barn (now converted into dwellings) occupies the site. Markham vividly drew attention to old trees 'of 200 or 300 years old' growing in abandoned marl-pits which indicated the decline in arable farming since the late Middle Ages, but we can correct the impression he gives that marling had ceased before he advocated its revival. The Sussex Coroners' inquests, 1485-1558, record four fatal accidents arising from marl-digging out of 48 accidents in total: those for 1558 to 1603 record five fatal accidents out of twenty-nine. (It is, incidentally, relevant to point out how dangerous was marling. The main cause of accidents was the toppling over of overhanging material being undercut by the digger at the bottom of the pit.) Markham is significant as being the first to remark on the disadvantages of small fields. He noted that, because Wealden farmers could only marl or drain a little land at a time, they were enforced to have many small enclosures which had such thick hedgerows that 'in unseasonable weather do keep both the sun and wind from the corn … so that it carneth not, nor eareth, nor prospereth …'. Markham was also the first writer to mention land-slipping.

Markham advised husbandmen to take advantage of high prices for both corn and dairy goods and so keep to mixed farming. He suggested that a farm of 100-120 acres should be divided into five or six equal parts, the plough being taken round the farm so that some 20-25 acres would be under corn in each year, by

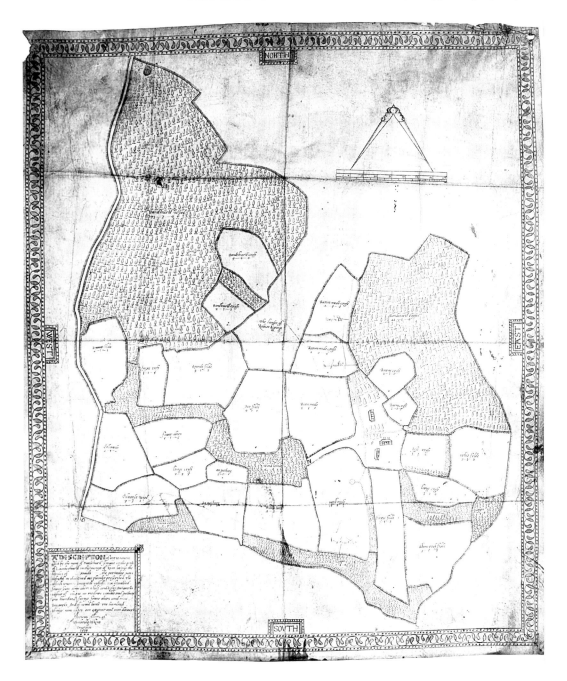

63 *A map of Sandhurst in Lamberhurst, by Henry Allinn, 1599. Extensive woods, including coppice, presumably feeding Lamberhurst Furnace, 'plocks' grubbed out of the woods in the later Middle Ages, two ox pastures, a 'cherye' and a 'stone' field are shown. All the enclosures were small, the tiniest being called crofts (CKS U 840 P6).*

turn, and the remainder laid to good pasture until its own time for tillage. Markham's suggested marling would have borne heavily on the farmer. To improve 'hazel mould' land for corn he advocated bestowing 600 cart loads of marl upon each acre, every load containing 10-12 bushels: on stiff, wet, cold clay, to serve for pasture and oats, 300 loads per acre: on sandy soils, 500-600 loads, 'at least'. As Fussell remarked, Markham evidently thought it was possible to 'cram' the ground to death with marl. He justified this enormous application on the grounds that it would make the field equal in fertility to the top-grade soil on the coastlands of north-east Kent (see p.59).[4]

In *Farewell to Husbandry*, Markham recommended lime for enriching barren clays, and minutely expresses the successive cultivations needed to reclaim ground for sowing. First, weeds were to be cut as close to the ground as possible and stacked to dry. Roots, grubbed, were also piled on these heaps and, covered with soil, leaving a vent-hole, were burned for ashes, which were spread over the ground. He advocated breaking up ground with a strong plough at the beginning of May, hacking the furrows in pieces with an iron hack, like a carpenter's adze, and reckoning half an acre as a good day's work. At midsummer he suggested that 60-80 bushels per acre of sea sand should be spread on it. In August farmers were to make a kiln of lime and bestow at least 40-50 bushels to the acre. In September dung and compost from ponds and ditches was to be applied, this being ploughed (evidently with eight oxen) deeper than before, and hackers following as in the first ploughing. After harrowing, 'Sow wheat plentifully not starving the ground for want of seed nor choking it with too much, but giving

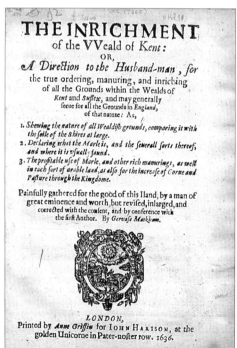

64 Markham's title page to his Inrichment of the Weald *(1636).*

65 A layered hedge, the agricultural improver's first consideration.

it its full due, leave it to the earth and God's blessing', seed was covered with a second harrowing in clods broken 'even to dust' with a clodding beetle (a wooden maul). Wooden nippers were used to pull up weeds when half a finger high and loose stones were gathered in heaps for paving.

His reclamation techniques, it will be noted, included burn-beating, referred to previously (p.116). This became known as 'devonshiring', from its first being revived in the West Country. Although Markham had little new to say, his books went through repeated editions, so we may assume that contemporary farmers found useful his suggested management of heavy clay. Eighteenth-century farmers judged his work differently. The agricultural writer, Arthur Young, thought a 'tolerable farmer' of the late 18th century would have been ashamed of it.[5] He failed to find any idea of a beneficial course of crops and considered the farming system founded entirely 'upon the plan of exhausting the land as fast as possible …' instead of 'the miserable management of all that hacking and clodding and mauling to reduce a clay soil to powder' before winter set in. Young reckoned that it should have been left for the rain, wind, sun and frost to have mellowed it during the winter, overlooking the fact that the Wealden farmer had difficulty in spring sowing (p.57).[6]

Young was also critical of Markham for not discussing draining clays. This is doubtless because on William Poole's land at Hooke in Chailey, Sussex, in 1771 evidence had been shown of under-draining ages before it was considered to have been adopted on heavy soils. Young wrote:

> Near an 100 years ago [i.e. *c.*1670] a very large oak, 200 years old, was cut down at Hook. In digging a ditch through the spot where the old stump was, on taking up the remains of it, a drain was discovered under it filled with alder branches: and it is very remarkable that the alder was perfectly round: the greeness of the bark was preserved, and even some leaves were found … it is from hence very evident that under-ground draining was practised more than 300 years ago in this kingdom.[7]

Thus, it is wrong to assume that under-draining was 'invented' in the 18th century.

Markham himself noted in *Inrichment* that in the Wealds of Kent and Sussex 'a great number of woody and over-grown grounds' had been converted of late to pasture and tillage, and the cartographer and surveyor, John Norden, confirms this:

> where in former times a farm stood in these parts wholly upon these unprofitable bushy and woody grounds, having only some small ragged pasture … now I see as I travel and where I have had business, that these unprofitable grounds are converted to beneficial tillage: in so much that the people lack not, but can to their great benefit yearly afford to others both butter, cheese and corn, even where there was little or none at all.[8]

A good deal of such activity is represented on contemporary estate maps and surveys. We can also glimpse examples of this from contemporary documents. Land improvement on the demesne of Sheffield manor in Fletching at the end of the 16th century was being undertaken by Richard Leche, a gentleman servant to Lord Buckhurst. When Leche leased a parcel of rough ground in 1592 Buckhurst did not raise the rent for four years, and in a similar example the lessee had five years to cut down trees and underwood (paying a lower rent than later) and then 'at his pleasure to ridd, medridd and grub up by the root all manner of stubbs, roots, bushes, brooms, brambles and such like now standing' and to leave the premises 'sufficiently fenced and enclosed'. Here a new farm was created from woody ground. Lord Buckhurst himself took a leading part in all this. He leased land in 1578, including rough ground and a decayed ironworks site at Fletching to Leche who was required to build two substantial corn mills 'most mete for the setting and placing thereof', to breed swans on the mill-pond and to plant six fruit trees annually, an early sign of post-industrial rehabilitation. In another lease to Leche 50 acres of Shipley Wood was reserved for underwood and timber, but 88 acres were to be grubbed up for the plough and sowed. Leche himself leased out Rough Croft, 11 acres of the newly-won land as a smallholding, and the tenant built himself a cottage on it. The annual planting of fruit trees was evidently a general requirement for tenants. In the mid-17th century William Wilson, a henchman of the Earl of Effingham, was doing the same thing on the manor of Barkham.[9]

66 *This scene of burn beating in Finland recalls the similar method of restoring fertility to worn-out land in the Weald.*

Another aspect of land improvement is Lord Buckhurst's requirement of his servant Leche to provision his household at Buckhurst or Lewes Priory, the rent being abated by the value of the provisions and one year's notice given. On the 16th week after Easter Buckhurst was assured of:

> two quarters of good, pure, clean, sweet, well winnowed and of the best wheat: three quarters of straw-dried malt, sweet and of the best: four quarters of good, pure and clean oats: twenty bushels of good and sweet peas: twelve fat capons, alive: ten good and fat green geese, alive of nine weeks old at the least: five good and fat pigs, alive: two hundred sound and good eggs.

Another lease prescribed for:

> two good and fat steers, alive: ten good and fat wethers: two good and fat calves: ... five good and fat stable geese: four hundred good and sound apples, mete to bake and roast and one hundred Wardon pears.

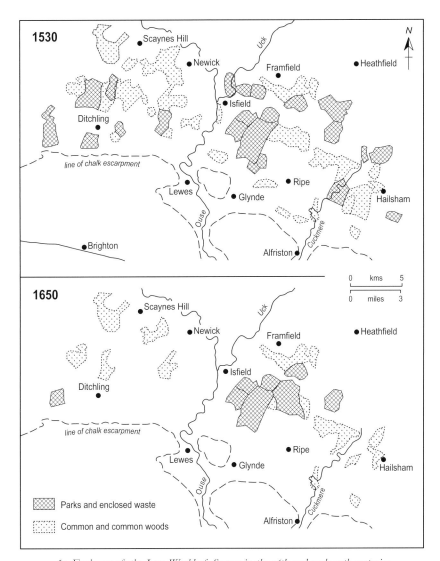

67 *Enclosure of the Low Weald of Sussex in the 16th and early 17th centuries.*

There are also signs that the 'floating' of water meadows had extended to the Weald by the mid-17th century. This was an early 17th-century innovation which provided a skilfully managed sheet of running water, about one inch deep, to flow over water meadows during the spring for the sake of the feed of grass or hay crop induced by its fertilising properties. Ingenuity lay in the accuracy with which the necessary amount of water was drawn from a catch-water system of drains. The earliest system recorded in the Weald relates to land at Crossways Farm, Abinger, Surrey, in 1622, initiated by Richard Evelyn, the diarist's father.[10] The Tillingbourne valley was ideal for this purpose, on account of the numerous springs which broke out along the valley sides at the conjunction of the clays. At Blackham, in 1659, upland meadow was valued at 12s. an acre, whilst 'flowed' (floated) meadow was priced at 18s.[11]

There is also much evidence of highly profitable commercial fisheries, apparently not widely practised nor understood until the publication of Mascall's book, after which a fish pond became as valuable as a garden, sale of carp becoming a considerable part of the revenue of the nobility and gentry. Old hammer and furnace ponds made excellent fish ponds. Carp, said to have been introduced by his forebear about 1514, were the principal species, but tench, perch, eel, and pike were raised. When artificially fed on peas, carp could reach a weight of 25lbs a brace. The one-year-old fish three inches long, used for stocking, ranged from 12-15 inches after four years and were worth 50-60 shillings the hundred. Tench grew slowly and were worth less. The enterprise needed a minimum of four ponds, one each for spawning, a nursery for feeding fish to maturity, and a stew pond to hold fish ready for eating. The nursery pond held carp up to one year old when they were transferred to the main pond for three to four years. Each fish needed a square of 15 feet, so that a pond needed to be about a minimum of 15 acres to hold a reasonable stock. A horse-shoe form was most convenient for removing fish. Once in 14 years or so the clay bottom was relaid. Pike were introduced in 1537. A four-acre water would produce 1,600 carp of 10-18 inches in two to three years, plus 40-50 tench and 600 perch, which made the fish pond one of the most profitable parts of the estate 'much superior to parks, bowling greens and billard tables'. It also had supplementary advantages: fibrous mould from the pond made good manure; stews were useful as cattle ponds; osiers for basket-making; and oats were cropped once in three to four years when the great pond was drained.

The Commons

Although innovations were significant at this period, much of the farming continued on traditional lines and was highly dependent on commons, their ferns and brakes growing on them being very accessible as a fertiliser. It was very general for tenants to claim the right to cut these 'to mend their lands'. This right was confirmed in custumals of Ashdown Forest, the Abergavenny manors, the Cowdray manors and the manors of Framfield, Graffham, Warningcamp-Byworth and Woolavington. On the Lower Greensand of West Sussex it was normal for the lord to allot a strip of fern, known as a 'fern layne', to commoners in proportion to their arable. This was then held in severalty for the period of each tenant's individual cutting, in just the same way that a common meadow was temporarily divided into lots for mowing. Fern and brakes were cut in August and, since repeated fern cutting prevented the regeneration of trees, attempts were made to stop the practice, but without avail. Norden, who was struck by the improvement of land in the Surrey and Sussex Wealds in this way, explained that, after being laid in the cattle fold, the fern was laid on the meadows to ensure a good growth of grass or, if laid down in the stockyards for the winter, it made excellent manure for ploughing into the arable. This was undoubtedly the cheapest and most general way of feeding land in the Weald in the 17th century. Arthur Young, who could find little to praise in Wealden farming, was highly impressed with the efficacy of this practice. Commons were also used for other purposes, apart from grazing animals which could not be sustained on holdings, such as for pannage and the cutting of turf and peat. Heath, fern, peat, and turf were dug: sand sold to glass-makers: part converted to warren: part sown with oats. Fir planting, presumably a reference to Scots pine, is an unusually early instance of conifer growing (1629).[12]

The Enclosure of Commons and Disparking of deer parks

The Low Weald

Changes resulting from these innovations can be illustrated with respect to the one hundred square miles on the Low Weald of Sussex between the Pevensey Levels and the river Adur (Fig.67), about one-third of which was in an unimproved state in 1500. By 1630 about ten per cent had been enclosed or disparked. New families, intent on improvement, had settled in the area, such as the Dobells of Street and established families, such as the Pelhams of Laughton, were similarly disposed and numerous commons became pawns amongst London speculators. A record number of high-handed attempts at enclosure occurred from the end of Henry VIII's reign into that of James I, which were met with violence from commoners. One practice was the extinguishing of customary holdings on the 'windy' side of the law, which resulted in the cessation of common rights. A less dubious practice was the partial enclosure of a common to allow for a new farm, woodland regeneration, or some industrial purpose, such as brick and tile manufacture. Numerous instances sparked off rioting, and the tearing up of newly planted hedges. In some cases, anger resulted in physical harm to persons, when inhabitants of Fletching pulled down the fences Sir Henry Compton had erected around part of Chailey Common, his stewards followed the men home and wounded one by gunfire.[13] This dispute was settled in the Court of the Star Chamber. The map by Edw. Gier and Clement Stoakes, 1651, of Great Lodge Farm, Chailey, shows that part of the demesnes of the manor of Brambletye were owned by Henry Compton (the present Great Lodge and Warrenwood farms). In 1619 Compton had acquired this manor through marriage with Cicely, daughter of the Earl of Dorset.

Chailey is of particular relevance on account of the exceptional extent of its commons and the inter-commoning between which had evolved various manors. A considerable acreage was enclosed at this period. The share of the Chailey commons possessed by Houndean manor was enclosed *c.*1622: that was held by Allington manor between 1659 and 1666: and Homewood was discommoned before 1650.[14]

The enclosure of Plumpton common, 240 acres, is particularly well documented. Francis Carew of Beddington, Surrey, Charles Howard, Earl of Effingham, London speculators John Layton and Humphrey Roberts and

Richard Leche were amongst the interested parties. In 1578 it was secured by Leche of Sheffield, who was pardoned by the Crown in 1589 for purchasing the common without licence. He then enclosed one third of it with the consent of some of the commoners. Following a dispute, the Court of Chancery appointed two commissioners, Thomas Bishop of Henfield (and Parham) and Henry Bowyer of Cuckfield, to arbitrate. They reported in 1595 to Sir John Puckering, Keeper of the Great Seal, as follows:

> We repaired to Plumpton Common and called before us the parties, plaintiff and defendant and heard allegations of both sides. We have got agreement [the parties agreed on the partial enclosure] and we so humbly take your leave, this first day of October in the 37th year of her Majesty's most happy reign.[15]

The Commissioners sent a draft Decree to the Court of Chancery, which was subsequently enacted. In 1623 John Mascall of Plumpton Place is found leasing the one-third of the common enclosed and Sir George Goring of Lewes had an interest in the remaining part.

In addition to the enclosure of commons, numerous deer parks were disparked. John Rowe, steward to Lord Abergavenny, observed that Ditchling and Cuckfield Parks had long before 1597 been converted 'to better uses'. The 300 acres of lightly wooded lawns had just been divided into fields in 1582. Cultivation also extended over Haley Park in Westmeston, in Kenward's, in Chiddingly, at Laughton and in Ewhurst. The Shortfrith and Frankbarrow Chase were also let out. Of particular interest is the immense area of parkland taken from the Archbishop of Canterbury. The More, Ringmer and Plashett Parks were disparked and over 2,000 acres in the Broyle were the subject of dissension for years. This served as common for tenants in the bailiwick of Ringmer, the southern part of the archbishop's manor of South Malling. An Act for enclosing the Broyle and Ashdown Forest was passed in 1662. Commissioners were appointed, and about 1,000 acres of the best land was taken by the holder under the Crown, the Earl of Bristol. Such violent opposition was incurred that he was obliged to throw it open again. The Duke of Dorset, who recovered the Park, curtailed the estover rights of tenants and raised a prodigious growth of timber which, by the late 18th century, Burrell estimated at 12,000 tons.

It should be borne in mind that land improvement normally proceeded by slow degrees. Unproductiveness in early stages of reclamation is implied by low rents. Thus, Ditchling and Cuckfield Parks were rented at only 3d. an acre between 1594-1606, whereas by 1696 the rent was 5s. 6d. an acre.

High Weald

'There be yet [1625] remaining in Sussex divers great forests and sundry commons or wastes, having five or six miles in length, which for the most part are not fit to be manured for corn and yieldeth but little profit in pasture.' So wrote Gervase Markham, and his estimate proved to be correct, although it did not deter farming enthusiasts, notably the Westons, and the over-optimistic Commonwealth surveyors of Ashdown Forest.

On the western margin of the High Weald stretched St Leonard's Forest and its bordering deer parks. Physically indistinguishable, though administratively part of Lewes rape, lay the smaller Worth Forest to the east. Waterdown and Dallington Forests lay close to the north-eastern edge of Ashdown Forest. In Kent lay the South Frith. In the southern High Weald the commons were less extensive but stretched almost continuously along the Heathfield-Burwash and Heathfield-Battle ridges as a strip averaging three-quarters of a mile wide. One motive behind enclosure of these 'wastes' was the preservation of timber. By the end of the 17th century commons enclosures for this purpose were made at Mayfield, Waldron, Netherfield and St Leonard's Forest and some 500 acres (The Five Hundred Acres) were enclosed from Ashdown Forest, probably in 1674. Yet with the decline of the Wealden iron industry from the first quarter of the 17th century afforestation was minimal, presumably because the high ridges were handicapped by distance and topography from the markets of London and the coast, as Samuel Hartlib observed in 1652.

The most important conversion to tillage occurred in St Leonard's Forest after it came into Crown hands in 1563. It then comprised only some 600 acres of improved ground and about 6,000 acres of barren land. During the succeeding half century a modest extension of arable took place in the Forest and adjoining parks. In the Forest itself, where the Crown had indirect control, the revenue was greatly increased by letting some 2,500 acres as farmland by 1609. About forty separate allotments had been made, some for small farms and cottage holdings, probably for part-time ironworkers.

The extent of improved land in these parcels was very substantial, possibly reduced gradually by unremitting exertion, though if the larger-scale attempts at reclamation of the heath by Sir Richard Weston in the mid-17th century are a guide, it was only partially successful. He was perhaps amongst the first of that large group of Wealden farmers who looked upon farming primarily as a hobby, and his main interest in St Leonard's Forest was probably the means it provided for experimenting with agricultural techniques he had observed on the sandy soils of Brabant and Flanders. Weston advocated intensive sheep folding, followed by devonshiring of the land in spring, and heavy applications of marl. After two crops he put the land down to grass 'as good grass as ever I saw in any meadow in England', and experimented with rotations including flax, turnips, clover and lucerne. The Westons, father and son, let their improved land for £20 annually, which does not suggest a large acreage. At any rate, these modest improvements did not survive a change of ownership. In 1662 Sir Edward Graves began to turn the property into a warren and repeatedly burnt the heath to foster the growth of grass for rabbits. The principle of light-land husbandry failed in the Forest, as elsewhere in the Weald, because the finely-grained sand behaved like heavy land in wet seasons, which made feeding sheep off turnips difficult until under-draining was introduced.

The same can be said of Ashdown Forest, which underwent a series of disruptions fiercely resisted by commoners. With the new-found optimism of the Commonwealth and the advocacy of such writers as Adam Moore, the first attempts were made to ameliorate the Forest for agriculture and forestry. A scheme for enclosing part of the Forest was proposed in 1658, by which some 4,500 acres were to be left as commonland. The greater part of the enclosed area was to be planted with wood; a part was proposed to be upgraded as sheep pasture, and that near sources of marl was to be brought under tillage. Charles II was restored before this scheme could be executed. Immediately after the Restoration the Keepership of the Forest was granted to the Earl of Dorset and his son, Lord Buckhurst, for their successive lives, so restoring the privilege granted to them by Charles I. The Earl was not satisfied with this and repeatedly petitioned the King with craven letters for an absolute grant of the Forest. The Earl of Bristol, however, who had the greater influence at Court, was granted a 99-year lease of the Forest and was granted permission to plough up, divide and enclose it, and to allot parts to those with rights of common. The commoners strenuously resisted. The Earl of Bristol eventually forfeited his lease because of non-payment of rent and a new lease was assigned to Sir Thomas Williams who proceeded with the enclosure of the Forest. During this period speculators such as Alexander Staples managed to set up warrens, to bring in large flocks of sheep and to create some new fields. This period of uncertainty ended with the Chancery Decree of 1693 which followed the suit of Sir Thomas Williams on behalf of himself and the Earl of Dorset, who had by then won his cherished goal of the Keepership, against 144 commoners. By the Decree about 6,400 acres were reserved as common pasture, the remainder, enclosed and freed from common rights, was to be used by the lessees of the Crown as they chose. In the main, the enclosed parts were centred upon existing lodges and were the areas of greatest agricultural potential. The high ridges were mainly left as common, and, for the convenience of the commoners, the commonland was laid out near the settlements on the periphery of the Forest, thus creating the unusual semi-enclosed aspect of the present-day Forest in which enclosed and open ground intermingle so attractively. Soon after the Decree the interests of Sir Thomas Williams passed through various persons until they were bought out by the Duke of Dorset in 1730, who became possessed of whatever rights remained with the Crown grantees. The Dorset family, later to be Earls De La Warr, eventually sought to restrict, or dispose of, commoners' rights (p.230).[16]

Although agricultural improvement became theoretically possible after the Decree, actually, it had only a long-term effect on the landscape. Only a small part of the enclosed portion was brought under tillage and nearly all the residue remained a vast rabbit warren, indistinguishable from the commons only in the somewhat greater amount of timber. It was not until the latter part of the 18th century that the enclosed portion was made more productive. As in St Leonard's Forest, the urge for improvement had spent itself.

The smaller Waterdown Forest had been improved earlier. This is confirmed by the plaintiffs in a Chancery suit of 1603 who objected to paying customary swine rents because the trees bearing mast were mostly cut down and 'the best ground in Waterdown Forest had been enclosed and converted to tillage'. In this legal battle, it was alleged that Edward Nevill, Lord Abergavenny, 'a man of great living and allied to kings' had molested tenants and kept privately to himself court rolls, ancient surveys and customs of the manor to hinder the defendants' case against him. About 1650 some of this land was being let for 30s. an acre and was used by Sir Richard Weston in an attempt to prove that wooded lands 'were a loss to the owner and this island', but it appears to have subsequently reverted to waste.

On the commons near Heathfield and Burwash the main form of improvement was the part enclosure permitted by the Statute of 13 Elizabeth for the preservation of timber. As in the Low Weald, former church property got into the hands of speculators and new landlords. Thus, the manor of Heathfield (originally the Wealden portion of the bishop of Chichester's manor of Bishopstone) was sold by the Crown to a London merchant, who resold to Lord Buckhurst, who recouped himself by enclosing the whole of the manorial commons. The large manor of Mayfield (formerly the northern beadlewick of the Archbishop of Canterbury's manor of South Malling) was likewise surrendered to the Crown and acquired subsequently by the famous financier, Thomas Gresham. Later, in 1596, it passed to Sir Henry Nevill, who promptly exploited its most realisable asset by disposing of all the commonland to Thomas Anyscombe. Meanwhile, the woods on the commons were totally devastated by ironworks (p.158). During the first half of the 17th century Anyscombe and his heirs enclosed the commons.[17]

Another aspect of enclosure was the granting of small plots of roadside waste to cottagers and the piecemeal intake of the waste by assarters. In this way the manor of Hammerden had granted out to cottagers the whole of Ticehurst Green before 1700, so creating the present picturesque village. In Hastings rape the Pelhams of Laughton claimed ownership of all the waste as the rapal lords. They granted cottage holdings to the poor along the ridges. The revenues were inconsequential, but evidently the linear settlement which is so conspicuous today was growing steadily through the 17th century. At some places the iron industry appears to have been directly responsible for a spate of smallholdings. This seems to be the case at Waldron Down Common, where assarting occurred in the late 16th century, and it is not likely to be coincidental that Means (Mens or Minns) Wood at Newpound in Wisborough Green was encroached upon by 19 cottagers in 1641 when Norden cited the place as one where the wood had been devastated for the furnaces. Yet had colonisation in association with the developing iron industry taken in any marked degree 'the form of assarting [or enclosing] the waste and woodland, or carving out blocks of land' as Worcester has asserted, or as envisaged by Fussell, some evidence of the process would have been discernible in manorial records. On the contrary, there are signs that lords declined to let out parcels to cottagers 'fearing that they would be an enemie to the prospering of the woods'.[18]

We can glimpse something of Wealden agriculture and society in Gervase Markham's day, by means of a case study of Framfield manor with lands in Framfield and adjoining parishes of Buxted, Uckfield and Withyham. The bases of this are the parish records of Buxted, Framfield and Uckfield and a manorial

survey or Terrier made for Richard Sackville, 3rd Earl of Dorset, of Knole in
1617. This is no ordinary manorial survey. It enumerates in unusual detail every
mansion, farmhouse, and cottage, and every field and its land-use over approximately 18,000 acres, 27 square miles. The most similar in style and minuteness
is the Buckhurst Terrier (1597-8), produced for the same lordship. With the aid
of the bounds given for fields, features mentioned only incidentally, such as
highways and byways, stretches of roadside waste, and ironworks, begin to
emerge. The cadaster map, which almost certainly accompanied the Framfield
manor Terrier, appears to have been lost, but the information recorded in the
survey is so extraordinarily comprehensive that to an unusual degree the

68 *Richard Sackville, 3rd Earl of
Dorset, a reckless spendthrift.*

geography of 1617 can be reconstructed as a kind of snapshot of the evolving Weald. The survey can do more. On account of the consistent recording of tenures going back to the Middle Ages, a reasonably accurate picture of the distribution of farmland and waste can be obtained for the period of the last major clearing of the woodland, the period 1250-1350.[19]

The basic pattern of land-holding clearly emerges (Fig.69). The larger holdings were mainly in the ownership of 45 minor gentry. In some instances persons were holding more than one tenement but overall it is plain that this was mainly a community of small family farmers, smallholders and cottagers. The smallest tenements tended to be concentrated in areas of late clearing of the woodland in the 13th and 14th centuries, such as High Hurstwood and Buxted Wood in Buxted and Langhurst Wood in Framfield. Of particular interest are some 30 cottages related to sites of ironworks, such as Pounsley and Tickerage. Very few of these are traceable on later maps or on the ground: the impression given is that the labouring ironworkers were housed in hovels. The village of Framfield did not exist: merely the cottages by the parish church, one of which was the only shop distinguished in the survey. At Buxted church was a small group of cottages which are now marked by earthworks in the Park.

The average field size was 4.5 acres (at the time of the Tithe Survey in 1840 it was only a little larger). The ridding up of hedges and amalgamation of fields does not appear to have made much headway by this time. The smallest fields tended to be on the land assarted in the final stages of the medieval clearings where fields of two to three acres were common. As for land-use, there was a broad consistency across all four parishes. Pasture and meadow hugely predomi-nated (Fig.69): arable comprised around 30 per cent: coppice and woodland ranged from just over 10 per cent in Framfield to 14 per cent in Uckfield and 20 per cent in Withyham: orchards and hop gardens were features of many farms but the total acreage was small. Some 4,000 acres of commonland had resisted the medieval clearances.

The survey of the manor of Possingworth in 1563 would appear to typify the land use in the high ridge country in the late 16th century. The manor

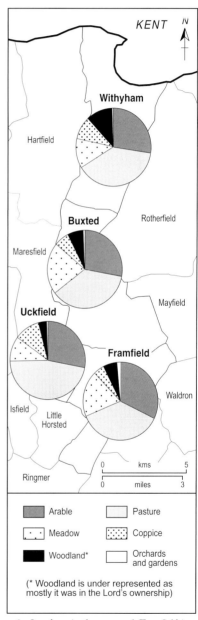

69 *Land use in the manor of Framfield in Framfield, Buxted and Uckfield, 1617.*

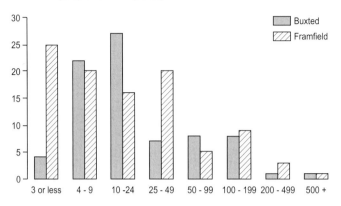

70 Size of holdings in the manor of Framfield, 1617.

comprised no arable, 120 acres of pasture, 39 acres of meadow, 112 acres of wood, 218 acres of heath and 600 acres of common. The meadows were watered by a 'fair fresh water spring or well continually rising', one of the many similar springs in the Hastings Beds. The pasture was either lying in 'divers plocks between woods', much in their shadow, or they were 'full of brome and brambles'. The main income of farmers was said to be derived from breeding cattle.

With the revival of marling and introduction of devonshiring towards the end of the 16th century, some of the better land was brought under the plough but the extent of changes was probably modest. At Possingworth, which had no arable in 1563, only 70 acres were under the plough as late as 1712, and even in Penhurst and Ninfield, on farms which were to become almost wholly arable in the early 19th century, the amount of tillage was still small in 1696. The over-riding importance of the iron industry at that time may have been partly responsible for the agricultural stagnation of the High Weald. The appalling roads were a contributory factor. Until turnpikes became general, the only produce which could be marketed easily was driven on the hoof.[20]

XIII (LEFT) *Droveway from Southwick and Kingston Buci descending the escarpment of the South Downs en route for the deep Weald near Horsham.*

XIV (ABOVE) *A fine example of a wide droveway from Tarring in West Worthing, approaching Crookhorn Farm in Shipley.*

XV (ABOVE LEFT) *Crookhorn Farm, Shipley, shown by Blunt to William Morris in 1896. Until the 1950s its only access was by this greenway. Like most farms in the district its foundations were built by digging a stone quarry adjacent to the site which then filled with water and became a cattle pond.*

XVI (BELOW LEFT) *William Gier's map of Wardsbrook, Ticehurst, 1612 (see p.176).*

XVII (ABOVE) *Pattenden, Goudhurst, a 'double Wealden', one of the finest examples of 15th-century house building.*

XVIII (RIGHT) *A beautifully carved crown post at Pattenden.*

XIX *An artist's representation of iron-ore mining in 'mine-pits'. (Mike Codd)*

XX *Reconstruction of a gunfoundry. An artist's reconstruction by Mike Codd.*

15

The Wealden Iron Industry

THE Weald was the premier iron-producing district in Britain during most of the Roman occupation. It was so again when the Sussex Weald became the cradle of British iron making during the 16th century, based on the blast furnace in place of the bloomery process, and a break-through in the casting of cannon, both facilitated by the expertise of immigrant French workers. The blast furnace introduced at the end of the 15th century was the small continental type developed mainly to make castings of cannon. Although in general use on the continent by the mid-15th century, it appears not to have been established in England until 1496 when Henry VII ordered its construction at Newbridge in Ashdown Forest to supply his artillery with iron shot on his Scottish campaign. This site is now regarded as the birthplace of the British iron industry. This new technique so greatly increased the production of iron that the bloomery process was ousted.

The earliest cannon consisted of wrought-iron bars welded together into a hollow tube and bound with iron hoops to prevent them splitting apart when stone balls (gunstones) were fired. A safer and more accurate weapon was made of cast bronze which fired cast-iron cannon balls, though this was very expensive. Up to this point all the improvements in cannon manufacture had occurred on the continent. However, in 1543 cannon were cast in one piece by drilling a solid bore with a steel-tipped drill on the edge of Ashdown Forest either at Buxted or in adjacent Maresfield with French assistance, and the improvement made England the acknowledged leader in armaments for about one hundred years. Three persons were associated with this first cast-iron muzzle-loading cannon – Ralph Hogge, Peter Baude, a bronze gunfounder of French extraction, and the Rev. William Levett, rector of Buxted parish 1533-45, whose elder brother was also an ironmaster.

Considering the historic importance of the breakthrough in casting cannon in 1543, it is strange that the generally accepted account of it has been proved

71 Replica of a medieval cannon, Pevensey Castle.

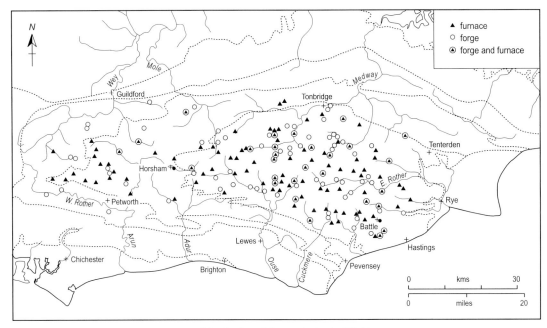

72 Distribution of ironworks in the Weald.

incorrect. The Elizabethan historian, Holinshed, attributed the credit for the casting of cannon to Hogge and his French assistant Baude, and they are commemorated in the popular jingle:

> Ralph Hogge and his man, John
> They did cast the first can-non

Yet by his own testimony in 1563 Ralph Hogge acknowledged that credit should go to his 'master', William Levett. Levett himself made bequests to both Hogge and Baude and referred to them as 'servants' and Edmund Pope of Hendall manor and furnace also described Hogge in his will as 'servant of Mr Pearson Levett'. Levett was appointed the King's Gunstonemaker by Henry VIII and was succeeded by Hogge. Levett has been regarded as an outstanding technical expert with the birthplace of the first cast-iron cannon being at Buxted. In a recent study Teesdale has accepted this view but considered Oldlands in Maresfield as the most likely furnace where the first cannon was cast. John Wrake has now re-opened the debate on both these points. He argues, unconvincingly, that Levett's role was as business manager, but he may be correct in his assertion that the real birthplace of the first cast cannon is likely to have been one of the several in Maresfield parish where Hogge was very active, and not at Huggett's Furnace in Buxted, as popularly supposed.[1]

A significant factor behind the rapid expansion of the Wealden iron industry from *c.*1510 was the immigration of French workers. The earliest came to England around 1490 and the stream continued steadily, with particularly heavy immigration in some years, as from 1522-25 (years of famine in Normandy). It is thought that some 300 immigrants may have been in the Weald in the 1540s, of whom about half became denizens, and that in the 1560s about half the furnace and forge workers in the Weald were of immigrant stock. Nine-tenths of these came from the ironworking district of the Pays de Bray, the truncated continuation of the Weald which stretches from the hinterland of Dieppe into the Beauvaisis (p.25). A single place, Neuville Ferrières, near Neufchâtel-en-Bray supplied about twenty per cent of them. The Lay Subsidy Roll for 1524-5 lists aliens in many east Sussex parishes. The Westminster Denization Roll of 1544 groups the Frenchmen under ironmasters. For example, William Levett was then employing 12, Sir William Sidney at Robertsbridge, six, Pelham, 17 Frenchmen. The occupations of a number of these are stated: these include miner, collier, hammerman, finer, joiner, smith and a 'gunner' working with Peter Baude.[2]

It has been possible to reconstruct a typical ironworks and its ancillary buildings to show what they looked like (Plate XX). The furnace often rose to a height of 30 feet and was more than 20 feet square at the bottom with walls five or six feet thick to withstand the great heat necessary to obtain molten iron. The heat was generated with large leathern bellows about 20 feet long, usually driven by an overshot wheel almost as high as the furnace itself. To obtain the power, the water from a dam was carried high above the ground along a wooden trough often 75 yards or more in length to a point above the wheel. Buildings included a furnace house of stone and timber for the manager, a bridge-house to protect the water-wheel, a number of smaller houses and cabins for workmen, stables for oxen used in hauling ore, storage space for the ore and charcoal, and, because a little farming was also associated with iron production, barns for housing livestock and farming implements.[3]

73 East Grinstead church: the earliest cast-iron grave slab (1570). The church also contains nine lines of one of the earliest monumental inscriptions in English (1505) which explains that Dame Katherine Grey and her second husband Richard Lewkenor of Brambletye 'fowndyd indued and Inorned this present church' which appears to be evidence of a rebuilding of the church towards the end of the 15th century.

74 Minepits at Stockland Farm, Hadlow Down.

In all periods the iron-making industry was to a considerable extent governed by the quality and availability of local ore supplies. Diggings for iron-ore are almost ubiquitous over iron-bearing rocks. They were commonly called 'Minepits', since 'mine' was the local name for ore and they are usually in the form of bell-pits at an horizon about 20-30 feet above the base of the Wadhurst Clay at its junction with the Ashdown Beds. The dimensions of a typical minepit are some six to nine feet at the top, widening at the bottom and rarely more than 15 feet deep. In woods, and on mined land, subsequently abandoned to woodland, they invariably remain as small water-filled ponds. Worsham has remarked: 'In some woods the craters are closely spaced, with rims about a foot or two apart, and the ground looks as if it has suffered a bombardment: in others the ground is merely slightly uneven, with well-formed craters scattered at wide intervals.' Numerous woods with pits, some providing ore for Roman bloomeries, are called Minepit Woods. Examples of the former type are in Stockland Wood, Hadlow Down and all round the village of Mark Cross near Rotherfield. A minor source of iron-ore was in sandstone beds of the Weald. On farmland, ore pits were generally filled in to prevent damage to farmers.[4] Many pits were filled in on land reclaimed for arable or pasture but, although once levelled, subsidence generally reveals the sites as saucer-shaped depressions two to three feet deep and when ploughed have patches of shale and sandstone fragments on the surface. It is possible that some thin limestone seams were also dug in the same pits and taken as flux for the furnaces or used as lime. Marly material would also have been extracted in the process of digging for ore. Recent radio-carbon dating has proved the existence of medieval mine-pits, and Roman ones have also been identified, including sites at Tuesnoad, previously mentioned.

The rapid expansion of the iron industry in Tudor times had its basis in centuries of smithing, though little is known at present of iron-working in Saxon times and in the early Middle Ages. By the 14th century iron-working was widespread but probably not more extensive than in other iron-making districts in England. The earliest known artifact is the 14th-century iron grave slab of John Collins in Burwash church and there is evidence for it at places such as

75 Portraits on wood of Richard the ironmaster and his wife Catherine Infield of Gravetye, placed in the master bedroom on their marriage at Gravetye near East Grinstead.

Alfold, Crawley, Thundersfield in Horley, Loxwood, Outwood, Penshurst, Petworth, Rotherfield, Tudeley, Wartling and Withyham. The only site where detailed information is extant is for Tudeley in the Park or Chase of the South Frith near Tonbridge, where four bloomeries producing iron commercially are mentioned in the 14th century, supplied from the extensive woodland. It is estimated that the iron production from such bloomeries was very small. A larger production became possible with the introduction of the water-powered bloomery forges by the 15th century at Ticehurst, Burwash, Newbridge and probably Buxted. An aspect, which has not been followed up since Lower mentioned it in 1849,[5] is that a 15th-century hooped gun, formerly at Bridge, may indicate that ordnance manufacture may have a longer history than is realised.

From the 1520s wealden iron-making expanded rapidly into the 1580s, attained a peak about 1610-35 and then stagnated before declining to near extinction by the middle of the 18th century. Ashburnham, the last remaining furnace, went out of use in 1812. The remarkable rise of the industry was due to the proximity to continental expertise, the ever-growing demands for ordnance from the Crown, and to the growth of London and the other south-eastern centres, needing ironmongery which could be supplied from its immense woods, the widespread availability of ironstone (its phosphorus content making it more suitable for casting cannon than for the manufacture of bar iron) and the water-power in the deep ghylls. These resources were eagerly exploited by landowners such as the earls of Northumberland, the Sidneys of Penshurst, the Duke of Norfolk at Sheffield Park and the Crown in Ashdown Forest.

The head-start in gunfounding proved to be the Weald's advantage. The Board of Ordnance granted a monopoly of production to Ralph Hogge, 'the Queen's gunstonemaker', who was involved in the earliest experiments at Buxted, and licensed him to sell cannon surplus to requirements abroad. His successors, Thomas and John Browne, father and son, were also Wealdsmen, dominating in iron ordnance for more than half a century, and in the industry's last stages the Fullers of Heathfield and Waldron were among the leading manufacturers of cannon in England. The continental technology put the Sussex Weald into the

DATE STONE
WITH
HOG REBUS

76 Ralph Hogge's retirement home at Buxted. (John Malton, 2002, pen and ink, 20.5 × 14.5cm [8 × 5¾in.])

vanguard of the 16th-century iron industry in England, and although after 1550 it spread into the neighbouring parts of Kent and Surrey, the Sussex supremacy persisted.

During wartime most of ordinary life continued to run along its established channels, but the gunfoundries were placed immediately on a war footing. At the onset of the Second Dutch War (1664-7) the British navy was far from being fully mobilised. In February 1664 George Browne, the king's gunfounder, sent news to his co-partner, Alexander Courthope, that the enemy fleet was already at sea, but so great was the shortage of cannon that the Board of Ordnance had required their works to expedite deliveries of ordnance in advance of their contract and to specifications which had been hastily revised. Although an experienced gunfounder, Browne was put under severe strain by the sudden changes and demands upon him. 'I pray God send us good service … for on it depends our well-being', he confided to Courthope. His anxieties proved to be needless. Contracts were duly met and Courthope was eventually able to get their London agent to invest for him £1,000 in securities and to take care of jewels and plate valued at a similar sum. The agent also sent a generous consignment of claret, sack, neat's tongues and Westphalian hams in anticipation of a celebratory visit by the King to Horsmonden furnace itself.

When between 1674 and 1677 we again glimpse details of Alexander Courthope's foundry operations, they disclose that he was casting guns at his two furnaces of Horsmonden and Bedgebury only during the winter, when there was sufficient water-power, and at one 'blowing' on each occasion. The 'blowings' were staggered a week or so apart, which suggests that a senior gunfounder supervised both furnaces. The total cast during this period was 768 cannon. Payments were made to numerous members of the landed aristocracy and gentry, evidently 'sleeping partners' in the enterprise. They included John Roberts of Boarzell (p.173).[6]

The Courthope family – comprising Sir George and Alexander, Charles, Henry, Peter and Richard – were also successfully gunfounding between 1678 and 1681, using hired furnaces at Brede, Frith, Hamsell, Hawkhurst, Horsmonden and Temple Mills to arm 30 new warships. Staged payments from the Ordnance Office amounted to over £30,000, which probably represented some 1,700 cannon. Guns and shot were taken overland to Milland on the Medway mainly during the summer when the roads were most practicable. The cost of ore was only £2,226. Cordwood at Brede cost five shillings a cord. Carriers took charge of ready money to pay for rents and labour. Christmas boxes were given to the warders and clerks at the Tower.

Furnaces also produced domestic ironwork, including decorative cast-iron fire-backs in an immense variety of designs. With the general use of chimneys from the 16th century, fireplaces were constructed with flues which made the protection of brick or stonework important. The adoption of the blast furnace

77 *Richard Lennard's fireback, early 17th-century. Lennard was an occupier of Brede Furnace and Forge and his fireback depicts him surrounded with his implements and products of his trade.*

with its castings in open sand moulds made possible the production of moulded firebacks.[7]

'Goodman', John Horsmonden's smithy of Goudhurst (works possibly on the River Teise between the village and Finchcocks) supplied scythes, cutlery and hardware to clients as far as Devon in the mid-16th century. The smith's wares were taken by carrier to stores at the *George* at Southwark or the *Star* in Bread Street, London, and payments were generally received in the same manner, although carriers were becoming increasingly reluctant to handle large sums on account of increased robbery.

In the Pays de Bray most ironworks were sited on rapidly flowing rivers yielding a plentiful and constant supply of water, such as the river Béthune, which reduced dependence on leats, dams and hammer-ponds. The Weald ironmaster had to go to great lengths to obtain a sufficient head of water, because most of the new furnaces and forges were sited on relatively quiet streams of gentle gradient which had insufficient water, particularly in the summer, to power large bellows or forge hammers. Water had to be diverted and impounded by building earthen dams ('bays') across the narrow valleys to create long hammer-ponds as reservoirs, frequently as an inter-connecting chain. Many of these are now dry, but those that remain are amongst the most beautiful features in the Weald. Some

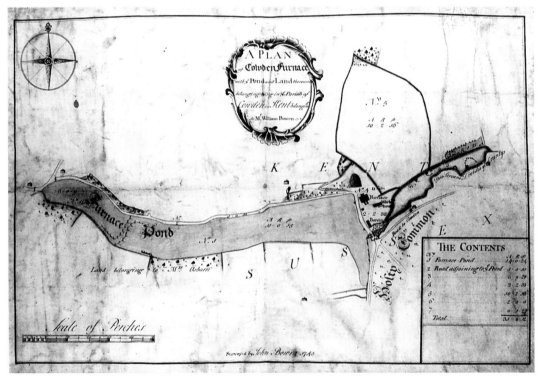

78 Plan of Cowden Furnace, 1743, by John Bowra showing the site of the furnace, a kiln, boring house, the bay, weirs, a slag heap, and a 14-acre pond working the bellows. (CKS U 650 P1)

of the leats needed to bring water to the dam were up to a mile or more long, such as that from the river Brede for the Crowham forge in Westfield, and that for the Ashburnham furnace.[8]

In stream beds or exposed in banks are numerous traces of glassy furnace slag, looking like bottle glass or forge refuse, which is quite different, being nubbly and known as cinder because it is mixed with fragments of ore and charcoal. Sunken lanes show where oxen dragged loads to and from the ironworks to tidewater. Artistic reproductions elucidate the working of a furnace or a forge (Plates XIX and XX). Glimpses of buildings are obtained at the Robertsbridge Abbey furnace in 1609 where a 'great stone bridge' crossed the two streams providing power at the pond bay: eight steel forges and various buildings for the steel-makers and a house for the hammerman existed: and the eastern gatehouse of the Abbey was used to store iron.[9]

The industry's irreversible decline and ultimate extinction was due to a number of interlinked causes. Towards the end of the 17th century it was undercut in price and generally excelled in quality by foreign imports, especially from Sweden, where wages were cheaper, water-power more regular and greater, and woodland more accessible. The steeply rising price of fuel, in competition with the cloth and hop industries, was another factor. The success of Abraham Darby at Coalbrookdale in 1735 to substitute pit coal for the expensive charcoal was another nail in the coffin, whilst the final blow was the loss of the valuable naval contracts to the Carron ironworks in Scotland, which had a coalmine and a sea port on the doorstep.

The industry produced numerous *nouveaux riches*, who purchased former gentlemen's estates and entered the ranks of the gentry themselves. Leonard Gale the elder, a blacksmith's son from near Sevenoaks, survived the plague which killed his parents and most of their children. Giving up his trade, he leased an iron forge in Worth Forest, and subsequently became a partner with Walter Burrell in other ironworks. Prospering during the Civil War, Gale amassed a fortune. His son had a university education and used his father's legacy to purchase the Crabbet Estate from the long-standing gentry family, the Smiths. He then spent his life as a country squire and MP for East Grinstead. The Fermors of Walsh Manor and the Fowles, both starting from the ranks of the yeomanry, became prominent gentry in Rotherfield for several generations. Robert Hodson of the Pounsley gun-foundry, also a yeoman initially, had two sons, Barnaby and Thomas, both gunfounders and termed as 'men of great wealth' whose offspring, Goldsmith and Susannah, married into the important families of Boorde and Morley of Lindfield and Glynde respectively.[10] Another family owing their rise from the yeomanry into the ranks of the gentry through interests in cloth and iron were the Streatfeilds of Chiddingstone.[11] Henry Streatfeild (d. 1591) was a 'woollendraper' and his son, Richard, ironmaster in 1594, leasing Cansiron Forge in Hartfield in 1589[12] and Pilbeams Forge in Chiddingstone and Withyham in 1590. He died in possession of Cansiron.[13] He purchased substantial property from a declining landed family, the Burghs of Lindfield, and his successors continued building up the estate.[14] A fine series of 18th-century estate maps shows the extent of the build-up. The dwelling house in High Street, Chidding-stone, was rebuilt in brick in 1702[15] and again as a mock Gothic castle in the mid-19th century, much of the village disappearing into the Park.[16]

Another way an ironmaster showed his wealth was by the purchase or building of a notable mansion. Gravetye in West Hoathly is a large stone Elizabethan mansion with broad mullioned windows, tall dormers and a stone porch. This was the new home of Richard Infield, who worked Mill Place Furnace and married Catherine Culpeper, daughter of Sir Edward Culpeper of Wakehurst Place. Portraits on wood in the master bedroom are of the newly married couple and bear the date of their marriage and an andiron bears the same motif (Fig.75). The porch bears the initials HF, which is explained by Infield's grand-daughter's marriage to Henry Faulconer who, in his day, also worked the furnace. The great Elizabethan mansion of Sir Walter Covert, who owned Slaugham Furnace, is now a picturesque ruin. Wadhurst and Ticehurst parishes are particularly rich in ironmaster's houses. Great Shoesmiths was the home of the Barhams who long worked Brooklands and Verrege forges and whose cast-iron grave slabs are in Wadhurst church. Nearby is Riverhall, built near his Riverhall Furnace by Nicholas Fowle in 1591. It has a fire-back with the initial EH, which may represent Edmund Hawes, a local ironmaster and perhaps a previous owner. Faircrouch was the home of William Benge, the builder of the Gloucester Furnace at Lamberhurst in 1695. Whiligh was built from 1583 for the Courthopes, and Pashley, with a beautiful early 17th-century façade with close studding, was built for the Mays who owned Pashley Furnace. Alexander Courthope, gunmaster to King Charles II, with George Browne, lived at Sprivers in Lamberhurst. With the profits of the iron trade, ironmasters climbed into the ranks of the gentry. Wadhurst church has no fewer than 30 iron grave-slabs in the floor of the nave and aisles commemorating the families of Porter, Fowle, Dunmott, Barham, Luck, Holland, Saunders and Benge, who were connected with the local iron trade. Hendall manor retains its Elizabethan atmosphere with its gables, mullions, courtyard garden and great stone barn on the lawn. It appears to have been largely rebuilt by the Pope family in stone on medieval cellars and passageways during the phase of the iron industry. Parts of the old timber-framed house can be identified and a later extension, shown in Grimm's drawings, has been demolished. The stone quarry providing material for house and barns is close by. The furnace site is marked by a prominent bay and a cinder bank. A wooden trough is visible in summer. Sandstone rock outcrops in the Rock Wood SSSI support Atlantic plants. It is difficult to believe that the ghyll woodland was not clear felled during the 16th century. In Wadhurst William Courthope, the antiquarian, noted the furnace and forge at Riverhall worked by the Fowles. Nicholas Fowle, who carried on these works, built in 1591 the fine mansion of Riverhall, which still exhibits traces of its former grandeur. Brookland Forge and Ferredge Forge, on the borders of Frant, at or near Bartley Mill, or Little Shoesmiths, were worked by the Barhams of Butts and Shoesmiths. John Barham, c.1630, built the spacious mansion of Great Shoesmiths, beautifully situated, and worked Bartley Mill and Brookland forges.[17]

79 Watercolour by Albrecht Dürer of an industrial complex in south Germany, late 15th-century. The scene in the Tillingbourne valley would have been broadly similar.

The late 16th-century concentration of blast-furnaces and gunfoundries in and around Ashdown Forest would also have contributed generally to local prosperity. Ralph Hogge's works made payments (including in kind in the form of herrings, wheat or iron) to 150 persons between 1576-78, mainly woodcutters, carriers, miners, colliers and skilled men, such as finers, hammermen and founders. According to Teesdale, the high level of economic activity resulted in generally lower ages at marriage, a high fertility rate, and a build-up of rural population. In a group of seven villages centred on Buxted, the aggregate surplus of baptism over burials contributed to a steady growth of population over a 30-year period, 1575-1605. For Maresfield alone the parish registers show a 46 per cent increase in baptisms in the decade 1570-79, as compared with the previous decade, and a 33 per cent increase in burials. This increase in population must be attributable, in part at least, directly or indirectly, to work opportunities and resulting prosperity generated by Hogge's and other ironworks. So evident was this to local families that Hogge's wife, Margaret, acted as sponsor 41 times at baptisms at Maresfield between 1557 and 1585. By the mid-'70s many of the French families who had formed prominent and close-knit communities had mostly moved away.[18]

The cutting of fuel for ironworks and glasshouses alone provided much extra employment. To cut nearly 2,000 cords of wood in Whitley Wood near Sevenoaks *c.*1595 required the services of 36 woodcutters. Mostly, they were paid 6d. per cord. So valuable was this taskwork to the poor, that Edward Turner's wife took over the cutting when he went to prison. Additionally, to the cutters paid at piecework rates, artisans such as the local baker, the smith and the trugger themselves cut the wood they needed, this evidently being the cheapest way to buy it. The owners accounted for every tree with meticulous care. Occasional carelessness shows up in the accounts, e.g. 'A young oak cut almost through by Wells and his boy as he hath confessed'. Petty pilfering was rife, no doubt on account of the rising cost of fuel. Edward Cranewell, the glassmaker, ruefully observed of local people that 'You shall not fail to find cordwood upon their fires in their houses'. George Bentyn continually carried out wood illicitly upon horseback by means of hooks slung upon each side of his horse. Four boys carried away an oak; another was seen to hide wood against an accomplice's hedge; a widow sent her daughter to steal wood regularly. More audacious thefts occurred; six cords were stolen by Richard Hayler's girls 'clean away on their necks', and 17 more were stolen in carts.[19]

16

Gunpowder, Wire, Glass and Cloth

THE importance of Sussex iron-making should not obscure the rise of other water-powered industries, for example, in the Tillingbourne valley of Surrey, where an archetypal rural workshop developed into a miniature industrial *pays* in the late 16th and 17th centuries.[1] The Tillingbourne is a small tributary of the river Wey which steadily acquired a new importance as a source of energy driving grain and textile mills, trip-hammers for iron, brass and wire manufacture, and also wheels for the making of gunpowder, saw-milling, paper-manufacture and knife-grinding.

80 John Evelyn, diarist, connoisseur and gardener. He wrote of the Tillingbourne in 1675: 'I do not remember to have seen such a variety of mills and works upon so narrow a brook and in so little a compass: there being mills for corn, cloth, brass, iron and powder, etc.'

Water-using industries also gravitated to the river, notably leather-tanning, and the regulated river was put to other uses, the floating of water meadows being a conspicuous example. The same skilful engineering techniques acquired in this industrial management of water were then applied to garden layouts with ornamental canals, serpentine rivers, cascades and waterfalls. There can scarcely be in south-east England a valley richer in historical associations with the art of directed sources of power in nature for the use and pleasure of man. Contemporaries were themselves self-consciously aware that they had created a sharply differentiated landscape. The diarist, John Evelyn, whose family was at the heart of the industrial development and who was himself responsible for garden-making in a new vogue, observed of the valley in 1675: 'I do not remember to have seen such a variety of mills and works upon so narrow a brook and in so little a compass; there being mills for corn, cloth, brass, iron, powder, etc ...'. The diarist's grandfather, the first George Evelyn, bought the Wotton Estate near Dorking in 1579 and became famous as a manufacturer of gunpowder. His youngest son, Richard, who succeeded to the Wotton inheritance in 1603, was remembered as a 'thriving, neat, silent and

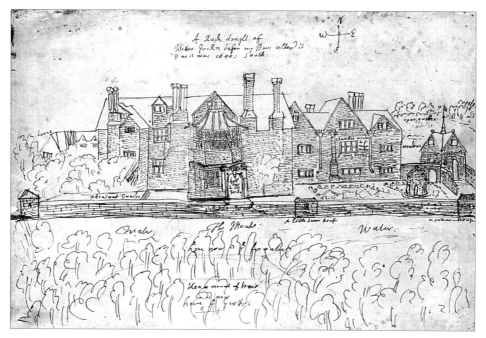

81 John Evelyn's birthplace at Wotton, near his grandfather's gunpowder works.

methodical genius' and diversified into brass, wire and iron. Although the Evelyns were the most successful of the local 'protectors', other local families were engaged in manufactures, including the Hills of Abinger, the Morgans and Randalls of Chilworth, the Brays of Shere and the Lee-Steeres of Wotton and Ockley. Apart from the latter, an old Surrey landed family, the others, including the Evelyns, were Tudor *arrivistes*, whose migration to the Tillingbourne valley was evidently primarily due to the opportunities it offered to the enterprising industrialist.

Although iron manufacture at Thomas Elrington's forge at Abinger Hammer, founded in 1557 (and famous on account of its special exemption from restrictions on fuel-cutting, despite being within the area of London), was the first new form of industrial activity, gunpowder making became more important because it had better condition of growth. The location and development of gunpowder manufacture was determined as much by a sufficiency of fuel supplies and of water-power, as by a sparsely populated remoteness which offered a greater safety in working. Sites were also favoured by the accessibility of London, then the chief source of imported saltpetre and the market for the powder. Wood was an important ingredient in gunpowder making, for, apart from the alder or dogwood used in manufacture, wood fuel was needed for drying the mill cake after it was granulated and glazed, and wood was used to burn pyrites to make sulphur. Water was needed in the re-crystalisation of saltpetre and as a drench to minimise explosion. The mix of saltpetre and sulphur was incorporated by means of grindstones operated by relatively small amounts of water-power. The dogwood

82 River Tillingbourne; site of the Elvix wire and brass mill.

was invariably disbarked after soaking in bundles in the water. Three early sites of gunpowder manufacture can be identified in the Tillingbourne valley, including that of the Evelyns and that of the East India Company, which was licensed in 1626 to make explosives for its own use. This project began badly at Chilworth, progressed uncertainly, and ended dismally. In their 10 years of operation the Company was accident-prone, even by the standards of contemporary gunpowder making. The company became involved in acrimonious disputes with highly litigious neighbours and finally disposed of the lease on the works in 1636 when George Evelyn's competitors, Samuel Cordwell and George Collins, erected new premises at Chilworth and operated successfully, as did Morgan Randall, their successor, who owned 18 powder mills at Chilworth in the 1670s.

When George Evelyn's powder mills were closed down, his son moved into brass-making in 1622. The brass industry had supplied products for the receptacles and tools used in gunpowder manufacture, and a brass foundry had begun unsuccessfully earlier in the valley by Thomas Street, whose works were closed down as a contravention of the monopoly of the works at Tintern. Richard Evelyn set up brass, copper and wire works at two separate locations along the river, producing brass and copper plate for consumer goods, such as pans, kettles, ladles and curtain rings. The diarist refers to his father's water-driven *ingenio* from Sweden. Evelyn's principal lessee, Pe(e)ter Brocklesby probably of alien extraction, also eventually fell foul of monopolists and was unable to sell his wares to the rich market of the Guinea coast and the Indies, which was their prerogative, and he himself was at the disadvantage of merchants from Aachen and Lunen-berg who exported more cheaply finished products of continental origin to London.

Although brief, the industrial era permanently altered the old pattern of rural settlement in the valley. A new element, the mill hamlet, was introduced, such as Broadmoor and Friday Street in Wotton; Abinger Bottom, Abinger Hammer and Sutton in Abinger; Sutton and Pitland Street (now part of Holmbury St Mary); and Chilworth in St Martha's. Other older centres expanded with milling, notably Weston in Albury. These hamlets are still criss-crossed with defunct leats and floodwater channels; they contain the site of a mill and a 'mill farm', numerous drained ponds and traces of spillways. The surrounding fields are of the small 'assart' type bounded by quickset hedges. Each mill-hamlet is built in the dominant architectural style of the 17th century, half-timbered dwellings subsequently brick-nogged. From documentary sources it is possible to date fairly precisely the origin of these mill-hamlets, now much loved places. Thus, Abinger Bottom was described as 'six newly erected cottages, enclosures and a mill' (at Friday Street) in 1607, and Shere forge at Abinger Hammer has cottages for the 'iron men' in existence by the last quarter of the 16th century. For the lasting effect of industry in the Tillingbourne valley on the woodland see pp.158-9.

Another characteristic Wealden industry, glassmaking, was dependent on a prodigious supply of wood fuel and readily fitted into the cycle of the farming year because it was too hot to work in the furnaces in summer.[2] Unlike the widespread charcoal iron industry, it was virtually confined to the densely wooded parishes in the north-west Weald around Chiddingfold on the Surrey-Sussex border, where it appears to have started in the Middle Ages in Chiddingfold and the two adjoining parishes of Hambledon and Kirdford and spread in the 16th century to Wisborough Green, its main centre then, and to Alfold, Ewhurst, Billingshurst and Lurgashall. It took more than 10 tons of wood billets to make one ton of glass. A large Elizabethan glass furnace burnt as much as a medium-sized iron furnace and more than many iron forges. Medieval glassmakers were so dependent on their fuel supply that they appear to have rented a woodland for a few years and built a rough temporary furnace on it before moving to another source of fuel. It is possible that this mobile glassmaking was being carried on as early as the mid-13th century, but the earliest documentary record of it is in Chiddingfold in 1351 when John Alemayne sent window glass to St Stephen's chapel at Westminster. Alemayne's property at Hazel Bridge was leased to John Schurterre, 'glasier', in 1367. Kenyon thought that possibly he was then the only glassmaker in the Weald. His glasshouse was sited in the woods from which it drew its fuel, namely Shuerewode (Shirewood) and Strowykeswode (Strudgwick). These woods lie in the still densely wooded valley of the Hambledon stream. After his death, c.1379, his widow carried on the family glassmaking with a Staffordshire glazier, possibly until her son John, also a glazier, was old enough to take over.

Beech billets were preferred for melting glass because of their greater heating effect. There are still many fine beeches on Idehurst Hurst, a woodland drawn

83 *The mill hamlet of Friday*
Street in Abinger parish, Surrey.
This arose from the various
industrial projects of the Evelyn
family. The trees that encroached
on the lakeside have recently been
felled, creating a scene similar to
that depicted by Victorian and
Edwardian artists.

84 *Stages in the manufacture of*
glass, 17th-century.

upon by Henry Strudwick of Kirdford, who was making glass in 1557 (possibly a 'rising land'), and Kenyon has noted that it is not often noticed that beech, given equal chances with oak, will thrive and often swamp oak, and make good, though not as fine trees as on the chalk. Strudwick used cleft wood, which suggests that it was the branches of pollarded beech and oak trees, probably cut at intervals of about 20 years, which would yield a good crop of small to medium sized firewood. It seems that the ample supplies of beech fuel were the attraction of Kirdford and Chiddingfold for glassmakers, though it is possible that some oak was also used. A main ingredient of glass is sand, and this was obtained locally, the white outcrops at Hambledon Common on the Folkestone Beds and at Lodsworth on the Hythe Beds being used, the latter source indicated on a map of 1629. This was not of a high quality by later standards, but furnished material for what was known as green forest glass, window and glass suitable for general domestic use but not luxury crystal glass, for which foreigners in Elizabethan London used soda from Spain and imported sand as ingredients. The flux needed to facilitate smelting was obtained from the ash of bracken and the wood ashes from their furnaces. Only long experience could teach the medieval glassmaker in what proportions to mix his ingredients in varying condition of wind direction, quality of fuel, and different pits, and so his product was very variable in quality.

There is little trace of the glass industry in the present landscape. Excavated sites, usually in or near coppice woodland, reveal merely a burnt patch and a few fragments of crucibles and glass. Only one glass-making site has been scientifically excavated. It is at Blundell's Wood, Hambledon, and this tells us in some detail what a 14th-century 'glasshouse' was like. A temporary wooden shed, roofed with tiles, probably covered the small rough furnaces in which the glass was melted and annealed. Two primitive kilns, a large sub-rectangular one and a smaller 'beehive' type, lay on either side of a small round oven and a working floor. E.S. Wood has suggested that the function of the main kiln was as a melting furnace and the smaller was for 'fritting' and annealing, whilst the smaller oven was probably for pre-heating pits. The pottery from this site is ascribed to c.1330.

In Tudor times two substantial yeoman-farmer families were engaged in glass-making, the Strudwicks of Kirdford and the Peytowes of Chiddingfold, but the rapid expansion and vastly improved methods of making glass during the reign of Elizabeth are associated with the immigration of craftsmen from the continent. The most famous of them was John Carré of Arras, who erected two glasshouses at Fernfold in Wisborough Green in 1567 with assistants from Lorraine. He was buried at Alfold in 1572. Representatives of two families from the traditional glass-making district of Normandy, the Forêt de Lyons, east of Rouen, the Cakerys and Bungars also set up works, as did Lorrainers Hennezels (Henseys) and Tytterys and Tysacks from the Forêt de Darney region in the Vosges, which has so many resemblances to the Wealden landscape. All the foreign glassmakers were probably Huguenot, though it appears that they settled in England not on account of persecution but owing to oppressive taxation. At least 26 entries in the parish registers of Wisborough Green between 1567 and 1624 relate to these French families, and a French priest was licensed to hold services in the church.[3]

85 An aerial view of Cranbrook, the centre of the Kent and East Sussex cloth industry.

Issac Bungar proudly came from one of the original glass-making families in Normandy and established himself in the Wisborough Green and Billingshurst district between 1600 and 1618. He took over Carré's works and attempted to solve his fuel supply, now scarcer because of the insatiable needs of glass- and iron-works, the clothing trade and farmers using lime kilns, by buying up woodlands in order to avoid constantly rising prices and intense competition of accessible fuel. Moreover, he sought to control both production and the market in window glass in the face of rising fuel costs. Nevertheless, he was forced to curtail production to no more than his own woods could support for fear of reprisals and restrictions from neighbours, his clients and Parliament. By 1612 technical change permitted the use of coal as a fuel in glass-making in Staffordshire, but Bungar did not surrender his manufacture in the Weald without a long and bitter battle with Admiral Sir Robert Mansell who held the monopoly of coal-fired furnaces. His hand was strengthened by a Royal Proclamation of 1615 expressly prohibiting the use of wood in melting glass. Bungar refused to work for Mansell and, since he continued to make glass at Wisborough Green, he was prosecuted by Mansell and, as a result, Bungar shut down his last wood-fired furnace in 1618, though his opposition to Mansell did not cease. His use of other methods included bribing workmen to spoil the products deliberately. A memorial to the industry are windows in Chiddingfold and Kirdford churches glazed with fragments of window glass discovered by Kenyon and other archaeologists. Some windows in the *Crown Inn* at Chiddingfold also contain local forest glass.

For more than 400 years, from the 13th to the 17th centuries, clothmaking was a staple industry of the western Weald. Almost every Surrey village had inhabitants engaged in one or more stages in the production of woollen cloth. The villages of Gomshall and Shere were outstanding as weaving centres. In 1380 they had between them 14 weavers and 42 spinners besides pelterers, shearers, dyers, fullers and so on. Drapers were mentioned there in 1436 and in Henry VIII's reign Shere is mentioned in a list of places where longcloths were made. The houses of clothmakers, together with the individual farmhouses and houses of village craftsmen, such as blacksmiths and wheelwrights, supporting this clothmaking community, explain the present character of Shere village and some details of its domestic architecture. The clothiers who controlled the dyeing and other finishing processes were mainly based in Godalming and Guildford, but their sphere of activity embraced Wealden villages and small towns as far afield as the South Downs. John Leland observed of Petworth *c.*1540 that it was 'right well encreasid syns the yerles of Northumbreland used little to ly there, for now the men there make good cloth'. Kirdford, Lodsworth, Midhurst, Haslemere, Wonersh and Steyning were also engaged in the Tudor industry. In the early 18th century the principal products were blue kerseys for the Canaries market sold through London agents.[4]

In east Sussex there is circumstantial evidence of the manufacture of cloth, hats and gloves for local markets at Uckfield, Wadhurst, Rotherfield and such places as Fletching in the 14th century, since, as already noted, there was a need for generations to offset modest agricultural returns with many domestic handicrafts. This industry was still continuing in 1649 when five weavers at Rotherfield, three in Mayfield, two in Frant and one each at Warbleton, Framfield, Burwash and Buxted combined to keep up the price of coarse linen cloth and woollen products.[5]

The main Wealden woollen industry was in the Kent Weald. This was well established by the 15th century and was growing throughout the 16th century, peaking *c.*1560, when it soon afterwards underwent a slow demise lasting to the 1670s. An estimate of output at 11,000 or 12,000 cloths in 1567 indicates that it was of the second rank behind the Wiltshire, Suffolk and Yorkshire manu-facturing regions. Zell has established that the majority of clothiers were confined to a limited district of nine parishes in the central Weald – Cranbrook (the highest concentration), Biddenden, Benenden, Goudhurst, Staplehurst, Rolvenden, Brenchley, Smarden, and Yalding. In these parishes production was mainly of high quality, heavy broadcloth, a minimum of 28 yards in length and weighing at least 86 pounds. Some outworkers who spun and wove yarn for the clothiers lived beyond the borders of these parishes, notably in the East Sussex Weald. An adjoining district to the north extending into the Chartland – Smarden, Hothfield, Egerton, Lenham, Pluckley, and Bethersden – mainly specialised in low-valued kerseys which were lighter in weight and only about 16 yards or so in length. Wool

86 High Hurstwood Mill (which retains its mill wheel).

was obtained principally from Romney Marsh and the North and South Downs. Dyestuffs and oil came from London import merchants or imported through the port of Rye.[6]

The various stages of manufacture were in the hands of outworking specialists who mainly worked in their own homes. The clothier washed the raw wool, sorted and culled it, weighted and then dyed it, using woad, copperas and later indigo for blues and madder, brazil and later cochineal for reds. Wood fuel was needed to heat the vats and coppers for the dyeing process. Clothiers owned or leased coppice for this purpose or purchased it from neighbouring owners. By the 1570s the expansion of both the cloth and iron industries led to rising prices and severe competition, which became a hot political issue (p.160).

The dyed wool was then distributed to the clothier's spinners, women working part-time in their cottages who may have spun an average of one pound of wool into yarn each working day. Zell estimates that at least 5,000 part-time spinners would probably have been needed to produce the annual output of cloth, which means that perhaps some 10 to 15 per cent of households in the central Weald had a resident spinner, and in the 'core' area mentioned above most households engaged in spinning as a spare-time occupation. Although paid significantly less than male adults, this work by women (and probably children) was a critical means of survival for the poor and a useful supplement for better-off families.

The yarn was collected by the clothiers and put out again to weavers to make up into cloth. Weavers were apprenticed men who normally worked full-time, though many had farms and smallholdings as well. Few weavers wove their cloth for sale. They used a broadloom which needed two persons to work it. They might have produced two yards of broadloom a day, so a single broad cloth would have taken them a fortnight to make. Zell found that of 104 weavers he was examining, 64 engaged in some agricultural activity. A total of some 1,300 weavers might have been employed in the 16th century.

WITH POSSESSION.

BUXTED, SUSSEX

About ½ mile from the Hamlet of High Hurst Wood, 2½ miles from Buxted Station, 4 from Uckfield and about 12 from Lewes and Tunbridge Wells.

PARTICULARS, PLAN & CONDITIONS OF SALE

. . OF A VALUABLE . .

Freehold Property,

KNOWN AS

UPPER NORDENS GREEN FARM,

COMPRISING A WELL-BUILT

MODERN COTTAGE RESIDENCE,

CONTAINING

Four Bedrooms, Box Room, Two Sitting Rooms, Kitchen, Larder, Dairy, &c , Good Garden, with Well of good Water, Fowl House, Meal Room, E. Closet.

CAPITAL FARM BUILDINGS,

ALL IN EXCELLENT ORDER, INCLUDING

Cow Stall for Ten Cows, Stabling for Three Horses, Feeding Room, Calving Box, Large Granary, Cart Shed, Piggeries, &c.

AND

28 a. 0 r. 22 p.

OF

PASTURE, ARABLE & WOODLAND,

The whole sloping to the South and possessing beautiful views over a lovely country.

WHICH WILL BE OFFERED FOR SALE BY AUCTION, BY

MR. WALTER F. INGRAM

AT THE

MAIDEN'S HEAD HOTEL, UCKFIELD,

On THURSDAY, the 28th day of SEPT., 1905,

AT THREE P.M. PRECISELY, IN TWO LOTS.

Particulars, Plan and Conditions of Sale may be obtained of Messrs. ATTREE, JOHNSON & WARD, 6, Raymond Buildings, Gray's Inn, London, W.C.; at the MAIDEN'S HEAD, Uckfield; of Mr. LEPPARD, Upper Nordens Green Farm, Buxted, who will show the Property; or of the AUCTIONEER, 2, St. Andrew's Place, Lewes.

FARNCOMBE AND CO., LIMITED, PRINTERS, LEWES.

87 Sale Particulars of a small farm at High Hurstwood. This tranquil and remote place retains to this day something of the character of the small farms assarted out of the woodland in the late 13th or early 14th centuries.

Fulling, the next process, was done at a fulling mill. There the cloth was scoured with fuller's earth, and thickened and steeped in a vat of urine, the hammers which battered the cloth being worked by water-powered mill wheels. Shearmen, who were paid piece rates, then raised the nap of the cloth by passing across teazels, mounted on a frame, after which a smooth surface was created by clipping rough wool and fluff with a large and heavy pair of shears.

It is evident from the Subsidy Rolls of the 1520s that some clothiers were wealthier than local landowning gentry. As Zell has remarked '… The wealthy clothier was the dominant economic force; on his good will – and financial resources – the well-being of thousands rested'. It appears that, initially, clothiers were landowners or substantial farmers who were able to afford the capital required to maintain a clothmaking business. They tended to enlarge their inherited estates out of the profits of clothmaking, and one, at least, John Roberts of Boarzell in Ticehurst, moved into the ranks of the gentry (pp.173-4). Although there were dozens of small master-clothiers, a small elite came to dominate the industry such as Stephen Draner of Cranbrook, the earliest example, whose assessment of £300 in goods was the highest in the Weald in 1524/5, and Stephen Sharpe and Alexander Dence, also of Cranbrook, active in the mid-16th century. Probably the wealthiest clothier when he died in 1567 was Peter Couthop, who owned 240 acres of land in Cranbrook and Biddenden and gross personal wealth of almost £1,800. The probate inventory of John Mayne, who died in 1566, reveals him to have been a remarkably wealthy man styled 'Esq', living in conditions of luxury in Biddenden. His house consisted of 20 rooms, and he had another house on property in High Halden and a London house in Holborn. His ready money alone was valued at £634 10s. He was rich in plate and his apparel included sumptuous satin gowns; his walls were hung with tapestries; he had a private chapel and a gallery, which must have been a showpiece for his armoury, some pictures, a mirror and a pair of virginals. In two chests bound with iron he kept his velvet shoes and the altar cloth and vestments. Thirty-three yards of broadcloth lay in the cellar. He farmed a little at Biddenden, doubtless for home consumption, and kept livestock at High Halden, and his wood and dyestuffs. Here he also bred horses and provided sanctuary for them in their old age.[7]

As previously noted, the Wealden broadcloth industry underwent a lingering decline from the 1620s. The reality of this was reflected in a petition from Benenden in 1673 – once the heart of the broadcloth region – which complained of the 'great and general poverty in respect of the trade of clothmaking' within the parish and in the report of the vicar of Biddenden in 1685 that the parish was 'not so populous now as formerly when the clothing trade there flourished'.

The demise of the Kentish broadcloth industry was due to various causes. The loss of continental markets during the Thirty Years War and increased production of woollens in central Europe were major factors. Also, competition for labour from the expanding dockyards and from fruit- and hop-growing in mid-Kent may have played a part. The most powerful explanation is thought to be connected with trends in clothmaking elsewhere in England during the 17th century. In

88 Maypole Farmhouse, High Hurstwood.

almost every major region, except the Weald, clothiers responded to overseas competition and declining domestic markets for broadcloth by modifying the commodities they produced in favour of the 'New Draperies', cheaper light worsted materials. This industry sprang up in towns such as Maidstone, Canterbury and Sandwich. The clothmakers failed because they did not diversify. As their industry declined some simply turned to commercial farming, while others leased out their lands to local farmers.

17

Iron-makers:
Woodland Exploiters or Conservers?

Now whether it [the iron industry] be as gainful and profitable to the commonwealth may be doubted; but the age ensuing will be better able to tell you.

Camden, 1586.

These iron times breed none that mind posterity.

Drayton, Poly-Olbion, 1612 (The Song of Sussex, xvii)

SHORTLY after his accession in 1660, Charles II was concerned that the devastation of England's forests and woods might jeopardise his ambitious warship-
building programme. He directed enquiries to the newly founded Royal Society
which deputed John Evelyn to respond under its patronage. This took the form
in 1664 of his famed *Sylva: or a Discourse of Forest Trees*, which passed through five
editions during the author's lifetime, and was republished in 1776 with five
impressions, the last in 1825. Evelyn extolled the place of woods in England's rise
to greatness and prosperity and sounded a trumpet call of alarm to the nation
about their contemporary condition. His book was a *tour de force* and a work of
love. The writer's soul was in his subject, and readers caught so much of his
enthusiasm for planting, that Evelyn boasted in the 1679 edition that millions of
trees had been planted 'at the instigation and by the sole direction' of his book.[1]

Evelyn's standpoint was that his and the previous generation had been
destroyers of woods without a thought for the future. He did not pull his
punches. He berated iron-works unsparingly (but stopped short of doing the
same to ironmasters, too). He regarded the devastation of trees as so evident that
he gave a single regional example, 'the prodigious waste which voracious iron and
glass-works have made in the Sussex Weald'.

The popular notion of Wealden history has always accepted that deforestation
to stoke the furnaces and forges actually occurred. The first historian of the iron
industry, M.A. Lower, came to this conclusion and W. Topley accepted it in his
Geology of the Weald (1875). Both attributed the industry's extinction largely to
exhaustion of fuel supplies.[2] Yet Defoe, writing in the early 18th century, regarded
Hampshire, Sussex and Kent as 'an inexhaustible storehouse of timber never to
be destroyed …', and in 1677 Andrew Yarranton affirmed that ironworks, so far
from destroying woods, had actually been a cause of their increase, notwithstanding the contrary opinion of a royal commission in 1548, an enquiry in 1574,
and sundry subsequent protective legislation.

In the face of these contrary opinions are ironmasters to be convicted as primary offenders, or accessories after the fact? Or exonerated, not to say congratulated for foresight? In reality, both destructive and constructive effects of the iron industry can be perceived. Seemingly conflicting accounts can be largely reconciled by distinguishing between earlier, i.e. to about 1570-80, and later phases of iron-making. We must also bring under the spotlight the monastic lands coming onto the market, whose new owners were looking to maximise the return on their purchases or grants, particularly of the most valuable assets, the woodlands. It is also important to contrast the effect of these events on grazed woods legally subject to various common rights, such as the right to mast (pannage) fallen wood for fuel (estovers) on the one hand, and privately-owned woodlands on the other, which could be fenced from browsing animals, so allowing rapid tree regeneration.

To take the latter case first, woodland is not a finite resource. A woodland cannot be destroyed by clear-felling its trees. Provided the stumps of oak or other species in the cut-over area were left with one shoot (known as a 'staddle'), and were fenced off from grazing animals (impracticable on commonlands), spontaneous regeneration would have occurred. By sparing the staddles, trees would have produced coppice within 20 years to provide more fuel wood for stoking the furnaces and forges. Continual careful management of the wood thereafter, including perhaps the replacement of exhausted stools, would have created high-yielding coppice fuel supply for ironworks indefinitely on a regular rotation.[3] This conservation of resources must have generally occurred in the Weald, beginning from the end of the 16th century, because a number of its charcoal blast furnaces and forges remained in use for a century or more, indicating sustained management of fuel resources rather than irreversible destruction. This emphasis on coppicing for industrial purposes does, however, appear to have curtailed the growth of standards for shipbuilding, Evelyn's prime concern.[4]

On commons the lord of the manor owned the trees and underwood, which could now be sold at high prices for ready money. The exercise of the customary common rights of pasturage and taking of wood as fuel, and so on, would have effectively either impeded or precluded the natural regeneration of trees on commonlands after 'once-for-all' felling because, once cut, the young regrowth of many species is very susceptible to browsing and therefore tree growth could be eliminated.[5] Such action, altering so entirely the character of a place which had remained relatively unchanged for hundreds of years, often became a highly emotive issue in the Weald where commonlands were invariably 'wood-pastures', i.e. relatively densely covered with trees. It brought commoners defending their rights to pannage and estover into conflict with suppliers to ironworks whose activities could result in irreversible changes in the rural economy and ecology, and invariably cause hardship to the rural community. An expedient adopted to overcome the problem of regenerating wood on commonlands was to enclose all or parts of them, which itself was deleterious to the poor and small farmers.

Wealden blast furnaces came rapidly into use in the first half of the 16th century and concern at fuel shortages along the south coast and in the London

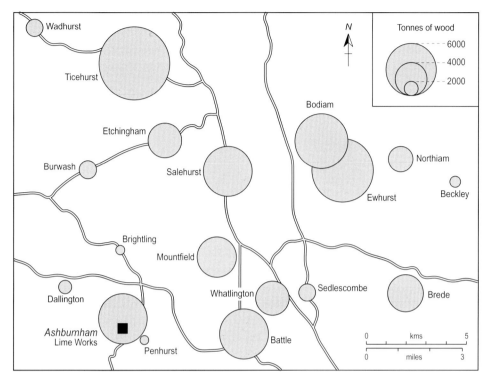

89 *Wood fuel supplied to the Ashburnham ironworks. The Ashburnham Furnace was supplied from the same sources. (Source: Ashburnham MSS, ESRO)*

area provoked a public outcry which led, in 1548, to a commission of enquiry. This reported that each of the fifty or so ironworks in East Sussex consumed, on average, annually 1,500 loads of 'great wood'. The presentments to the Commission indicate that the main source of fuel was at that time once-and-for-all clear-felling.[6] It is relevant to note that the Act of 35 Hen VIII, the earliest attempt to protect woodland, whilst exempting privately-owned woodlands in the Weald, was applied to 'common' woodlands. The Weald was similarly exempted from the Act of 1558-9 which prohibited the felling of 'great trees' for iron making.[7] The Act of 1581 similarly exempted the Weald generally, though protecting timber near ports, the Downs and within 22 miles of London except for the ironworks of Christopher Darell at Newdigate, Surrey, who was carefully coppicing his woods. The first legislation to affect the entire Weald was in 1585. Entitled 'An Act for the preservation of timber in the wilds of the counties of Sussex, Surrey and Kent …', it prohibited the erection of new ironworks, except upon old sites, or where 'the owner can supply fuel from his own woods'. No one was allowed to fell timber more than one foot square at the stub but the treetops could be used as fuel. This was rather like shutting the stable door after the horse had bolted.

What of the ironmasters' defence? This is very strong but is not irreconcilable with the exploitative case considered below. The transition from an exploitative strategy to coppice management is evident in the case of the Sidney ironworks at Pallingridge in Dallington established in 1541-2. Sir William Sidney's first step was to lease woodlands for 19 years from Sir John Baker. All oaks and the bark and tannin, together with 160 of the best beeches, were reserved to Sir John. Sidney was required to use the top and lop off 60 oaks to make the necessary fencing to protect the 'spring' (i.e. the shoots from the base of the felled trees) from cattle. He also undertook to fill in pits dug for iron ore before new ones were made. The length of the lease was evidently determined to provide coppice available for cutting from the end of the period.[8]

The same development is traceable in Sidney's accounts for the Robertsbridge ironworks established about the same time. For a while the large reserves of old woodland would have supplied fuel. This is suggested by entries in the ironworks account mentioning various sources of wood, including coppice and 'great wood', but not the regular cutting of named parcels of coppice which would indicate a substantial acreage of woodland under sustained management.[9] In c.1570 some exploitation was still occurring for, amongst woodland 'appointed to the iron forge', were 'great oaks and beech' standing in hedgerows and woods on local copyholds. Possingworth, one of the demesne woodlands, is described as 'wasted' but it had been divided into parcels and cutting was to begin between 1585-89, suggesting that growth from tree stumps was anticipated. The other demesne woodlands were brought under a 20-year rotation of cutting; this relatively slow growth suggests an early stage of coppicing before even-aged blocks and trees and other refinements had been introduced. It was estimated that the combined forge and furnace could make 140 tonnes of iron annually 'for ever', with sustained management of 1,100 acres of woodland cut at the rate of 55 acres per year on the 20-year rotation. Coppice management was thus probably being operated in woodlands where little attention had been previously paid to it. Leases of Robertsbridge Abbey forge and furnace in the 17th century indicate that they were then entirely operated by means of underwoods which had been

90 A petition to Lord Cobham, the Lord Lieutenant of Kent, 1595, urging that the furnace of the Queen's gunfounder, Thomas Johnson, at Horsmonden should not be threatened with damage by Cranbrook clothworkers and others. At a time of corn shortage and scarcity of wood fuel, numerous weavers were reported to be conspiring to destroy ironworks in the vicinity of Cranbrook, including Horsmonden and Barden furnaces. Horsmonden had easy access to the Medway for the carriage of guns. (CKS TR 1538)

successfully brought under a 14-year rotation.[10] About a decade after Sir William Sidney, Sir John Pelham was also about to adopt coppicing to supply his iron-works after exhausting other sources since his will provided that his wife '… shall not take or employ any of my great woods [for iron smelting] … as hath not been cut down heretofore within this forty years last past … that the places where the woods stand to be incopsed, for the preservation of the spring of the wood for the better continuance of the wood there'. On the Ashburnham estate more than 50 coppices were cut on a 20-year rotation, supplying the Ashburnham forge and furnace in the 17th century. Presumably due to better forestry management, yields were substantially higher in the 1690s than in the 1670s.[11] This practice evidently became general in the Weald and higher standards of management were increasingly adopted, making it possible to operate ironworks indefinitely on given sites. Such sustained management was an important source of income to landowners.[12]

What of the case for the prosecution? A frenzy of destruction in the 16th century with pernicious consequences fell upon the forests. Ralph Hogge's iron-works on the southern fringes of Ashdown Forest, producing cannon and shot for Tudor navies and for sale abroad, were not using coppice wood, but 'top' wood and 'log' wood from the Forest and from Etchingwood, a common in Framfield. Other ironmasters were simultaneously clearing timber from the Forest with striking speed and scale of degradation. 'Waste and spoil' was reported on many occasions, as in 1558 when 2,000 beeches, 100 oaks and several thousand birch had been recently felled. By 1632 great timber in the neigh-bourhood of Ashdown was scarce. By 1658 none at all was to be found and the Forest was the least valued of all the Crown Forests.[13]

The small amount of wood in Ashdown in the late 16th century probably accounts for the Crown's interest in iron-making in St Leonard's Forest after 1563. Again, trees were cut down wholesale to feed six furnaces and it was rapidly reduced to a 'vast unfrequented place, heathie, vaultie, of unwholesome shades and overgrown hollows', where locals reported large serpents roaming freely. Nor did Waterdown Forest fare any better. Tenants objected to paying customary swine rents for pannage on the grounds that the old oak and beech woods, pre-viously bearing mast, had been used prior to 1575 by Lord Bergavenny for his five local iron-works.[14] Worth Forest was similarly devastated.

It was not only the forests that suffered in this way. Common woods were given no mercy. In addition to buying all hedgerow and copyhold woods he could from the 196 tenants of Framfield manor for ironworks, Lord Buckhurst cracked down c.1570 on takers of 'customary wood' from the commons and sought out those who sold it illicitly or falsely underestimated the amounts they took. He was also concerned at the damage to woodlands caused by tenants who haphazardly picked out trees for 'custom wood'. A survey of the common woodlands was ordered with a view to enclosures, preparatory to supplying with fuel some of the six furnaces and five forges in the vicinity.[15] That the common woods lost their tree cover is implied by the changing during the 17th century of the common's ancient wood names: Pounsley Wood became Pounsley Common;

Langhurst Wood, Blackboys Common; West Wood became Palehouse Common; Martin's Wood, Highlands Common; Etchingwood, Etching Common. The 1623 custumal of the manor significantly refers to pannage rights 'if trees shall be there'.

The same havoc was wrought on the commons of Wadhurst, where ironworks were also particularly numerous. One incident is well documented. Alexander Collins was reported to have felled most of the oaks on Coursley Common, Wadhurst in 1548. Crossley defends this action on the grounds that an experienced ironmaster, such as Collins, would have re-established the wood as coppice; but tree regeneration would have been greatly hampered, if not completely foiled, by the exercise of common rights.[16] It is noteworthy that in the specimens of charcoal from Tudor and Stuart ironworks sites discussed by Straker – birch, beech, oak and poplar took precedence over hazel and hornbeam, the preferred coppiced species, and include that made from large timber.[17]

The ironworks also destroyed outright woodland at other places. Norden's list of devastated woods included Burningfold, 'Lopwood Green', 'the Minns' (the Menn's common in Wisborough Green), Kirdford, Petworth Park, Ebernoe

91 This tool was used traditionally by cottagers to cut turf where woodland had been devastated by water-powered industry. The operator threw the whole weight of his body against the heavy cross-handle.

Wassals, Rusper, Balcombe, the Dicker and *other places infinite* (author's italics).[18] These places appear to have been mainly wood commons, mostly in West Sussex. Other sources for East Sussex also reported devastation: in Clarige Forest in Waldron, the Broyle, Hayley Park in Westmeston, and Homewood in Chailey, mainly properties which fell into lay hands with the Dissolution of the Monasteries. Part of Pounsley Wood and Broadreed Wood were enclosed for the preservation of wood about 1600.[19] The commons belonging to the manor of Mayfield and Wadhurst were enclosed between 1600 and 1660.[20]

The fullest information about woodland management concerns the Wotton estate near Dorking, Evelyn's birthplace and his inheritance late in life, which supported various industrial enterprises requiring wood fuel. Distinct phases can be identified. The first phase was marked by the frenzied cutting of extensive common woodlands. In the second phase, from c.1580, considerable areas of the stripped commons were enclosed with a view to increasing by encoppicing the rapidly depleted wood store. One such large enclosure eventually became the main source of fuel for Abinger forge. Another successful venture was the creation of seven new smallholdings on grubbed up ground (a sign of the growing need of industrial workers). A further enterprise was a model project of 1597 with the dual purpose of securing a regular supply of fuel and enhanced agricultural rents by a lease of 60 acres of cleared woodland, on which shaws were created round the new fields by the simple provision that the lessee was not to grub up wood or bushes standing or growing upon any of the ditches, banks or hedges, 'as are with three score feet of assize from any such ditch or hedge'.

Although by 1640 a steady crop of coppice timber had been contrived for the various local mills, the over-use of the dwindling woodland on unenclosed parts of the commonlands mainly for industrial purposes continued. This put increasing pressure on supplies of domestic fire-wood traditionally drawn from the commons by the poorer classes. Exploitative processes in combination discouraged tree regeneration to the extent that much once-open woodland degenerated to typical heathland flora. In this stage of woodland management, the virtual destruction of principal sources of domestic fuel in parts of the commons within convenient distance from settlements left some districts without accessible supplies. They sundered traditions and obliged the poor, in conditions of some hardship, to seek alternative domestic fuels, even in such districts as the Tillingbourne valley where woodlands had for centuries been a part of people's lives, thoughts and sentiments. Alternative wood-fuel could only be derived from the products of heath-peat, turves, heather and bracken – which had tended to

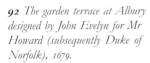

92 The garden terrace at Albury designed by John Evelyn for Mr Howard (subsequently Duke of Norfolk), 1679.

replace woodland on poorer soils. Additionally, new industries using large quantities of firewood as the primary fuel, such as lime-burning and brick-making, had also to find alternatives to wood. This fuel-cutting pressure was the final contributory factor to the further progressive degradation of the environment with irreversible ecological consequences. The shortage of wood fuel in west Surrey is corroborated by Emanuel Bowen's elaborate cartouche on his map of Surrey (1749) which includes, among other symbolic portraits of local activities, a peat-digger stacking peats to dry on an open moor, with the statement that for the inhabitants of Surrey 'the fuel for firing was formerly mostly wood, but that being now almost destroyed, they burn peat, turf and cole'. In short, a devastated terrain in west Surrey was the consequence of environmental changes brought about by man for industrial purposes.[21]

To return to the Weald in general, a significant consequence of woodland clearances on commonlands was the cessation of pannage. John Norden wrote

93 *The* bason *at Albury fed by the Silent Pool spring, an ingenious achievement of John Evelyn, drawing upon his family's experience in water technology and his own researches in Italy. The grotto on the right is modelled on the Grotto of Posilipo at Naples.*

that one need not enquire of pannage 'for oaks and beech that have been formerly very fair in many parts of the kingdom for feeding … are fallen to the ground'. This is amply corroborated. Pannage receipts for the manors of Framfield and Mayfield and Wadhurst, the Broyle, and on the Dicker and in Ashdown Forest, invariably show a marked decline in the later 16th century, and during the 17th century the custom died out altogether after hundreds of years.[22] Pannage in the Broyle, still valuable in 1506, was apparently not worth mentioning in 1603. After 1560 there is no mention of pannage in the court books of Alciston manor, which formerly enjoyed pannage in the common woods of Starnash, Lignash and Abbots Wood, and none in the records of Laughton after the early 17th century or of Ashdown Forest after 1600. The resort to alternative sources of fuel by wood-starved rustics was more general than formerly supposed. For example, the devastation of the Menn's Wood, previously mentioned, obliged tenants of Amberley manor to dig peat on the Amberley Wild Brooks, and peat was also dug in the Adur valley near Steyning, where wood was scarce. Turves had to be cut at Thakeham in default of wood fuel in the mid-17th century.[23]

We can now reach some conclusion. Defoe and Yarranton were correct in their refutation of mismanagement on privately-owned woodlands. But coppice did not produce shipbuilding timber nor mast for pigs. It also considerably raised fuel prices, being subject to competition from the cloth trade and other users. Hammersley reckoned that fuel comprised between 58 and 75 per cent of the total iron production costs in the last stage of the Wealden iron industry, which must have had an important bearing on its decline.[24] Was it shame that accounts for contemporaries' silence on the exploitative strategy on the commonlands which eroded traditional patterns of life and has left scars on heathland which have never healed?

18

The Farmer and Labourer 1700-1815

BECAUSE of the nature of its rural community and somewhat isolated location, the Weald was not well organised for innovation. Numerous farmers were only part-time, having supplementary businesses for attention. Then because the full-time farmer held his own plough and performed all the manual work himself with his wife and a little extra labour, he did not have time to think, read, to meet with his neighbours or to ride through the region or outside it, to see and get information about better farming practices. Even going to market or a fair was not frequent because he had little to sell. Arthur Young noted that nothing retarded agriculture so much as one farmer not knowing what another was doing at a distance from him.[1] These circumstances exacerbated the wealdsmen's inborn aversion to everything that was new, even if it was good. Moreover, the effect of one-year leases was pernicious. From the point of view of innovation, it had the effect of tying

94 Arthur Young, the sternest, but not the wisest, critic of Wealden husbandry.

a man's hand behind his back and the tenant was under the strongest temptation to wear out the land. Young pondered on what was the greater evil, a badly-managed large farm, or a cluster of small ones, and concluded that the most baleful was the latter, there being 'a greater number of hands and heads at work to spoil the land … here is not so much idleness that is to be dreaded as mischief'.

Agricultural innovators were generally outsiders with capital. One of the most outstanding in the 18th century was William Poole of Hooke at Chailey in Sussex. After purchasing the farm in 1732, he systematically built up an estate of some 600 acres, largely in the Low Weald. With paid offices supporting him in a gentlemanly way of life, initially in the Pelham interest, agriculture became the frame of his way of life. Yet he was not too proud to put his four coach horses to the plough during the week and in the coach on Sunday. He apparently devoted much time to direct farming of his estate. From the outset he kept meticulous farm accounts and between 1763 and his death in 1779 maintained a farming diary which recorded on a daily basis his agricultural activities in minute detail and particulars of the weather. This reveals him as an assiduous cultivator of his mediocre soil and a champion of innovation in agricultural rotations and equipment.[2] Although he played his part in local affairs, he does not appear to have been a leading figure of any group attempting to promote the improvement of the Low Weald, as Lord Sheffield was to become a generation later. This is doubtless because when he took over his farm the 'new' farming had not reached the heavy clays and his pioneering work as a private individual at the beginning of the Agrarian Revolution was left to be publicised by Arthur Young.

Poole began farming in Chailey in the customary Sussex manner on strong clay lands, but progressively the old system was abandoned in favour of new techniques. His Cheshire origin would have accustomed him to heavy soil. Poole was using horses for ploughing from the outset, though oxen were retained for carting. He superseded sowing 'at random' by drilling in 1750. He introduced heavy rollers for use on wet land. Turnips prepared the land for wheat occasionally. He noted that the narrow chisel point of the standard

95 *William Cobbett, defender extraordinary of the small man and a fearless antagonist of injustice.*

turnwrest plough was very deficient in cutting weeds, and improved it. He experimented with manures on a scientific basis. He used a trenching plough for hollow draining. In the deep trench cut by the plough a small spit was dug with the spade, leaving a shoulder on either side on which was put blackthorn with other stumpy bushes on the top of which pea haulm was placed (see p.117).

Apart from these innovations, his husbandry on the cold, wet clay was traditional. For wheat he would turn land up in early spring for a summer fallow and give it two more ploughings before sowing in the autumn after an application of lime from Plumpton. Beat-burning (devonshiring) was used to convert worn out pastures to arable. Clover seed (cow grass) was sown, and when ploughed up dung, mud and compost was carted on to it. Two ploughings were sufficient for barley and one for peas and beans. Picking up stones made it easier to harrow and reduced damage to the plough. Spring ploughing began late, presumably on account of the coldness of the soil. In 1732 he began ploughing for barley on Poor Field until March, and was making final sowings on 10 April. Regular winter work included scouring the river, pond-scouring, cleaning of water-furrows, ditching, draining, guttering and hedge-laying. April was hop-planting time and for dressing meadows with soap ashes. Poole's woods provided work for nine men in winter and the value of fuel for poles, stakes and faggots for domestic use and for kilns is implied by the regular grubbing-up of wood and scrub which had encroached as unruly hedges or shaws on the sides of his fields. A notable feature of his farming is the immense care taken of every particle of manure. The scouring of a pond would produce 'full 300 loads of mud and marl'. Parts of a meadow which had not been treated the previous year with soap ashes was covered over with 30 loads to an acre of mould, dung and lime. Other fields were 'mended' with peat and ashes from the 'amonet hills on ye common'. When he changed oat seed it came from Devon by sea. A significant feature of his husbandry was his use of the commons for grazing of oxen and sheep in rainy weather so as to avoid poaching his heavy land. This was doubtless also a custom of other local farmers, and may explain the survival of the Chailey commons to this day.

Poole's weather observations provide vivid evidence of the unpredictability of weather and the hazards of farming on heavy clay:

> 1-14 January. 1767. Deep snow and severe weather. Very little outdoor work done. Poor labourers greatly distressed by high prices of corn and provisions.

> 1767. This year very wet, especially summer. Wheat yielded very badly. … Never known land dirtier nor roads worse.

> 16/22 December, 1771. Rain in the last quarter of the last year (1770) has been the worst remembered by the oldest people and the worst season ever for sowing winter corn and for carting and getting out manure. In general scarcely half the wheat season completed.

> 1772. January 20. Poor people can do little work. Sheep confined to the common because of wet fields.

> June 1772. A fine season after a great deal of work

> Oct 1773. Fallows so wet that they cannot be sown (as in 1774). Obliged to leave fallows for spring crops or turnips next year. Lime would be in a slop before we can spread it. Working horses to the common. November. Fallows will not bear a man's weight. All in a sea and puddle. Floods. No attempt at plowing.

> October 17. 1774. Glorious week of weather for the husbandman, particularly for the Wilds of Sussex, both for getting in winter corn in the ground and carting of the after grass.

> 24 November, 1774. No fallows sown with wheat as so wet. A very wet and troublesome season for all sorts of labour ever since the autumn. Little wheat sowing on fallows. Could not land up because of slub, and for fear of burning up my horses, terribly bad for sheep. (1773).

> January 18, 1775. Mild weather, primroses appearing in woods. March very cold, mostly dry, frosts. Ground as dry as in summer, fallows so hard as to prevent sowing till some rain came.

> January 1-21. 1776. Deepest snow remembered by people here. Roads bestrewn with carts broken and overturned. Turnpike managers employed many hands to clear a passage through the hollows. The carrier's wagon with great difficulty and

danger got into Lewes with twelve horses. Turnips sent to the Parsonage to provide soup for the poor.

March 1776 very wet. No frosts to mellow land, soil too wet to plow and harrow, hard on top, and wet at bottom. Ground so wet that horses harrowing the seed would have sunk their footsteps so deep a light sweep of bushes was drawn over it by two men.

April 1776 fallows excessive hard, one might harrow among bricks, monstrous hardclods.

September 1776 (16/26) Last week very wet. Difficult harvest, continuous rain, storms, and floods. Men and horses up to their knees in such a slub.

General Murray was another outstandingly successful innovator with over 1,600 acres of cultivated land, including 500 on Romney Marsh. He housed Arthur Young for five days in 1789 at Beauport near Hastings and, confined for 30 hours by a snowstorm, Young spent the time poring over the General's accounts of his whole enterprise. It transpired that the General had thrown down hedges, lain several of his small fields into larger closes and abolished summer fallows by introducing fallow crops such as potatoes (for foddering his flock of 4,000 sheep), turnips (drilled and horse-hoed), and tares; fattened Welsh bullocks on his marsh; pared and burnt on a large scale; grubbed up woods; and spread 12,000 bushels of lime. His wheat yielded four quarters of an acre. He earned himself £7,311 in a year on an outlay of £1,744. This was largely due to the prodigious fertility of Romney Marsh which, in summer, supported six sheep to an acre.

96 A derelict limekiln below Duncton Hill, supplying lime to the Wealden portion of Lord Egremont's estate before the construction of canals.

97 Lord Sheffield's model farm at Sheffield Park. Lord Sheffield was a President of the Board of Agriculture and his re-organised home farm was intended to influence similar developments elsewhere.

Major-General Beatson has undeservedly been neglected by the agricultural historian. He employed his retirement in farming at Knowle Farm, Mayfield. He made many different farming experiments on the effects on crops of varying manures and cultivation techniques (he listed 128 different combinations in all) on almost all his fields. He may have been one of the first 'scientific' farmers in the South East, if not in England, fulfilling an ideal which had been for so long the frustrated plea of Arthur Young.[3]

In 1820 he published details of his experiments in *A New System of Cultivation*. This appeared at a time of sharply falling agricultural prices and Beatson realised that the future of wealden agriculture depended on cheapening production. As a newcomer, he was struck by the adherence of local farmers to practices which he perceived to be ruinous, and should have long since been abolished. By the medium of experiment he aimed to devise a farm system for the Weald which would incur the smallest possible expenditure on fertiliser, animal exertion and farm management in general. To avoid expensive liming to which farmers were becoming addicted, he calcined marl dug on the farm. He also abolished another expensive and traditional feature, the summer fallow, with a rotation of: (1) tares, beans and peas; (2) wheat; (3) oats or barley; (4) clover and ray grass. He also advocated methods of cultivation which obviated the exceptional amount of ploughing and stirring undertaken by local farmers. He costed the cultivation of an acre of wheat by the old husbandry at more than three-fold his inexpensive new system. Beatson's book shows that he was a man of great vision, sound judgement and strong character – and a pioneer in several directions, but, alas, he was no new Columella. Beatson was aware that the success of his system depended on landowners modifying covenants in leases in favour of it, instead of specifying fallows and lime. Through inertia this did not happen and local farmers were, in general, wholly unwilling to try new methods. Beatson was thus far in advance of his times with his inexpensive cultivation. Indeed, 'the times' have still not caught up with a good many of his ideas.

The mainstay of the small farmer was the sale of beef cattle fattened for market. From Hickstead Place, in the Sussex Low Weald, James Wood sent cattle, sheep and lambs several times a year to Smithfield in the mid-18th century. Their number, up to 30 cattle and sheep at a time, were such that the driver, Henry Woolven, could easily manage them on his own with the help of his dog. The drove probably spent several days travelling, and on the way would have been pastured nightly on commons away from tolled roads. The animals would have been fatigued on arrival at the market; the cattle were 'no longer the proud animals who bounded and frisked about coming out of the barn, struck with their horns everything they met, made the ground fly into the air with their feet, and seemed to threaten all the villagers'.[4] Londoners considered that their tiredness made for tastier meat.[5]

The traditional Red Sussex breed were being replaced with lean Welsh runts, which were more adaptable. Cobbett stressed how invaluable they had become to the Wealden farmer and recalled having seen

> hundreds of thousands. They now go over Normandy Common [near Farnham] in droves of a thousand, or more, in a drove, on their way to the fairs in Kent and Sussex, where they are great favourites; and, if kept to a proper age, they make fine oxen and very good milch cows, whole dairies of which are to be seen in those counties and in the weald of Surrey … As they increase in age they move on towards England, and towards the food which is not to be had at their homes; and thus they come off at last, two, three, or four years old, to work, to be fatted, or give milk, and fat calves, in the south of England, where they cannot be raised with profit. Hence the herds of fine oxen, with which I have seen the rich marshes in Kent and Sussex covered over; and hence the fine teams of oxen, which plough and harrow and roll no small part of the lands at the foot of the South Downs. If one of those careful and laborious and frugal Welsh women who raise these cattle, could see one of her diminutive calves become a fat ox in Pevensey Level; or if she could see six or eight of them in the wealds, drawing a timber-carriage with ten tons weight upon it, what would be her surprise![6]

The Welsh not only supplied young beasts, for Peter Kalm reported that from the hay-making season, large numbers of them, mainly women and girls, came into Kent to work for wages. After haying they would work in the cornfields, then they became casual labourers in the hop gardens and gathered the various kinds of beautiful Kentish fruit. They ended by re-making hop grounds.

Kalm also describes some aspects of everyday life on farms in the mid-18th century. The shoes which the labouring man commonly used were strongly armed with iron. Under the heel was set an iron plate following the shape of the heel, and somewhat resembled a horseshoe. Round about the soles were nails knocked in quite close and it was also knocked full of nails under the middle of the sole,

98 Finchcocks, Goudhurst, looking towards Spelmonden. (John Malton, May 2002, pen and ink, 20 x 12cm [8 x 4¾ in.]). Until recently this was one of the largest hop-farms. The outbuildings are now used as workshops and warehouses and the oasts are being converted to other uses.

so that it was a long time before shoes wore out. They commonly also wore gaiters strapped on the outside of the leg. (The smock-frock was the traditional garb of the small farmer and labourer.) Women wore pattens under their shoes when they went out so that dirt did not spoil them. They also always wore a straw hat, made by themselves from wheat-straw. Kalm was startled to find that the farmer's wife and daughters had hardly any outdoor duties (he was probably referring to life on a yeoman's farm) and that they did little bread baking, because there was a baker in every parish, nor did they do much brewing beer which also was bought in. Weaving and spinning had also become obsolete because manufactured goods were available in shops. It was all so different in Sweden where women milked cows and worked in the arable and meadows, as well as being busy with evening occupations. The English ways do not seem to have had his approval but he gave the credit to English country women for being very handsome and lively in society.[7]

Another discerning observer in the next generation was Arthur Young, who, uncharacteristically for one who heaped censure after censure on its farmers, compared life in the Weald very favourably with the outside world, and attributed much of this credit to the cottager and small farmer. In 1771 he was thrilled to find between Rye and Hawkhurst remarkably neat, well-built, clean, snug cottages, with well kept little gardens and tidy hedges ('even the pigsties tiled') and all filled with the happiest people imaginable. He was touched to wish that all industrious Britons could live so, perhaps thinking of the wretches suffering from enclosures and the Industrial Revolution. Very unfashionably he added, 'A country so

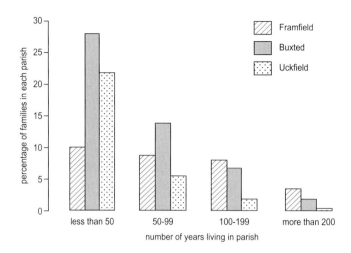

99 *Mobility of population, Framfield, Buxted and Uckfield, 1550-1750. (After A.J. Winser)*

decorated is beautiful indeed, and more entertaining to travel through, than if splendid temples and proud turrets arose on every hill'. Young's picture may be thought too idyllic to be true, yet it is corroborated in many ways by William Cobbett in the 1820s, who similarly thought of the small man as the essence of the Weald (pp.188-9).[8]

On most farms, building was done in a manner which now would be called leisurely, but it was done well. John Stapley recorded with pride and satisfaction in his journal every stage in the erection of his new 40ft. by 20ft. barn at Hickstead. In March 1746 he bought 16 standing trees on Widow Martin's Pucknowle Farm nearby and received permission to make two saw-pits. Credit was given until midsummer the following year, when Stapley proposed to erect his barn, and it was arranged that the felling and removal of the trees could be deferred up to Michaelmas should 'the road be not good'. In fact, Stapley's men, Thomas Reeve and Richard Burtenshaw, were able to fell, flaw, and saw the trees and get them to the site in April 1747, some six months after felling, by which time they were in the best condition to cut. By early May the roads were good enough to bring in stone for the foundations. Towards the end of the month the two men spent five days framing the barn and Stapley went to Lewes specially for nails. The frame was then raised by the same pair with the assistance of Henry Fowler. Thirty days' work by the two men was needed to finish the structure which was thatched by Henry Morley.[9]

19

The Later Gentry

As we have seen, a notable feature of the Weald was its concentration of gentry families. The Commissioners for the maintenance of the rich grazing grounds of the Pevensey Levels, sworn in 1801, comprised 17 members of the nobility, four baronets, a knight, four esquires, eight clerks in Holy Orders, 66 gentlemen and five town mayors.[1] The origin of many of the estates owned by these persons is to be found in the numerous little medieval lordships on the uplands, the most famous being those of the Etchinghams or Etchingham, and doubtless lies in an episode after the Conquest determined by military considerations. The Count of Eu, the holder of Hastings Rape, deliberately established small knightly manors for the defence of Hastings Castle. The manorial lords performed 'castleward' for a month at a time, each being responsible for a particular part of the castle. In the 13th century the Calendars of the Close and Patent Rolls record a remarkable concentration of gentry.[2] Of the 29 Sussex landed families, some elevated to the peerage, selected for biographical treatment by Lower, all but four of them were located at ancestral places in the Weald.

The presence of woods famed for their superb timber and the pleasures of hunting and hawking doubtless account for the unusual numbers of gentry. In the 17th century their estates were noted for salubrious air, fine herds of Red Sussex cattle, hops, trout streams and fish-ponds. They pronounced their residences to be as pleasant as any in England, an opinion which appears to have been generally held by their forbears over many previous centuries.

We can take an example from Ticehurst and district. Here was an exceptional number of lesser gentry in Tudor and Stuart times. The Robertses of Boarzell

100 Barns, Ockley Court Farm, Surrey, the focus of an extensive under-draining project. (John Malton, June 2002, pen and ink, 19 x 11.5cm [7½ x 4½ in.]) (see pxx)

101 Ornamental cottages, Ockley Green, Surrey, erected by the Calverts of Ockley Court Farm. (John Malton, July 2000, pen and ink with watercolour wash, 13 × 10cm [5 × 4in.])

had numerous like-minded gentry in their parish of Ticehurst and its neighbourhood, such as the Apsleys of Wardsbrook, the Mays at Pashley, the Shoyswells of Shoyswell, the Courthopes of Whiligh. The earliest lords of these manors took their cognomen from their home. Thus, the first recorded owner of Wigsell in Salehurst was William de Wikeshulle, who held one knight's fee of John Count of Eu in 1166. He may have descended from the 'William' in Domesday Book holding an unnamed piece of land with one plough, six acres of meadow, woodland yielding 6 swine … Ticehurst stands pleasantly on a high ridge affording uninterrupted views across miles of open country to the South Downs. An 18th-century clergyman declared that 'one might without fear of censure or contradiction pronounce Ticehurst to be as pleasant a residence as any in Sussex'.

By the 15th century a number of the original families were being replaced by newcomers. The family of Roberts is a classic example of Wealden gentry who rose socially from wealth founded on the cloth trade. John Roberts of Glassenbury in Cranbrook purchased Boarzell in Ticehurst in 1459 and subsequent purchases were made by the family of Warbleton Priory.

The Boarzell Estate was held by a branch of the Roberts family for nearly 400 years, the Glassenbury Estate until within living memory; although Tudor members of the family held local government office and received knighthoods, later heirs seldom pursued ambition, or indeed a profession, and were content instead to be gentlemen of leisure in their charming countryside in the ranks of the lesser gentry, intermarrying with Kentish and Sussex families.[3] Generations of the Boarzell Robertses appear to have leased out the largest part of their estate to local husbandmen and yeomen and, by means of virtually unvarying prescriptive covenants in their leases, presided over an almost unchanging land management during the course of their centuries-old ownership.[4]

The Courthopes were established in Wadhurst and Lamberhurst at the time of the 1296 Subsidy, when William de Courthope, of 'Curthope', was evidently a member of the gentry. In 1573 John Courthope acquired the Whiligh estate in Ticehurst and Wadhurst by virtue of his wife and rebuilt the mansion. Most of the succeeding Courthopes, who descended from father to son for nearly four centuries, were barristers. The most eminent of the early Courthopes was Sir George (b.1616). After an adventurous youth on the continent, he became an MP during the Protectorate of Cromwell and at the same time supplied the exiled King with money. He had earlier demonstrated his prudence by missing his father's funeral in order to establish at Charles I's court his virtually inherited right to a useful sinecure. He subsequently increased his wealth by gun-founding for Charles II's navy. A number of the later Courthopes became notable foresters (p.8).

As for the Ashburnhams of Ashburnham, the 17th-century Fuller of the 'Worthies' declared that his 'poor and plain pen is willing, though unable, to add any lustre to this family of stupendous antiquity', they claiming descent from Bertram, the High Sheriff of Sussex and Surrey whom King Harold commanded to make resistance against Duke William of Normandy. John Ashburnham, who built the church at Ashburnham, was gentleman of the chamber to both Charles I and II, and accompanied the former to the scaffold, taking possession of the King's blood-stained shirt. A result of the long-continued connection between families with the same place is extensive family archives which, for example, in the case of the Robertses, contain much information on persons, while the Courthopes have the biggest single collection of pre-1650 estate maps. The Evelyns have resided at Wotton in Surrey for more than 400 years. It was the birthplace of the diarist who makes numerous references to it in the *Sylva* and eulogised it as bearing comparison with the most beautifully situated estates in the nation. The Bartelots claim descent from Adam de Barttelot who was buried at their paternal estate of Stopham in 1100. They seldom sought distinction in state, church or army.

In the early 17th century Wigsell manor was sold to Henry English, yeoman of Salehurst. He is almost certainly the rebuilder of the manor house. The initials 'HP E' for Henry English and his wife, Persis, together with the date 1625 are on a fire-back in one of the rooms, and the dates of other initials are to be found on the wooden door of the front entrance. English lived at Wigsell until his death in 1649. The funeral service was conducted by John Bradshaw, preacher at Etchingham, a sufferer in the Civil War who seems to have found protection with

102 A retired 18th-century sportsman, owner of a little property in the Kent Low Weald. (CKS P 614 P3)

the family. In a letter to Henry English's son he wrote: 'Your country was …
recommended to me as the most quiet of all England, your Family as religious
and courteous …'. The site of Wigsell has great natural charm and, saving that
in the course of centuries a good deal of timber has been cut down and grubbed
up, the surroundings and distant views can have altered but little since the first
house was built there. The old brick boundary walls, the barns and farm buildings,
orchards and broken ground at the approach add to the charm of the house. The
17th-century house appears to be fairly complete and is a typical example of the
Sussex gentleman's home of the first half of the century.[5]

There was another group of anciently established gentry in Framfield and
Buxted. For more than four centuries the Stones had seats in this district. One
family mansion built in the reign of Queen Elizabeth replaced an earlier dwelling
and parts of this Tudor structure are incorporated in the present residence at
New Place. The main seat was at Stone Bridge. The grant of a coat of arms was
made in 1628. Stone Bridge was still owned by a member of the family in 1850.
The Warnetts were established at Hempstead from the 1450s. Robert de
Hempstead, manumitted from villein to freeman by Archbishop Peckham, was

living there in 1284, and a descendant of the same name was collecting taxes in 1332 and 1340. A memorial brass dated 1486 of John Warnett of Furnivals Inn with his coat of arms and Joan his wife is in Buxted church. John (2), married to the sister of the Bishop of Winchester, was also a distinguished lawyer assisting Edmund Dudley to replenish the royal exchequer. His daughter married a Stone of Framfield. John (2) rebuilt Hempstead in the late 15th or early 16th century, and John (4) was probably responsible for building a range early in the 1600s of at least three bays, including a high quality room and a grand staircase. A chapel and gatehouse are mentioned in wills. The Hearth Tax of 1664 records 10 hearths. A drawing by Grimm in 1785 shows the old hall which still survives unspoiled. The Tudor Warnetts were socially successful and married into families with important connections – the Owens, the Ernleys, Guilfords, and Dudleys. For generations the family appear to have been lawyers. The last of the descendants of the Warnetts to own Hempstead sold it to Lord Liverpool in 1841 and built Uckfield House (now demolished) nearby.[6]

By the early 17th century the older farmhouses had grown by successive accretions around their households 'like the fur round a cat' in a size and form finely adjusted to their owner's wealth, changing habits, interests and needs. The exceptionally detailed probate inventory drawn up in June 1639 on the death of John Roberts throws much light on this gentleman's moated farmhouse at Boarzell in Ticehurst. By his death his mansion had grown to 30 rooms, of which 11 were bedrooms, seven were used as storerooms or lumber places and eight were 'utility' rooms with special functions.[7] There appear to have been nine hearths. There is no sign of luxury or ostentation. There was no furniture that was not strictly necessary and little in the way of ornament. Great oak chests and tables were characteristic. There were some comfortable 'great' chairs but the sitting rooms were largely furnished with stools and forms. Curtains with rods and brass hooks adorned the windows but there were few rugs and carpets, and no portraits. Thirty-six various beds were needed for the family, their servants and visitors but there was only one close-stool (in the beer cellar). Stored within the farmhouse were hops, wheat and oat malt from the estate for self-contained domestic use. Two maps, two bibles and three prayer-books are recorded but no other books or musical instruments. Hemp, lambs' wool, bar iron, lathes, timber and tiles tell of domestic occupations and house repairs. Seven bacon flitches were in the half chimney, and the milk-cellar, cheese-house, brew-house and meat-cellar were full of equipment. John Roberts had no carriages and travelled everywhere on horseback, as did his wife, either side-saddle or pillion. Three fowling pieces and gear in his 'Hunting room' reveal Roberts' playing of the Sussex country gentleman. There is not much more that can be gleaned from this source. How much would we like to learn more of its habitableness, particularly of the material objects that had arisen from a family consciousness already going back at Boarzell for many generations. Going back to Roberts' grandfather one is particularly struck by the richness and variety of the foodstuffs at the Roberts' table. Aside from the striking amount of meat consumed, there were at least 15 specific varieties of fish, shellfish etc., obtained from Rye and Hastings. The

WHILIGH.

From a Drawing *done in 1722 in Possession of* George Courthop *Esq.*

103 Whiligh, the home of the Courthopes, ironmasters and foresters, from a drawing of 1722.

carrier regularly brought from London spices, wines, raisins, currants, prunes, and oranges. Minstrels, who must have frequented the London to Hastings road, entertained frequently.[8]

The contentment of Wealden country gentlemen and their ladies with their estates appears evident from their lifestyle. They supervised their flower and

104 Ring Cottage, Odiam, at one time in the occupation of gamekeepers. (John Malton, spring 2002, pen and ink, 17 × 12cm [6¾ × 4¾ in.])

kitchen gardens and were proud of the breeds of horses and cattle they kept up. Their home and its old rooms, and their barns and stables, the sight of the ancestral fields and woods, coppices and ponds gave them many special joys. Planting, and later, land drainage, together with replenishing fish ponds and game stocks, kept gentlemen busily employed, but what most pleasantly occupied their time and gave life meaning to them were the field sports of hunting, fishing, hawking, shooting and fowling. Their ladies were as satisfied as their men with country pursuits and amusements. Some country house owners consented to be 'mere' country gentlemen and were resident on their little estates more or less throughout the year. Mostly, they combined country life with professional practice in London or at some local market town. Many had the financial security of some sinecure which intruded little into their scenes of friendly repose and beauty. By the end of the 17th century gentlemen acquired an apartment by the name of a study which was sacred to the master of the house. This was lined with a few books for pious or other reading and was the repository for his journals, account books, correspondence and the estate maps, which were indispensible to his letting, planting and overall management of his property.

It is the surviving estate maps of the period which are amongst the best evidence we have of the vanished way of life of these 17th- and 18th-century gentry families. The finest Tudor estate map is Thomas Marshall's great map of the Barony of Buckhurst in 1597.[8] The Apsleys of Wardsbrook in Ticehurst are memorialised by William Gier's exquisite estate map of 1612 which is exuberantly decorated with honeysuckles, wild roses, wild strawberries, acorns and several other wild fruits and plants around a fine bird's eye view of the mansion, and the landscape is liberally sprinkled with various species of trees. Thus, the maps are part landscape and part map. Giles Burden's map of part of Ashburnham and Ninfield conveys a pastoral idyll with representations of horses, cattle or sheep in every field.[9] Such maps, which also depict numerous marl pits and ponds, gardens and orchards, whappleways, bridleways, shaws and hedges, are amongst the earliest accurate representations of the Weald. They vividly convey the pride and loving eye of the landowner commissioning the map, as well as that of the map-maker. As Francis Steer has rightly said, these maps were to contemporaries the basis of economic planning – husbandry, leasing and forestry depended on them. He has also noted that some map-makers tried to capture the very feel of the landscape under their scrutiny, 'for they took with them into the field not only the plane-table, measuring wheel and chain, but also a loving eye. The very colour of the Weald and Marsh shimmers in their varied greens'.[10]

20

Transport

Roads

Roads provided the framework for economic development but in the Weald their badness crippled it. Marshall in 1798 declared that, apart from a few public roads, the Weald was roadless, and Malcolm at the same time had to find a guide to take him from Ockley to Rudgwick. Although only 30 miles from London, the distance of six miles took him four hours with good horses. In the 1820s Cobbett encountered in the same area the deepest clay he had experienced.[1] Little wonder that, when the clayland community in nearby Cranleigh was 'rescued' by a new turnpike, it celebrated with a tall obelisk. It was possible to go over the surface in summer and in the dry; in winter and in the wet, hardly at all.

The infamous roads disadvantaged farmers in several ways. They were frequently denied access to markets by wagon, and struggled to reach them by pack-horse along rough bridle-roads. Consequently, as Defoe noted in 1727, corn

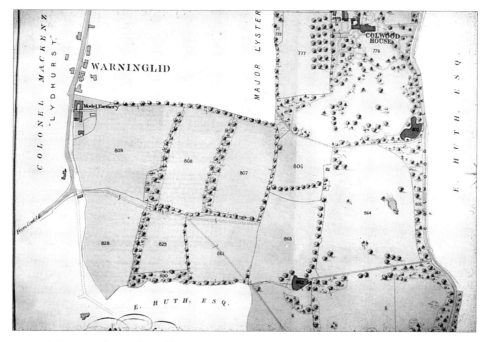

105 A Victorian Pleasure Farm. The primary object was economically to combine pleasure and utility. Hence hedgerows were planted with ornamental trees and not grubbed to make a landscape park.

in the Low Weald was cheap at the barn because it could not be carried out, and dear at the market because it could not be brought in. Wheat, for example, fetched lower prices in Horsham than in Guildford because the former had no water carriage. On account of the heavy going, fat steers driven to Smithfield in the traditional way, 'on the hoof', lost three to four per cent in weight during the journey. Others were as inconvenienced. Carrier services were disrupted in winter and the appalling state of the roads emptied Tunbridge Wells of its visitors in autumn. Roman roads had been struck through the Wealden forest, but from Saxon times until the desire to reach seaside towns in the early modern period, main roads skirted it. This has again been the situation since the last war. The best roads were on the ridges; down in the valleys the parish ('cross') roads even in summer were to a degree impassable. The carriage of timber from the woods and of iron-ore and cannon caused great damage to the roads and necessitated deviatory routes. Enormous animal exertion was also needed. Defoe witnessed an oak being conveyed on a vehicle expressively called a 'tug(g)' hauled by a team of 22 oxen. The Biddenden to Ashford Turnpike in 1829 doubled its tolls for horses drawing wagons laden with timber between 1 October and 1 May, presumably because of damage to the road.[2]

The countryside was isolated by bad weather in summer and for much of the winter by impassability over heavy land by horse, coach or wagon. When Parson Gray of Southwick, Sussex, wanted to travel on horseback to London in the 18th century he would pick a spell of fine summer weather, but on one occasion he was caught out badly and spent two days travelling home by carrier's cart. In the previous century the Sackvilles gave up residence at Buckhurst, their ancestral home in Withyham, in favour of Knole, partly because it had all-the-year-round roads to London (even today people living on the Weald clay have difficulty in persuading 'townee' friends to visit them before midsummer). The roads were so dangerous that the sinking of a chaise wheel in a mud-hole, or the breakage of a carriage, was an ordinary and oft-recurring incident. Early visitors by coach to Tunbridge Wells travelled at the hazard of their bones, and from frequent overturns thought a bone-setter a necessary part of the equipage for country visiting. They also wanted an armed escort. The country people were so unused to strangers that they hid behind curtains.[3]

For Horace Walpole travelling in Sussex was undertaken with a sense of foreboding. Returning from holiday in August 1752, he wrote:

> … if you love good roads, conveniences, good inns, plenty of postilions and horses, be so kind as never to go into Sussex. We thought ourselves in the northest part of England; the whole county has a Saxon air, and the inhabitants are as savage, as if King George the Second was the first monarch of the East Angles. Coaches grow there no more than balm and spices; we were forced to drop our post-chaise, that resembled nothing so much as a harlequin's calash, which was occasionally a chaise or a baker's cart. We journeyed over Alpine mountains, drenched in clouds, and thought of harlequin again, when he was driving the chariot of the sun through the morning clouds, and so was glad to hear the aqua vita man crying a dram … I have set up my staff, and finished my pilgrimages for this year. Sussex is a great damper of curiosity.

106 Limekilns near Dorking, by George Scharf, c.1830.

After a visit to the ruins of Bayham Abbey on another occasion the challenges were even greater:

> Here our woes increase. The roads grew bad beyond all badness, the night dark beyond all darkness, our guide frightened beyond all frightfulness. However, without being killed, we got up, or down – I forget which, it was so dark – a famous precipice called Silver Hill, and about ten at night arrived at a wretched village called Rotherbridge [Robertsbridge]. We had still six miles hither, but determined to stop, as it would be a pity to break our necks before we had seen all we intended. But, alas! There was only one bed to be had; all the rest were inhabited by smugglers, whom the people of the house called mountebanks and with one the lady of the den told Mr Chute he might lie. We did not at all take to this society, but, armed with links and lanthorns, set out again upon this impracticable journey. At two o'clock in the morning we got hither [to Battle] to a still worse inn, and that crammed with excise officers, one of whom had just shot a smuggler ...[4]

Both highways and local roads were invariably 10 to 15 feet below the level of adjacent fields so that they looked like a stream course. Two processes accounted for such deeply sunken lanes. Whilst the bottom of the road was constantly being worn down to rock by the wear and tear of heavy ox and horse-drawn wagons, aided by the fretting of the loosened surface by rain and frost, the top of the bank rose higher year by year with accumulations of dust, mould and stones thrown to the edge of the field and the accumulation of soil resulting from soil shovelled against the roots of a newly laid hedge. Thus, the two processes, one of removal and one of accretion, operated simultaneously, so

107 Turner's sketch of a Sussex broad-wheeled wagon. This was strongly built with broad wheels to enable it to be pulled through heavy clay. Its length and strength were designed for large and heavy loads, and its shape gave it better than average manoeuvrability. The frame was usually painted blue, the wheels, red.

constantly adding to the depth of the road below the field.[5] When roads were improved it was often considered advisable to abandon the old track altogether and replace it with a new one alongside. The depth of a road is broadly related to the degree of its usage over time but geology plays a large part, soft sandstone being more easily worn down than heavy clay. There was commonly a footpath on one of the high sides or on top of the bank. When snow fell deeply it filled these defiles and cut off market towns and farms.[6]

Most long-distance roads in the Weald were droving roads from peripheral manors but by the 13th century their original function had virtually ceased through settlement and colonisation. Nevertheless, as we have seen, they had influenced the location of much medieval building and consequently many had become important internal highways. The main access into the Weald came from natural ridgeways and were also best for internal circulation. The roads into the Weald from the seaports of Hythe, Rye and Hastings followed ridges, leaving the hollows (where was almost all the human activity) to the mercies of local 'roads'.

The latter formed a labyrinth of minor lanes, mostly deep hollow-ways, almost every field being bordered by a public right of way. A distinction was made between a 'highway' and the 'King's highway', the latter statutorily maintained by the parish. The present network of minor lanes is only a remnant of what formerly existed (Fig.135). Lane closures have occurred with later road-making, particularly since local Enclosure Awards in the mid-19th century, and the Road Traffic Act of 1875. They are mostly unmetalled, being largely obsolete 'greenways'. Among the most distinctive and charming features of the Wealden landscape, they are a wonderful heritage for the rambler and botanist. Parts of the old network have been joined together to make long-distance walking routes, such as the Weald Way and the Vanguard Way.

These old ways can lead the historian into the very bones of the landscape, as it were. Many of the remaining twisting byways are seemingly illogical, but need to be put into their historical context. A key to the labyrinth is the small farm. Each little family farm needed its own local access to a cart road and packway to link it to its church, water- and windmill, commons, markets, forests, woods, furnaces and forges, as well as to navigable water and to droving roads taking livestock along the east-west ridges and to London. These fed into a tree-like system of byways. A number of these were duplicated, for 'summer roads' were utterly impassable in winter. On the ground a number of by-roads clearly had a causeway at the side as a pack-saddle way, e.g. at Queen's Stockbridge Lane in Buxted. Wagons did not carry breakable goods; these were carried by packmen whose goods were hung on crooks slung over the pack-saddle. Their courses were traceable by hollowed-out, narrow, lanes known as packways or whappleways, and now as bridleways, i.e. suitable for horses which could pass, but not for carts or wagons.

Ironmasters were required by an Act of Parliament to repair roads damaged by the transport of cannon and other products. Such roads led to the nearest tide-water for the conveyance to Woolwich or London. It is possible to reconstruct the route via the river Ouse to Newhaven used by the furnaces and forges around Ashdown Forest and between the gunfoundries on the Kent border which made for the river Medway. From the 18th century all farms possessed both narrow- and broad-gauge wagons, the wheels of the latter being wider. These were used on farms during miry weather and on the highways in winter. Six horses or eight oxen were necessary to pull them. Four roads converged on the Hundred House Green in Framfield before the Enclosure Award of 1862. Pound Lane survives as a metalled road with wide green verges on either side (Fig.135). Another lane was part of a long-distance droving route and 'iron-way' extending from Crowborough Common to the north, down to the Downs at Bishopstone near Seaford, another ran to Tickerage Forge and a third was stopped up in 1862; the present footpath runs to the south.

By the mid-18th century economic and social development called for better communications, especially be-tween London and the spa of Tun-bridge Wells and the coast. The rise of Brighton and the other seaside towns generated roadmaking as did the migra-tion of newcomers searching for sites for new country houses and parks accessible to London. Turnpike trusts therefore competed to provide the best surfaces, easiest gradients and most direct routes, best provided with hostelries. In Kent the first turnpike act was passed in 1709 for improved access to Tunbridge Wells. By the end of the

108 *The Cranleigh obelisk marks the ecstatic relief of a community at their 'rescue' by a new road across the most appalling clay country in winter.*

century trusts were constructing roads with hard, rolled stone surfaces in the manner of Telford and McAdam and by 1837 there were 50 such trusts responsible for over 650 miles of turnpiking. Kent parishes 'stoned' roads from material at Coxheath, e.g. Staplehurst to Frittenden was 'stoned' in 1836.

Surrey changes were even more dramatic. The dearth of roads was replaced within a century by a virtually new system of direct trunk routes to London and a close network of cross-country connections. The first stretch improved was the ten miles between Reigate and Crawley over the Low Weald authorised in 1696 as a saddle-horse road, although not upgraded for carriages until 1755.[7] Between the first Sussex turnpike in 1749 and the 1841 London-Brighton railway the hub of the new roads was Brighton, but the other resorts were eventually similarly served.

The economic effects of turnpikes in the Weald, however, should not be over-rated. The frequency of toll-gates made carriage of bulky goods expensive. Moreover, although main highways were subject to improvement, the incompetent management of many of them invited strong censure. Malcolm in 1805 found the Brighton road between Reigate and the Sussex boundary rated by farmers as 'extremely defective' with sections where it was dangerous to pass; that between Godalming and Milford was 'scandalous and dangerous in a very high degree'; and that from Guildford leading to the county boundary at Alfold was 'in places very bad'. Meanwhile, local parish roads remained lamentable for much longer. Malcolm's list of Surrey parishes in 1805, with local roads as bad as 'some of the most inaccessible and uninhabited parts of Ireland', numbers 37, mostly in the Weald, where the farther one went from London the deeper one stuck in the mire. Exceptionally, a magistrate strictly enforced the repair of local roads. An example was Sir Thomas Turton, who had the road from Lingfield to Edenbridge opened up during winter at the end of the 18th century by threatening the luckless parish surveyors with prosecution. On account of the bad state of the local roads the more minor turnpike trusts attracted little traffic at the end of the 18th century. The Traffic receipts for the Ticehurst Town Turnpike, which took tolls on the road from Flimwell (on the Hastings-London road) to Wadhurst, are extant for 1769-70. They reveal a great increase in summer traffic compared with that in winter for both wheeled vehicles and the movement of livestock. The relatively large numbers of cattle passing the toll gate in May and June were probably Welsh runts being driven to markets in Kent.

An eagerness for 'improvement' by turnpike trustees could be inconsistent with the just rights of users. The local opposition to the wrongful closure by the London to Hastings turnpike trustees of a feeder road running through Robertsbridge, so forcing local landowners to make a circuitous route of up to two miles, led to a court case in 1821 won by the plaintiffs. The evidence of witnesses provides an engrossing picture of the uses of the road from c.1760 when the local community was still partly industrial. The action was triggered off when a servant of Mr Allfrey of Park Farm found the road barred to his wagon laden with stone from the ruins of Robertsbridge Abbey intended for the making of a cottage. One witness recalled carting bricks from the Park Farm kiln to repair Etchingham

109 Cowfold, delightful half-timbered and brick cottages around the parish church before the A272 road opened up the village from the 1820s. (John Malton, May 2002, pencil sketch, 21 × 14cm [8¼ × 5½ in.])

Bridge. Another reported that 30-40 ox teams made for the Robertsbridge furnace and forge in a single day, conveying heavy cannon to Maidstone, iron ore from the sandstone near Silver Hill, manufactured goods to London, coals from local woods, bricks and lime for the ironworks and cinder for use on the roads. David Duck took ore to the ironworks four times a day. Cart loads of wood for the inhabitants of Robertsbridge also regularly passed along the road, as did corn to Robertsbridge mill, with malt flour returning.[8]

Many landowners intent on building a mansion and laying out a park bore heavy costs of road-making themselves before carting in their building materials. As Malcolm observed of Surrey roads, if none happened to lead to a gentleman's house 'in the worse order and the more impassable are they and the lower will be the rents of the farms'. Thus, the Horsham-Crawley turnpike, seven miles in length, was constructed in the 1820s under the direction, and almost entirely at the expense of, Broadwood, a London piano manufacturer, who then built Holmbush as his country seat. Similarly, the builder of Mabledon, a fine new seat served by the turnpike from Tunbridge Wells to East Grinstead, bore the cost of reducing the incline on this road where it passed near his estate. A further example is the work of the brothers Burrell, who built the fashionable residences of Knepp Castle and West Grinstead Park after financing the Horsham-Worthing turnpike which gave them access to their seats. By the late 19th century on the heavy clay of the Surrey Weald, a newcomer would build himself a house on a farm at and around Cranleigh and make himself unpopular with local inhabitants by compelling the parish to make the green lanes into hard roads, which in turn accelerated the invasion of other *nouveaux riches*.[9] In the 19th century highways deemed obsolete were legally closed by magistrates at Quarter Sessions if a case was not made out for their continuance. In 1860, for example, four highways were stopped in Biddenden parish. Appeals made in respect of three more were accepted.[10]

110 Nineteenth-century barges on the River Adur near Bines Bridge. An artist's reconstruction by Mike Codd.

Canals

On account of the deficiencies of roads, it became the avowed aim of improvers to construct canals so as to bring corn to market and carry lime and other manures for farming. This was the express purpose of the improvement of the western Rother to Midhurst in 1791 and successive schemes embraced the Royal Military Canal between Hythe and Winchelsea (1804), the Adur (1804), the Ouse (1805) and the Wey and Arun Canal (1813). The latter was constructed on the strategic consideration of taking valuables overland, by-passing the passage by sea round the North Foreland, then a prey to enemy shipping and storms. The 3rd Earl of Egremont was particularly identified with such projects. He personally financed the Rother navigation to serve his Petworth estates, and projected the other West Sussex canals where he also had estate interests. The Newbridge-Pallingham Lock section of the Wey and Arun Navigation was excavated in 1787 and is notable for the Lording's aqueduct carrying the canal over the river Arun at Lording's Lock. A water-wheel was constructed to lift water into the canal from the river. The use of water transport encouraged landowners to fell timber near the canal during the Napoleonic Wars and the substitution of coal for wood fuel. Numerous lime kilns used raw chalk brought from Amberley. The restoration of peace in 1815 removed the immediate need for an inland water-route to London and after a brief heyday railways sapped canal trade, as they also did that of the turnpikes. One after another the canals closed. Imposing monuments of the old waterways include the tunnel to avoid the wide meander of the Arun near Pulborough and the Orfold viaduct, which has partially collapsed, that took barges to Guildford and northwards to the Thames.[11]

21

The Crisis Years, 1816-33

'I would not have the whole Weald to farm', exclaimed one witness, 'if they would
give it to me.'

George Smallpiece giving evidence before the
Select Committee on Agriculture, 1833.[1]

WHEN Smallpiece, a farmer, land agent, broker and sheep dealer, made his
exclamation, the Sussex and Surrey Wealds were still in a very bad state after a
triple agricultural disaster. The sharp fall in corn prices, following the end of the
Napoleonic wars, had been accompanied by the three wet seasons of 1816, 1817
and 1821 which had prevented farmers making their fallows for wheat and led
to widespread foot-rot which had wiped out sheep flocks. Additionally, farmers
had been eaten up with high poor rates which had risen substantially since 1822.
This, on heavy land expensive to cultivate, had resulted in the depressed state of
farms and greater poverty amongst farmers than on the Downs. Smallpiece
himself had thrown up a farm at Billingshurst because it was not worth half the
poor rate. A great deal of land was not occupied at all and much land which had
become sterile through over-cropping in wartime had still not completely
recovered owing to the lack of farmers' capital to improve it. To an earlier Select
Committee in 1822, John Ellman jnr of Glynde had demonstrated that Weald
farmers were then losing money by conventional methods of cultivation – three

*111 Yeoman's farmhouse tenanted
by labourers in the late 18th
century. (Source: Kenneth Gravett,*
Timber and Brick Building in
Kent, *1971)*

or four ploughings, 12 harrowings, two rollings, liming and dunging and cited a Lewes lime-burner who had lost money by failures of Weald farmers.[2]

Nor was the Kent Weald any better. John Neve, a large farmer and land agent of Tenterden, reported in 1833 that the farmers' situation there was very bad and that land was deteriorating. Landlords were advancing rent to tenants to induce them to take up farms. They were handicapped in a period of low prices by the heavy costs of lime, exacerbated by a 15-mile journey to water carriage.

Other sources help us to recreate the living conditions of the small farmer and labourer. To cultivate 100 acres required the constant employment of four able-bodied men, a big lad and a boy able to drive the plough. Single men came to farmhouses for hire but the custom was dying out, for masters and their wives disliked the trouble and the youths the restraint. They were provided with board and lodging elsewhere. In the Sussex and Surrey Wealds women had found much extra work in the fields during the wartime years but this was no longer available, so they helped their husbands 'flawing' bark in the woods in May. Almost every cottager fattened chickens for the London market. Owing to the great number of small farms, many labourers migrated seasonally for work, a custom detectable as far back as the 14th century. Taking advantage of the varying times of harvest in different places, they could begin with well-paid haymaking on the edge of London, returning to their own hay-harvest before setting off for the big corn farms in the 'hill country' on or at the foot of the Downs, and again returning for the harvest in their native parish which was two or three weeks later owing to elevation or coldness of the soil. There was still time to go fruit or hop-picking in Kent and Sussex before going on parish relief for the winter. In the Kent Weald one result of hop cultivation was that many men obtained highly-paid piece-work in summer and wives contributed to their husbands' earnings by tying hops and hop-picking, followed by making hop pockets, shaving poles or tearing up rags for manure in winter.

Boys were expected to take up daily work on farms as soon as they had the strength to work stiff, cold clays, usually about the age of ten or eleven. Thomas Orton had just had his 12th birthday in 1836 when he spoke of his 12-hour day with his father, leading the horse at plough and harrow and doing other jobs according to the season. For meals he had bread and cheese or bread and butter for breakfast and sometimes, but not often, bread and meat or meat and potatoes for dinner. The nine children (five boys and four girls) slept in one room. He had attended school for only a week and could not read. He admitted that few were so badly off. Until that age most had the irregular education in a dame or other local school, punctuated by spells of bird scaring, potato and bean sowing and acorn collecting. In the Kent Weald girls and boys as young as seven or eight were employed shaving hop poles and every child who could walk was wanted at hop-picking.[3]

The migratory hop-pickers came from all parts of England and Ireland and on the whole were reckoned to be people of good character. The most 'vicious and refractory' coming from St Giles (then a ghetto near the Charing Cross Road), Saffron Hill, Whitechapel and Kent Street. Cottages for labourers were

112 Cottagers near Cranbrook (c.1850) by Frederick Hardy. This and the next illustration date before the marked improvement in the standard of living which resulted from the Repeal of the Corn Laws and Free Trade.

variable in condition, as were the rents. At Albury, for example, Mr Drummond offered good cottages with ample gardens at low rents, whereas, in the neighbouring parish of Shere, landowners did not, which, it was claimed, led to the notorious activities of the 'Shere Gang', whom farmers were frightened to employ. Numerous 'cottages' were, in fact, apartments in former substantial timber-framed farmhouses which had become redundant with the amalgamation of holdings. There are endless examples of such dwellings which, from the early 20th century, blossomed again as single residences of city people and are now on the market for a million pounds or more. At the bottom level were turf huts, as in St Leonard's Forest, and those erected by squatters along the Forest Ridges. At Lindfield the benevolent William Allen had started a system of small allotments and advanced money to buy pigs, manure and seed. The tenant repaid the loan out of the proceeds of his crop.[4]

As for the way of life of the 'leather-legged race' or 'the clay-and-coppice people', as Cobbett called Wealdsmen, he rejoiced to see the continuance of old-fashioned ways of life which critical outsiders considered backward. The woman at Wisborough Green bleaching her home-spun wool and home-woven linen reminded him that, although he had travelled across England, he had not seen such a sight since leaving America. He also noted that most labourers still wore smock-frocks. He thought that they were better off than farm labourers without woods, because coppices gave them profitable work in winter and it was warmer working in woods then than in farmyards. He cited, in contrast, the Isle of Thanet, with its prodigious crops, efficient cultivation, huge barns, enormous ricks and yet with 'labourers' houses beggarly in the extreme. The people 'dirty, poor-looking; ragged'.⁵

'What a difference between a labouring man in the forests and woodlands of Hampshire and Sussex! Ironically, I have observed that the richer the soil, and the more destitute the woods, that is to say, the more purely a corn country, the more miserable the labourers.' Cobbett went on to inveigh against the big farmer and the landlord in other parts of England grasping hedges, ditches, commons and grassy lanes. 'The wretched labourer has not a stick of wood, and has no place for a pig or cow to grass.' Whenever he saw misery he thought of what he had observed of the endless strings of vine-covered cottages around

113 Frederick Hardy, cottagers near Cranbrook (c.1850). A closeness of detail in an assiduously wrought imitation of a rustic cottage interior as in illustration 111.

Lamberhurst, Goudhurst and Rolvenden. These villages were not like those on the chalklands. There were gardens in front and behind and a 'good deal of show and finery about them'. Echoing Arthur Young's comment earlier (p.168), he considered that there was more human happiness in the Weald than anywhere he had been. He was completely at odds with contemporary agricultural writers, such as Arthur Young and William Marshall, who regarded Wealden agriculture as so contemptible as to warrant radical change. Their views were extreme, but there was room for improvement. Cobbett himself observed that 'the Weald was indeed not much of a land for turnips' (Young's cornerstone of progressive farming) and he had only seen a few fields of swedes, another crude index of improvement. Yet, unlike Young and Marshall, and other experts from outside, he understood that Wealdsmen had not succumbed to the materialistic outlook measuring everything in terms of yield and profit, and that much of the land could not be regarded as wholly commercial. Consequently, it was free of 'wen-engendered' people (except at Tunbridge Wells) 'and unchoked by smoke and unstunned by the infernal rattle of coaches and drays'. He observed, 'What an at once horrible and ridiculous thing this country would become if this thing [London's sprawl] would go on for a few years'; he was pleased to note little by way of the townsmen's invasion into the Weald 'for whenever any of them go into the country, they look upon it that they are to begin a sort of warfare against anything around them. They invariably look upon every labourer as a thief'. How remarkably Cobbett's point of view has again gained growing support over the past 70 years or so.

Cobbett, in fact, perceived the Weald as a kind of Garden of Eden before the Fall. The countryside was pretty but with little variety in it and not strikingly beautiful. What more than compensated for merit in scenery was the air of neatness, warmth and comfort breathing the whole. He relished fine oaks scattered in the hedges, the comfortable farm houses covered in tiles, cottages with little gardens, coops for poultry and sties for pigs. One gains the impression that every labourer had a fowl in the pot. Above all, he rejoiced that the land was mainly in the hands of little proprietors and tenants (small yeomen yet remaining) yet the farms were not too small to be unviable. In fact, to him, the Weald was the embodiment of all the traditions and virtues which he cherished as most truly English. Through a lifetime of pugnacious political writing, he clung with fanatical devotion to the countryside and ways of life of old England. Amongst Cobbett's most vivid figures in *Rural Rides* are the 'clay and coppice people' inhabiting the Weald. In this poor and slow-changing countryside the self-supporting labourer was living close to the soil with his bakehouse, brewhouse, pig-sty and rabbit warren. The cheerful, hard-working and comparatively well-off Wealden labourer symbolised his idea of the perfect English countryman. Strong as the soil he worked upon, he still formed part of a recognisable community, all but inaccessible to strangers, still holding his own in the self-sufficiency which was for generations in the Weald the condition of survival. His very dress proclaimed his battle with the soil:

> As God has made the back to the burthen, so then clay and coppice people make the dress to the stubs and bushes. Under the sole of the shoe is iron; from the sole six inches upwards is a high-low; then comes a pair of leather breeches; then comes a stout doublet; over this comes a smock-frock; and the wearer sets brush and stubs and thorns and mire at defiance.

Cobbett took pride in the old farmhouses with their furnishings of oak tables, bedsteads, oak chests of drawers and oak clothes-chests, and the very scent of the air upon them was to him expressive of all the qualities of an admired past. In the presence of these old houses and their furnishing Cobbett felt some intangible essence linger of an earlier, homelier, England and they so vividly recalled to him an association with generations of farming folk that we can almost hear the farm labourers clumping in with their loud-sounding hob-nailed boots and dining cheerily at the side-table. All this, of course, was within Cobbett's experience, the touchstone to him of everything. In the unaltered old farmhouses he recovered a trace of the Surrey of his childhood and nostalgia swept over him. Hence his inflexible censure of 'Jews and Jobbers' who had begun to buy up farmhouses and building land nearer London and were furnishing in the new-

114 Inglenook, Stockland Farm.

fangled style of the age. Coming in the wake of this Cockney invasion were Parlours, 'aye, and with a carpet and bell-push, too', mahogany chairs, sofas, fine glass, wine decanters, dinner and breakfast sets, dessert knives.

In reality, the labourer was not always this high moral sort. Beershops were generally considered mischievous and corrupting. Being in secluded situations they allowed of secret meetings and tended to be brothels and receiving houses of stolen goods resorted to by 'abandoned characters'. It was often remarked that hard-working small farmers or labourers in their cottages lived more frugally than idle and profligate workhouse inmates who would be supplied with meat on five days a week. Inferior quality bread was rejected by paupers near Uckfield, while small farmers were feeding their families on refuse corn. Ardingly was said to be the worst run parish in Sussex, itself claimed to be the worst county in England for Poor Law administration. Its superabundant population put great pressure on an ill-run workhouse. The high poor rates induced farmers to leave the parish when their leases expired and their land was left in the most wretched state of cultivation.

Meanwhile, the Weald farmer was not ignoring new implements and ways of working the land. Two new types of plough were increasing the productivity of stiff land. One was the draining plough introduced about 1828 into the Kent Weald, which had rapidly come into use in the Weald generally by 1836. This greatly lessened the expense of under-draining and rendered land more productive of wheat. Hitherto brushwood had been placed in trenches. In the new process a drain about 2½-3 inches deep was placed about nine feet apart, clay taken out by the plough being rammed against a wooden slide which gradually was drawn forward. Although the land ploughed lighter after this under-draining, it does not appear that the farmer ploughed with fewer oxen or horses.

The other innovation was the subsoil plough. This was regarded as one of the most beneficial implements of husbandry invented for many years. Invented by James Smith of Deanston in Perthshire *c.*1824, it was in use in the Isle of Thanet in 1836 but not generally in the Weald until rather later. It was particularly beneficial to the Weald because it was applicable to soil hitherto intractable and the most expensive to cultivate. By it, wet land hitherto hopeless for cultivation was rendered mellow and friable. The resulting increase in yields was substantial; land which might have produced a precarious 20-24 bushels of wheat now was capable of up to one third more, and turnips and swedes could be raised. This plough stirred the subsoil without raising it to the surface, thus giving a much greater depth for rain to sink into. Any obdurate undercrust was broken up, making the soil more permeable. An ordinary plough went before and turned over a furrow six to eight inches deep and the subsoil plough followed in the same track to a further depth of 12 to 16 inches. Subsoil ploughing eradicated the need for the traditional ridging which had given the corrugated washboard effect to the fields.[6]

As Cobbett had observed, the early 19th century was still the era of the small family farm but great losses occurred in the first half of the 19th century. In Chiddingly parish small farms thrived up to 1815; between 1816 and 1842, when agricultural distress followed the Napoleonic wars, nearly half were lost and many of the remainder changed from owner-occupancy to tenancy.[7] At the end of the 18th century in Chiddingly there were a small number of what were locally considered large farms, alongside a large number of smaller holdings. Some small farms had disappeared before 1800; nevertheless, the survivors still occupied around 30 per cent of Chiddingly's enclosed land in the early 19th century. The traditional Wealden cattle farming system, involving retention of all male calves, their use as plough oxen between the ages of three and six, followed by fattening for the butcher, may still have been practised on some of the larger farms. These farmers found the abundant supplies of manure which the winter stall-fed cattle provided very beneficial for their hop fields. By this time, however, horses had replaced oxen as plough animals on many farms and the emphasis of the cattle economy had shifted towards rearing and dairying. In addition, many small farmers would have undertaken seasonal or occasional paid employment on larger farms (both local and in other regions, such as the South Downs), or in the wood-coppice industries. Farmers with small acreages were thus not necessarily those with the smallest incomes. In places, the decline of the small farm had begun earlier. R. Grover studied seven parishes in Hastings Rape between 1702 and 1781, and his tables indicate that the number of small farms as defined in his article fell by 33 per cent, but he does not tell us precisely when the changes occurred.[6] At Laughton the main period when farms increased in size appears to have been 1740-60, mostly a period of depression. Throughout the 18th and 19th centuries most small Wealden farmers sold only as much produce as was necessary to support their simple life-style. What made the post-Napoleonic depression exceptionally testing was the requirement to pay regularly, in cash, the high poor rates then prevailing in Wealden parishes. Like most open parishes in southern England, Wealden parishes had seen a marked growth in the number of persons dependent on parish relief during the late 18th and early 19th centuries. The charge fell on all occupiers of land roughly in proportion to the acreage held, so small farmers paid less than large ones. However, larger farmers were in a sense also beneficiaries, for many employed each summer a number of casual labourers whom they could leave the parish to support during the winter.

Small farms, worked largely by family labour, gained little from this pool of casual labour, yet were still required to contribute to parish relief. Year after year the small farmer's cash and savings were drained away, and his traditional resilience undermined.

On his way to visit Augustus Hare at Herstmonceux in August 1840, to escape the 'bricks and reck' of the damnable Cockneydom in the 'green country' for a week or two, Thomas Carlyle found 'starving' labourers in the Surrey Weald below Leith Hill but was enthralled by the East Sussex countryside, 'very beautiful, very strange', with its neat villages, red-brick houses and smallish farms with high-pitched barns and immense roofs all looking clean, smart and fruitful. He particularly sought out local people and thought them very civil, with plenty of sense, and not at all destitute. There were no threshing machines but many labourers were out of work. Although farming was depressed, farmers were struggling to keep wages at 12s. a week on a point of honour based on a general understanding that a man could not keep a family under that wage 'in their own thriftless way'. As a lowland Scot and a countryman at heart, he was interested in practical details of farming new to him. Men threshed with flails face to back and not face to face, as Carlyle had himself done, and they also stooped more than his countrymen did. Their reaping was different too; they built stooks with 12 sheaves, not 10, put no hood on them and worked round the skirts of a mass of corn, chipping at it, guiding it lightly by the tops and mowing at it until the whole sheaf was done at once. The Rev. Hare planned to preach against the farmers' unchristian decision to put an end to gleaning. As Carlyle explained, by way of reaping in the way he described 'a good many ears were left and the poor mothers with all their children come gleaning here, and sometimes amassed a winchester or two or wheat'. Nevertheless, he thought the people's lives were for the most part more supportable than he had seen it elsewhere and that nobody suffered continual hunger as did his own folk in Nithsdale.[8]

Smuggling had been greatly reduced by the preventive service, but this had the effect of increasing the poor rate. Labourers near Bexhill, for example, had formerly no difficulty in working on farms in summer and smuggling during the winter. Carriers were paid 5s. a night and upwards, according to the number of tubs they secured. Whereas the batmen, so called after their bludgeon, who disguised themselves and possessed firearms, could earn £1 a night but were mostly at the same time in receipt of parish relief. Many smaller farmers, if they did not participate, had connived at smuggling. It was asserted that 'beyond all doubt' smuggling had been the main cause of the riots and fires in Sussex and east Kent. Labourers had acquired the habit of acting in large gangs by night, and systematic aversion to authority. High living had become essential to them and they could not reconcile themselves to the moderate pay of lawful industry.

XXI *A hammer pond and bay – an artist's reconstruction by Mike Codd.*

XXII *An abandoned road to Inchreed near Hadlow Down, summer 2001.*

XXIII *The Weald as paradise: John Linnell's arcadian vision from his studio near Redhill. The South Downs close the view in the far distance (1887). By this date the Weald's great wooded expanse had come to be accepted as the great foil to advancing London.*

xxiv *Samuel Palmer,* The Gleaning Field, *1833.*

xxv *Helen Allingham,* The Wild Garden, c.*1885, a painting inspired by William Robinson.*

XXVI (LEFT) *Bedgebury with its great estate was the medieval home of the Culpepers. Field Marshal Beresford, Lord Wellington's deputy commander, built the present mansion, now a girls' school.*

XXVII (BELOW LEFT) *Kilndown church, the most striking Victorian Wealden church, the creation of Alexander James Beresford Hope.*

XXVIII (BELOW RIGHT) *Bexhill parish church, 1850, before restoration. The church contains the Bexhill Stone, thought to be the lid of a reliquary containing the relics of a Saxon saint. Its most ancient stained glass was removed by Horace Walpole to his chapel at Strawberry Hill but was returned in the 1920s by its conscience-stricken owner and has been re-set.*

22

The Swing Riots

THE 'Swing Riots' were rural disturbances which began in east Kent in August 1830 and reached their peak in November, when they had spread into Sussex, Surrey and most of southern and eastern England. They were so called because of threatening letters to farmers purporting to come from a 'Captain Swing' (Fig.115) but, in fact, there was no overall leadership, the riots being purely local and spontaneous, though highly contagious. The violence included the destruction of threshing machines, burning of ricks and barns, attacks on Overseers of the Poor, and intimidation of farmers and landowners to force up wages. The whole countryside was convulsed by the destruction of property and every peaceable family alarmed. For a time tracts of country fell into the hands of labourers.

William Cobbett had often predicted in his *Weekly Political Register* that the burning and destroying would happen and that it would begin in Sussex or Kent, not on account of discontent being greater there than elsewhere, but because the radically-minded agricultural labourers would be the first to rise in protest.[1] To Kent farmers he cited John Ellman Senior's evidence to a Committee of the House of Commons that 45 years before 1821 every man in his parish of Glynde brewed his own beer, and that in 1830 not a single man could afford to do it. Cobbett added that no one who had read his *Rural Rides* (1821-30) could have been surprised at the current discontent and resentment or have failed to foresee the violence that had occurred.[2]

The primary cause of the revolts was the extreme poverty of agricultural labourers and artisans, and the inattention of the government to their distress, hitherto borne with patience and fortitude, since the peace of 1815. A correspondent of Sir Edward Knatchbull, an MP and prominent Kent magistrate, complained of the enclosure of commons, the decline of small farms and the rise of the 'overgrown farmer (a hog) and his slaves'.[3] A Kent writer purporting to be Swing himself explained the violence by the loss of farms, ferocious game laws, harshness of tithes and ill-treatment and indignities suffered at the hands of the Poor Law officers.[4] Labourers joining a meeting on Benenden Heath had an extremely wretched appearance; some wore no shoes or stockings. An emigrant from Sedlescombe, writing from the United States, told his father that if he joined him he would not need the strap he wound round his stomach when he was hungry. A gentleman resident at Hawkhurst condemned the violence but admitted that 'no reasonable person was disposed to deny an increase in wages'.[5]

Cobbett compared the adverse change in the labourers' condition with impressions of them in his childhood. A barrel of ale was then kept ready for

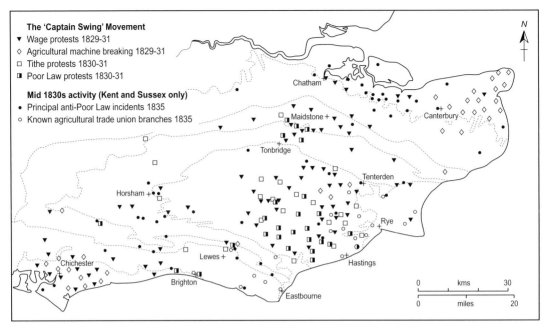

The 'Captain Swing' Movement
▼ Wage protests 1829-31
◇ Agricultural machine breaking 1829-31
□ Tithe protests 1830-31
◨ Poor Law protests 1830-31

Mid 1830s activity (Kent and Sussex only)
● Principal anti-Poor Law incidents 1835
○ Known agricultural trade union branches 1835

115 Rural protest in south-east England in the 1830s (after Short).

a wedding or a christening. Money was saved before marriage to purchase decent furniture and a bastard was a rarity. Every sober and industrious labourer had his Sunday coat, a silk handkerchief round his neck, worsted stockings tied under the knee with a red garter, and handsome shoes fastened on his feet with silver buckles. He also took his wife and children to church decently dressed. Men did not shift about as they then did unshaven on Sunday in ragged smock-frocks, unwashed shirts and scruffy shoes.[6]

Poverty was so extreme that arsonists looked upon themselves as waging a just war. Farmers generally took common cause with the labourers because they were unable to sustain higher wages on account of tithes, high rents and taxes, which included duties on malt for home brewing, soap, candles and coal, together with other necessaries. Indeed the discontent spread even wider. Nine months before the riots broke out, the 23 members of the Grand Jury at Maidstone unanimously communicated to the Prime Minister, the Duke of Wellington, 'the deep and unprecedented distress which ... prevails among all classes throughout this county ...'. Farmers at Staplehurst petitioned Parliament, declaring that they had raised their labourers' wages, as was their due, but 'that their burdens were such that they could bear them no longer'. So solid was the feeling in Kent against the government that people refused to be sworn as Special Constables.[7] The discontent was not solely economically motivated. The year 1830 was one of bitter controversy over Parliamentary Reform, a movement itself accentuated by the revolutions in France and Belgium in that year. Outbursts of violence immediately followed the Duke of Wellington's speech on 2 November, declaring against Parliamentary Reform. There were other grievances. The victimisation of paupers by Overseers of the Poor was an issue in Sussex. In his *Two-Penny Trash*, published from July 1830 'to show the working people what are the causes of their being poor', Cobbett maintained that the scandal of sinecures held by the ruling classes, including that still held by Lord Camden of Bayham Park, the Lord Lieutenant of Kent, had 'more to do with the disturbances than all the tri-coloured ribbons in the world'.[8]

There was thus a heightened expectation of change in all men. These various strands were brought together, for example, by a labourers' spokesman at Boughton Monchelsea, Kent:

> These people want bread and not powder and shot; we blame not the farmers – they are oppressed with enormous taxes, and cannot pay the labourer. We want therefore a removal of taxation and abuses ... all we want is our rights, and that we may live by our labour ...

It is also manifest in the petition presented by Hampshire labourers to King William IV at Brighton:

> ... many of us have not food sufficient to satisfy our hunger; our drink is chiefly of the crystal element; we have not clothes to hide the nakedness of ourselves, our wives, and our children, nor fuel wherewith to warm us; while at the same time our barns are filled with corn, our garners with wool, our pastures abound with cattle, and our land yields us an abundance of wood and coal; all of which display the wisdom, the kindness, and mercy of a great Creator on the one hand, and the cruelty, the injustice, and the depravity of his creatures on the other ...

Insurgents were not exclusively agricultural labourers. The numerous craftsmen were also of the same mind. The occupations of persons attending Cobbett's lecture at Battle in October 1830 included:

Shoemaker 6; grocer 2; tailor 4; saddler 2; clockmaker; cabinet maker 3; mason; carpenter 9; farmer 15; labourer 13; druggist 2; brickmaker 2; gardener 2; schoolmaster 2; tanner; wheelwright 2; blacksmith 6; bricklayer; miller; cordwainer; currier; auctioneer 2; basket-maker 2; baker; brewer; innkeeper.

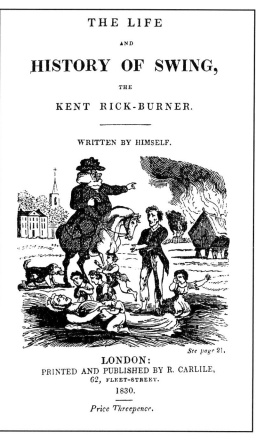

THE LIFE

AND

HISTORY OF SWING,

THE

KENT RICK-BURNER.

WRITTEN BY HIMSELF.

See page 21.

LONDON:
PRINTED AND PUBLISHED BY R. CARLILE,
62, FLEET-STREET.
1830.

Price Threepence.

116 A pamphlet supporting the cause of agricultural labourers.

The high level of winter unemployment explains the attacks on threshing machines. These were less common in the Kent and East Sussex Weald, though 'improving' farmers had them, and they were destroyed, for example, at Hawkhurst and Crowborough. Most farmers hurriedly hid them away. In the western Weald of Surrey and Sussex they had been recently introduced on larger estates. Under threats of destruction, Lord Egremont of Petworth observed that farmers had decided that, 'They were bad things and of no use to them, of which opinion I have always been, and I wish the farmers had found it out before'.

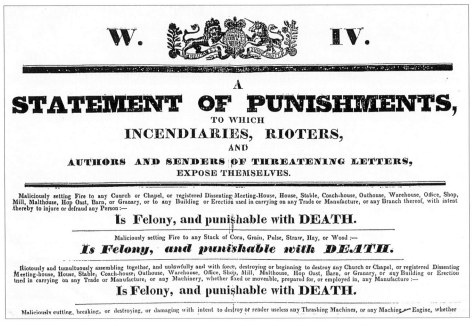

117 A government poster warning of punishment for arson and rioting.

As examples of local disturbances, the following is a summary. On 10 November four fires occurred at Robertsbridge and the labourers of Burwash assembled *en masse* and drove the Assistant Overseer over the parish boundary. At Brede the paupers had been so distressed by the actions of the Overseer that they brought the cart they had been compelled to drag laden with beech, seized the Overseer, and 12 women drew him out of the parish to 'rough music', accompanied by nearly 5,000 men, women and children. At numerous parishes clergymen were told to reduce their tithes. At Mayfield an estate bailiff was mounted on his horse, and escorted out of the parish, accompanied by drum and fife and followed by hundreds of people. Much good-humour existed even in tense incidents. Labourers who informed Lord Liverpool, soon to be Prime Minister, that they would dine with him, were provided with entertainment by his lordship at a public house.

In Buxted, Mrs Courthope of Whiligh at Wadhurst, on discovering that her haying machine was to be spared, gave refreshments to the invaders. As G.D.H. Cole remarked: 'This revolt was carried on by the labourers with quite extraordinary absence of violence. They killed no one; even the harshest overseer was only ducked and trundled out of the village in a barrow.' The gentry were unmolested, and many met the rioters and negotiated with them. At Ringmer 60 workmen invaded a farm and took all the labourers with them, then proceeding to four more farms they did the same. Going on from farm to farm they had three to four hundred strong by nightfall when incendiarism started. At Pulborough a meeting was convened to consider wages. A deputation entered from the labourers outside and said, in a tone that indicated strong feeling: 'Have you, gentlemen, a mind to give us two shillings a-day? We are come here tonight for an answer, and an answer we must have before we go. We have been starving on potatoes long enough, and there must be an alteration; we are come here peaceably; but we must have 2s. a day for our labour.' The demand was met. Arson was on a considerable scale. It began at Ardingly in October 1829 and in July 1830 a barn was set alight at Forest Row and a similar outbreak occurred at Ewhurst on 4 October. From 3 November disturbances commenced in earnest. Within a fortnight the disturbances had spread to the western Weald and from there into neighbouring counties. Rioters assembled in large numbers. At Etchingham 400 gathered; 500 in the Battle area and in Battle itself an estimated 1,000 rioters. The maladministration of the Poor Law led to the manhandling of an overseer at Robertsbridge, and the relieving of the officer at Ringmer of his duties. The Burwash labourers called for 2s. 6d. a day for a man supporting a wife and three children with a weekly allowance of 1s. 6d. for each additional child. A similar demand was made at Etchingham which acknowledged a lower winter rate of pay. At Hawkhurst on 9 November 1830 a crowd of two to three hundred destroyed a threshing machine at Conghurst Farm. Five men were sent for trial; the youngest was acquitted, another imprisoned for a year and the rest were transported for seven years. In the afternoon 400 men assembled at Highgate and demanded higher wages, which were agreed.[9]

A petition presented on Ringmer Green to Lord Gage in November 1830, on behalf of labourers of Ringmer and surrounding villages, mentioned the current wages of 9s. a week and asked for 'Our wages to be advanced to such a degree that will enable us to provide for ourselves and our families without being driven to the overseer'. On reading the petition Lord Gage went into the church vestry with local gentry and farmers to discuss it, the crowd of 150 men waiting quietly outside. When Lord Gage returned he conceded the wages demanded and approved the discharge of the Overseer of the Poor. At Horsham a meeting of the labourers was held in the parish church. The church doors were locked until the men's demands were met. In West Sussex generally wages were also settled under compulsion, but Lord Egremont reported that it was usually done amiably and 'with a friendly disposition on the part of the labourers'. In November, when matters had come to a head, magistrates and local landowners were requesting Sir Robert Peel to send in cavalry and foot soldiers to protect Horsham Gaol and frightened proprietors. Such armed reinforcements were kept as a deterrent; the riots were handled with minimum force and bloodletting through the existing machinery of policing and justice.

The Sussex Association for Improving the Condition of the Labouring Classes was formed in 1831 with the Duke of Sussex as President and with members drawn from the aristocracy and large landowners. It acknowledged the gradual deterioration of the condition of agricultural labourers in Sussex and adjoining counties owing to inadequate wages and the misapplication of the poor rate. It drew attention to the experiments carried on by W. Allen on the Gravelye estate at Lindfield allowing a labourer an acre of land at a fair rent for spade husbandry in order to supplement his wages from a farmer and so support his family in independence and some comfort without the necessity of being a burden on his parish. Upon the Gravelye estate labourers had an acre and a quarter of land close to their cottages but it was not taken up on a significant scale. The quarter of an acre was for garden and the acre was cultivated half in potatoes and half in corn. The keeping of a cow was recommended. Collecting of every vegetable substance, night soil and animal manure in a pit lined with clay was advised, as recommended by William Cobbett, as 'a very good authority upon such subjects, though not upon all'. It was pointed out that this careful management of manure would make little bits of land produce more than the farmers' large ones and that digging with the spade also produced much better yields, particularly in stiff soils. If this proposal had been acted upon on any significant scale, it would have created an independent peasantry working partially on their own account, similar to that on the continent.[10]

Cobbett had great cause to regard the honesty and spirit of the people of Battle with affection. Every effort was made by the authorities to incriminate him directly with the revolts. Thomas Goodman, who was convicted of setting a barn on fire near Battle shortly after Cobbett's lecture there on 16 October 1830, was browbeaten into giving a false testimony that he acted under Cobbett's instigation. A declaration signed by over 100 persons present at the lecture belonging to 14 different parishes, including the prosecutor of Goodman himself, whose barn he burned, testified to the contrary and Goodman was transported. The Goodman 'confession' was again used against Cobbett when he was acquitted on 7 July 1831 of the charge of raising discontent in the minds of labourers in his *Weekly Political Register* of 11 December 1830.[11] When he received congratulations from Battle on his election as a member of Parliament, Cobbett's pleasure was evident in his reply:

> I shall never forget the zealous, the prudent, and the truly just and humane conduct of the people of the town of Battle … It was my endeavours to put a stop to the conflagrations in the country made for this purpose, at that town, which was to have been made the means of my own destruction, and which might have been caused to effect that destruction, had it not been for the honesty of and the spirit of the people of that town.[12]

23

Emigration

DURING the first three decades of the 19th century Surrey's population increased by 65 per cent and that of Sussex and Kent by little less. Meanwhile, the distress and decay of farmers in the 1820s resulting from great mortality among sheep, total failure of hops in 1825 and the collapse of country banks, led to much land going out of cultivation and a reduction in work available for agricultural labourers. As previously noted, the Weald was furnishing a supply of agricultural labourers far in excess of demand and increasingly their maintenance as paupers became a dead loss to landowners and occupiers. Parish relief was received almost as a matter of course by a labourer with three children, whether or not he was able to support them; because no shame was then attached to being upon the poor-rates or for residence in the workhouses. It was claimed that, whenever an able-bodied pauper and his family got into a workhouse, they became so dependent on the supply of rations and blankets, that it was very difficult on any terms to get them out again. So rife was immorality at this time that 'a workhouse may very properly be called a receptacle for the maintenance and propagation of bastards'.[1] At Headcorn near Maidstone in 1826 nearly half the population of 1,190 was on parish relief; and at Bexhill and Northiam it was almost as bad. At Pulborough in West Sussex several landowners had spent large sums in making roads and canals in order to keep men employed and yet in a cold winter 70-80 people would be in the poorhouse. It was much the same at West Grinstead, despite having 'cut down every hill and made 16 miles of turnpike road' with the unemployed.

Emigration was adopted as a cure with a mixture of humanitarianism and economic and social expediency. In 1829 William Cobbett published his *Emigrant's Guide* with the explanation that for 11 years he had advised people not to emigrate but to remain at home in the hope that in a few years some change for the better would come. As this had not happened, and things had gradually become worse and worse, he now thought it advisable for some people to emigrate. 'No toil or frugality,' he declared, 'can save the labourer from hunger and rags, their toil being greater and their food less than those of the slaves in any part of the world that I have ever seen or ever heard of.'

As early as 1819 the parishes of Robertsbridge, Mountfield, Ewhurst and Sedlescombe near Battle had given financial assistance to emigrants as a way of shifting the burden of the Poor Rate off the backs of the remaining population. In 1824 Headcorn in Kent paid for the passage to America of six men, three women and 14 children via Liverpool, and within three years 80 persons

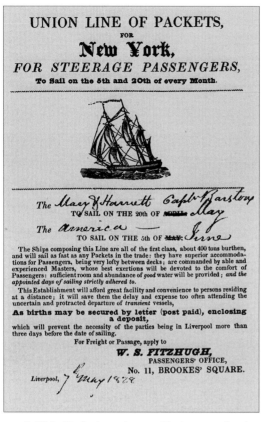

UNION LINE OF PACKETS,

FOR

New York,

FOR STEERAGE PASSENGERS,

To Sail on the 5th and 20th of every Month.

The *Mary & Harriett* Capt. *Marston*
TO SAIL ON THE 20th OF ~~APRIL~~ *May*

The *America* — *June*
TO SAIL ON THE 5th OF ~~MAY~~ *June*

The Ships composing this Line are all of the first class, about 400 tons burthen, and will sail as fast as any Packets in the trade: they have superior accommodations for Passengers, being very lofty between decks; are commanded by able and experienced Masters, whose best exertions will be devoted to the comfort of Passengers: sufficient room and abundance of *good* water will be provided; *and the appointed days of sailing strictly adhered to.*

This Establishment will afford great facility and convenience to persons residing at a distance; it will save them the delay and expense too often attending the uncertain and protracted departure of *transient* vessels.

As births may be secured by letter (post paid), enclosing a deposit,

which will prevent the necessity of the parties being in Liverpool more than three days before the date of sailing.

For Freight or Passage, apply to

W. S. FITZHUGH,

PASSENGERS' OFFICE,

No. 11, BROOKES' SQUARE.

Liverpool, *7 May 1828*

118 W.S. Fitzhugh acted as a shipping agent for the American government at Liverpool and offered an efficient and economical service to prospective emigrants.

chargeable upon the parish had been got rid of, all of whom subsequently did well and none wished to return. The parish had correctly concluded that it could borrow money and pay it off at less cost than if the persons had been kept at home, and that, with a diminishing poor rate, farmers could pay their labourers a higher wage.[2]

One of Cobbett's ways of assisting prospective emigrants was by publishing letters to Sedlescombe, Mountfield, Robertsbridge and Ewhurst in East Sussex from relatives who had emigrated by means of assisted passages. These letters present former paupers in the vivid act of survival. They had one fixed idea, to acquire land and settle on it in a distant place. In doing this they were not easily intimidated or frightened. Mostly, their reports of life in the United States were favourable and some had done very well as farmers or businessmen. (Their next generation began to flood English markets with produce which kept down the prices of English meat and corn.) The letters throw light on the hardship in England by comparison. One reported that the common people in America were as well off as the farmers of Kent, each 'as good as his master, sitting at his table, and with no person to tithe us'.

By 1834 emigration had made considerable progress, with annually increasing disbursements to the poor. The exodus of 56 from Tenterden in 1828 was also to America. Further groups went in 1829 and 1830. Biddenden and Sandhurst, amongst others, were sending emigrants in the 1820s, as were neighbouring East Sussex parishes. Amongst the emigrants from Tenterden in 1828 was a wife sent to join her convict husband in Botany Bay.[3] A remarkable migration which affected farming in Australia was the departure of William Shoobridge, born in Tenterden. His wife and three children died on the long passage to Van Diemen's Land (Tasmania) in 1822, but the hop plants he brought from Kent survived and were successfully harvested by him in Providence Valley near Hobart in 1825, so founding hop culture on the island which continues to this day.[4]

By the late 1820s passages to New York via Liverpool had preference over migrant ships operating from Rye or Dover. The American Chamber of

Commerce had opened an office in Liverpool from 1823, which provided free information and advice for steerage passengers and protected them from the fraudulence and incompetence of ship-owners and captains engaged in the Atlantic trade, which had become scandalous. W.S. Fitzhugh, shipping agent for the American government, who also acted for the Quebec passage, offered purpose-built, twice-monthly, packets of about 400 tons with extra space between decks which were commanded by able and experienced masters. He dealt directly with parish clergymen and Poor Law officers about every detail of passages from arrival in Liverpool (the conveyance of paupers and others from London being separately arranged through Pickford's), and he circulated in 1828 to Staplehurst and other parishes the advertisement for 10,000 labourers wanted for the construction of the Chesapeake and Ohio Canal for which tempting wages and an abundance of bread, meat, vegetables and 'good whiskey' were on offer.

119 George Obrien Wyndham, 3rd Earl of Egremont, by Thomas Phillips.

Emigration was organised in the Petworth district on a scale and standard exceeding anywhere else. This was due to the 3rd Earl of Egremont, who provided most of the financial support, and its redoubtable director, the Rev. Thomas Sockett, Rector of Petworth, who was the prime-mover and spared neither time nor trouble to supply the safety, wants and comforts of emigrants. He obtained the services of Surgeon Superintendent James Marr Brydone who tempered firm naval discipline with the physical and spiritual welfare of his passengers, assisted their travel inland beyond the Great Lakes and in getting employment. One of his reports is of having left Portsmouth with 135 emigrants, some unwell, and having first anchored off Grosse Island in the St Lawrence after 35 days; 136 persons eventually arrived in Montreal, all in good health and spirits, a birth having occurred on the journey.

In all, 1,800 men, women and children sailed to Upper Canada (Ontario) between 1832-7 before Lord Egremont's death ended the scheme. Lord Egremont defrayed £5 towards the cost of clothing and other necessaries for prospective emigrants from parishes in which he owned most of the land and the Emigration Committee urged other parishes and sponsors to do the same.

Additionally, Lord Egremont paid the fare of £10 for the voyage for people from Petworth and the neighbouring parishes of Duncton, Tillington, Egdean and Northchapel and in proportion to the amount of land he owned in other parishes. Financial assistance was also provided by other parishes in the Petworth scheme, notably the Dorking Emigration Committee, sponsored by Charles Barclay of Bury Hill, and some east Sussex parishes were sponsored by the Earl of Chichester of Stanmer and Thomas Calverley of Hellingly. The Duke of Richmond, a minister in the Whig government, whose father had been Governor General of Canada in 1818-19, also supported the Petworth scheme.

Emigration on a parish basis was facilitated a great deal further under the Poor Law Amendment Act (1834), Section 62, which empowered properly constituted vestries, following agreed procedures, to raise or borrow money for funding the emigration of paupers not exceeding the average yearly poor-rate of the three preceding years. This scheme for allowing parishes to mortgage a portion of their rates to off-load their surplus population was the idea of R. Horton and won the support of the Duke of Wellington, the Prime Minister, who refused to offer any financial assistance for the purpose at public expense. This scheme proved to be as great a benefit to those who remained, as to those who emigrated. Parishes all over the Weald took advantage of it, including borrowing from a government agency, e.g. the steady trickle of emigrants who left Frittenden and Benenden between 1834 and 1850.[5] It should be noted, however, that this account has been confined to 'assisted' passages. Additionally, large numbers emigrated by their own means. The Rev. Edmund Moore of Frittenden estimated that as many as 500 persons had emigrated from his parish between 1820 and 1850.

As the 19th century advanced, Australia and New Zealand (and occasionally the Cape) came more into focus, but as successive governments gave no financial encouragement to emigration, the numbers assisted by Wealden parishes remained small. The Providence Chapel in Cranbrook, in a notable dissenting district, circulated details of a colony of 1,000 nonconformists being established near Auckland. A social mix of 'capitalists, persons of small means and labourers' was planned, each adult receiving a free grant of 40 acres and 20 acres for a child. An 'agricultural instructor' was appointed and arrangements made for a doctor, minister and teacher to take up posts. A pioneer party had left in 1861 to make the necessary arrangements with local authorities. The primary object was to mitigate the hardships of the first years of an emigrant's life by bringing together those who would wisely help themselves, by helping one another. The necessary kit for the colonies could then be purchased from Coy, Evans and Co. of Cornhill and Piccadilly or from Lobbs of Cheapside, both of whom shipped baggage. By then the institution of the migrant ship had given way to the steamer in which working-class men and women mixed freely without the need to be kept segregated under lock and key.[6]

24

Wealden Churches and Chapels

AT Worth is one of the more remarkable churches in England. It is transeptal, large, elaborate and stone-built with the characteristics of late Saxon workmanship – long, narrow openings, pilaster strips and 'long and short' quoins. It has an extended apsed chancel, a large chancel arch, and three notable windows formed by twin arched lights separated by robust stone balusters set in the centre of the wall. These balusters stand on square stone bases. The design and bold details of the church are quite unlike the little unpretentious Saxon downland churches. It moves one by its grand proportions and the impressiveness of its components. In Desmond Seward's view, it is the most beautiful thing in Sussex.[1]

Nothing illustrates more clearly the darkness still surrounding much early Wealden development than that the existence of this grand church in what was then presumably a simple clearing in the forest cannot be explained. No documentary evidence for its building has been traced and consequently we know nothing about its patrons or functions. It is without a history. The Domesday Book entry for Worth is in the Surrey folios, the boundary between Surrey and Sussex then apparently still indeterminate. There is thus the probability that the church's origins are associated with Surrey. It has been suggested that it was a foundation of Edward the Confessor as an outpost of the Abbey of Chertsey.[2] It is, however, more likely that the church is not Anglo-Saxon but post-Conquest in date which would link it with the Earls Warenne of Lewes, the local landholders.[3]

120 Worth church.

The first Wealden churches usually had quite different history. They were often half-timbered buildings in the simple vernacular tradition within clearings in the forest typically rebuilt in stone with the population growth in the 12th and 13th centuries, by when after a dozen generations of human effort parishes were fast outgrowing their 'colonial' character as an appendage to the earlier developed south. The most famous example is that of Mayfield which, according to the historian Eadmer, was built as a little wooden church in the 10th century by St Dunstan, Archbishop of Canterbury. The present large church is Perpendicular, after a fire in 1389. Kirdford is a classic example of a parish church which had to be successively enlarged to accommodate the increased congregation of the largest parish in West Sussex so as to maintain its intimate associations with the daily life of the local community of which it was the centre and focus. The original 12th-century nave and chancel, presumably successors of a still smaller wooden building, were almost doubled in size in the 13th century by building a wide north aisle the whole length of the original nave and chancel and an arcade of three beautiful pointed arches took the place of the nave's north wall. The blocked south door and part of the south wall of the nave, with its herringbone masonry, survive from the earlier church. The chancel was again rebuilt and extended in the 14th century and a vaulted sacristy added. The square tower is 15th-century, a period when the symbolism of a steeple with its bells had taken on a renewed spiritual force. The porch has a medieval bargeboard and Elizabethan balusters. The stonework is largely Bargate Stone, quarried locally. There is a Horsham stone roof and Sussex 'marble' (last dug in the parish *c*.1880) has been used for paving and fittings. Overall, the church is described by Ian Nairn as 'Admirably solid and straightforward, an epitome of Wealden building'.[4]

The story of Kirdford is broadly repeated the Weald over. At Fletching, for example, the tower has traces of Saxo-Norman work but the present large structure is in the Early English style, and was completed about 1230. The graceful shingled spire was added about 1340. Another church rebuilding, symbolising Wealden prosperity, is at Lindfield, which was an important iron and cloth centre at least from the 13th century. Extensive rebuilding was also required for churches at Buxted, Heathfield, Rotherfield and Waldron to accommodate the huge congregations which came to settle in these parishes during the last phase of woodland clearance. West Hoathly church records particularly well this progressive enlargement to keep pace with forest clearing. Originally a little rectangular Norman building, an aisle and chapel was added and the chancel most unusually was extended to make it larger than the nave in the 12th and 13th centuries. Old Pembury, Lamberhurst, Capel and Tudeley were Kentish churches which underwent much the same progression and for the same reasons.

Another distinctive regional characteristic of Wealden churches is the further rebuilding from the 15th century in a period of rapid growth of population and wealth, mainly as a consequence of the cloth trade. This did not result in great 'wool churches' as in East Anglia, Somerset or Northamptonshire. An exception is the remodelling of Cranbrook parish church between *c*.1475-1530 on an enlarged and grander scale. More typical of the period are the widespread great west towers set up from the late 14th century. They are particularly prominent in Kent, Tenterden being an outstanding example of good workmanship, visible for miles. For one of these towers a detailed churchwarden's account book survives. The parishioners of Bolney built the 66ft. square tower to their church in 1536-8. The moving spirit was John Bolney, churchwarden and leading landowner, whose family can be traced back to the 13th century. He was the overall administrator of an inspired community effort involving the whole village. Benefactions, big and small, were offered according to people's means. A bridge and roadway had first to be constructed from the stone quarries to the church. Payment was made for this to local men, but some gave back a proportion of their wages. Even skilled men of the village joined others in quarrying and carting the stone. The tower was raised by an itinerant gang of masons, who

121 Cowden church timbers. (John Malton, September 2002, ink and pencil sketch, 12.5 x 18cm [5 x 7¼ in.])

skilfully cut large blocks of sandstone. Timber was cut for scaffolding and beams and every tool and implement was made on the spot. Engraved on a stone by the west door are the triumphant words 'This Stepl is 66 Foot high'. This episode is a fascinating story of collective devotion on the part of all sections of a local community.[5]

In thinly inhabited woodland districts where good building stone was lacking, medieval constructions are notable for the amount of timber used in bell towers or turrets in the 14th and 15th centuries, as at Burstow, Horne, Horley, Leigh and Newdigate on the Weald Clay in Surrey, and at Cowden and High Halden in Kent. Such timber towers are fine specimens of medieval carpentry, retaining massive beams and posts hewn from locally grown oak. Surrey churches are also distinguished by their finely carved wooden screens, the finest being at Charlwood. In some Kent churches the carpenter's skill is also well executed as at Headcorn, where the huge span of the roof is acknowledged to be a great achievement. Charlwood has a particularly fine medieval wooden screen. Ticehurst has a font with a beautifully carved 16th-century oak cover which opens on hinges and has panels carved with delicately wrought designs.

The former palace of the archbishops of Canterbury at Mayfield includes the spectacular Great Hall (now the chapel of the public school belonging to the Sisters of the Holy Child Jesus), probably built by Archbishop Reynolds

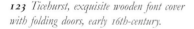

122 The interior of Newdigate timber tower.

123 Ticehurst, exquisite wooden font cover with folding doors, early 16th-century.

(1313-27). Its glory is the great span of nearly 40 feet of the three tremendous pointed stone arches, the widest built in the medieval period, which spring from corbels in the form of foliated capitals on short shafts supported by grotesque figures. The usual three doorways to the former kitchen, buttery and pantry survive and diaper carving is well preserved where the archbishop's throne stood. Fifteenth-century archbishops tended to reside at Knole but the fine gatehouse on the village street and the porch to the Great Hall bear the arms of Archbishop Warham (1503-32).

Battle Abbey, founded by King William in 1076, fulfilled his vow on the eve of the Battle of Hastings that if he were successful he would found a monastery on the battlefield. Despite the entreaties of monks from Marmoutier on the Loire that a ridge lacking in water was an impracticable site, the king refused to countenance any change in his resolution and insisted that the high altar should be placed on the very spot where King Harold's ensign fell. From the beginning

124 The Archbishops' Palace, Mayfield, gateway of Archbishop Warham, c.1520.

he endowed Battle as a wealthy house, making it 15th in order of wealth of monasteries recorded in Domesday Book. It was also granted a *banlieu*, or 'leuga', a roughly circular estate three miles in diameter for its maintenance. Thus, the Abbey rapidly developed (p.91). The conventual buildings were initially completed by Abbot Ralph (1107-24), whose rounded apse, ambulatory and radiating chapels, more common in the Loire valley than in Normandy, were repeated later at Canterbury and other cathedrals. Almost all the monastic buildings were rebuilt on a grandiose scale during the 13th century out of wealth generated by astute land management. This was achieved with considerable difficulty on account of the narrow hilltop and its steeply sloping sides. The new buildings expanded into the hillsides in the form of cellars and crypts, and the creation of specially constructed earthen platforms was necessary.[6] In 1338 one of the most splendid gatehouses in England was built, signifying the threat of French raids and internal rebellion. A sumptuous abbot's hall was the main addition in the 15th century.

125 The magnificently restored tomb of Sir Anthony Browne and his wife in Battle parish church. Browne took possession of the Abbey at the Dissolution.

The ruined site, which, glimpsed from Ninfield to the east, is spectacular, comprises substantial parts of the dormitory block, refectory, common and novices' rooms and guest house. An outstanding official in the 15th century was Bartholomew Bolney who served the monastery as steward from the 1420s to his death in 1477. He rose from a modest family background by the legal profession to marry a daughter of Sir John Gage of Firle whose grandson, Sir John Gage, took possession of Battle's manor of Alciston at the Dissolution in 1538 where his grandfather had so often held the manorial court as the abbot's steward. The king's close friend and guardian of Edward VI, Sir Anthony Browne, son in law of Sir John Gage, who received the site of the Abbey and manors in East Sussex, razed the church, cloisters and chapter house. He and his wife have a magnificent tomb, recently restored, in Battle church.[7]

Robertsbridge Abbey was a Cistercian house founded by Alured de St Martin in 1176. Originally built at Salehurst with monks from Boxley, the Abbey was removed because of floods. The village of Robertsbridge grew up around the Abbey which, by means of granges – barns with an oratory and rudimentary sleeping accommodation for two or three lay brethren – successfully cleared the surrounding wild country of forest and marsh. Little survives apart from Abbey Farm which was probably the abbot's lodging. The most picturesque abbey ruin in the Weald is Bayham, a Premonstratensian house founded c.1208 which, like Robertsbridge, created a small estate out of uninhabited country. The church was rebuilt during the 13th century on conventional Cistercian lines but with a polygonal apse, and clustered around it is a complex of monastic buildings that stood before Cardinal Wolsey dissolved the abbey in 1525. Humphry Repton made use of the ruins in his landscape design of 1799-1800 (p.244).

Very characteristic of the Weald were the small Augustinian priories and nunneries, small communities whose primary purpose was prayer. Their solitary and simple vision of life, in deep woodlands, preserved the monastery's seclusion, and acted as a place for recreation and exercise and provided fuel for heating and other needs. Michelham was founded in 1229 by Gilbert of Aquila, lord of Pevensey rape, within a wide moat. By the last quarter of the 14th century the priory had run into debt through flood damage to its buildings and lands, and grants of the churches of Alfriston and Fletching by the Bishop of Chichester in 1398 provided funds for repairs. The priory had been a target of the Peasants' Revolt in 1381 and the gatehouse was built to give greater protection in 1395. The frater, refectory and other parts of the south range of the priory were converted into a Tudor mansion on the Dissolution. Warbleton Priory, which was transferred from Hastings by Sir John Pelham in 1413, is now a charming house mainly fronted in 17th-century ashlar but with a medieval half-timbered wing. An outbuilding, once part of the priory, contains medieval arches. Easebourne was a small nunnery founded by John de Bohun whose castle mound rises in woodland above Midhurst. The refectory was converted into a barn at the Dissolution and now serves the community. There was no monastic church; the nuns heard mass through internal windows connecting the priory with the south aisle of the parish church. Repeated scandals marked the last one hundred years of its existence.

Shulbrede, near Fernhurst in West Sussex, was founded by Sir Ralph de Arderne *c*.1200. The church was destroyed at the Dissolution and the rest of the buildings turned into a farmhouse. These were sensitively restored by Arthur Ponsonby from 1902. The stone staircase leading to a large upper room, known as the Prior's chamber, and the vaulted undercroft still preserve their medieval character. In the Prior's room is a 16th- or early 17th-century mural with paintings

126 Shulbrede Priory restored by Arthur Ponsonby.

of animals rejoicing at the birth of Christ. On the outside wall of the refectory, originally one hall, but now divided into two floors, is the lavatorium of three trefoiled arches. As at Easebourne, the administration appears to have been very lax on the eve of the Dissolution. The historian Horsfield remarked in 1835 that the priory 'is buried in a dingle or small valley, surrounded by hills covered with wood, and not to be approached even in summer, but with difficulty'.[8] It is still one of the most rewarding places to find.

In the Weald the losses from Victorian 'restoration' were great. Fernhurst and Loxwood in West Sussex were both demolished and replaced by one described by Ian Nairn in *The Buildings of England* as 'deadly dull', and the other as 'horribly fiddly'. Another razed to the ground was the chapel at Plaistow, formerly in Kirdford parish, shown in early watercolours as timber-framed and thatched in the same style as surrounding farmhouses, until replaced by the present stone building in 1851.[9] Other once simple little buildings before the advent of *nouveaux riches* in their parishes include Balcombe, Crawley, Crowborough, Wivelsfield and Woodmancote. Harsh restorations abound. Lindfield's monuments were treated with no regard for propriety or respect of antiquity.[10] William Morris vainly protested at the spoliation of the dramatic axial design of the Knight Templars' church at Shipley by the addition of a north aisle in 1893 to the design of J.L. Pearson.

A drastic change was the rebuilding of Hurstpierpoint church. An 11th-century tower was all that remained of the church referred to in Domesday Book when John Urry, rector from 1419-44, rebuilt the church largely at his own expense. This was completely razed to the ground and replaced by the present church built under the auspices of Canon Borrer, rector for 57 years. He considered the church in a very dilapidated state and too small for the expanding parish, then attracting wealthy residents from Brighton's hinterland. He sought the services of one of the leading architects of that time, Charles Barry, who built the parish church of St Peter's, Brighton, the first portion of the Royal Sussex County Hospital and whose design was selected for the House of Commons destroyed by fire. Although this occurred in 1843 during a great epoch of church building, this cannot condone the entire demolition of the old church. Even the dedication was changed from St Lawrence to that of the Holy Trinity because Borrer did not consider that the minor saint was any longer appropriate for his grand edifice.[11]

The architect, Philip Webb (1831-1915), the co-founder with William Morris of the Society for the Protection of Ancient Buildings, retired to Caxtons, a half-timbered house, weatherboarded on its upper storey, on the ridge in Worth parish, and not far from Standen, the house he designed for the Beales. He had a lifelong familiarity with the buildings and landscapes of the Weald and one of the main themes of his surviving correspondence was the needless destruction of the legacy of historic buildings during the last quarter of the 19th century, and of the rapid changes taking place in town and countryside which were making them almost into new places. Slaugham was a lost cause by 1905, as far as Webb was concerned, because the lovely church had been ravished and 'sickled over'. His strongest strictures were reserved for 'restoration' at the beautiful church at Worth, where he always lost his temper at the stupid 'smalling down' of the

127 *Warbleton Priory, a delightful house with outbuildings bearing traces of the medieval monastery.*

128 *Rotherfield church pulpit. In the bottom right-hand corner stands the cross blown off the spire by the great storm of 1987. (John Malton, May 1999, pen and ink with watercolour wash, 12.5 × 16.5cm [5 × 6½ in.])*

ancient vigour of the interior (even more sweeping destruction was defeated by protests). Webb's trip to Burwash church was spoiled by recent 'witless fiddling' but he was able to pass on the good news in one of the last letters he was to write to William Morris (1896) about Etchingham church, which had been entirely rebuilt by Sir William de Etchingham in the late 14th century and had suffered least at Victorian hands:

> The church just one of those placid 14th-century Sussex pieces of serious village building; a kind of happy sing-song of labour and unconscious feeling; which was as of picked-up manna in the wilderness to me. The tracery part of all the nave and aisle windows (is) still holding untouched glass of its date – all masculine and of colour none better anywhere in the world.[12]

In Kent, Marden church was saved from drastic change by the Society for the Protection of Ancient Buildings.[13]

In compensation for much drastic restoration, the Weald was also to gain from some splendid Victorian church building. The most talked-about early Victorian rural parish church was that of Kilndown near Goudhurst in Kent. This was the creation of Alexander James Beresford Hope, the owner of the Bedgebury estate and from the late 1840s the dominant force within the ecclesiological movement. Between 1840-5 Hope transformed Kilndown, a recently built pre-Camdenian church designed by Anthony Salvin, by means of a chancel of crowded sumptuousness by Roos, an Italian architect, with woodwork designed by R.C. Carpenter, metalwork by William Butterfield and decorations by Willement. The timber used came from the estate and much of the carving was done by local carpenters. The gilded rood-screen and roof, the coloured wall, the lustre on all fittings and the universal stained glass was acclaimed by *The Ecclesiologist* as 'a whole of colour such as is to be seen … in no other English church at the present time'.[14] Lit for evensong, this marvellous change represented the resurgent note of High Anglicanism and was the model which the Cambridge Camden Society was urging on Anglicans nationally. Such 'Squire's churches' were expensive and their single-source funding was a direct assertion of wealth and local patrimony. In Beresford Hope's case he poured so much of his energies and money into the Cambridge Camden Society and into other architectural projects, such as his estate village at Kilndown, and numerous other estate cottages, that his impoverished descendants had to sell the estate, its country house and fittings. An altogether quieter, but admirable complex of early Victorian buildings is that financed by Edmund Moore, the grandson of an archbishop, at Frittenden. This comprised a rebuilt church by R.C. Hussey (who discovered that the old church was too decayed for restoration), a school, 'like an overgrown cottage orné, two Gothic cottages, a large country house and a model farm. Much more typical of churches paid for by wealthy residents is the little church of Mark Beech, paid for by the Hon. John Talbot whose architect, David Brandon 'poorly seconded the wishes of the founder'.[15]

In 1877 the Weald became the home of the only English order of Carthusians since the Reformation when St Hugh's Charterhouse was founded at Shermanbury in West Sussex. In this quiet part of the Low Weald was found the isolation from

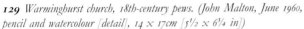

129 Warminghurst church, 18th-century pews. (John Malton, June 1960, pencil and watercolour [detail], 14 × 17cm [5½ × 6¾ in])

130 Frittenden church. The Revd Edmund Moore, a grandson of an archbishop, and his wife, Lady Harriet, a daughter of the 4th Duke of Buccleuch and Queensberry, paid for the rebuilding of the neglected church in 1848 and around it additionally built the Rectory and created a home farm with model buildings, a school and cottages. The architect R.C. Hussey was responsible for the sensitive restoration of the church in a rather dull Headcorn stone. At its re-opening over one thousand people were provided with roast beef and plum pudding and medals were struck for the children.

the outside world the order required. Built by a French architect for French monks persecuted in France, the tall steeple is a landmark for miles and the enormous cloister, with the separate monks' cells opening onto it, is in the style of the French Gothic Revival. The monks pass their lives in cells, except when they are going directly through the great cloister into the church, chapterhouse and library, and for their weekly walk and dining in the frater on Sundays. Recently founded monasteries include an Anglican institution on Benedictine lines buried in woodland in East Sussex near Crawley Down and Worth Priory in a former imitation Tudor mansion.

Nonconformist Chapels

Meanwhile, the forest country was pullulating with fundamentalist religious sects. The Society of Dependents (the 'Cokelers'), was an intensely religious local sect founded in 1850 when James Sirgood arrived in Loxwood, then a small, remote

131 Cade Street Chapel. The cross was erected in the early 20th century to commemorate seven of the martyrs burnt at Lewes.

hamlet on the Weald clay of West Sussex. Sirgood was a shoemaker, a disciple of William Bridges who in 1838 had formed a religious group of the urban poor in south London known as the Plumstead Peculiars. Sirgood's charismatic and deceptively simple evangelicalism proved to be a salvation for the rural poor, many of whom were farm workers in summer, and copse-cutters in winter. Their localities were bywords for inaccessibility in winter owing to heavy clay, and Loxwood was not then an ecclesiastical parish, having a chapel-of-ease where services were only held fortnightly by a minister from Wisborough Green, four miles away. The rural poor in neighbouring hamlets off the main roads experienced an even greater religious dearth. Peter Jerrome has called the district 'effectively a lost world'. By means of open-air meetings on commons or in the cottage homes of his followers within walking distance of Loxwood, Sirgood rapidly built up a substantial following, which local magnates and ministers failed to suppress. As congregations grew, meetings in tied cottages tended to be replaced by tiny chapels which were less vulnerable to hostile landowners and 'rough music' at the hands of village thugs. By his death in 1885, Sirgood had attracted about 2,000 adherents.[16]

The Dependents, so named because they depended on Christ for everything, utterly rejected the indulgence of their contemporary world for ascetic living. They were honest, plain living people who valued poverty and humility and eschewed marriage. There were no sacraments and no catechism. They discouraged matrimony on religious grounds, understanding this as a charter for celibacy,

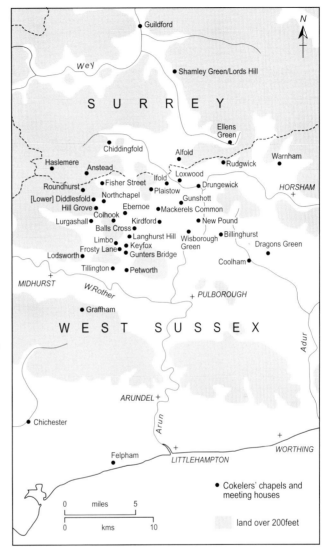

132 The chapels and meeting places of the Cokelers (after Peter Jerrome).

not promiscuity. They were traditionally abstemious and an alleged habit of drinking cocoa as a substitute for alcohol is often said to have given rise to their local name of 'Cokelers', but Peter Jerrome suggests that this term is a corruption of 'Cuckolders', used in constantly repeated accusations that Dependents 'went about with other men's wives'. They denied themselves cultural and sporting entertainments and the reading of published works, except the Bible.

A remarkable feature was the opening of local stores from about 1878 to provide an alternative to service for young women, so freeing them for evening services, and also to bind the community together. Through their cleanliness, hard work and business acumen, the Dependents threw off much of the contempt and derision they had suffered and became respected for sincerity and clean living.

133 Cokelers' chapel at Northchapel. The Cokelers ran a general store and a bicycle shop in the village.

By means of the stores, the Dependents were also able to practise the agricultural self-sufficiency which has always been the mark of the Wealden smallholder and family farmer, butter, milk, bacon, eggs and cheese being produced on local farms run by Cokeler families and maintained in tandem with retail 'department' stores, as at Northchapel, thus cutting out the middleman. Their practice of agricultural co-operation without a middleman was well in advance of the rest of England and noted as a possible model for improving the small farmers' position everywhere.

After Sirgood's death in 1885 the strength of the Dependents declined inexorably to some 600 in 1916, an estimated 200 in 1942, some 60 or 70 in 1981. The sect is now extinct. The chapels have been demolished or converted into private residences, with the exception of that at Loxwood which is used by another church. As recently as 1942 the Cokeler women would have been seen at Loxwood, walking in twos and threes, wearing tiny bonnets of black straw and black velvet shawls, black coats and black skirts reaching the ground, accompanied by soberly dressed men with mutton chop whiskers and little beards who had only recently discarded the Sussex smock frock.[17]

25

The Wildness Pleases:

The Changed Appreciation of the Weald

WHEN 18th-century foreigners expressed admiration for the 'Garden of England', it was that part of Kent along Watling Street near Sittingbourne, Rochester and Greenwich that they had in mind. There they found nursery gardens, orchards, hop fields, hay meadows and corn fields supplying all kinds of produce in a time-orderly, garden-like setting in the mainstream of landscape taste, embodying the useful and the habitable, traceable back through time in western European literature. To the mid-18th-century Duke of Nivernois, Kent, between Rochester and London, was 'the finest country in the universe, the most populous, the most animated, the most cultivated …'. Newly-returned English travellers were also quick to conceive this image of north-east Kent as a terrestrial paradise when the great sweeping vistas of northern France were still fresh enough in their mind's eye to point the contrast. Horace Walpole, who travelled through the district in 1741 with eyes newly opened by the experience of the Grand Tour, stumbled to the realisation that its intimate domestic atmosphere

134 Balcombe viaduct, opened in 1841, is a splendid monument to the general engineer of the London Brighton and South Coast Railway, Arthur Raistrick and the company's architect, Mocatta. En route to and from Brighton passengers were entranced by newly discovered scenery. An artist's reconstruction by Mike Codd.

was due to the littleness of its natural and man-made features, a quality lacking in the France he had just left. In the same way, he detected, by similar analogy and contrast, that another notable omission across the Channel was the comfortable 'middling' farmhouse on the scale of the Kentish yeoman's hall.[1]

Yet, as we have noted, the few 18th-century or earlier travellers who penetrated the Wealds of Kent, Sussex and Surrey had little admiration to bestow. It is significant, for example, that Horace Walpole was so preoccupied by the dangers and discomforts of his tours that he has not a word to say about the Weald's landscape. Cobbett's intense relish in the 1820s for the 'heaths, the miry coppices, the wild woods and the forests of Sussex and Hampshire' was typical of a man who, in almost every respect, was a rebel against the conventions of his age. Representative of the early 19th-century assessment of the Weald is W.H. Ireland's *New and Complete History of Kent* (1829), which closely followed Hasted's (p.11). He warmed to the varied prospects from elevated ground around the Weald and from the hilly districts of Goudhurst, Hemsted in Benenden, Rolvenden, Staplehurst and Cranbrook, but 'deep and miry' country overspread with woods wearied him either to reside at or to travel through, and Tenterden was considered too near marshes to be healthy.

This lack of appreciation for much of the Weald changed, but a long time elapsed before it happened. As Vaughan Cornish has written, the appeal of a swelling mass of woodland borne upon the English lowland was less clamorous than the more inspiring spectacle of nature in upland Britain, which inspired the first Romantic poets and artists, but gained strength as the eye became 'educated to its subtler charms'.[2]

This was very true of the Weald. Its landscape did not conform to the conventional notion of the beautiful, until the impulse of the Romantic and Picturesque movements from the end of the 18th century, and it was not until it became better known with improved roads, and later by railways, that the lushness and greenness of its ordinary, everyday scenery created the impression of a kind of enlarged landscaped park and at the same time a domesticity speaking of home pleasures and comforts. Lovers of wooded glens, rocky outcrops and cascades became enchanted by the hillier parts of the High Weald. It was found to be wilder and stranger than almost any other part of lowland England. This touch of 'wildness', so reproachful to Stuart commentators (p.10), was now recognised, with newly-opened eyes, as a distinct and uncommon genre of human landscape which excited admiration and wonder. In this new mood was written this description of the central Weald, only a year or two after the completion of one of the first railways:

> The ordinary traveller from London to Brighton by the express train is probably entirely unaware that he passes through some of the wildest and most beautiful country in the three kingdoms; he may, particularly about the Balcombe station, get glimpses of almost unrivalled forest scenery which remind him strongly of the run into Namur through the Ardennes, but he does not know, or does not care to inquire, anything about it … within thirty-five miles of London you get a country as primitive and almost as lonely as that of the Adirondack …[3]

Meanwhile, Turner had been representing in watercolour the faint but palpable tang of wildness in the surviving Sussex woodland and Samuel Palmer had dreamily called up reveries of the prodigal Wealden garden, teeming with life and produce at Shoreham in Kent. John Linnell, with the aid of the newly-opened Brighton railway, made detailed sketches of woodland scenes at Balcombe and then stationed himself on the summit of the sandstone hills near Redhill to capture the panoramic beauty of the Weald. This spiriting of a new, imagined, wildness out of what wooded nature survived in a shrunken form after medieval clearings was to become an inexhaustible source of enrichment to urban life. As Élisée Reclus observed of the Sussex Weald in 1881 it 'abounds in wild woodland scenery unsurpassed in any part of England'.[4]

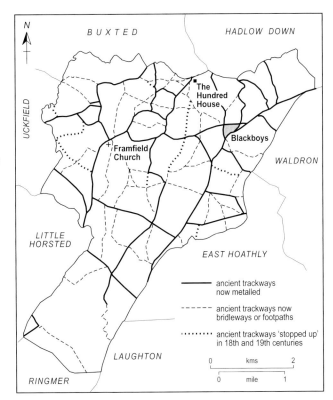

135 Network of former roads in Framfield parish.

Italy in England

This growing appreciation of Wealden landscape was also connected with perceptions of beauty, for ever changed for many English travellers as a consequence of the Grand Tour. When lowland English scenery began to be considered from the Picturesque point of view it was commonly judged against much loved scenes around Rome and Florence, or had been made famous by Claude Lorrain and Nicholas Poussin. An observer, dreamily looking out at a grey

English horizon and fervently wishing he was in Italy, would try to turn it in imagination into the sweeping backdrop of his Italian models.

So deeply did the love of Italy burn in their hearts that few admitted that Wealden views surpassed anything they had seen in Italy itself. Yet this John Dennis did in 1717 in one of the earliest surviving appreciations of the beauty of a man-made English lowland landscape:

> … The Prospects that in Italy pleas'd me most, were that of the Valdarno from the Appenines, that of Rome and the Mediterranean from the Mountain of Viterbo … But from a Hill which I pass'd in my late Journey into Sussex, I had a prospect more extensive than any of these, and which surpass'd them at once in Rural Charms, in Pomp and in Magnificence … call'd Lethe Hill [Leith Hill in Surrey].[5]

Another who compared the Weald favourably with Italy was 18th-century John Macky, who praised the Weald because it resembled Lombardy.[6]

As David Watkin has remarked:

> There can be no doubt that the steep hills and rolling woods of central Surrey are still, and must have been much more so when in a condition of relatively wild remoteness as in the 1800s, amongst the most 'Picturesque' parts of the country, in the precise sense in which the word was used in 1800. That is to say they are like an 'excited' version of a Capability Brown park on the grandest scale. Thus Leith Hill is the highest point in SE England: and a topographer recently described how from Newlands Corner one sees 'range after range of hills composing themselves as elegantly and harmoniously as a Claude landscape'.[7]

This association of the Weald with Italian landscape becomes stronger in the 19th century and the Edwardian period. Tennyson admired his favourite view of the Downs at Shoreham because, when he returned from abroad and looked from the terrace of his home on Blackdown, he thought it was exactly like Italy, and visitors after his death were in agreement:[8]

> In the rich sunshine the terrace had a curiously Italian look. There were the scarlet flowers blazing on the balustrade where he loved to see them against the blue of fifty miles away. Tall cypress-like trees flank the terrace, and between them you gaze at that wonderful view across the chequered green of the Sussex Weald to the grey-blue of Chanctonbury Ring and the South Downs. English as the scene is, one could easily imagine oneself looking down from the terrace of a villa raised over the Lombardy plain …[9]

E.M. Forster playfully puts this same sentiment in *A Room with a View* (1908):

> Ah, how beautiful the Weald looks! The hills stood out above its radiance, as Fiesole stands above the Tuscan plain, and the South Downs, if one chose, were the mountains of Carrara. She might be forgetting her Italy, but she was noticing more things in her England. One could play a new game with a view, and try to find in its innumerable folds, some town or village that would do for Florence …[10]

'Bungalow Briggs' at Bellagio at Dormansland went a stage further and built an Italianate speculative development named after a settlement on Lake Como.

The 'discovery' of heathland

Another reason for a growing love for the Weald was a changed perception of heathland. According to 18th-century and earlier taste, heaths were 'sullen', 'scenically tiresome', a foil to the beauty of the rest of England and 'horrid and frightful' to look upon. Agricultural writers bewailed their lack of enclosure and cultivation. Villages had an evil reputation as the haunts of lawless people. Going over Hindhead was tedious and dangerous as Pepys reported in August 1668:

> At Gilford we dined ... So to coach again, and got to Lippock, late over Hindhead, having an old man, a guide, in the coach with us; but got thither with great fear of being out of the way, it being ten at night ...[11]

William Cobbett had a pact with himself never to set foot on Hindhead, which he regarded as an affront to the agricultural improver. He amuses in *Rural Rides* with various devices to keep faith with this resolution but on one occasion he was beaten by a young guide who either did not know the way round it or was dishonest enough not to tell him.[12] Thomas Allen, author of *A History of Surrey*

136 Heathland, by George Vicat Cole.

and Sussex, in 1829 could find between Albury and Ewhurst 'no object on which the eye can repose with pleasure, even for a moment'.

Yet, soon after Cobbett's day, heaths were coming to be admired under the influence of the Picturesque movement for their hint of the primeval. Ruskin's preference for wilder scenery than the polished neatness of the Richmond river-side had much to do with young artists such as Birket Foster and Helen Allingham sketching in the Weald. Mrs Mary (Humphry) Ward, who spent summers at Grayswood near Haslemere, struck a new note:

> A nature wild and solitary indeed but still rich, luxuriant and friendly to the sense of the traveller, even in its loneliest places. The heaths and woods of some districts of Surrey scarcely are more thickly populated than the fells of Westmoreland; the walker may wander for miles, and still enjoy an untamed primitive earth, guiltless of boundary or furrow, the undisturbed home of all that grows and flies, where the rabbits, the lizards, and the birds live their life as they please, either ignorant of intruding man or strangely little incommoded by his neighbourhood. And yet there is nothing forbidding or austere in these wild solitudes. The patches of graceful birch-wood; the miniature lakes nestling among them; the brakes of ling-pink, faintly scented, a feast for every sense; the stretches of purple heather, glowing into scarlet under the touch of the sun; the scattered farm-houses, so mellow in colour, so pleasant in outline; the general softness and lavishness of the earth and all it bears makes these Surrey commons not a wilderness but a paradise ...[13]

Charles Kingsley, rector of Eversley, explained this new fascination with heathland in terms of natural science coupled with a growing sense of 'wildness' as an antidote to modernisation:

> In countless thousands the winged seeds [of Scots pine] float down the south-west gales from the older trees ... Till as you stand upon some eminence, you see, stretching to the eastward of each tract of older trees, a long cloud of younger ones, like a green comet's tail ... Truly beautiful – grand indeed to me it is – to see young live nature thus carrying on a great savage process in the heart of this old and seemingly all-artificial English land; and reproducing here, as surely as in the Australian bush, a native forest, careless of mankind ...[14]

The desolate aspect of heaths was being changed by the extraordinary spread of these self-seeded Scots pine originally planted in clumps or knolls from the 17th century for the dual purpose of ornament and game conservation. That late Victorians took this tree to their hearts, is clear from its frequent presence beside cottages and from the popularity of Leader's watercolours, caught within a frame of close stands of pine on a Surrey common with 'smouldering' purple heather or the brazen illumination of a gorse-clad moor in the foreground. The late Victorian middle class was seized with such a compelling perception of 'pine country' as providing the best soil, the purest air and the healthiest surroundings that the 'rush to the pine woods' in the wild and previously almost undiscovered corners of the Surrey Weald became a minor urban exodus. By the 1890s any yeoman's farmhouse lying within four to five miles of a railway station could be easily let in summer as a 'second home' to wealthy London businessmen.[15]

The appreciation of the Weald's vernacular architecture also developed from the late 18th century when Hasted and others took the then conventional view

137 J.C. Dibdin's sketch of Haxted Farm near Edenbridge, Kent, 1874. This is an example of the vernacular which inspired late Victorian and Edwardian architects.

that it was 'too mean' for consideration. Sensitivity to it was first stimulated by the Picturesque movement which led sketchers like John T. Smith to search for ruinous cottages as elements of 'pleasing decay' on the edges of remote Surrey commons. As early as 1803 the professional architect, Richard Elsam, considered that in Kent and Surrey, designers of houses required 'no other guide' than the surviving examples of simple, traditional building. The histrionic style of the Gothic Revival was soon to overshadow completely the quieter 'Wealden' and other traditional styles but in the 1860s attitudes shifted and the heritage of domestic building was eagerly studied once more, revealing the proportion, balance and graceful simplicity of half-timbered and stone-built houses. The masterly attention given by traditional builders to details such as chamfers, stops, beams and joists was also noted, as were the 'organic' settings of the houses themselves. The so-called Wealden with its two-storeyed ends jutting out laterally seemed to provide visual proof that conscious aesthetic effect in domestic building had been a consideration in the region for centuries.[16]

Vernacular architecture was especially fascinating to members of the William Morris group (including the architects Philip Webb and William Lethaby) who aimed to preserve old buildings, revive handicrafts and build imitatively in regional styles between about 1560 and 1720. Philip Webb's Red House at Bexley, built for Morris in 1869, was a forerunner in the revival of the vernacular, but the true leader of the movement was Norman Shaw who in the 1870s built country houses in the 'Old English' style in Withyham and Cranbrook. The style then became *à la mode* and young architects wishing to make a national reputation drove or cycled down deep woody Wealden byways searching at every lane's turning for vernacular survivals for their pattern books. Nothing better illustrates this new admiration for medieval half-timbered houses than the fashion for exposing again the exterior beams which in the Georgian period had been hidden under plaster.

26

Agriculture and Forestry on the Wane

THE 19th-century peak of agricultural prosperity and landed rents in the South East was around the time of the Crimean War and into the 1860s. Every farmer who had capital enough to manage a clay farm successfully went travelling around in search of a 'sheep and turnip' farm on the Downs.[1] Land hunger prevailed there and rents went higher than was reasonable. In the Weald tenants offered higher rents to the Dering estate to be freed of the stipulations against ploughing up old pastures.[2] For a time arable farming paid well but within 30 years the import of foreign and Empire wheat and meat, kept frozen on ships and in the butcher's ice chamber, together with the disastrous wet year of 1879 and great drought of 1893, hit large farmers on the chalklands very hard. Profits from sheep and corn fell by up to 50 per cent and landlords had to abate rents by a similar proportion. Poorer land was practically unsaleable, worth nothing except for rabbits. It was said that a square mile near Winchester was rented for a sovereign. Much downland turf broken up with rising prices from the 1840s was left uncultivated, some crops left in the ground, the farmer not troubling to harvest them. The land took decades to recover a good sward. It would have been much better if downland had not been broken up. Poor farms literally went a-begging as farmers at their wit's end were trying to find profitable substitutes for sheep and corn.

The Weald also suffered from agricultural depression, but not to the same extent as downland. The small farmer consumed part of his own produce at falling prices, had little labour to pay, and often combined farming with another occupation. To combat hard times he tended to work still harder. He was also able more readily than downland farmers to adapt his farm to purposes other than corn and meat. This was to the advantage of large landowners such as the Ashburnhams who had assarted the 325-acre Rushlake Coppice into 51 small-holdings before 1830.[3] The worst effects of the depression were on the Low Wealds of Surrey and West Sussex where much pasture had been brought under the plough since the 1850s. Falling wheat prices, exacerbated by floods, more frequent and prolonged than previously, put much arable out of cultivation and the great expenditure on under-draining was rapidly being lost.

In the Kent and East Sussex Wealds and around Farnham the staple of hops did better than meat and corn; farmers here could not have existed or paid their rent without hops. All their money, skill and hopes were expended on them and they made their profit out of them. Production expanded; in Farnham one seventh of the parish was devoted to it which came up to the very doors of houses and encroached on vegetable gardens and pleasure grounds. Hop farmers

138 Hops at Farnham (c.1820) by George Scharf.

were criticised for giving hops all their energy and attention to the neglect of the rest of the farm.

The much maligned High Weald farmer also introduced specially new ideas for farming. Smallholders planted bush fruits and their families spent entire autumns harvesting them and turning them into preserves, jams, relishes and pickles, aided by cheap colonial sugar. Instead of losing money, the smallholders' land paid its way. The most important innovation was poultry farming. Chickens for market as an adjunct to farming had been kept in the High Weald since time immemorial, but increased yearly with agricultural depression and largely accounted for the district suffering less than others. A smallholder with poultry was often better off than a larger farm without it. It was said that a farmer who kept 100 hens properly looked after, earned more from them than from the same number of breeding ewes. Given fair land, a man, his wife and four to six children needed a minimum of about 50 acres to make a living at this period. Typically he lived harder and worked harder than the average labourer. He sowed a few acres of corn, kept a few cows and used the commons for the younger stock. In the winter a marsh farmer sent him some sheep which got a precarious living running all over the farm and with this he could pay his rent. A chicken farm could be more profitable, and smaller, and accordingly, some landlords split up larger farms for them.[4]

Poultry farming was especially suited to small farms because of the amount of skill and supervision required, but its success was largely due to the degree of organisation amongst the small producers. There were two distinct divisions, rearing and fattening, because specialist poultry farms did not exist, owing principally to the fear of disease. Fatteners (long called also higglers) collected 'lean' fowls from rearers by means of light carts over a wide area between Uckfield and the Kent border, kept them for a month or so in cages (cramming them for the last part of the period), and sold them deadweight principally to Leadenhall and the central markets in London by highly successful marketing using special vans attached to passenger trains at Heathfield and Uckfield. More than one million fowls were sent by rail to London in 1893. To fetch the highest prices the chickens were marketed as 'Surrey fowls'. Oats and separated milk produced on the farm were fed to the poultry and their manure rapidly revived exhausted soil. Thus cows and chickens went well together. To dispense with labour, cramming, which was previously performed by hand, was now done by means of a cramming machine worked by a treadle. Rather oddly the speckled Sussex fowl, so good for the table with his white legs and heavy body, was allowed to die out. The vicar of Heathfield stated that poultry farming tended to early marriages as young men saved money quickly and also offered employment to women and children. Indeed an intelligent, thrifty young man, labourer or smallholder, working week in and week out as long as there was daylight, found the means to rise. The want of a similar organisation for eggs deprived the English farmer of an egg market, for which there was an enormous unsupplied demand, and which would have enabled Wealdsmen to compete successfully with the foreigner.

Nevertheless, the depression worsened in the years up to the First World War. To the misfortune of the Weald, the value of every kind of woodland produce declined more rapidly than corn from the late 1870s with increased imports of timber and the substitution of other materials for wood. This blow fell mainly upon the larger landowners who were simultaneously reducing rents. On the extensive Ashburnham estate, there was no incentive to convert woodlands, largely coppice since the 16th century, to high forest, although E. Driver, in 1830, had recommended that the neglected parts should be drained and filled up with oaks and softwoods, using the labour of the poor.[5] This graphically illustrates the innate conservatism of the Wealden landowner and the backwardness of English forestry. This was to prove a factor in the break up of estates from 1900. It also had a disastrous effect on rural employment and on the small farmer. In the Weald the 'underwood' industry had furnished a vast field of employment from October to May by felling timber and flawing, cutting coppice, shaving hoops, plashing hurdles, splitting wattles, basket-making, or binding faggots. Men earned high wages at this time but the industry was virtually at its end by the early 1900s and the skills needed, transmitted from father to son, were being lost. By 1906 even underwood used for sporting purposes was deteriorating for want of labour, so marked was the exodus to towns. Uncut coppice rapidly deteriorates. Left neglected 20 or 30 years, it provides poor shooting cover, precludes the cutting or thinning of timber and dies off if it does not put out new shoots.[6]

This had severe effects on the small farmer and cottager, the key to his pros-perity being his supplementary sources of income, apart from tilling his own fields, especially in winter when his land was more or less idle. To the failure of one after another of these side sources his vanishing presence can be traced. The small man was also being hit in other ways. The enclosure of commons and the taking in of roadside verges meant that cows could no longer be grazed or geese wander. Sanitary rules also restricted the cottagers' pigsties. All this worked to the doom of small farmers. The trend was inexorable; the eradication was to have repercussions long afterwards.

These various setbacks soon left indelible marks of decay on the landscape. Land, which had been under corn to a large extent, was tumbling down into good-for-nothing pasture in the 1880s and 1890s.[7] On particularly poor strips, a starved and shiftless type of farming prevailed, allowing the land to slip back to its natural aspect of oak saplings, 6ft. bracken and bramble tangles. Even on better land there were poor thistly pastures and half-tilled fields. Gates and fences showed the indolent neglect of successive tenants, and gapped and ragged hedges were not plashed and laid-down as customarily but casually mended with stumps, rails and wire as a last resort to prevent straying stock. Drains were only meddled with when waterlogged meadows became unusable. Plodding along at a jog-trot to a rail-head, a running commentary would be heard from old labourers recalling the time when the grazing land had, piece-by-piece, replaced the plough and where first the horses had ousted the immemorial ox teams. The miller now only ran the stones at the watermill half the time of 20 years earlier, and owing to greater water abstraction he was obliged to send corn in dry summers to a neighbouring mill which had an auxiliary steam engine.[8]

The Great Ashdown Forest case

One of the most distinctive of rural communities was that of the cottagers and smallholders on the edges of Ashdown Forest who cut for fuel the black, peaty earth, which, held together by root-fibres, was miscalled turf. They were a heterogeneous lot. They included the poachers of woods and game that Coventry Patmore encountered at Heron's Ghyll in the 1870s and 1880s. There was nothing unconscientious or underhand about them; offenders paid their fines or went to

139 Uckfield went through an orgy of rebuilding between the 1830s and the 1860s which included the church and almost all the old buildings.

prison with no grudges and then did the same crime again. In other respects Patmore found them 'very simple, amiable and companionable persons' and was never robbed by them in any other way. This apparently arose from a mutual good-humoured understanding of the 'take and give' kind between cottagers and long-suffering landowners, gamekeepers and magistrates.[9] In his Forest home the cottager was a simple child of nature. His way of life was primitive. 'When we ran short, we were obliged to make shift. When there was plenty we had plenty.' Patmore considered their Arcadian simplicity was due to 'almost total absence of a soul-disturbing faith.' Baptism was not commonly practised among even the more settled of the country-folk. 'When I asked my ploughman if he had had his baby baptised, his answer was "No, I don't hold with baptism; it never did me no good"'. Some of these strange characters were bearded tinkers, gypsies, and turf-cutters who lived with bare-footed children in sod huts – dwellings made from a hole cut into a bank which was covered over with poles and brushwood overlaid with growing turf, or 'benders' constructed of hazel rods and bent over to form a dome shape, covered with canvas. Sod huts and 'benders' were still being erected as late as the 1880s because the new Sanitary Acts were not enforced beyond legally settled districts, a matter not finalised until the formation of Conservators in 1886. Their owners were adept at encroaching ('cribbing') upon the Forest. It was standard practice for a forester to increase his smallholding by nibbling away at the boundary until he was found out and had to pay a small fee to the lord of the manor. Squatting was also rife in the early and mid-19th century. When the Board of Conservators was established in 1886 a total of 104 persons was found to have cribbed 156 little enclosures from the Forest since 1869.[10]

Yet Patmore's godless rapscallions mixed with the frugal and hardworking members of the Reverend Ebenezer Littleton's chapel in Withyham. He regarded his flock as paragons amongst smallholders, so frugal and hardworking that they had saved a little and borrowed a little to raise enough money to purchase a holding enfranchised by the lord of the manor. Many prospered better than some larger farmers in the same district. Many cottagers had half-an-acre, others up to four or five acres. They were able to exist in this way because they could turn out on to the Forest what few cattle and sheep they had, as commoners had done for centuries. People with the smaller acreages supplemented their livelihood by working for someone else; holders of five or six acres lived entirely on it. Some found a market for their produce in Tunbridge Wells or took it by railway from Crowborough to Hastings and St Leonards. Littleton reported that smallholdings had greatly increased in recent times, enclosed from the Forest by people who found it paid them better than working fulltime for a farmer.[11]

The way of life of these people was threatened by the attempts of the Dorset (De La Warr) family to curtail or dispose of commoners' rights, which culminated in the legal action against them known as the 'Great Ashdown Forest case' of 1880-82. This tested the right of commoners to cut brakes and litter on the Forest – 'brakes' being the common brake fern.[12] Wealthy commoners had also taken many loads of turf off the Forest to make lawns and gravel for carriage roads. Bernard Hale of Holly Hill at Coleman's Hatch, who was Deputy Lieutenant of

Sussex, took from the Forest as common rights stone for stables, gravel for paths, heather for thatching and peat for rhododendron beds and for heating green houses. Sir Spencer Maryon Wilson, of Searles in Fletching, was sued by the 7th Earl De La Warr for taking stone and turf for lawn-making, contrary to the Decree of 1693. He submitted 'without prejudice' before the case went into court.

By the 1870s the management of the Forest had become totally out of control. Persons living near enough took from the Forest anything useful they wanted, whether commoners or not. Encroachment was rife. The Forest, worked too hard by a robber economy, had taken on a forlorn appearance. The 7th Earl De La Warr, who succeeded as lord of the manor of Duddleswell, the controlling authority of the Forest, in 1873, can be seen in retrospect to have been sorely tried. But his tactics were in error. Had he attempted to draw up a management plan for the Forest on the lines of that in 1830, to which his predecessor, the 5th Earl, had given moral support, which had reserved areas against litter-cutting for the sake of tree preservation and game, he may have won acceptance from legitimate commoners. Instead, he allowed himself to be caricatured as a litigious, selfish and oppressive person. Litter meant anything else that fell to the scythe – heather, furze, gorse, broom, and coarse grass, together with seedling trees to a careless cutter. It would seem that the cutting of brakes and litter had been carried on for generations without interruption from lords of the manor. It was also customary on commons in Sussex generally (p.120). Nevertheless, the practice was extremely harmful to the growth of trees on common lands and from time to time it was not recognised by manorial lords as a common right. In 1795 the then Duke of Dorset had determined to put a stop to it.

Legal opinion does not appear to have favoured the Duke's view in 1795, but the matter arose again in 1816 when fir clumps planted as coverts for game aroused much ill feeling amongst commoners, and yet again in 1830. At this time there was a great deal of illicit depredation of the Forest by those with no common rights. Some commoners were also using the Forest on a much larger scale, and for different purposes, from those envisaged in the 1693 Decree. This arose from a new type of 'gentleman' commoner who built a mansion and created an estate on the fringes of the Forest from the late 18th century. The estates included Kidbrooke Park (now Michael Hall), whose owner, Lord Colchester, the former Speaker of the House of Commons, took trees from the Forest for his hedges and pleasure grounds and made an artificial cascade, taking all the largest stone he could find on the Forest.

The 'Great Ashdown Forest case' came to trial in 1880 when Bernard Hale and John Miles, his labourer, were defendants in the High Court of the Chancery Division. The judgment of Vice-Chancellor Bacon was for Lord De La Warr, on the grounds that there was no trace in the Decree of 1693 of the claims of commoners to cut and carry away litter. On appeal in 1881 the judgment was reversed by virtue of the provisions of the Prescription Act, by which it was deemed that litter-cutting had been enjoyed as of right for more than 60 years, although the notion that the commoners were entitled to it under the Decree was mistaken. A cross-action was instituted by Hale and other prominent commoners to ensure that the rights that he had won for himself could be enjoyed by other commoners.

The successful outcome for the commoners proved to be another milestone in the battle for public rights over the commons and Forests of England and Wales. Had Lord De La Warr won his case, there is little doubt that ultimately he would have been able to force the commoners to enclose the Forest. The vindication of the commoners' rights had saved the Forest, as had happened several times previously. A great debt is owed to solicitors who amassed a huge body of documentary evidence pertinent to the case and the highly experienced and committed lawyers who argued it for the commoners. Of the counsel, the amusing and witty Sir William Harcourt had experience of common rights in the New Forest and elsewhere and was a leading authority, guiding the Commons Act, 1876, to the statute book. Sir Joshua Williams was also greatly learned on commons. M.P. Lawrence was a son of P.H. Lawrence who had suggested the formation of the Commons Preservation Society, which came into being in 1865.[13] Indefatigable in gathering evidence of litter-cutting on the Forest was William A. Raper, a Battle solicitor who was assisted in litigation by Sir Robert Hunter, a former honorary solicitor to the Commons Preservation Society and later a joint founder of the National Trust.[14] Raper's notebooks containing the depositions, and invaluable insight into contemporary rural life on the edge of the Forest, have been transcribed by Brian Short for the Sussex Record Society. A special Act of Parliament (1885) regulated the Forest through a representative body of Conservators, which remains the controlling organisation to this day and the means by which the protection and enhancement of its beauty is maintained.

Yet peace was not restored to the Forest for many years. The numerous persons who held Forest encroachments made in the anarchic period of its history in the 19th century were left without any gains from the legal case just concluded. The first lively issue was the high level of valuations of their properties made by Raper which were substantially reduced on representations to the Land Commissioners by the leaders of the Ashdown Forest Protection Association, founded in 1886 to promote the smallholders' cause, many of whom were very poor and known as cottagers, crofters, 'cottiers' or foresters. Another major issue was that few of these had any common rights as defined by the 1885 Act. A number of court cases brought by the Conservators against poor people and their connivance at similar offences by well-to-do commoners, packed up to 400 persons in the school room at Nutley, caused Raper's popularity to decline sharply and led to resentment and allegations that the Forest was being run 'as a happy hunting ground for lawyers and rich men'. As a result of the influence of such persons as T.C. Thompson, C.J. Heald, Elphinstone Barchard and Jesse Ridley, the smallholders managed to hold their ground. Their guile also served them well. John Hobbs, who could not sign his name when he took on a yearly tenancy of a patch of the Forest in 1919, was served with notices to quit after 1928 for failure to farm in a husbandlike manner, but was clever enough to create new tenancies of the same property, his landlady taking a lenient view, and not wanting to be too hard on him.[15]

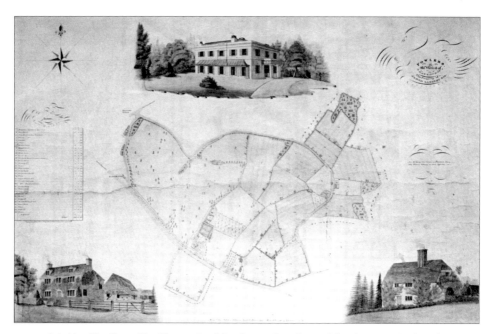

140 *A fashionable villa at Hawkhurst, 1830. Note layout of gardens and farmhouses retained on the estate. (CKS, U78 P13)*

The decay of the countryside and rural unemployment was greatly arrested by the creation of country estates and building of country houses by *nouveaux riches* (p.244). As an example, H.F. Locke King, a wealthy entrepreneur, notable for his involvement with Brooklands racing track and holidays in Egypt, built up a sporting estate of 2,700 acres in a compact block of 14 farms on the Low Weald near Billingshurst in West Sussex. At Okehurst he developed large-scale dairying, laid down a railway track to take corn to his water mill, and added modern buildings and equipment. The hedgerows and river and canal banks were planted up with trees. A great portion of the property was 'wild woodland', practically given up to 'teeming' game. Three thousand pheasants or more were raised annually; 266 mallard and teal were reared on flooded meadows and three miles of river provided coarse fishing. The scenic quality was summed up as 'glorious wilderness woodlands', grand old thorn hedges and immense oak shaws, rush-fringed ponds and prettily broken countryside, offering perfect shooting coverts equal to the isolated game reserves in the eastern counties and possessing the great charm of exceptional quiet and 'a sense of being alone with nature in her wildest mood'.[16]

A short-lived dairying enterprise was at Stammerham, now part of Christ's Hospital, from 1885. Taking advantage of the railway facilities, the Southern Counties Dairy Association purchased the Stammerham estate of over 900 acres and ran it as a single unit dairy with model farm buildings. A specially constructed platform was provided by the railway company for the purpose of supplying London. In 1892 Christ's Hospital School bought the estate from the bankrupt company but the farm buildings still exist.[17]

27

'We are all Londoners now'

IN 1915 Grahame Robertson, owner of artist Helen Allingham's house at Sandhills, Witley, compared her local landscapes and the watercolours of Birket Foster, who had preceded her at Witley, with the changed countryside and rural life then around him. He concluded that their works were not only a delight to the eye but lasting memorials to the old Surrey Weald now so changed as already to have become a kind of dream world, fabulous and remote as Lyonesse or Atlantis. 'What would they think of it now?', he mused, without the commons, village greens and rustics in their cottage gardens which they had loved and fought hard to protect against the 'improving' and destructive jerry-builder. It was a similar thought that inspired Gertrude Jekyll to write about 'lost' things in her *Old West Surrey* (1904).[1]

It was George 'Bourne' (Sturt), the wheelwright from Bourne in the parish of Farnham, Surrey, who most clearly described the social and environmental changes at the end of the 19th century which were destroying the old rural way of life. He was a shrewd and loving observer of his countryside and few writers

141 Vann, Chiddingfold, Surrey, a fine example of the sensitive integration of old and new buildings in a vernacular style in the spirit of the Arts and Crafts movement.

have so felicitously described the everyday life of the country labourer and his family in its last phase. Although he would write only of changes which were part of his own experience, they had begun to operate so generally in London's countryside as to make his observations of wider significance.

He attributed these changes to the new 'grasping, hustling, competitive' newcomers from London, and other cities and towns, whose demand for building land made them ready from the 1890s 'to sell or break up or cut down or level away anything on any sites'. He contrasted the new rural society of his day with the old 'peasant' tradition when local people had subsisted in the main upon what their industry could produce out of the soil and material of their own countryside. Then craftsmen had worked unhurriedly 'taking time to make their products comely', and the villager was closely linked to his own countryside in many ways. 'He did not merely reside in it; he was part of it, and it was part of him.'

He identified the enclosure of the common, essential for the well-being of the smallholder and cottager, as the catalyst of change in his village.

> … To the enclosure of the common more than to any other cause may be traced all the changes that have subsequently passed over the village. It was like knocking the keystone out of an arch. The keystone is not the arch; but, once it is gone, all sorts of forces, previously resisted, begin to operate towards ruin, and gradually the whole structure crumbles down. This fairly illustrated what has happened to the village, in consequence of the loss of the common. The direct results have been perhaps the least important in themselves; but indirectly the enclosure mattered, because it left the people helpless against influences which have sapped away their interests, robbed them of security and peace, rendered their knowledge and skill of small value, and seriously affected their personal pride and character. Observe it well. The enclosure itself, I say, was not actually the cause of all this; but it was the opening, so to speak, through which all this was let in. The other causes which have been at work could hardly have operated as they have done if the village had not been weakened by the changes directly due to the loss of the common …

It was because of the common

> that people were enabled to keep cows and get milk and butter; it was only with the turf-firing cut on the common that they could smoke their bacon, hanging it in the wide chimneys over those old open hearths where none but such fuel could be used; and, again, it was only because they could get furze from the common to heat their bread ovens that it was worth their while to grow a little wheat at home, and have it ground into flour for making bread.

With the common the poorest labourer could practise the traditional crafts which Cobbett, in his little book on Cottage Economy had advocated as the one hope for labourers, and the whole system, with the common at its heart, was still 'in full swing' at Bourne within living memory of 1912.[2]

At about the same time John Halsham (a pseudonym of Forrester Scott) was recording similar changes wrought by urban taste overrunning much of the then still rural central Sussex around Haywards Heath. He noted that urbanisation in thought and habit occupied once rural territory more widely and quickly than bricks and mortar spread across fields. 'We are all Londoners now in our cradles

142 Battle survived the Dissolution of its Abbey and is now one of the most charming of the small towns of Sussex. The old market place has recently been freed from motor cars.

from Bow Bells to Berwick.' He had a mental map of future 'Londonisation':

> 'Sheringham' is not half so large a place as 'Arnington', and is some ten years behind it in its stage of growth ... Here also are larger remnants of the old life and ways ... Above all things the place owns the priceless gift of a character ... In due time the rising tide will no doubt overflow this higher ridge... but meanwhile here is some dozen years respite from the crawling invasion ...

Halsham vividly recreates the Weald as he perceived it around the turn of the 20th century around Ardingly, Lindfield, West Hoathly, Worth and Balcombe. The life of the country was invisible to the traveller along the ridgeways, for woodland masked everything except the church spires, bone-white in the sun, which marked the villages. Down there, between the gable-end of the Baptist chapel and the little bell-turret of the school, decrepit ancients dozed at cottage doors and crept about the street. Numerous outlying farms were only served by narrow lanes ending in a green ride through a wood. Flagged paths led to little thatched cottages, brick-nogged below and weather-boarded above. Reactionaries were constantly shaking their heads at the heavy changes in the village architecture as wattle and daub walls, artless drains and unsavoury wells were hidden or cleared away, and dreaded the day when the postmaster who ran a corn chandlery and used the lid of a meal bin to dispense stamps and postal orders, would be replaced by lady assistants behind a rosewood counter and brass wire trellis. Meanwhile, the church had been restored 'to a yawning vacancy' and the picturesque hump-backed bridge had been fitted with iron girders. The baker's cart now came several times a week because the old cottage bread ovens had gone cold.

Not all the old ways had changed. A clocksmith still practised his trade. The leisurely hearse-like wagonnette, which served as an omnibus, was interrupted by flocks of sheep and droves of bullocks, hay waggons or timber tugs. Passengers patiently conversed whilst boxes were brought down from flagged paths and farewells made in porches, and a prolonged whistling would bring a lad across several fields to collect a parcel of a couple of rabbits and some medicine. Halsham was disturbed at the physical appearance of the rural population which had resisted the exodus to London and other towns and cities. A too common sight was of old men with sunk toothless mouths, rheumy eyes and grey-stubbled chins, yet he was struck by the power of their slow, tireless gardening despite lean arms and crooked knees. It was not only the men who were unlovely. He found the women plain and thought the boys and girls would grow up to have the same worn eyes and fallen mouths.[3]

Another who deplored recent changes was Wilfrid Scawen Blunt, the estate owner of Crabbet Park near Crawley and Newbuildings in Shipley. He predicted, correctly, that his district would drift 'into the condition of a continuous pleasure ground, serving all classes from the great manufacturing cities for health resorts and places of weekend amusement, and the rich for opportunities of spending their money on amateur agriculture with the help of amateur rural dependents'. He was angered at the decline of small farmers and cottagers due to the decline in the woodland use and the drying up in recent times of one after another of the side sources of income needed to eke out a living despite the Weald being an ideal country for peasant ownership and small tenant holdings.[4]

Blunt (and Hilaire Belloc) believed that with changes in government policy and other circumstances the small man's prosperity might be retrieved from decline and 'the age of gold for our peasantry might come again'. The undoubted ability of the small farmer to weather the worst effects of agricultural depression better than the big farmer was not lost on observers. The respective merits of large and small farms waxed strongly. It was generally agreed that larger farms in proportion yielded the most surplus food and freed more people for employment in other industries. Accordingly, the large farm system was held to be the most conducive to Britain's national prosperity.

28

Londoners and their Weald

> Home is the hunter, home from the hill, and the Wolves are back from Monks House. And much refreshed into the bargain. Three solitary nights. Think of that! Was there ever such a miracle? Not a voice, not a telephone. Only the owl calling; perhaps a clap of thunder, the horses coming down to the Brooks and Mr Botten calling with the milk in the morning …

So Virginia Woolf wrote in her diary under 28 June 1937, on her return to Tavistock Square from a long weekend at her Sussex refuge. She was writing again before noon, hoping to drive her pen the harder on her return. Her delight in a brief, invigorating release into the Weald and her relish for the return to the city expresses the dual raptures on departure and return, which were the same two tunes that generations of real lovers of London had sung over centuries. Amongst others who oscillated between departure and return, there were those who counted themselves lucky, such as Mr Eager in E.M. Forster's *A Room with a View*, who, when in London felt he could never live out of it, and when in the country felt the same about the country; or those who lived in the Weald who felt that what made going to London worthwhile was the joy of coming back again.

The first to combine in relative comfort the double-life of working in London with living in the countryside were well-to-do Victorian households. Their response was largely due to the transformation of London's character and the practical details of everyday life there since Samuel Johnson expressed his famous aphorism, 'When a man is tired of London he is tired of life; for there is in London all that life can afford'. Later generations had to come to terms with a spectacular outward

143 London, Gustave Doré's vision of late Victorian London as the capital of the British empire with its congestion, noise and pollution.

expansion of the metropolis, the first world capital to have grown so hugely and rapidly that in the 1860s it was 'more excavated, more cut about, more rebuilt and more extended than at any time in its previous history'. With its unchallenged eminence among English cities as the centre of English culture and political and economic life, London more than doubled its built-up area between 1746, the date of John Rocque's map, and Cary's in 1822. By 1851 it had exploded into the then uniquely big, widespread and haphazard metropolis, the world's largest city, covering 50 square miles, more than five times the size of the city of one hundred years earlier. London, in effect, became a new city and its sheer immensity dispersed people from their places of work and leisure, whether by choice or not.

Moreover, broadly in proportion to its growing size, London became so much blacker and more acridly smoky that 'Smoke' became cockney slang for the capital. Londoners began to need more of the country so as to lay in a stock of health for the winter, sufficient, said ardently London-hating Cobbett, to enable them to withstand the suffocation of the smoking and stinking Wen.

As representative of the 1870s, as was Dr Johnson a hundred years earlier, was (Sir) Leslie Stephen, whose daily experience of London was an endurance test, especially in the penitential gloom of winter. This needed the compensation of an annual holiday and weekend breaks away from London as a restorative from dirt and grind and the entanglements and interruptions of urban life. For relaxation in middle age he founded one of the earliest known walking clubs, The Sunday Tramps (1879), which devoted the Sabbath to explorations of London's countryside.

As early as 1770 Gilbert White of Selborne noted in his diary that the smell of coal smoke pervaded the village some 30 miles away when the wind blew from the north-east. In the 1820s Thomas Carlyle hated living under the smoke canopy. By the early 1860s he spoke of going out farther from the pursuit of London smoke. The journalist Leigh Hunt could then find 'a glass of veritable home-brewed country ale' as near as Putney Common and novelist George Eliot had earlier found rural solace as near as Walworth and East Sheen. By the 1880s 'going beyond the smoke' meant much longer journeys into London's countryside because its accompanying smoke-laden cloud, mainly caused by domestic coal burning, had mushroomed still further. It was then regarded as the master evil oppressing the city which yearly increased in intensity. In December 1890 *The Times* newspaper had lamented:

> ... Can we dispel that overhanging canopy of gloom which makes London in winter a city of dreadful and almost everlasting night? Can we divest ourselves of that fetid shroud which makes us all wanderers in an Inferno even more dreary than Dante ever imagined? It is difficult to give even a hopeful answer ... What would London give, what indeed, would it not give, if some man of science would tell it how to get rid of that intolerable winter gloom which destroys now so unnecessarily lowers its vitality, impedes its labour and destroys its happiness?[1]

Despite all their Londonisation (or more correctly, because of it), well-to-do Victorian and later Londoners, many of whom were countrymen by birth but working in the City by necessity, periodically wearied of the city and sought, however briefly, an alternative in the country or at the sea-side. The more urbanised they became, the greater was the aim of living away from the scene of business and of escaping from smoke, noise and hurry. Nevertheless, they could never forgo London entirely. Modern city life, in fact, exercised a continuous double pressure of attraction and repulsion. It was only by making long daily journeys to London that most professional and businessmen could enjoy country life at all. Juxtaposed with the world's largest and most artificial environment, the Weald increasingly became a restorative for faded urban-dwellers, thus satisfying some of the various physical and spiritual needs of its citizens.

Paradoxically, an advantage of living in London was the ease of getting out of it. If London made escape necessary, the Weald made it practicable by its very accessibility. The turnpike roads had made parts conveniently accessible earlier. By the 1870s the dense network of suburban and long-distance trains running in and out of London termini, unmatched anywhere in the world, made travel from hot and dusty streets into cool woodland glades feel like an enchantment and the breath of life.

Yet the Weald was not valued solely for its intrinsic qualities. The new outlook on nature was conceived as a restorative. With a deep sense of estrangement from natural life, and with London as a foil and background, the cockney's vision was not of ordinary country but one where light, air, greenness and beauty had something of the supernatural. For the Londoner every bush was a burning bush and he found it difficult to imagine anywhere else breezier, greener or more fragrant or where butter could be yellower, cream thicker, or honey sweeter than in the Weald. In those living in London lodgings amidst boundless streets who had never seen a meadow for years or were unaware of the change of seasons, a maddening desire could arise for countryside or sea-beach. The Weald thus became a permanent part of the equipment for dealing with psychological problems accompanying technological progress. Foreigners, who generally saw little out of the ordinary in the Wealden landscape, failed to appreciate what a tremendous difference London made to the perceived freshness of the air, the beauty of the views and the feeling of repose.

The estrangement from natural life had a powerful effect on London artists. Amongst the earliest was Samuel Palmer, who dreamily called up reveries of the prodigal Weald at Shoreham in Kent. By the 1840s many artists, alienated from the city, developed a fanatical passion for 'the country'. Although several rural districts near London were brought into a general artistic consciousness for the first time, most would-be landscapists drifted into the Weald. The first of the breakaway artists was the academician, Richard Redgrave, who in 1849 gave up a successful career as a genre painter in the city and was to spend no fewer than 37 successive summers painting directly in the open air at Abinger, Surrey. Also in the same year John Linnell independently abandoned portraiture in Bayswater and removed to Redstone, near Redhill, to recover his first love of landscape. At the same time John C. Horsley was 'painting from nature' at the old wool town of Cranbrook, Kent and invited fellow artist, Thomas Webster, to join him. Shortly afterwards the pair invited Frederick Hardy and his brother George to

144 Richard Redgrave, deputy director of the Victoria and Albert Museum, and painter at Abinger for 37 successive summers.

settle there. About the same time John Millais and William Hunt of the Pre-Raphaelite Brotherhood were painting minutely from nature backgrounds at Hastings and Winchelsea respectively. J.C. Hook joined Redgrave at Abinger from 1853 and then settled for a while at Witley. Redgrave's discovery of the Abinger woods and heaths led to the arrival of George Vicat Cole, Edmund Warren, G.P. Boyce and Cole's friend Benjamin W. Leader, though he did not take up permanent residence there until 20 years later. Meanwhile, further artists' migration was converting the Surrey heathland at Witley into a third artists' colony in the Weald. At Hook's suggestion, Birket Foster, long frustrated as an illustrative draughtsman in London, joined him at Witley in 1861. Frederick Walker also joined him there and the Witley circle soon included Sir Henry Cole, Redgrave's superior at the South Kensington Museum (Victoria and Albert), and these were followed by Helen Allingham and by writers and poets, including George Eliot and Tennyson. Subsequently, multiplying artists' colonies in the Victorian period ultimately turned the Weald into a vast open-air studio. Many artists who chose the Weald as a major arena came to identify its uncommon profusion and diversity as matching to perfection the spirit of the age which rejoiced in exuberance, intricacy, opulence and smallness of detail. Just as in the world of natural science, the Weald was adopted as the first general model of landscape (p.2), so in the realm of landscape art was it imaged as English scenic beauty in a kind of *édition de luxe*.[2]

Beyond the Smoke

To some Londoners their longing for the 'green country' of the Weald was simply ravenous – an almost painful craving, in a preternatural sleepiness mood induced by mental stress. Thomas Carlyle's escape beyond the smoke, reek and brick of London in 1840 to Herstmonceux opened up a country of miracle to him. This was also the mood of J.C. Hook at Brompton in the mid-1850s before he came to paint in Surrey. The burden of London pressed hard on Samuel Palmer in North Kensington at much the same time, suffering from acute despondence and irresolution as an artist at the loss of nature which was the sustaining impulse of his life. He found it almost impossible to function away from the country and was haunted for years by the thought of 'wide prospects and a range like that of Leith Hill' with which he could recapture something of the spirit of his brilliant decade at Shoreham: '… Surely,' he wrote, when his discontent with his London surroundings was reaching its climax, 'the sight and smell of sunshine and new mown hay are more congenial with our pursuits than those of smoke and sewers.'[3]

No record evokes such an intense and lengthy longing for the country than the letters of George Eliot, regarded at the end of her life as the leading English novelist. She suffered great ill-health, being periodically rendered helpless with nausea and headache when in London. She was forever going into London's countryside (principally the Weald) as a cure. A dun-coloured fog left her ailing, oppressed and chilled. With the first hour of stillness among the fields, lanes and commons she got a delicious sense of repose and refreshment. The countryside she wanted was 'true country air, free of London haze' with wide horizons giving her a sense of 'standing on a round world' and not impractically far off from frequent trains. The western Weald met her needs precisely. A summer spent there would send her back to town with a sense of renewed strength. Much of her life was spent searching for fresh air 'and the thoughts that come with it'. The Surrey Weald became her favourite location and she eventually settled at Witley near Haslemere, though not forgoing fish and other little luxuries which came by train from Waterloo.[4]

At about the same time the diaries and other works of the struggling novelist George Gissing tell of his maddening desire for the countryside and sea-beach. He wrote from his prison of two rooms in a London lodging hemmed in by boundless streets, of how he would give a year of his life for six months of true country and the leisure to read under a cottage roof.[5]

At the turn of the century Grant Allen and others had colonised Hindhead in a deliberate attempt to escape from London, which they considered baneful to the human spirit:

> I am writing in my study on a heather-clad hilltop. When I raise my eyes from my sheet of foolscap, it falls upon miles of broad open moorland. My window looks out upon unsullied nature. Everything around is fresh and clean and wholesome … But away down in the valley, as night draws on, a lurid glare reddens the north-eastern horizon. It marks the spot where the great wen of London heaves and festers. Up here on the free hills, the sharp air blows in upon us, limpid and clear from a thousand leagues of open ocean; down here in the crowded town, it stagnates and ferments, polluted with the diseases and vices of centuries.[6]

To the Victorian and Edwardian businessman's mind the Weald was the land of his dreams, a great beckoning landscape of verdant charm to which he irresistibly surrendered. To select a fair and elevated locality, not too far away from London, and to make there a modish place where his family could enjoy fresh air and country luxuries, was the overriding ambition of the successful. On this Eden was expended the wealth accumulated in the city, or on the coalfields and industrial cities and overseas. Traditionally, the rich had moved westwards out of London in search of the freshest air and Surrey had a special place in this national psyche as one of the prettiest and most accessible of the Home Counties.

Nineteenth-century London life also inspired the weekend holiday, a British institution since adopted by almost every country in the world. Many professional and business people indulged by week-ending, in the romantic notion that they were country gentlemen. By 1914 the habit of owning or renting a country cottage or wooden cabin, for weekend use during the summer by physically exhausted Londoners for recreation, exercise, or simply for a change of air and scene, had become a middle-class cult.

This perception of the countryside as an alternative world to London led to an element of social nonconformity which expressed itself from the 1880s as 'a back-to-the-land' movement. This was a reaffirmation of rural values on the part of those unable, or unwilling, to accede to the growing complexity, and what was judged the falsity and unjustness, of modern city life and its physical and moral corrupting influences. Its principal objective was the moral, physical, political and economic regeneration of England through the revival of agriculture and country life, seen as destroyed by laissez-faire industrialism based on the division of labour in the factory system in towns.

The rural idyll which inspired 'Simple Lifers' was inextricably linked with another contemporary nonconformist movement, that of the rural Arts and Crafts. Inspired by William Morris, farmer-craftsmen, including sculptors, metal-workers, bookbinders, calligraphers, furniture-makers and handloom weavers, migrated from London to found rural workplaces at Steep, near Petersfield, where Bedales School was founded on Arts and Crafts principles, and at places such as Haslemere, South Harting, and Shere. The best-known was at Ditchling, associated with the sculptor, calligrapher and typographer, Eric Gill and his followers.[7]

29

Parks and Gardens

… Perhaps you'll park it? … turn it all into a fine new park … It was four farms, and Mr Sangres made a fine park of them, with a herd of fallow deer … How did Mr Sangres make his money?… It was pepper an' spices, or it may ha' been gloves. No, Gloves was Sir Reginald Liss at Marley End. Spices was Mr Sangres. He's a Brazilian gentleman …

Rudyard Kipling,
An Habitation Enforced in Actions and Reactions (1909), 27-8.

The carriage wheels of newly-moneyed parvenus pressed hard on the road-maker and with the coming of railways their invasion became a flood. Almost all the newcomers caught the spirit of landscaping and this was so widespread in districts accessible to London, or particularly favourable to landscape design and tree planting, that by 1910 it gave parts of the Weald a new countryside, and led to profound social changes.

Much land previously held by established gentry passed into the hands of upstart landlords who did not value land for its own sake but as a place where, when down from London, they could admire the scenery and their pedigree livestock. To them an estate was a picture to be looked at. The focal point of their attention was their new landscape park, created from one or more farms, bought at falling prices on account of the agricultural depression, but their aesthetic interest extended to some degree over their estate at large, or at least over the land visible from the mansion. This is what J.C. Loudon, the mid-Victorian landscape designer, called the inter-connection of the parts. The fashionable idea was to work woods, farms, fields and meadows into a composite picture, by planting timber freely for pleasure and profit, and with an eye to opening up vistas in thick woods, planting out eyesores, softening hard lines and stiff banks, and planting up hedgerows and the tail-ends of fields.

Thus the more inspired creators closely interwove the various components of an estate – country house, garden and terrace, park, home farm, woods, tenanted farms and estate villages – into a continuous series of new scenes in a single all-embracing composition which pictorially, as well as economically, was conceived as indivisible. This functioned in their owners' minds as a kingdom in miniature which, until the advent of planning and other regulations, could be administered at will. A later vogue by late Victorian and Edward *nouveaux riches* was to plant exotic trees in pineta, arboreta and 'wild' gardens. Trees thus came into their own again.[1] Owen Johnson has remarked of the central Weald, the scene of the most

145 Humphry Repton's intended landscape design at Bayham. The mansion ultimately built was less ostentatious than proposed, but the informal landscaping of the grounds kept closely to the submitted plan. Note the retention of standing oaks after the removal of hedgerows and plantings to conceal straight lines.

intense landscaping activity, that 'you could almost imagine that some heavenly gardener had scattered a huge packet of seeds over the Ouse headwaters'.[2] Christopher Hussey, heir to the estate of Scotney Castle (which itself had earlier played an important part in the movement), observed that the spread of the various and contrasting, but inter-connected, kinds of landscaping was to reshape woods, ponds and fields on many estates into 'a vast, created landscape, natural enough to our eyes, but in reality managed as much for picturesque appearances as for economic returns'. We must recall that Hussey's comment was made in 1927 when estates were already fast dissolving. A long period of neglect and austerity ensued during which the landscaping spirit died out completely and only fragments of the movement remain. Yet, on estates of the super-rich landscaping has recently undergone a revival.[3]

As early as 1825, William Cobbett drew a distinction between the unselfconscious face of the traditional Wealden farming landscape and the 'artificial' landscapes of the new gentry spreading out of London in the wake of the turnpikes. Sarcastically, he cast his exact, quick glance over the 'improvements' which frustrated his express aim of seeing the country's agriculture and its working farmers and labourers. The experience of a day's journey across Surrey led him to conclude that the traditional habits and sights of rural England survived there only along rutted hollow-ways, unusable to carriages. Beside the high roads from London the parvenus, who were his aversion, were expelling yeomanry and rearranging landscape for their sensuous delight, activities associated in Cobbett's mind with the topsy-turvydom created by the repulsive eruption of the Great Wen.

> Those that travel on turnpike roads know nothing of England – From Hascombe to Thursley almost the whole way is across fields or commons, or along narrow lanes. Here we see the people without any disguise or affectation. Against a great road things are made for show.

Cobbett's distinction between two contending forces in the landscape of South-East England, the one sustaining a working landscape of mean farm buildings rented by round-smocked farmers, and the other creating a new design worked on for pleasure like a piece of stage scenery, is amply borne out by other writers.[4]

These include two contemporary French travellers who ecstatically described the new landscapes that Cobbett abhorred. In the eyes of Pichot, who in 1825 kept closely to the well-used turnpikes near Brighton, the landscape presented an array of almost uninterrupted parks and *fermes ornées*:

> From every knoll the eye surveys parkland which stretches from hillsides to valleys and from valleys to hillsides, over meadows of a delicious green and gently wandering streams … Far and wide there reigns an air of security, prosperity and even happiness.[5]

The Comte de la Garde was similarly enchanted by the ravishing beauty of a picture-book landscape seen on his journey from Brighton to London through the Wealds of Sussex and Surrey in 1834. Here and there were shoals of weekend cottages (*maisons de plaisance*), simple thatched cottages bedecked with roses, neat and tidy villages, and hop fields which reminded him of Lombardy, all seeming to radiate an air of ease and well-being.

> … We roll along a smooth sandy road as if in a garden; on every side we are ravished with enchanting views. Here the immense parks have a lushness and variety due to the genius of successors to Kent and Brown. These clever imitators of Nature have had the talent to re-unite in an intricate tracery widely-scattered and different beauties, so offering at the same time sombre forests, rocky outcrops, gushing springs, and winding streams sometimes turning into azure lakes which flow through wide expanses of meadowland covered with flocks of sheep, and assorted breeds of cows, roebuck and fallow deer; all seems to unite beauty with the useful.[6]

Soon afterwards the villa-owning class of city financiers, merchants and tradesmen was also invading the Weald. Their first choice of location was a naturally beautiful and unpretentious countryside lying close to a railway station within daily travelling distance of London. To 'make a place', the villa architect looked ideally for a rising knoll, a patch of woodland, some park-like fields and meadows, and wanted a small head of pure water. A southward-facing villa was then raised upon the summit, the hill became a small park (leaving tell-tale field banks and the roots of grubbed-up trees along sunk fences), the road a tree-lined gravel drive and the home farm was hidden in some wooded dingle. This was so stereotyped a formula that artistically minded guests on the round of Victorian visiting were wearied in house after house by the same views from the windows as well as by the same interior design and furniture. From afar, former 'villa' country is easily identified today by risings crowned with pines, providing shelter for houses on north and east. Forrester Scott observed that such a group of conifers around a hilltop was a sign to half the county of Sussex. He tells of a 'Mrs Latimer of Blackpatch', who, 'for inscrutable reasons' built a flamboyant mansion surmounting a lonely hill 'all red gables and chimneys … with sweeps of bare gravel drive and groves of eighteen inch laurustinus and arbor-vitae …'. 'Now of course', remarked this lady, 'we had to make all the gardens out of fields … we really beat you in the view … it only wants a few more good houses on the best sites to be really perfect …'. Her idea of perfection duly happened around Haywards Heath with the coming of the railway.[7]

We should imagine the Weald in the early to mid-19th century as strips of land traversed by turnpikes to the coast. Within a narrow belt of a mile or two on either side of a great road migrants were building their country houses and parks. Beyond lay bands of still working landscapes, served by deeply worn tracks and left aside by the high roads. These 'backlands' did not attract Cockneys until they fell progressively within the purview of the developer with the advent of railways. An example of 'deep-lane' country which held out against 'improvements' was the Haywards Heath and Lindfield district where the entirely different attitudes and ways of life of the old village farming families and the wealthy Cockney newcomers is the subject of John Halsham's brilliant *Idlehurst*.[8] Ruskin explained how, in the heavy clay country around Cranleigh in Surrey, a newcomer would build himself a house on a farm, and then become unpopular with local inhabitants by compelling the parish to make the green lanes into hard roads, which, in turn, accelerated the invasions of other *nouveaux riches* so making the place a paradise for trades men. George Sturt also wrote about the lost character of places by reason of newcomers hailing from towns and making them as countrified as Wimbledon or Blackheath.[9]

> Witmore Bottom has been changed to Whitmore Vale. To old inhabitants of the neighbourhood the original name was associated with stirring memories of sheep-stealers and smugglers … of sailors trudging the long hill road above it, to and from Portsmouth for the French Wars, and of much other stern and sturdy English life; but what can one make of the new-fangled polite substitute of it? If anything at all, it suggests the transitory existence of the modern discoverers of Hindhead, whose villas seen from distance seem to have broken out upon the once majestic hill like a red skin eruption, and in certain slants of the sunshine make it an uplifted horror visible for miles. There was a time when I could not see Hindhead without gladness; there are times now when I rather look away from it than endure to think of what has gone from it for ever.[10]

Others have vivid comments to make about the changes. Prince Kropotkin took a knapsack and went on foot out of London into Sussex in the 1880s. He expected to find a soil busily cultivated, but neither near London nor further south did he see men in the fields. On the Weald he could walk for twenty miles without seeing anything but heath and woodlands rented as pheasant shooting grounds to 'London gentlemen', as the labourers said.[11] A generation later the Czech playwright and journalist, Karel Capek, had much the same to say after a visit to the Surrey countryside:

Half-open gates led you to ancient lanes in a park deeper than a forest and here there is a little, red house with high chimneys, a church steeple among the trees, a meadow ... a pathway which looks as if it has been swept, velvet pools with water lilies and irises, parks, country houses, meadows and meadows, not a single field, nothing which might cry of human toil ... The English countryside isn't for working in; it is for looking at.[12]

As a variation on the same theme, Nancy Mitford in *The Pursuit of Love* (1945) observed:

The great difference between Surrey and proper, real country, is that in Surrey, when you see blossom you know there will be no fruit. Think of the Vale of Evesham and then look at all this pointless pink stuff – it gives you quite a different feeling ...

Reference to sale particulars of country properties sold between the 1880s and the 1920s confirms these generalised pictures. Repeated expressions such as 'tracts of picturesque woodland', 'fine building sites', 'sporting estate', 'first-class pheasant shooting', 'natural beauties in a healthy bracing climate', park-like lands', 'weekend cottages', and 'pleasure grounds' abound, for the Weald nearest to London was by then regarded as the heart of one of the most favoured residential districts in England.

Although the spread of country houses to a particular district was dependent on turnpike roads and, later, railways to and from London, it was not simply in direct ratio to them. A widening taste in scenery also helps to account for the radiation outwards of parvenus from London into the Weald. As we have noted, the Weald had earlier had a bad image, partly created by its appalling roads. As the Weald became better known in the 19th century, a deeper appreciation of its restfulness and homeliness (essential qualities of a garden) became publicised as was the cosiness imparted by its cottages and farmhouses. Another change, as we have noted, was admiration extended to woodland, a new taste which was fed into the mass media by artists (see p.219).

One new landowner who gave an account of his management over some 15 years from *c*.1865 was the poet and writer Coventry Patmore, who bought two farms at Heron's Ghyll near Uckfield.[13] The beautifully wooded ghylls, superb views, trout streams, access to a turnpike and the nearness to London were its attractions when he bought the property from Lord Abergavenny's estate at merely its agricultural value. Within 15 years he had converted it into a modish residential property. In our mind's eye we can envisage him with axe and saw joyously releasing 'into the blue distance' trees and underwood which hid the great line of the South Downs. He quarried his own stone with which to extend and refront a former farmhouse and sold 'at almost any price' more stone to neighbouring incomers building their own mansions or for local church-building and restoration. Removing farm buildings and stabling out of sight, he made gardens and terraces. He then cut around the house, leaving the best trees for ornament, so making what he considered to be a beautiful little park of 60 acres abounding in well-grouped trees and clear sweeps of grass. He also superintended personally the planting of 120,000 forest trees in his neglected woods with the aim of both profit and pleasure. Meanwhile, a chain of five ponds was made with earth dams, looking like a stretch of winding river from the house, and hundreds of loads of peat were carted from Ashdown Forest to prepare the soil for banks of rhododendrons. Finally, five miles of paths were constructed through shrubberies and woods. He was lucky to buy on a sharply rising market, selling his property in c.1880 for more than five times the purchase price, and meanwhile he had thoroughly enjoyed life as an English country gentleman. Patmore's experience was far from unique. It was a story that was repeated, with various degrees of inspiration and expenditure, across the face of the Weald of his day.

A more modest type of playground was the 'pleasure farm', earlier known as the *ferme ornée*, a term which Victorians added to sale catalogues from about 1870 and which continued in vogue up to the Second World War, when it abruptly disappeared, though millionaires are bringing it back in a new genre firmly today. The 'pleasure farm' was a small agricultural estate largely turned over to ornament and leisure. Typically, an attractive half-timbered or stone-clad yeoman's farmstead would be renovated and extended, or a small 'manor house' or new villa built, usually designed in the regional style. Such farms came cheaply on to the market in the last quarter of the 19th century as the prices of mediocre heavy land tumbled with the increasing imports of overseas grain. With the growth of trans-wealden railways between London and the coast, 'pleasure farms' became intensely characteristic of the clays of the Low Weald of Surrey and Sussex, which lacked the high ground esteemed by the wealthier. On these 'toy' estates the simplest way of ornamenting was by planting up the hedgerows (often turning them into shaws), and the 'tail-ends' of fields, and adding a specimen tree or two to the lawns.[14]

Clergy also caught the landscaping spirit in rectories, parsonages, glebelands and churchyards. The Rev. Anthony Dale, mid-century rector of Bolney, Sussex, was so practical an artist as to record details of his planting in the parish registers. Three of his 'Bhutan pines', sown from seed obtained from a local director of the East India Company, survive, as do most of his Luccombe oaks (now tall handsome specimens) and the 200 'fine young tellers' planted in the glebe hedgerows, still enhancing the verge of the former highway to Brighton.[15]

By the 1830s the park as the leading form of landscaping had been carried through to perfection by Kent, Brown and Repton and their imitators. New inspiration was needed. Wealthy merchants and professional people began to use the vast reservoir of hardy plants brought back by collectors from the cool and temperate parts of the world. The best artistic medium for this purpose proved to be the 'wild' and other natural gardens introduced from the 1870s by William Robinson (1838-1935), followed by Gertrude Jekyll, an early convert.[16] This movement is of particular significance in the history of the Weald because it increasingly drew inspiration directly from trees, the traditional pre-occupation of Wealdsmen, and of the Weald's vestigial semi-wildness. Unlike early creators of designed landscapes who had seen them through the eyes of Claude and Poussin's transcripts of scenery around Rome and Tivoli, Robinson's inspiration came from the 'genius' of the historic wildness of the Weald itself. 'I am never concerned with Claude', he wrote, 'but seek the best expression I can secure of our English rural landscapes, which are far finer than Claude's.'[17]

Robinson was an opinionated and irascible Irishman who moved to England and was elected a member of the Linnaean Society of London in his twenties. He became a most prolific writer on gardening and a successful editor of gardening periodicals. Charles Quest-Ritson has remarked that his *The English Flower Garden*, published in 1883 and reprinted 15 times during Robinson's lifetime, 'was the book of books – the gardener's bible'. In this book, which developed from his earlier *Wild Garden* (1870), Robinson was the undisputed leading proponent of natural gardening as opposed to the standard formal 'bedding-out' long practised in England.

Robinson always attracted controversy. The garden historian, Quest-Ritson, refers to him as 'a popularizer who seldom jumped on a band wagon before it had already been rolling for at least a decade', and considers that his writings are full of contradictions and *volte-faces*. Nevertheless, his exceptional energy and uncommon gifts, touching every aspect of the arrangement of bold natural groups of plants and trees, captured the mood of the nation.[18]

146 Gravetye, the home of the Elizabethan ironmaster Richard Infield, which became the home of William Robinson and the centre of his gardening and publishing activities. The country house hotel splendidly maintains the Robinsonian traditions.

This is particularly true of the central Weald where he bought Gravetye Manor near East Grinstead in 1884 (originally built in 1598 for the ironmaster Richard Infield and his bride Catharine) and it was here that Robinson pioneered many of his ideas for the creation of the English natural garden, which became admired and copied all over the world. Aided by Ernest Markham, Robinson's talented head gardener, he raised clematis and many other plants, and introduced in miniature something of Swiss mountain scenery by making use of rocky outcrops in deep natural ravines. Several old mill streams, marl and mine pits, and disused hammer ponds were transformed into water gardens enhanced by naturalising early bulbs along the watersides and in meadows. He added a heath garden and, true to the spirit of his *Wild Garden*, extended ornament to fields, hedgerows and woods. Nearer the house, Robinson established the herbaceous border.[19]

Robinson abhorred the thick park belts of Capability Brown and his 'pudding-like clumps' and decided against turning fields into a park-like expanse, considering that a park without great breadth and dignity of old trees was not beautiful (alas that so many other place-makers did not follow suit!). 'Almost every field was dealt with; beauty was not lost sight of, nothing from making a road to forming a fence was done without considering its effect on the landscape from every point of view.' The scale of his plantings can be gauged from the 120,000 trees set out in 1889-90, the 4,000 cedar of Lebanon, Riga pine, Austrian pine and Corsican pine in 1892 and the 100,000 narcissus along the margin of the Lower Lake in 1897-8.

Most affected by Robinson's style of gardening was the Forest Ridge of the High Weald of Kent and Sussex. As this imitated nature's work in a clearing within open woodland, and its acid soil, rich in leaf mould, was such an excellent medium for all ericaceous plants and trees, this district provided a perfect setting for the movement. Moreover, the cheapness of land which had never been turned to full account facilitated the purchase of the extensive spaces needed for natural gardening. The Weald's own spirit of place contributed to the new design, for the ways in which woodland gradually gave way to cultivation provided ample suggestions for naturally arranged plants and trees. Great care was taken to produce fine colour effects without losing the natural woodland character of the setting.

Numerous gardens amongst the greatest in England and of international reputation still embellish the Weald, many influenced by Robinson's achievements at Gravetye. Leonard Messel's Nymans, created mainly between 1890-1915, and lying on the Forest Ridge relatively free from frost, was one of the first to collect all the hardy heathers native to Britain and 'living in a cool forest district with too many dark days' he experimented in a paddock near his house with shrubs and rare trees he had personally collected from New Zealand, Australia, South Africa and America, plus trees introduced from China by Wilson. The *Flora*, published in 1918, comprises almost 200 pages.[20] Leonardslee is a spectacular woodland garden including a series of hammer ponds and with one of the finest collections of mature rhododendrons, azaleas, choice trees and shrubs. It was begun by Sir Edmund Loder, great-grandfather of the present owner, who

147 Leonardslee, the creation of the Loder family, was devastated by the Great Storm of 16 October 1987 but has been enhanced by new plantings and design.

planted the garden himself. It is understood that Millais at Compton Brow near Blackdown was Loder's 'advisor'. The Bedgebury National Pinetum, which was established as the National Conifer Collection in 1923 as part of Kew Gardens, was largely the work of William Dallimore in the inter-war years, but its origin is owed to Alexander Beresford Hope who planted exotic trees on part of his 2,000 acres of woodland on the Bedgebury estate. At an estimated cost of nearly £3 million, the conifer collection, already recognised as the best in the world, is to be increased to 100 per cent of the world's conifers capable of being cultivated in the temperate zone, and superior visitor facilities and educational projects are planned. Colonel R. Stephenson Clarke, who began to plant at Borde Hill near Haywards Heath in the 1890s, has recorded his first efforts at shutting out unsightly views and improving the landscape generally. Sheffield Park has some of the finest landscaping. Much of Brown's work where John Baker Holroyd, 1st

Earl of Sheffield, built Sheffield House, a neo-Gothic building, in 1775, and the studied chiaroscuro effect that Repton aimed at, has given way to Soames's 'wild gardening' and informal woodlands.[21]

The Weald was also notable for its old fashioned cottage flower gardens crowded with informally grouped hardy plants amidst vegetable patches. We first learn of the extraordinary pains Wealden agricultural labourers and their wives took with their gardens from the pens of Arthur Young, William Cobbett and the Comte de la Garde (pp.167, 187, 245).[22] In the 19th century local horticultural societies sprang up, such as those of Battle and Ditchling, regularly offered prizes to labourers. Through Helen Allingham and Birket Foster's water-colours and later through transcripts of nature by H.B. Brabazon, as well as by the Impressionists, such cottage gardens became more widely known and appreciated. As mentioned previously, Gertrude Jekyll drew greatly upon them for her teaching of colour planning and grouping.

30

The Present and the Uncertain Future

IN 1933 the equipment and livestock for sale at Home Farm, Heron's Ghyll near Uckfield, included three broad-wheeled Sussex wagons with iron arms, skid pan and chains; a 3½-inch wheeled wagon; a light spring Market cart; a turn-wrest plough; a wood shim (for making hills for hops); seven dairy cows (each named); five horses (named); some beef cattle; and five breeding pigs and 100 head of poultry. A nearly new 'Albion' mowing machine and a 5hp Ruston Hornby oil engine were the only evidence of modernity. Everything else symbolised mixed farming as it had been practised in the Weald for hundreds of years.[1]

Since then the Weald has undergone immense changes, not all for the better. Until the 1950s farmers groped about barns with lanterns, lacked mains water and had no electricity in the farmhouse. Yet times were good for the young family taking up farming. The mixed farm disappeared with subsidised agriculture, but a reasonably good living could be had from 15 dairy cows, as a step-up to a larger farm. Large estates were being put on the market and sold as freeholds, giving opportunities for unprecedented owner occupation. Orchards and hops were still holding their own.

148 Derelict hop-handling plant, Barkham Court, Withyham.

Over the past 20 years the Weald, like other rural areas, has been facing unprecedented pressures. Farming and forestry, always difficult on the heavy clays, have been pushed to the economic margins by soaring land values, competition from cheaper products from abroad and changing consumer preferences. The number of people employed in Wealden agriculture has fallen by one third in the last ten years as economic activity has been declining, particularly in the High Weald. Since 1987 the area occupied by orchards in the Weald has fallen by more than one third and the area occupied by hops has declined by more than three-quarters. Dairy farming, buoyant until recently, is now in rapid retreat. Meanwhile, a revolution in retailing has occurred. In 1959 in Smarden parish retail shops totalled 13; in 1999 there were only two. Data from the same parish also records the bare details of changes in farming which are typical of the Weald as a whole. In 1881 there were 60 farmers; in 1950, 32; and only 12 in 1999. In 1881, 4,000 acres were being farmed but now only 2,500 acres. Hops, a major crop until the last war, are no longer grown in the parish and orchards are almost extinct. Meanwhile, half-timbered farmhouses are almost all owned by commuting business and professional people, an exception being one owned by a time-share company based in Singapore.[2] Consequently, although the landscape still looks much the same, its important features – woodland, hedgerows and pasture – are no longer being fully taken into account and in some cases are no longer being managed at all. Never since clearing woodland for agriculture began has the question had to be raised as to whether the cultivated land of the Weald, which we take as much for granted as the air we breathe, could be abandoned by its farmers. Now this is a real possibility. The big farmer will doubtless survive and get bigger. It is the small farmer, now being driven to the wall, who is most at risk. If all the small farmers go under, the wonderful mix of small fields and scattered farmsteads surrounded by small woodlands and hedgerows will eventually disappear with them.

This poses a great threat to the Weald. It must change to survive, but somehow its special character must continue and flourish, insulated from the worst of the 21st century commercial pressures in the busy South East. Only by acceptable new land use and the revival of traditional ways of managing its landscape – such as hedge-laying and coppicing, pond maintenance, skilful tree pruning and the productive use of the patchwork of fields and herb-rich meadows, together with restraints on the townsman's concept of countryside – will there be a distinctively beautiful landscape to pass on to future generations. The lack of traditional skills is endangering this revival. There is scope, for example, for a massive expansion of hedge-laying as a remunerative hobby, the part-time worker obtaining his material from some 'derelict' or 'uneconomic' wood, so helping to restore it in the process. This would greatly benefit the economy and the landscape but it would need an infrastructure to re-train and encourage potential workers.[3]

In Praise of Trees

The worst possible scenario has been reserved for forestry. Commercial coppicing has virtually died out and the timber dray bearing great oaks and beech, the most familiar sight in the Weald since colonisation began, is hardly ever seen. Yet four-fifths of Britain's timber is imported. Anyone conscious of the Weald's traditional place in national forestry and woodsmanship is filled with a sense of shame and disbelief at the waste of indigenous resources, which, in the Weald's continuation into the Pays de Bray, pursues exemplary forestry providing much rural employment. Yet there are some grounds for optimism. A commercial and wildlife-friendly vision for woodlands is now held by some builders, interior designers, architects and artists who use timber. Their aim is to encourage people to rediscover the delights of natural building materials that are sustainable.[4] There is at present more interest in the renovation of woodland than there has been for half a century. One aspect of this is a renewed activity in coppicing. This has regularly taken on a new lease of life in earlier phases of alternative agriculture, as it offered a good income when farming hit bad times. Each cut is beneficial to wildlife. The canopy of leaves is opened up, encouraging wild flowers that need light and water and cannot grow under the trees. These in turn attract insects to feed on the pollen and nectar and birds feed on the insects. As coppicing moves from compartment to compartment there are always areas which provide food, cover and nesting sites for birds and animals. The 1990s has seen a revival and this in turn is inspiring pride and interest in woodland management for both a market and for wildlife, and it is nurturing traditional woodland crafts such as the making of fencing, tool handles, basket making, garden furniture using oak and chestnut, and timber building. Funding from the EU is available to help long-term unemployed who want to become self-employed coppice workers.

A remunerative outlet for wood products is a first step in the revival of sustained management of woodland which has preserved the distinctive landscape of the Weald. The decision in 1995 of the East Sussex County Council, in conjunction with other organisations, to promote new uses for 19,000 acres of neglected chestnut coppice is a praiseworthy initiative which partly owes its inspiration to vigorous French forestry practice in Normandy. It is hoped that the construction of the visitor centre at the Woodland Enterprise Centre at Flimwell in short scantlings of coppiced sweet chestnut will stimulate architects and builders to use an indigenous natural resource, which is capable of producing wood as rapidly as softwoods while being virtually as strong and durable as oak and requiring no preservative or protective coating for external use. Its timber thus provides excellent material for the construction of buildings and for furniture; such use would again make chestnut one of the most valuable assets to this countryside. The West Sussex County Council has also been active in putting forward a vision for the county's woodlands, including the use of wood as an energy source to reduce the effects of pollutant gas emissions and oil crises. Many woodland owners are not motivated by the prospect of economic returns but most are sufficiently concerned with stewardship to lend support to projects which aim at generating rural employment.

In Kent, where 40 per cent of woodland is coppice, a Centenary Community Woodland Project was started in 1992 to encourage parish councils to create and manage their own woodlands, and to value the produce, whether coppice stools

149 The late Dame Jean Dowling bought Balcombe Farmhouse in 1969 as one of the earliest homes for week-ending and retirement. It was sensitively restored, with advice from the Society for the Protection of Ancient Buildings, to make it more livable after a long period of neglect and has been made into a delightful home without spoiling its character. A notable achievement was the removal of plaster from the original oak beams. (John Malton, summer 2002, pencil sketch, 21 × 14cm [8¼ × 5½ in.])

or holly for Christmas or blackberries. A Charcoal Project is aimed at encouraging the purchase of locally-made charcoal which is superior to imported produce and not detrimental to tropical forests in the developing world. Environmentally-conscious owners are beginning to set examples for others to follow. On Stockland Farm at Hadlow Down two acres of neglected coppice is being cleared annually, which besides creating bio-diversity is exposing to view old woodbanks, ponds and other historical features. Although coppice is the present priority, it may be feasible to increase the acreage under managed high forest in the 21st century now that we are re-establishing links with some of the oldest elements on the Wealden landscape.

Another means of a further increase in well-managed woodland will shortly be the tangible result of the modern conservation movement, e.g. the proposed plantings by the Sussex Wildlife Trust at Ebernoe Common and the Menn's Wood. Meanwhile, the Woodscape Project, just begun by the Forestry Commission, aims to take out conifers and to restore native trees to ancient woodland, broadly defined as ground covered by trees since at least 1600. This will return the woods to something like how they looked in past times. As David Streeter has remarked, such woodlands are as much part of the past English heritage and as worthy of preservation as 'chalk grassland or Stonehenge'.[5]

Alternative Farming – new crops for old

The rapid decline in many of the traditional Wealden crops has stimulated the production of entirely new, or revived, alternatives. The wine renaissance has been a striking success. The vine was grown in the South East in Roman times. In the Middle Ages there were innumerable vineyards attached to monastic houses. Climate change has meant that some centuries were better than others. The present English wine-making has been madly, almost dementedly, experimental, with results that the French claimed tasted like rain, but it is now no longer being depicted as a pantomime horse gamely running a marathon. Against the odds, it is producing high quality wines, in some cases superior to similarly priced wines from Saumur or Australia, which are being served at official functions and which, drunk on a warm summer's day amid some of the loveliest countryside in England, is one of life's greatest pleasures.

A pioneer in viticulture was George Ordish who planted a few vines at Yalding in 1938. After 1945 Edward Hyams and Ray Barrington Brock followed his example, the latter setting up at his own expense the Viticultural Research Station at Oxted in 1946. One of the most celebrated of the new generation of vineyards is Lamberhurst, started in 1972 and now with 60 acres of vines. Vineyards spread swiftly in the 1980s, the High Weald being one of the best areas for growing grapes, its comparatively warm climate approximating to that of Champagne, and this is reflected in the number of vineyards.[6] The Seyval grape, which ripens earlier, is more or less perfect for English conditions, the most northerly in the world. It is frost resistant (late frosts in June are a problem) and has a flavour which improves with age. One has to be prepared to spend long back-breaking hours pruning vines on a cold January day and be resigned to losing an awful lot of money in bad years.

Other forms of alternative farming, first brought to a head by the food mountains of 1983-4, are strongly developing in place of conventional agricultural production. The growing of varied plants for industrial, medicinal and aromatic use, and more diversified foodstuffs, including vegetable, fruit, dairy produce, unusual meats and fish, all seem to have fresh potential. A store in Goudhurst was stocking over 60 locally produced foodstuffs in 2000 which, by their very production, help to maintain employment and the rich wildlife habitats and scenic qualities. A directory issued by the High Weald AONB Unit in 2000 lists almost 50 suppliers of local woodland products, nine producers of yoghurt and cheeses, 25 of meat, 28 of fruit and vegetables, and 26 of wine, cider, beer and juices, including 16 vineyards. Attempts are being made to increase products derived from heathland, e.g. Scots pine, Christmas trees, bracken mulch, honey and heather. Recent concern – over pesticide residues in fresh fruit and vegetables, excessive antibiotic use in poultry, the dangers of genetically modified crops and contaminated livestock feed – has led to a mushrooming interest in organic farming. Such village shops are increasingly developing specialised goods and a strong customer focus to counter the pull of the large supermarkets. They offer a very personal service and, like all good shopkeepers, know which farms have supplied particular goods. Farmers' markets have been established (usually

150 Tenterden: its townscape reflects its historic role as a market and administrative centre of the Kent Weald.

on Saturdays) at Hailsham, Lewes, Tunbridge Wells, and Horsham, with others, such as Heathfield, due shortly.

Nut trees, neglected since the 1880s and 1890s in Ightham and Plaxtol parishes, are being revived with funds from the EC. A Kentish Cobnuts Association was formed in 1990 and, in 1993, 10 cobnut growers in Kent were offered stewardship grants. Ightham has bestowed a new sign on its *Cobtree Inn*, removing the image of a cob horse and restoring the tree. Walnut trees are also due for a revival.[7] Frances Smith, an early pioneer of farm-to-restaurant, from 1987 has grown an unusual variety of vegetables and herbs on 23 acres at Appledore, inspired by Joy Larcom's *The Salad Garden* (1984). In the past 20 years a remarkable number of small proprietors, who have not been totally wiped out of existence, have tackled new farming pursuits, whether lavender and other aromatic herbs, snails, poultry, goat-keeping, mushrooms, organic vegetables, or a return to farmhouse cheese-making. A modest start in these activities offers the best of beginnings of many pioneers of new farming pursuits.

Small specialist fruit growers also still exist. Old orchards are characterised by taller, spreading, well-spaced trees, often in sheep-grazed meadows. They support a far greater variety of wildlife, such as lichens, invertebrates, owls, and woodpeckers, than modern orchards but cost much more to maintain and harvest. Under the Countryside Stewardship Scheme there is a funded plan for the restoration of the traditional management of older orchards.

Buying locally-produced goods benefits the Weald countryside in various ways. It contributes to the survival of local distinctiveness and the sense of place which

151 The Chestnut House at Flimwell, built of sweet chestnut to promote its use as a building material.

is fast diminishing across the country and, in particular, it gives support to farming and forestry management. It reduces long distance transport and energy use and minimises packaging, waste and storage. It helps maintain habitats for wildlife and landscape character in general. It supports and helps create local jobs and the investment in local services. In short, it will help stave off what we all despair of – a soulless, emptied, countryside. As Sally Marsh, the High Weald AONB Officer, has said, 'Today, consumer spending can help to reverse the declines and threats to several local types of countryside'. It is thus in the Weald's interest that all its products bear characteristic imprint of the region as deep as the French *terroir.*

Another serious threat to the Weald arises from modern development. Until recently the low lying, damp heavy clay of the Low Weald has protected it against house building but it is now being regarded as a housing reserve for the future, notwithstanding its susceptibility to floods. Unlike the High Weald, which was designated an Area of Outstanding Natural Beauty on account of the exaggerated degree of importance attributed to its panoramic views in 1983, this quintessence of the Weald is workaday, honest-to-goodness country which has not been granted any major landscape protection against development, although a part of the Kent Low Weald has been recently given a 'lower-tier' designation as a Special Landscape Area, which may reduce somewhat its vulnerability. Although there is a national target of building 60 per cent of new housing on brown field sites, we must expect that substantially more than 40 per cent of all new housing in the South East will be built on greenfield land because of the enormous demand for housing. Future housing demand could be met outside the South East, if only employment and career aspirations could also be met in other regions. Only a national policy for improving regional economies will counter-balance the unsustainable growth of the South East. Failing this, there will be no option but to build on this comfortable and congenial land. There are plenty of people to praise beauty spots but few to laud this ordinary country, though there are more than a few who love it. To defend its small-scale beauty, as delicate as fine bone china, is more necessary than ever.

An ancient, unspoilt landscape like the Weald could continue to provide sustenance for those who need the privacy and protectiveness of a haven with a ring fence round it for a refuge, as did Kipling, and as Adam Nicolson and monks at Crawley Down have recently done. It could also attract the man or woman who aims 'to break the unkindly spirit of the clay', if only to leave a pathetic monument like the giant silo at Burnt Oak Farm near Rotherfield, hoisted over the valley of the river Uck in the 1920s to store maize that rarely ripened. Provided the traditional crafts of hedging and ditching are kept up, there would also be the Old Hobdens of the future, as for generations past, the archetypal Wealdsmen, who would teach newcomers that although they may own the premises it is they who actually possess it. Above all, it could remain home to those conquered by the sheer miracle of the distinguished, mellow, humanised beauty of its sylvan pastoral landscape. But for all this to happen the Weald's traditional small family farmer would need to survive and the small woods of its richly timbered countryside be actively managed and we should not simply look back into the past, but, as Bryn Green has reminded us, we should take the opportunity 'to conceive, design, create and maintain new landscapes fit for the social, economic and environmental needs of the 21st century'.[8] By these means the old farmhouses, red-roofed villages, churches with their tall towers and the network of narrow lanes will continue to be where one can escape from the hustle and bustle of city life and have the feeling of entering a world of unspoiled nature.

Notes

Manuscript sources are given in full. Articles and books are given by author and date, by which they can be located in the Bibliography.

Manuscript abbreviations:

ESRO	East Sussex Record Office, Lewes
CKS	Kent Centre for Local Studies, Maidstone
PRO	Public Record Office, Kew
WSRO	West Sussex Record Office, Chichester

Other abbreviations:

SRS	Sussex Record Society
SAC	Sussex Archaeological Collections
Agric. Hist. Rev.	Agricultural History Review
BPP	British Parliamentary Papers (Irish University Press edition)

Chapter 1: A Perspective

1. Mantell, 1822, 1825, 1833. These works clearly established for the first time the extraordinary changes in the surface of the Weald and of its climate, vegetation and fauna and that it was one of the best places in England for their study; Wooldridge, 1949.
2. ESRO, ASHB. Ms. 1173.
3. Halsham (Forrester Scott), 1898, 22-4.
4. Stephen, 1874.
5. Halsham, 1898, 22-4.
6. ESRO, ASHB. 4409.
7. Harvey, 1997, 2001.
8. Hardcastle, 1999.
9. Kendon, 1930.
10. Sassoon, 1960.
11. Blunden, 1932, 107-22.
12. Everitt, 1986, 55-6.
13. Witney, 1976, 30.
14. Norden, 1636 ed.
15. BM Lansdown Ms.53 f.165.
16. Hasted, 1797-1801.
17. Dearn, 1814; Ireland, 1829.
18. KS U3345/F1.
19. Nicolson, 2000.
20. Cobbett, 1930, 61.

Chapter 2: Historical Bounds

1. This is the 'real Weald' of William Cobbett and it might be called the Weald proper or the historic Weald. Cobbett, *op.cit*, 157.
2. Furley, 1871-4, vol. 2ii, 638-48, 833.

Chapter 3: The Natural Setting

1. Coppedhall PSSSI.
2. Martin, 1828. Martin, the first geologist of the area, noted that the presence of underlying calcareous sandstone below the clay was generally denoted by elms.
3. Blunt (1932 edn.), 242.
4. Blunt, Collected Works.
5. Gissing, ed. Mattheisen under date 1889.
6. Robinson, in Williams, 1971, 51-60.
7. Rose, 1995.
8. Fitton, 1824, 1833. Fitton was a brilliant stratigrapher who, although informed in 1821 that there was nothing of geological interest at Hastings, established it as one of the most important sites in South-East England.

Chapter 4: Soils and Earth History

1. Rev. Gilbert White, 1816 edn., Chapter 1.
2. Cobbett, 1930, 237.
3. Rev. Arthur Young, 1813.
4. Kaye-Smith, 1916, 266-7.
5. Topley, 1875.
6. CKS, E 173/1-2A.
7. I am indebted to Mr James Overy for much of this paragraph.
8. Markham, 1636 edn., 7.
9. Evans, 1999, 56-7.

10. Jones, 1980; Allen 1975, 1976, 1981; Gallois, 1965.
11. CKS, E 173/1-2A.
12. Alec Clifton-Taylor in John Newman, *West Kent and the Weald* (1969), 23.
13. CKS, 477/1-10.
14. Lower, 1849.
15. Report of Professor Gregory to Earl Sheffield, 1 March 1908, SAS Library.

Chapter 5: The Wildwood

1. Harrison, 1928.
2. Prestwich, 1869, 127-297; *ibid.*, 1895, 617-28
3. Cleere, 1976, 239.
4. Rackham, 1980, 27, 97, 109, 319.
5. Gardiner, 1990, 33-53.
6. Tebbutt, 1975.
7. Dimbleby, 1962; *idem*, 1965, 85-92.
8. Scaife and Burrin, 1985, 27-34; *idem*, 1987, 1-9.
9. Gardiner, Ashdown Forest.
10. Margary, 1948.
11. Cleere, 1976, 233-46; *idem*, 1977.
12. Cleere and Crossley, 1985, 279-83.
13. Tebbutt, 1974, 34-43.
14. Rackham, 1980, 108-9.
15. Cleere and Crossley, 1985, Figs. 16 and 17.
16. Tom Williamson, 1987, 53, 419-31.
17. Jones, 1979.

Chapter 6: The Saxon and Jutish Andredesweald

1. Rivet and Smith, 1979, 250-2; Mawer and Stenton, 1929, 1-2.
2. Vera, 2000, 109.
3. Everitt, 1976.
4. Witney (1976), Chapter Six.
5. Everitt, 1986, 18.
6. Gelling and Cole, 200, 314.
7. *Ibid.*, 224-6; 234-6; 235.
8. Brandon (ed.), 1978, 138-59.
9. Gelling and Cole, *op. cit.*, 226, 314.
10. Ward, 1936; Everitt, *op. cit.*, 1986, 27.
11. Everitt, 1986, 27.
12. Douglas (ed.), 1944.
13. Hearne, 1720.
14. Blair, 1991.
15. Darby and Campbell, 1962.
16. Cf. Sawyer, 1965, 64, 145; 1978, 137.
17. Loyn, 1982.

Chapter 7: The 'Custom of the Country' – Agriculture

1. Saunders and Chatters, 82.

2. M.F. Wallis De Vries, 1998, 113.
3. Arthur Young, 1792-4, 291.
4. Sackville West, 1933.
5. Gollancz (ed), 1950, 85.
6. James Overy, pers. comm.
7. Briault, 1942.
8. Arthur Young (ed.), *Annals of Agriculture*, 5, 1786, 107.
9. Brandon and Short, 1990, 64.
10. Markham, 1636, 80.
11. Brandon and Short, 1990, 65.
12. Dyer, *Agric. Hist. Rev.* 49, 2001, 98; cf. Topley, *op. cit.*, 262-3.
13. ESRO, Add. Ms. 3924, 1878.
14. Bishop, 1938, 38-44.
15. ESRO, SAS CO/631, 2.
16. Brandon, 1969, 135.
17. ESRO, Dunn Ms. 6077/15/21.
18. Streeter and Richardson, 58, 101-2.
19. Grant, 1845, 420-9.
20. Marshall, 1798.

Chapter 8: 'Custom of the Country' – Woodcraft

1. Roberts, 1999.
2. Vera, 2001, 159, 272.
3. Hardcastle, 1999, 105-9.

Chapter 9: The Medieval Woodland

1. ESRO, SRL Ms. 1373, 1623.
2. Du Boulay, 1966.
3. Bise, 1978.
4. Du Boulay, 1966, 104.
5. Cantor, 1982, 77-8.
6. Peckham, 1925.
7. Brandon, 1963.
8. Redwood and Wilson, 1958, 36.
9. PRO, E 101/1361.
10. Hunter, 1902, 197.

Chapter 10: How was the Land Won?

1. Rackham, 1986.
2. Ministry of Agriculture, Technical Report No. I, 'The reclamation of derelict woodland for agricultural use', 1957.
3. Edlin, 1958, 50.
4. Searle, 1974, 22, 64.
5. SRS, 34, 1928, 238-9.
6. ESRO, SAT LB 34.
7. Godfrey, SRS, 34; Hallam, 1981, 93; Brandon and Short, 1990, 53.
8. English Nature, Kent, File TQ/54-9.

Chapter 11: The Great Clearing c.1050-1348

1. Searle, *op. cit.*, 22.

2. Witney, 1976, 121-3.
3. ESRO, SAT LB 34.
4. Peckham, 1925, 87-98.
5. Brandon and Short, 1990.
6. Brandon, 1969.
7. ESRO, SAT LB 34.
8. CKS, 1475/M242.

Chapter 12: The Retreat of Settlement

1. Baker, 1966, 1-5.
2. Brandon, 1969, 135-53.
3. Tebbutt, 1981.
4. Glasscock, 1965; Sheail, 1972; Cornwall, 1956; C.F. Tebbutt, 1981, 107-116.
5. CKS, U1475/M251 Fodiland, Reeve's Acct., 1388-9.
6. Brandon, 1971, 1-17.

Chapter 13: Timber-framed Buildings

1. Melling, 1965, 1.
2. Chatwin, 1996.
3. Harris, 1978.
4. Warren and Hallam in John Warren, 1990.
5. Chatwin, *op. cit.*
6. Roberts, *op. cit.*, 81-3, re. horizontal woven work in hazel.
7. Rigold, 1963, 211-16.
8. Coutin, in John Warren (ed.), 1990, 74, 80.
9. Rigold, 1963.
10. D. Martin, pers. comm.
11. Rigold, 1963.
12. D. Martin, pers. comm.
13. Brandon, 1974, 142-5.
14. Du Boulay, 1966.
15. Pearson, 1994.
16. Aberg, 1978; West, 2002.
17. Rigold, 1962, 27-47.
18. Mason, 1964, 50.
19. West, 2001.
20. Thirsk, 1997, 14-15.
21. Joan Shelley, pers. comm.
22. Chatwin, 1996, 48.
23. *Sunday Telegraph*, 1991.
24. Law, 2001.

Chapter 14: The Age of the Improvers, c.1550-1650

1. Aldis, 1909, 370.
2. Fussell, 1952, 60-102.
3. Evans, 1999, 21.
4. Fussell, 1952, 69.
5. Young (ed.), *Annals of Agriculture*, 5, 1785, 107.
6. Young (ed.), *Annals of Agriculture*, 21, 1794, 467.

7. Young, *The Farmer's Tour through the East of England,* vol. III (1771), 141-2.
8. Norden, 1636 edn.
9. ESRO, SRL Ms. 1/1/29.
10. Brandon, 1984(b).
11. CKS, 0269/189, 1659.
12. WSRO, Mitford Ms. Map of Fitzlee, 1629.
13. ESRO, Add. Ms. 64997; PRO STA C9/104/79.
14. SAT ABER 27, f.16; SAT SH 384, f.ii, et. seq.; thesis 161.
15. ESRO, SRL. Ms. 179/1.
16. ESRO, ACC 2953/99.
17. Brandon, 1963.
18. *Ibid.*
19. ESRO, ADA 137.
20. ESRO, SAT J 606.

Chapter 15: The Wealden Iron Industry

1. Wrake, Maresfield Historical Society, Occasional Papers, No. 2, June 1999.
2. Awty, *Wealden Iron* XIII, 1978, 17-19; XVI, 1979, 2-11.
3. NEF. Ec. Hist. Rev. 5, 1934, 13-24.
4. ESRO, Dunn Ms. 29/1.
5. Lower, 1849, 183.
6. ESRO, Co/631
7. *Architecture Review*, 1925, 58.
8. WIRG newsletter, Spring 2000.
9. Lower, 1849, 197.
10. Teesdale, 1991, 90-2.
11. CKS, U968, T 251.
12. CKS, T 24/3.
13. CKS, T 461.
14. CKS, T 218.
15. CKS, T 303.
16. CKS, T3.
17. CKS, P1.
18. Teesdale, 1991, 66-9.
19. CKS, U 1450/D/DI/E 15, 1582-95.

Chapter 16: Gunpowder, Wire, Glass and Cloth

1. Brandon, 1984, 75-107.
2. Kenyon, 1967, 122, 137.
3. *Ibid.*
4. Brandon, 1984(b).
5. CKS, 1934/21.
6. Zell, 1994, 189.
7. CKS, LHC U 301/F3.

Chapter 17: Iron-makers: Woodland Exploiters or Conservers?

1. Evelyn, *Sylva*, 1679 edn., 12, 34.

2. Lower, 1849, 190-7, 204; Topley, 1875, 332.
3. Roberts, 95.
4. This was evidently the case on the Ash-burnham Estate. Moffatt, 1883, 4.
5. Chatters and Saunders, 1994.
6. Straker, 1931, 114-21.
7. *Ibid.*, 12.
8. CKS, U1475/T267.
9. Crossley (ed.), 1975, 129-34.
10. CKS, U1475/T287; T274.
11. ESRO, ASHB. Ms., 1178.
12. CKS, U1475 E20(2).
13. Crossley, 1974, 48-79; Teesdale, 1984, 72.
14. PRO Chancery.
15. Suit, 1603, Pullein, 1926, 80; PRO Star Chamber 5/A2/25.
16. Crossley, 1974; Teesdale, 1984, 72.
17. Straker, 1931, 123.
18. Brandon, 1984(b).
19. ESRO, SRL Ms. 1371.
20. ESRO, SRL Ms. 13/3.
21. Cleere and Crossley, 1995 edn., 136.
22. Straker, *op. cit.*, 109-11.
23. PRO Star Chamber, Jas I, 872, 13, 16.
24. Hammersley, 1984, 610.

Chapter 18: The Farmer and Labourer 1700-1815

1. Young (ed.), *Annals of Agriculture*, 26, 1796, 521.
2. Brent, 1970, 69-80.
3. Young (ed.), *Annals of Agriculture*, 4, 1785, 454.
4. ESRO, Hickstead 474.
5. Young (ed.), *Annals of Agriculture*, 18, 1792, 22.
6. Cobbett, 1930, 481.
7. Lucas, 1892.
8. Young, *The Farmer's Tour through the East of England*, vol. III, 1771, 124-6.
9. ESRO, Hickstead 474.

Chapter 19: The Later Gentry

1. ESRO, AMS 141.
2. Everitt, 1966; Du Boulay, 1966, 92-113.
3. ESRO, Dunn Ms. 49/22.
4. ESRO, Dunn Ms. 47/24.
5. W.E. Bowen, SAC 29 (1879), 149-52.
6. R.G. Lucas, 'The History of the Warnett Family' (unpub.)
7. ESRO, Dunn Ms. 49/22.
8. Will and inventory of Roberts, PRO/PROB/11/58/27; PRO/PROB/11/71/326.
9. SRS, 39 (1933).

10. Steer, D982/2/5, f8.

Chapter 20: Transport

1. Cobbett, 1930 edn., 198.
2. CKS, U1293 01/7.
3. Montagu, *Letters* (1777); vol. I, 1736, 60; 1738, 49.
4. Walpole, *Letters*, vol. II, August 26, 1749, 178-9; August 5, 1752, 299.
5. J. Lucas (ed.), 1892, 381.
6. CKS, P152/8/2.
7. Malcolm, vol. III, 1805, 298.
8. ESRO, ALF 9/1-12.
9. Brandon, 1979, 176.
10. CKS, P26/22-4.
11. Vine, 1965.

Chapter 21: The Crisis Years, 1816-33

1. BPP Agriculture, vol.2, 1833, 608-617.
2. BPP Agriculture, vol.1, 1820, 110-124.
3. BPP Agriculture, vol.3, 1836, 244-54.
4. BPP Poor Law, 17, 1834, 152-4.
5. Cobbett, 1830.
6. Baxter, vol. I, 1846, 228-41.
7. Sheppard, 'Small Farms in a Sussex Weald Parish, 1800-1860', *Agric. Hist. Rev.*, 40, 1992, 127-41.
8. Sanders, *Letters*, vol.12, 1970-2001, 167, 236, etc.

Chapter 22: The Swing Riots

1. Cobbett, *Political Register*, 3 Nov. 1830, 712.
2. Cobbett, *Two-Penny Trash*, Dec. 1830, 121-44.
3. CKS, 0951/C14.
4. CKS, Anon., *The Life and History of Swing*, 1830.
5. CKS, Anon., *Address to Men of Hawkhurst*, 1830.
6. Cobbett, 1834, 41-4.
7. Cobbett, *Political Register*, 2 Jan. 1830, 26.
8. Cobbett (ed. Nattrass.), *Peasant Politics*, vol. 6, 1998, 124-8.
9. CKS, Cresswell, 2003.
10. ESRO, AMS 5784.
11. Cobbett, *Political Register*, 13, 29 Dec. 1832, 803.
12. Like Cobbett, the geologist and surgeon, Gideon Mantell, sought the cause of incendiarism in the distress and despair of the agricultural labourers. See E. Cecil Curwen (ed.), *The Journal of Gideon Mantell*, 1940, 89.

Chapter 23: Emigration

1. BPP Emigration, vol.1, 1826, 117.
2. BPP Emigration, vol.2, 1826-7, 331.
3. CKS, 364/8/4.
4. Walton, 1998, 183.
5. CKS, P 152/8/2.
6. CKS, P 157/8/6, re: the Cape and the Govt. Emigration Office.

Chapter 24: Wealden Churches and Chapels

1. Sewell, 1995, 141.
2. Jenkins, 1999, 765.
3. Blair, pers. comm.
4. Nairn and Pevsner, 1964, 253.
5. Howell-Thomas, *West Sussex History*, 28, May 1984, 13-19.
6. Hare, 1981.
7. Clough, SRS 63.
8. Horsfield, 1835, vol. 2, 104.
9. Smith, 1979.
10. Lower, 1870.
11. J.L. Denman, articles in parish magazine, 1955, collected by R.A. Packham 1991.
12. Brandon, 1981, 8-14.
13. CKS, P102/3.
14. *The Ecclesiologist*, 1864, 60-1.
15. Frittenden Parish Council Ms.
16. Turnour, *National Review*, 1904, 106-12.
17. Jerrome, 1998.

Chapter 25: The Wildness Pleases: The Changed Appreciation of the Weald

1. Brandon, 1979, 167.
2. Cornish, 1937, 2.
3. Thorne, 1844.
4. Brandon, 1979, 184.
5. Dennis, 1721, 32.
6. Macky, *A Journey through England*, vol. 1, 971.
7. Watkin, 1968, 158-9.
8. Allingham, 1907, 301.
9. *Poetry Review*, vol. 16, 1925, 363-67.
10. E.M. Forster, 1908 edn., 15.
11. Latham and Matthews (eds.), vol. 9, 1976, 274.
12. Cobbett, *Life*, 1831, 359.
13. Ward, 1888, 295-6.
14. Charles Kingsley, 1859, 134-63.
15. Brandon, 1979, 170.
16. *Ibid.*, 171.

Chapter 26: Agriculture and Forestry on the Wane

1. Hoskyns, 1856.

2. CKS, Pamphlet by J. Homfray on farming *c.*1885.
3. ESRO, ASHB Ms., 1173.
4. Brandon and Short, 327.
5. ESRO, ASHB Ms., 1173.
6. Blunt, 1906, 955-67; Wilberforce, 1906, 678-9.
7. Haggard, *Rural England*, vol. 1, 1902, 104-36.
8. Halsham (Forrester-Scott), *Old Standards*, 35-45; 106-15; 154-61.
9. Patmore, 1886, 10.
10. Kirby, 1998.
11. ESRO, Ashdown Forest Ms.
12. Short, SRS 67.
13. ESRO, Add. Ms. 3978.
14. Eversley, 1894, vii, 170.
15. ESRO, Acc. 6815.
16. Sale Particulars, 1907. In 1912 the property was purchased by Sir Charles William Fielding, then Chairman of Rio Tinto.
17. Tim Hoof.

Chapter 27: 'We are all Londoners now'

1. Robertson, 12-13.
2. Bourne (Sturt), 1912, 115-26; Mackerness (ed.), 1967 edn.
3. Halsham, 1898, 123-4.
4. Blunt, 1906, 955-67.

Chapter 28: Londoners and their Weald

1. *The Times*, 27 December 1890, 7d.
2. Brandon, 1984(c), 53-74.
3. *Ibid.*
4. Eliot.
5. Mattheisen (ed.), *Letters*, April 16, 1882; August, 1885.
6. Allen, 1896, 2-3.
7. Brandon and Short, 1990, 346.

Chapter 29: Parks and Gardens

1. Brandon, 1979, 180-2.
2. Johnson, 18-19.
3. Hussey, 1967 edn., 129. See also J.C. Loudon, 1830, 790-821 and plate between pp.814-15.
4. Cobbett, 1930, 288.
5. Pichot, 1825, 16, 20-1.
6. Comte A. de la Garde, *Brighton*, 1834, in translation.
7. Brandon, 1974, 260.
8. Brandon, 1979, 176.
9. *Ibid.*, 176.
10. Sturt, 1912, 148.

11. Kropotkin, 1974 edn.
12. Karel Capek, *Letters from England*, 2001, 74-5.
13. Patmore, 1986.
14. Brandon, 1979, 179.
15. Brandon, 1979, 177.
16. Jekyll, *Wood and Garden*, 1899, 4.
17. W. Robinson, *The Wild Garden*, 1870.
18. Quest-Ritson, 2001, 116-17.
19. Robinson, *Gravetye Manor*, 1911; *Home Landscapes*, 1914.
20. Messel, 1916.
21. Brandon, 1979, 182-3.
22. Young, *op. cit.*, 1771, 124-6; Cobbett, *Rural Rides, op. cit.*, 546-7; de la Garde, 1834.

Chapter 30: The Present and the Uncertain Future
1. Sale Particulars.
2. Smarden Millennium Publication and pers. comm.
3. *The Times*, 28 January 2002.
4. In Praise of Trees: Conference, Salisbury, June 2002.
5. Christian, 1966, 56.
6. *The Observer*, May 1992.
7. *The Times*, 22 April 2002, 23.
8. Jenkins, 2002, 210.

Bibliography

Manuscript sources are cited in full. Articles and books are given by author and date, for ease of identification from the Notes. Unless otherwise stated, the place of publication is London.

Abbreviations

MANUSCRIPT: CKS   Centre for Kent Studies, Maidstone
               ESRO   East Sussex Record Office, Lewes
               PRO   Public Record Office (The National Archives)
               WSRO   West Sussex Record Office

PRINTED: *Agric. Hist. Rev.*   *Agricultural History Review*
         Ann. Phil. Soc.   *Annals of the Philosophical Society*
         Arch. Cant.   *Archaeologia Cantiana*
         Bull. Inst. Arch.   *Bulletin of the Institute of Archaeology*
         Econ. Hist. Rev.   *Economic History Review*
         Journ. Hist. Geog.   *Journal of Historical Geography*
         Phil. Trans. Roy. Soc. *Philosophical Transactions of the Royal Society*
         Proc. Geol. Assoc.   *Proceedings of the Geological Association*
         Proc. Prehist. Soc.   *Proceedings of the Prehistoric Society*
         Quart. Journ. Geol. Soc. *Quarterly Journal of the Geological Society*
         SAC   *Sussex Archaeological Collections*
         SRS   *Sussex Record Society*

Aberg, F.A., 'Medieval Moated Sites', *Council for British Archaeology, Research Report* (1978)

Aldis, H.G., in *Cambridge History of English Literature*, vol. 4 (1909)

Allen, P., 'The Wealden Environment: Anglo-Paris Basin', *Phil. Trans. Roy. Soc.* 104 (1959), 242, 283-346

—, 'Wealden of the Weald: a new model', *Proc. Geol. Assoc.* 86 (1975), 389-437

—, 'Pursuit of Wealden Models', *Quart. Journ. Geol. Soc.* 138 (1981), 375-405

Allingham, H. and Radford, D. (eds.), *A Diary of William Allingham* (1907)

Anon., *The Life and History of Swing: The Kent Rick-burner* (KCS, Maidstone, 1830)

Anon., *Address to Men of Hawkhurst* (CKS, Maidstone, 1830)

Aston, Michael, *Interpreting the Landscape* (1985)

Awty, Brian, 'Denization returns and lay subsidy rolls and sources of French ironworkers in the Weald', *Wealden Iron Research Group* 13 (1978), 17-19; 16 (1979), 2-11

—, 'The continental origins of Wealden ironworkers', *Econ. Hist. Rev.* 34 (1981), 13-24

Bailey, Mark, 'The Rabbit in Medieval East Anglian Economy', *Agric. Hist. Rev.* 36 (1988), 1-20

Baker, A.R.H., 'Some evidence of a reduction in the acreage of cultivated land in Sussex during the early fourteenth century', *SAC* 104 (1966), 1-23

Barker, Eric, 'Sussex Anglo-Saxon Charters', *SAC* 86 (1947), 42-101; 87 (1949), 112-63; 88 (1950), 43-69

Batchelor, Gordon W., *The Beresfords of Bedgebury Park* (Goudhurst, 1996)

Baxter, John, *Library of Practical Agriculture*, 2 vols. (Lewes, 1846)

Beckett, Arthur, *The Spirit of the Weald* (1911)

Belloc, Hilaire, *The County of Sussex* (1936)

Bise, Gabriel (ed.), *Gaston Foix's Hunting Book* (Geneva, 1978)

Bishop, T.A.M., 'The rotation of crops at Westerham, 1297-1356', *Econ. Hist. Rev.* 9 (1938)

Blair, John, *Early Medieval Surrey* (1991)

Blunden, Edmund, *The Face of England* (1932)

Blunt, Wilfrid Scawen, *Collected Works* (1914)

—, 'Possiblities of peasant ownership in Sussex', *Nineteenth Century*, vol. 59 (1906), 955-67

—, *My Diaries* (1932 edn.)

Bourne (Sturt), George, *Change in the Village* (1912)

Boxall, J.P., 'The Sussex breed of cattle in the nineteenth century', *Agric. Hist. Rev.* 20 (1972), 17-29

Brandon, P.F., 'The enclosure of Keymer Commons', *Sussex Notes and Queries*, 15 (1960), 181-6

—, 'The Commonlands and Wastes of Sussex', unpub. Ph.D. Thesis, University of London (1963)

—, 'Medieval clearances in the east Sussex Weald', *Transactions of the Institute of British Geographers* 48 (1969), 135-53

—, 'Agriculture and the effects of floods and weather at Barnhorne, Sussex during the late Middle Ages', *SAC* 109 (1971a), 94-106

—, 'Late-Medieval weather in Sussex and its agricultural significance', *Transactions of the Institute of British Geographers* 54 (1971b), 1-17

—, *The Sussex Landscape* (1974)

— (ed.), *The South Saxons* (Chichester, 1978)

—, 'Designed landscapes in South-East England', *Transactions of the Institute of British Geographers*, Special Number, 10 (1979)

—, 'Philip Webb, the Morris circle and Sussex', *Sussex History* 2 (1979b), 8-14

—, *The Tillingbourne River Story* (Shere, 1984a)

—, 'Land, Technology and water management in the Tillingbourne valley, Surrey', *Southern History* 6 (1984b), 75-107

—, 'Wealden nature and the role of London in the nineteenth-century artistic imagination', *Journ. Hist. Geog.* 10 (1984c), 53-74

— (with Brian Short), *The South East from AD 1000* (1990)

—, *The South Downs* (Phillimore & Co. Ltd., Chichester, West Sussex, 1998)

Brent, Colin, 'Rural population in Sussex between 1550-1640', *SAC* Part 1, 116

(1978), 41-56

Brent, Judith, 'The Pooles of Chailey and Lewes: the establishment and influence of a gentry family, 1732-1739', *SAC* 114 (1970), 69-80

Briault, E.W.H., *The Land of Britain: Sussex (East and West)* (1942)

Bridbury, A.R., 'The Black Death', *Econ. Hist. Rev.* 26 (1973), 577-92

Buckatzsch, E.J., 'The geographical distribution of wealth in England, 1086-1843', *Econ. Hist. Rev.* 2nd series, 3 (1950), 180-202

Burleigh, G.R., 'An introduction to deserted medieval villages in east Sussex', *SAC* 91 (1973), 45-83

—, 'Further notes of deserted and shrunken medieval villages in Sussex', *SAC* 114 (1976), 61-8

Caird, J., *English Agriculture in 1851-2* (1852)

Cameron, Wendy and Maude, Mary McDougall, *Assisting Emigration to Upper Canada: The Petworth Project, 1832-7* (2000)

Cantor, L., *The English Medieval Landscape* (1982)

Capek, Karel, *Letters from England* (2001 edn.)

Carlyle, Thomas, *Collected Letters of Thomas and Jane Carlyle*, ed. Charles Sanders (North Carolina, 1970-2001)

Cattell, C.S., 'The historical geography of the Wealden iron industry', unpub. M.A. Dissertation, University of London (1973)

—, 'The 1574 lists of Wealden ironworks', *SAC* 117 (1979), 161-72

Charlesworth, A., 'Social protest in a rural society; the spatial diffusion of the Captain Swing disturbances of 1830-1831', *Historical Geography Research Group monographs*, I (Norwich, 1969)

— (ed.), *An Atlas of Rural Protest in Britain, 1548-1900* (1983)

Chatters, C. and Sanderson, N., 'Grazing Lowland Pasture Woods', *British Wildlife* 6,2 (1998), 78-88

Chatwin, Diana, *The development of timber-framed building in the Sussex Weald* (1996)

Christian, Garth, *Tomorrow's Countryside* (1966)

Cleere, H., 'Some operating parameters for Roman ironworks', *Bull. Inst. Arch.* 13 (1976), 233-46

—, 'Classis Britannica' in D.E. Johnston (ed.), *The Saxon Shore: Council for British Archaeology Report*, 18 (1977)

— and Crossley, D.C., *The Iron Industry of the Weald* (Leicester, 1985)

Clifton-Taylor, Alec in John Newman, *Pevsner's Buildings of England: West Kent* (1969), 23-9

Clough, M. (ed.), *The Book of Bartholomew Bolney*, SRS 63 (1964)

Clough, M. (ed.), *Two Fitzalan Surveys*, SRS 67 (1969)

Cobbett, William (Cole, G.D.H. and M., eds.), *Rural Rides* (1930)

—, *A Legacy for Labourers* (1834)

—, *Political Register* (1802-35)

—, *Two-Penny Trash* (1830-32)

—, *A Life* (1835)

—, *Selected Writings*, ed. Nattrass, Leonora, vol.6: Peasant Politics (1998)

Cooper, J.H., 'A religious census of Sussex in 1676', *SAC* 45 (1902), 142-8

Cooper, W.D., 'Participation of Sussex in Cade's rising', *SAC* 18 (1866), 17-36

Copley, G.J., *William Camden's Britannia: Kent* (1977a)

—, *Surrey and Sussex* (1977b)

Cornwall, J., 'Sussex Lay Subsidy Rolls, 1524-5', *SRS* 56 (1956)

—, 'Sussex wealth and society in the reign of Henry VIII', *SAC* 114 (1976), 1-26

Cresswell, Alison, *The Swing Riots* (CKS, Maidstone, 2003)

Crocker, Alan, *Paper Mills of the Tillingbourne* (Oxshott, 1988)

Crossley, D.W., 'The performance of the glass industry in sixteenth-century England', *Econ. Hist. Rev.* 25 (1972a), 421-33

—, 'A sixteenth-century Wealden blast furnace at Panningridge, Sussex', *Post Medieval Archaeology* 6 (1972b), 42-68

—, 'Ralph Hogge's Ironworks Accounts, 1576-81', *SAC* 112 (1974)

— (ed.), 'Sidney Ironworks accounts, 1541-1573', *Camden Fourth Series* 6, 15 (1975)

Curwen, E.C., *The Archaeology of Sussex* (1936)

—, *The Journal of Gideon Mantell* (1940)

Darby, H.C. and Campbell, E.M.J., *The Domesday Geography of South-East England* (1962)

Davis, J., 'Lollard survival and the textile industry in the South-east of England' in Cumming, J.G. (ed.), *Studies in Church History* (1966), 191-201

Dearn, T.D.W., *An Historical and Topographical Descriptive Account of the Weald of Kent* (1814)

Defoe, Daniel, *A Tour through the Whole Island of Great Britain* (1738 edn., repr. 1927)

Denman, J., articles in Hurstpierpoint Church magazine (1955), collected by Packham, R.A. (1991)

Dennis, John, *Original Letters* (1721)

Dimbleby, G.W., *The Development of British Heathlands and their Soils* (1962)

—, 'A Mesolithic site on Iping Common, Sussex, England', *Proc. Prehist. Soc.* 31 (1965), 85-92

Douglas, D.C. (ed.), *The Domesday Monachorum of Christ Church, Canterbury* (1944)

Drewett, P., Rudling, D. and Gardiner, M., *The South East to AD 1000* (1988)

Du Boulay, F.R.H., *The Lordship of Canterbury; An Essay in Medieval Society* (1966)

Dyer, C., *Making a Living in the Middle Ages: The People of Britain, 850-1520* (2002)

Edlin, H.L., *The Living Forest* (1958)

Eliot, George, *Letters*, ed. Gordon C. Haight, 5 vols. (1954-6)

English Nature, *Landscape Profile: The Greensand* (Lewes, 1999)

Evelyn, John, *Sylva or a Discourse of Forest Trees* (1679 edn.)

Evans, J., *Rusthall* (Tunbridge Wells, 1999)

Everitt, Alan, *The Pattern of Rural Dissent: The Nineteenth Century* (Leicester, 1972)

—, 'The making of the agrarian landscape of Kent', *Arch. Cant.* 92 (1976), 1-31

—, *Continuity and Colonization: The Evolution of Kentish Settlement* (Leicester, 1986)

Eversley, Lord, *England's Commons and Forests* (1894)

Fitton, William H., 'Notes on the opposite coasts of the English Channel', *Ann. Phil. Soc.*, new series, vol. 8 (1824)

—, *A Geological sketch of the vicinity of Hastings* (1833)

Forster, E.M., *A Room with a View* (1980 edn.)

Fuller, G.J., 'The development of roads in the Surrey and Sussex Weald and coastlands between 1700 and 1900', *Transactions of the Institute of British Geographers* 19 (1953), 37-49

Furley, Robert, *A History of the Weald of Kent* (1871-4)

Fussell, G.E., 'Four centuries of farming systems in Sussex', *SAC* 90 (1952)

Gallois, R.W., *The Wealden District*, 4th edn., British Regional Geology, Geological Survey (1965)

Garde, de la, Comte, *Brighton: Scénes detachés d'un voyage en Angleterre*, 2nd edn. (Paris, 1834)

Gardiner, Mark, 'The Archaeology of the Weald', *SAC* 128 (1990), 33-54

Garrad, G.H., *A Survey of the Agriculture of Kent* (1954)

Gelling, Margaret, *Signposts to the Past: Place-names and the History of England* (Chichester, 1988 edn.)

— and Cole, Ann, *The Landscape of Place-Names* (2000)

Gissing, G. (Mattheisen, P., Young, A. and Coustillas, P., eds.), *Collected Letters*, 4 vols. (Athens, Ohio, 1990-3)

Godfrey, Walter (ed.), *The Book of John Rowe*, SRS 34 (1828)

Gollancz, Victor (ed.), *A Year of Grace* (1950)

Grant, J., 'On large hedges and small enclosures in Devon', *The Journal of the Royal Agricultural Society of England*, vol.5 (1845), 420-9

Grant, John, 'The distribution of lay wealth in Kent, Surrey and Sussex in the early fourteenth century', *Arch. Cant.* 80 (1965), 61-8

Green, Bryn, 'Towards a more sustainable agriculture: time for a rural land-use strategy', *Biologist 40*, 2 (1993), 81-5

—, 'Plenty of Wilderness: creating a new countryside', *ECOS* 16 (2) (1995)

—, 'The farmed landscape: the ecology and conservation of diversity' in Jennifer Jenkins (ed.), *Remaking the Landscape: The Changing Face of Britain* (2002), 183-210

Gregory, Professor, 'Report to Earl of Sheffield (1908)', Library, Sussex Archaeological Society

Haggard, H. Rider, *Rural England: Being an Account of agriculture and social researches carried out in the years 1901 and 1902* (1906)

Hall, A.D. and Russell, E.J., *A Report on the Agriculture and Soils of Kent, Surrey and Sussex* (1911)

—, *A Pilgrimage of English Farming, 1910-12* (1914)

Hallam, H. E., *Rural England, 1066-1348* (1981)

Halsham, John (Forrester Scott), *Idlehurst: A Journey into the Country* (1898)

—, *Lonewood Corner* (1907)

—, *Old Standards: South Country Sketches* (1913)

Hammersley, G.F., 'The charcoal iron industry and its fuel', *Econ. Hist. Rev.* 26 (1977), 593-613

Hardcastle, John, 'Regeneration of oak with a historical incentive', *Quarterly Journal of Forestry* 93, No. 2 (1999), 105-9

Hare, J.N., 'The buildings of Battle Abbey', *Proceedings of Battle Conference* 3 (1981), 71-95

Harris, R., *Discovering Timber-Framed Buildings* (1978)

Harrison, Sir Edward R., *Benjamin Harrison of Ightham* (1928)

Harvey, Graham, *The Killing of the Countryside* (1997)

—, National Trust Newsletter (2001)

Hasted, Edward, *The History and Topographical Survey of the County of Kent* (Canterbury, 1797-1801, repr. 1972)

Hawes, S., 'Notes of the Weald Clay of Sussex and its cultivation', *Journal of the Royal Agricultural Society of England*, 19 (1858), 182-98

Hearne, T., *Textus Roffensis* (Oxford, 1720)

High Weald AONB Management Plan (1995), High Weald Forum, Lewes

Hobsbawm, E. and Rude, G., *Captain Swing* (1973)

Hoof, Tim, *Christ's Hospital*, undergraduate dissertation, Wye College, University of London (1988)

Horsfield, T.W., *The History, Antiquities and Topography of the County of Sussex*, 2 vols. (Lewes, 1835)

Hoskyns, W., *Talpa* (1856)

Howell-Thomas, D., 'Bolney Church Tower', *West Sussex History* 28 (May, 1984)

Hunter, John, *Preservation of the Commons* (1902)

Hussey, Christopher, *The Picturesque* (1927, repr. 1967)

Ireland, W.H., *A New and Complete History of Kent* (1829)

Jekyll, G., *Wood and Garden* (1899)

Jenkins, Simon, *England's Thousand Best Churches* (1995)

Jerrome, Peter, *John Sirgood's Way* (1998)

Johnson, Owen, *The Sussex Tree Book* (Westmeston, Sussex, 1998)

Jones, D.K.C. (ed.), *The Shaping of Southern England* (1980), 10-13

Kalm, Peter, *A Visit to England*, ed. J. Lucas (1892)

Kaye-Smith, Sheila, *Sussex Gorse* (1916)

Kendon, Frank, *The Small Years* (1930)

Kenyon, G.H., *The Glass Industry of the Weald* (Leicester, 1967)

King, S.H., 'Domesday Sussex' in H.C. Darby and E.M.J. Campbell, *The Domesday Geography of South-East England* (Cambridge, 1971)

Kingsley, Charles, *Miscellanies* (1859)

Kirby, Peter, *Forest Camera: A Portrait of Ashdown* (1998)

Kropotkin, Prince, P. (Ward, Colin, ed.), *Factories, Fields and Workshops* (1974 edn.)

Lambarde, W., *A Perambulation of Kent; Containing the Description, Historie and Customes of that Shire* (1576, repr. 1970)

Latham, R.C. and Matthews, W. (eds.), *The Diary of Samuel Pepys*, vol. 9 (1976)

Lavergne, L. de, *The Rural Economy of England, Scotland and Ireland* (1865)

Law, Ben, *The Woodland Way* (East Meon, Hampshire, 2001)

Lennard, R.V., *Rural England, 1086-1135* (1959)

Loudon, C., *Illustrations of Landscape Gardening and Architecture* (1830)

—, *An Encyclopaedia of Cottage, Farm and Villa Architecture* (1842 edn.)

Lower, M.A., 'On the Ironworks of Sussex', *SAC* 2 (1849)

Lower, M.A., *A Compendious History of Sussex*, 2 vols. (1870)

Loyn, H.R., *The Norman Conquest* (1982)

Mackerness, M.D. (ed.), *The Journals of George Sturt* (1967 edn.)

Macky, John, *A Journey Through England*, vol. 1 (1732 edn.)

Malcolm, J.A., *A Compendium of Modern Husbandry* (1805)

Manley, John, *A.D. 43; A Reassessment* (2002)

Mantell, Gideon, *The Fossils of the South Downs or Illustrations of the Geology of Sussex* (1822)

—, 'Notice of the Iguanodon, a newly discovered fossil of an herbivorous reptile from the sandstone of Tilgate Forest, *Phil. Trans.* (1825), 179

—, *The Geology of the South-East of England* (1833)

Markham, Gervase, *The Inrichment of the Weald of Kent* (1636 edn.)

—, *Farewell to Husbandry* (1638 edn.)

Marshall, W., *The Rural Economy of the Southern Counties*, 2 vols. (1798)

Martin, David, *Historic Buildings in Eastern Sussex*, vols. 1-4 (on-going)

Martin, P.I., *A Geological Memoir on a part of Western Sussex* (1828)

Mason, R.T., *Framed Buildings of the Weald* (1969 edn.)

Mate, Mavis, 'Agrarian economy after the Black Death; the manors of Canterbury Cathedral Priory, 1348-91', *Econ. Hist. Rev.* 37 (1984), 341-54

Mawer, A. and Stenton, F.M., *The Place-Names of Sussex*, Part 1 (1929)

Melling, E., *Kentish Sources, V: Some Kentish Houses: Maidstone* (1965)

Messel, O., *An Inventory of trees and plants at Nymans* (1916)

Mill, J.S., *Account of a Tour in Sussex in July 1827, The Worthing Parade*, 1 (1951 repr.), 159-183

Mingay, G., *English Landed Society in the Eighteenth Century* (1963)

Moffat, B., 'Output of the Woodlands of the Ashburnham estate in the late 18th and early 19th centuries', *Quarterly Journal of Forestry* (October, 1983), 255-7

—, 'Species cut in woods on the Ashburnham estate', *Quarterly Journal of Forestry* (1984), 225-59

Montagu, Lady Mary Wortley, *Letters (1777)*, vol. 1 (1736), 60; (1738), 49

Moore, J.S., *Laughton: A Study in the Evolution of the Wealden Landscape* (Leicester, 1965)

Morris, John (ed.), *Domesday Book: Surrey* (Chichester, 1975)

—, *Domesday Book: Kent* (Chichester, 1976)

—, *Domesday Book: Sussex* (Chichester, 1976)

Nairn, I. and Pevsner, N., *The Buildings of England: Sussex East and West* (1965)

Nef, J.U., 'The progress of technology and the growth of large scale industry in Great Britain, 1540-1640', *Econ. Hist. Rev.* 5 (1934)

Newman, John, *West Kent and the Weald*, Pevsner's Buildings of England series (1969)

Nicolson, Nigel, *Watching over the Weald* (Kent Preservation Society, 2000)

Norden, J., *The Surveyor's Dialogue* (1610 edn.)

Patmore, Coventry, *How I Managed my Estate* (1886)

Pearson, S., *The Medieval Houses of Kent: An Historical Analysis* (1994)

Peckham, W.D., 'Thirteen Custumals of the Sussex manors of the Bishop of

Chichester', *SRS* 31 (1925)

Pichot, M.W., *Voyage historique … en Angleterre …* (Paris, 1825)

Prestwich, Joseph, 'On the occurrence of Paleolithic flint implements in the neighbourhood of Ightham, Kent', *Geological Journal* 45 (1869), 127-297

—, 'The greater antiquity of Man', *Nineteenth Century* 37 (1895), 617-28

Pullein, M., *Rotherfield* (1926)

Quest-Ritson, C., *The English Garden in Social History* (2001)

Rackham, Oliver, *Ancient Woodland* (1980)

—, *The History of the Countryside* (1986)

'Reclamation of derelict land for agricultural use', *Ministry of Agriculture, Technical Report No. 1* (1957)

Redwood, B.C. and Wilson, A.E., *Custumals of Sussex Manors of the Archbishop of Canterbury*, *SRS* 57 (1958)

Reid, I.G., *The Small Farm on Heavy Land* (Wye College, Dept. of Agricultural Economics, 1958)

Repton, H., *Observations on the Theory and Practice of Landscape Gardening* (1803)

Rigold, S.E., 'Excavation of a Moated site at Pivington', *Arch. Cant.* 77 (1962), 27-47

—, 'The Distribution of the Wealden House' in Foster, I.L.L. and Awcock, L. (eds.), *Culture and Environment, Essays in Honour of Cyril Oman* (1963)

Rivet, A.F. and Smith, Colin, *The Place-Names of Roman Britain* (1979)

Roberts, Geoffrey, *Woodlands of Kent* (1999)

Robertson, W. Graham, *Time Was* (1931)

Robinson, D.A. in Williams, R.B.G., *Guide to Sussex Excursions* (Institute of British Geographers, 1971), 51-60

Robinson, W., *The Wild Garden* (1870)

—, *Gravetye Manor* (1911)

—, *Home Landscapes* (1914)

Rose, Francis, *Habitat and Vegetation of Sussex* (Booth Museum, Brighton, 1995)

Sackville-West, V., *Collected Works*, vol. 1 (1933)

Salzman, L.F., *The Cartulary of Sele* (Lewes, 1921)

—, *The Cartulary of the Priory of St Pancras at Lewes*, Part 1, *SRS* 38 (1932)

—, *The Ministers' Accounts of the Manor of Petworth*, *SRS* 55 (1955)

Sassoon, S., *The Memoirs of a Fox-hunting Man* (1960 edn.)

Saville, R.V., 'Gentry wealth on the Weald in the eighteenth century: the Fullers of Brightling Park', *SAC* 121 (1983), 129-47

Sawyer, P.H., 'The Wealth of England in the eleventh century', *Trans. Roy. Hist. Soc.,* 5th series, 15 (1965), 145-64

—, *Medieval Settlement: Continuity and Change* (1976)

—, *From Roman Britain to Norman England* (1978)

Scaife, R.G. and Burrin, P.J., 'The environmental impact of prehistoric man as recorded in the Upper Cuckmere valley at Stream Farm, Chiddingly', *SAC* 123 (1985), 27-34

Schofield, R.S., 'The geographical distribution of wealth in England, 1344-1649', *Econ. Hist. Rev.* 18 (1965), 483-510

Searle, E., 'Hides, virgates and tenants; settlements of Battle Abbey', *Econ. Hist. Rev.* 16 (1963), 290-300

—, *Lordship and Community: Battle Abbey and its Banlieu, 1066-1538* (Toronto, 1974)

Sheail, J., 'The distribution of taxable population and wealth in England during the early sixteenth century', *Transactions of the Institute of British Geographers* 55 (1972), 111-26

Sewell, Desmond, *Sussex* (1995)

Sheppard, June, 'Small farms in a Sussex Weald parish, 1800-1860', *Agric. Hist. Rev.* 40 (1992), 127-141

Short, B.M., 'The turnover of tenants on the Ashburnham estate, 1830-50', *SAC* 113 (1975), 157-74

—, 'The art and craft of chicken cramming: poultry in the Weald of Sussex, 1850-1950', *Agric. Hist. Rev.* 30 (1982), 19-30

—, 'South-east England, Kent, Surrey and Sussex' in Thirsk, Joan (ed.), *The Agrarian History of England and Wales*, vol. 5(i), 1640-1750 (Cambridge, 1985), 270-313

— (with Brandon, Peter), *The South East from AD 1000* (1990)

—, *The Ashdown Forest Dispute, 1876-1882: Environmental Politics and Custom*, *SRS* 80 (1997)

Smith, Verena, *The Sharpe Collection of Watercolours and Drawings, 1797-1809* (Lewes, 1979)

Stamp, L.D., *The Land of Britain: Kent* (1943)

Stamp, L.D. and Willatts, E.C., *The Land of Britain: Surrey* (1941)

Stephen, Leslie, 'On landscape', *Cornhill Magazine* 29 (1974), 512-30

Stevenson, W., *A General View of the Agriculture of the County of Surrey* (1809)

Straker, E., *Wealden Iron* (1931)

—, *The Buckhurst Terrier, 1597-8*, *SRS* 39 (1933)

Streeter, David and Richardson, Rosamund, *Discovering Hedgerows* (1983)

Tebbutt, C.F., 'The prehistoric occupation of the Ashdown Forest area of the Weald', *SAC* 112 (1974), 34-43

—, 'A deserted medieval farm settlement at Faulkner's Farm, Hartfield', *SAC* 119 (1981)

Teesdale, E.M., *The Queen's Gunstonemaker* (1984)

Thirsk, Joan (ed.), *The Agrarian History of England and Wales, 1500-1640*, vol. 4 (Cambridge, 1967)

—, *Alternative Agriculture* (1997)

Thorne, J., *The Environs of London* (1844), 1-4

Tomlinson, H.L., 'Wealden gunfounding; an analysis of its demise in the eighteenth century', *Econ. Hist. Rev.* 39 (1976), 383-99

Topley, W., *The Geology of the Weald* (1875)

Turner, D.J., 'Moated sites in Surrey: a provisional list', *Surrey Archaeological Collections* 71 (1977), 88-94

Turnour, Viscount, 'The Cokelers', *National Review* (1904), 106-12

University of Sussex, *Sussex: Environment, Landscape and Society* (1983)

Vera, F.W.M., *Grazing and Ecology and Forest History* (2000)

Vine, P.A.L., *London's Lost Route to the Sea* (1965)

—, *The Royal Military Canal* (1972)

Wagner, A.R., 'The Wagners of Brighton', *SAC* 98 (1959), 35-57

Wallis, M.F. and De Vries, Y., *Grazing and Conservation Management* (1998)

Walpole, Horace (Cunningham, P., ed.), *Letters* (Edinburgh, 1906 edn.)

Walton, Robin and Ivan, *Kentish Oasts* (1998)

Ward, G., 'The *Haeselerse* charter of 1018', *SAC* 78 (1936), 18-29

Ward, Mrs Humphry, *Robert Elsmere* (1888)

Warren, John and Hallam, Marjorie in John Warren (ed.), *Wealden Buildings* (1990)

Watkin, David, *Thomas Hope and the Neo-Classical Idea* (1968)

West, Mike, *Moated Sites and the Medieval Manor: Evidence from Western Sussex*, Centre for Continuing Education, University of Sussex (2001)

White, Rev. Gilbert, *The Natural History and Antiquities of Selborne* (1816 edn.)

Wilberforce, R.G., 'Education for country children', *Nineteenth Century*, vol. 59 (1906), 678-9

Williams, Ann, 'Land and power in the eleventh century; the estate of Harold Godwinson', *Proceedings of the Battle Conference* 3 (1981), 171-87

Williamson, Tom and Bellamy, Liz, *Property and Landscape* (1987)

Witney, K.P., *The Jutish Forest: A Study of the Weald of Kent from 450-1350 A.D.* (1982)

—, 'The economic position of husbandmen at the time of Domesday Book: a Kentish perspective', *Econ. Hist. Rev.* 37 (1988), 23-34

—, 'Woodland economy of Kent, 1066-1348, *Agric. Hist. Rev.* 38 (1990), 1-18

Wooldridge, S.W., *The Weald and the Field Sciences*, British Association for Advancement of Science, new series, 1 (1949), 3-11

— and Goldring, F., *The Weald* (1953)

Wrake, John, *Maresfield Historical Society, Occasional Paper* 2 (1999)

Yates, E.M., *The History of the Landscape in the parishes of South Harting and Rogate* (Chichester, 1972)

Yates, N., 'The condition of Kent churches before Victorian restoration', *Arch. Cant.* 103 (1986), 119-125

Young, Arthur, *The Farmer's Tour through the East of England*, vol. 3 (1771)

—, 'A Tour in Sussex', *Annals of Agriculture* 11 (1789), 170-304

—, *Annals of Agriculture*

—, *Travels During the Years 1787, 1788 and 1789 in the Kingdom of France* (1792-4)

Young, Rev. A., *General View of the Agriculture of the County of Sussex* (1813)

Zell, M., 'A wood-pasture regime: The Kentish Weald in the sixteenth century', *Southern History* 7 (1985a), 69-93

—, 'Population and family structure in the sixteenth century Weald', *Arch. Cant.* 100 (1985b), 231-57

—, *Industry in the Countryside: Wealden Society in the Sixteenth Century* (1994)

Index

Page numbers in **bold** refer to illustrations; Roman numerals at end of entries refer to colour plates

John Norden's map of Sussex engraved by Christopher Schwytzer, 1595. Like Saxton's map this shows no roads but has more symbols, including those for windmills, beacons and antiquities. The arms are of Thomas Sackville, Lord Buckhurst, whose family seat was at Old Buckhurst, Withyham.